EXPERIMENTS IN SELF-DETERMINATION

Histories of the outstation movement in Australia

EXPERIMENTS IN SELF-DETERMINATION

Histories of the outstation movement in Australia

Edited by Nicolas Peterson and Fred Myers

MONOGRAPHS IN
ANTHROPOLOGY SERIES

Australian
National
University

PRESS

ANU PRESS

Published by ANU Press
The Australian National University
Acton ACT 2601, Australia
Email: anupress@anu.edu.au
This title is also available online at press.anu.edu.au

National Library of Australia Cataloguing-in-Publication entry

Title:	Experiments in self-determination : histories of the outstation movement in Australia / editors: Nicolas Peterson, Fred Myers.
ISBN:	9781925022896 (paperback) 9781925022902 (ebook)
Subjects:	Community life. Community organization. Aboriginal Australians--Social conditions--20th century. Aboriginal Australians--Social life and customs--20th century.
Other Creators/Contributors:	Peterson, Nicolas, 1941- editor. Myers, Fred R., 1948- editor.
Dewey Number:	305.89915

Cover design and layout by ANU Press

Contents

History and memory

Western Desert complexities

Policy visions and their realisation

Frustrated aspirations

List of maps

List of figures

List of tables

Preface and acknowledgements

This volume has its origins in an Australian Research Council (ARC) Linkage Project (LP1000200359), 'Pintupi dialogues: reconstructing memories of art, land and community through the visual record'. The project brought together Nicolas Peterson and Pip Deveson from The Australian National University, Peter Thorley from the National Museum of Australia, Fred Myers from New York University and Papunya Tula Limited to work on 13 hours of archival footage shot by Ian Dunlop at the Central Australian outstation of Yayayi in 1974. The footage was of particular interest not only because it recorded the lives of people who had only settled down in the previous 12 years, but also because it documented one of the first outstations that was established following the election of the Whitlam Government in 1972. Self-determination was the focus of the ARC project, with outstations seen as a major manifestation of Indigenous aspirations in this respect. Understanding Indigenous views is crucial to avoid trivialising this complex and highly contested policy area.

The original footage was divided into a number of shorter edited sequences dealing with different topics for community use, and also made into an hour-long film, *Remembering Yayayi*. Marlene Nampitjinpa, who was born in the bush in 1959 and was three years old at the time of first meeting Europeans, comments on the 1974 footage in which she features along with her parents and many other relatives.

Towards the conclusion of the ARC project, it was planned to hold a conference that would explore the early history of the establishment of outstations across northern Australia as manifestations of Aboriginal-led self-determination. The papers published here were originally presented at The Australian National University on 16 and 17 December 2013 in a lively proceedings that brought together a number of retired employees of the Department of Aboriginal Affairs, an older generation of anthropologists who had been in the field during the 1970s and an audience of younger scholars working with people in the existing and transformed outstations.

We would like to acknowledge the generous support we have received from the National Museum of Australia, particularly the support of three of its directors, Craddock Morton, Andrew Sayers and Mathew Trinca. The ongoing support of Paul Sweeney from Papunya Tula Limited has been crucial to the success of the project. The comments of the anonymous referees have done much to strengthen the volume and were extremely helpful. Thanks are also due to Karina Pelling for the maps and Christine Huber for assistance with the publishing process.

It is with great sadness that we report the death of the Reverend Bill Edwards on 24 July 2015.

1

The origins and history
of outstations as Aboriginal
life projects

Fred Myers and Nicolas Peterson

In recent years, there has been an acrimonious debate about the existence and significance of outstations or 'homeland communities' as they are sometimes called. These debates have cast various interpretations on the motivations for the establishment and support of these small and remote Indigenous residential formations. For example, outstations have sometimes been characterised by traditionalists as a *retreat* from modernisation, and from time to time they have been characterised in very negative terms. Indeed, one government minister called them 'cultural museums' (Eastley 2005; see Kowal 2010: 182). We hope to show, however, that such views give little hearing for an Aboriginal perspective, and trivialise complex policy issues and deeply held views. In these debates, we fear, something of the lived experiences, motivations and histories of existing communities is missing. For this reason, we invited a number of anthropological witnesses to the early period in which outstations gained a purchase in remote Australia to provide accounts of what these communities were like, and what their residents' aspirations and experiences were.

Our hope is that these closer-to-the ground accounts can provide insight into and illumination of what Indigenous aspirations were in the establishment and organisation of these communities. Indeed, we think that in delineating what took place in this earlier period, it is possible to understand these aspirations. However, it is not easy to do so. Often, we have to infer such aspirations, as historians have not infrequently done in seeing 'resistance' in the past. More importantly, we find that William Stanner's famous essay 'The Dreaming' reflects the sense of many observers of remote communities that an *explicit* discourse of a future imagined, or of a future collective aspiration beyond 'life is a one-possibility thing' (Stanner 2011: 68), was rare. Certainly, we have come to understand that where such aspirations existed they could be embedded in and expressed through a range of religious formations such as the Elcho Island movement reported by Ronald Berndt (1962) or *Tjulurru* ('Balgo Business') of the 1970s and 1980s in the Central and Western deserts (Kolig 1979; Myers n.d.; Glowczewski 1983), and were concerned with renewal and revitalisation (for example, see Austin-Broos, in this volume). Nonetheless, as an explicitly formulated aspiration, the outstation movement, we think, stands out for its clarity.

We use the term 'outstation' with a certain understanding. While some writers prefer 'homelands' to emphasise the link of many outstations with the founders' ancestral lands, appreciable numbers of outstations are not on such lands, but are, by agreement, elsewhere. Further, some conservative writers such as Helen Hughes (2007) have muddied the usage as they have sometimes used the term 'homelands' to refer to *all* Aboriginal settlements on remote Aboriginal lands, including what are today the Aboriginal 'townships' that have formed from the old mission and government settlements.

Outstations are small, decentralised and relatively permanent communities of kin established by Aboriginal people on land that has social, cultural or economic significance to them (cf. Blanchard 1987: 7). Generally speaking, the majority of them have fewer than 40 people. The term has a distinctly Australian history. It comes from the cattle industry and was used for a subsidiary homestead or other dwelling that was more than a day's return travel from the main homestead. It suggests a dependent relationship between the outstation and the main homestead, but with a degree of separation. While outstations in the cattle industry were presumably planned and sanctioned by the owner or manager of the property, the majority of outstations in the Aboriginal context are entirely Aboriginal 'life projects'.[1] By 'life projects', we refer to the desires of those Indigenous people who sought and seek autonomy in deciding the meaning of their life independently of projects promoted by the state and market, and to

---

1   In the absence of the idea of a career among most remote-dwelling Aboriginal people (see Austin-Broos 2006), the nature of most Aboriginal people's life projects is obscure to outsiders. Some few do work as teachers or health workers over a normal working life, and in the past a career as a stockman was not uncommon, but grander ideas beyond such individual aspirations are harder to discern, except in one area: that of the outstation.

people developing their own situation-based knowledge and practices in the contemporary world (cf. Blaser 2004). These are not simply projects of isolation from outside influences or some sort of cultural apartheid. Mario Blaser's use of the term, in fact, draws specific attention to the ways in which Indigenous people might ally themselves with various categories of outsider in order to protect or sustain values or concerns of their own. But the term draws attention to directions of life that emanate from Indigenous histories that are not free of outside influences but are nonetheless distinctive in their shape, as in the example of Ntaria (see Austin-Broos, this volume) and in the case of the Yolngu outstations in eastern Arnhem Land, which Frances Morphy and Howard Morphy (this volume) describe as struggling to re-emplace a regional system of relationships through engagements with various outsiders. Many of the chapters in this volume note that government enthusiasm for and support of these life projects have waxed and waned, often with destructive consequences (see, for example, Cane; Morphy and Morphy; and White, this volume).

As a result of his research for the influential *Destruction of Aboriginal Society* (1970), C. D. Rowley, and Jeremy Long, who worked with him, felt the dissolution of the mission and settlement institutions was an important step forward in Aboriginal advancement. According to the eminent historian of Aboriginal policy Tim Rowse (1993: 34), they saw this deinstitutionalisation as liberating people to eventually move to the towns. It was an influential view, not only because of Rowley's standing, but also because Long was a key adviser to the Council for Aboriginal Affairs, which was the main source of policy at the time of the move to outstations. Rowley's likening of settlements to what sociologist Erving Goffman called 'total institutions'—delineated in his book on *Asylums* (1961)—gained ideological purchase among many critics during a period in which such enclosed social systems were widely challenged (see Rowley 1970: 48–9). This critique of institutionalisation, and its implicit assumptions about the significance of autonomy in well-being, was to provide fertile ground for the support of outstations in the following years, when evidence emerged that living in small groups was enormously positive for health because it allowed people to live life at a scale that gave them much greater control over their lives. The idea of population movement away from the centralised communities was eventually to raise real questions regarding the future role of the larger settlements and mission stations, although this concern did not emerge publicly for some time.[2] Thirty years later, however, the outstation movement was coming under attack, represented at this point as a *backward* step that was

---

2   Dexter (2015: 154) reports that the Department of the Interior, which had responsibility for Aboriginal issues and the Northern Territory, did not support decentralisation and was opposed to this 'setting back the clock'.

unsustainable economically—a criticism that was renewed in 2014. At the same time, however, others have strongly defended the sustainability of outstations with their mixed economies (for example, Altman 2012).

Policy for remote Aboriginal communities is a complex field of political debate, fraught with difficulty, not least because there are few clear or obvious directions for policy to take. This makes outstations of particular interest even if they seem to be going in a countervailing direction not only to current government policy, but also to what many Aboriginal people have done in the past by moving to regional centres and metropolitan areas. Interestingly, however, it is evident that since the 1970s there has been no great movement to metropolitan centres, where the natural growth in numbers has been greatly boosted by changes in self-identification, and living away from cities is by far the preferred option (Taylor and Bell 2004).

As Aboriginal life projects, outstations are one of the clearest manifestations of self-determination, and have been a rallying point for supporters of Aboriginal people as recognition of their aspirations.[3] If governments have, at times, supported the outstation movement, it has also been an area where policy can and has changed quite rapidly—indeed, right up to the time of writing when Western Australia and South Australia have announced they will withdraw financial and logistical support from many small communities that they say are too costly to service. And, in response, Australia has seen a revitalised movement—in capital cities and on social media—of protest against the 'closure' of Indigenous communities. The majority of these small communities are Aboriginal. Thus, outstations also provide an excellent lens through which to look at larger policy issues in Aboriginal affairs.

The chapters in this volume, then, examine the origins and history of specific outstations to explore the interaction of Aboriginal agency with policy, and to better understand Aboriginal engagement with the specific historical circumstances they faced. One might ask why we do not just record the history of these movements directly, as oral history. In our experience, this kind of historical framework—that is, of oral history—is culturally specific. The historical consciousness of many older Aboriginal people in remote communities seems to take a very different form. Their accounts of past events are usually encompassed in a rich array of contextually elicited or triggered stories about particular events. Such accounts, when gathered, are more commonly episodic, fragmented and reactive—not driven by the chronological narrative forms of historical discourse. Such a formulation of memory, or memories, may

---

3   This is very noticeably the case in recent political demonstrations and social media campaigns against the threat of closure of or withdrawal of governmental support for contemporary remote communities in Western Australia and elsewhere.

in fact veil the persistence of people's motivations, their long-term commitment to particular courses of action and the way they have consistently worked towards specific goals—commitments and persistence registered in activity and movement as much as in discourse.

Here we proceed by outlining the origins of outstations and then the subsequent growth in numbers following the end of the policy of 'assimilation' and the passing of the *Aboriginal Land Rights (Northern Territory) Act 1976*. We will follow this with a brief examination of the twists and turns of government policy in relation to them, and will conclude with a consideration of the implications of this history for the insight it provides into government policy for remote Aboriginal people more generally.

The origins of outstations

If something like a 'movement' began in the 1970s, it is nonetheless the case that not all outstations have their origins in this moment, as the contributions by Bill Edwards, Jeremy Long, Peter Sutton and Neville White make clear. Some group locations thought of as outstations in the 1970s originated from groups of people who had never permanently left the bush. A case in point was eastern Arnhem Land, discussed by Neville White, where the Reverend Harold Shepherdson encouraged Aboriginal people living in the bush to stay there, telling them that if they cleared an airstrip, he would fly out to visit them so that they had access to the basic commodities they wanted. Originally, their wants were limited: mainly flour, sugar, tea and tobacco, with a few other items of material culture such as clothing, knives and mosquito nets. In her memoir of life as a missionary's wife, Ella Shepherdson refers to Gattji as the first outstation in eastern Arnhem Land (established in 1936), although her husband was unable to fly there, as the airstrip was not long enough (Shepherdson 1981: 35). The next outstation mentioned in this memoir was established in 1947 at Buckingham Bay, followed by one in Arnhem Bay and another in the Wessel Islands in 1953. Subsequently, a number of others were established.

A common feature of these outstation localities, including the original Gattji site, was that they were good for making gardens, although none of the gardens seems to have been long lasting (Shepherdson 1981: 32; see also Peterson 1976; Kimber 1977: 3). Indeed, it is a common feature of both Aboriginal and non-Aboriginal advocacy for most outstations that there were opportunities for and a keenness to make gardens (for example, see Austin-Broos; Edwards; Peterson; Sutton, this volume). This is a trope. Most such gardens, if ever established, had a short life, and thus the significance of gardening has to be understood in terms of indicating a recognition that people needed to contribute to their self-sufficiency and as a plan for activity, rather than as a manifestation of a social evolutionary view of the development process that Aboriginal people had to progress through in their transition from hunting and gathering. The emphasis on gardens also bears some relationship to the muscular Christian concern that modern subjects learn the value of 'work'. The emphasis on 'gardens' can be understood as a comprehensible mediation between Indigenous aspirations for autonomy and governmental/mission concerns for learning to labour as a basis for 'self-sufficiency'.

There were many forces at work that one can recognise in the broad movement to smaller and dispersed communities. Decentralisation encouraged by the person in charge of some missions was one. Thus, in 1953, the priest in charge of the Tiwi Mission at Bathurst Island encouraged some Aboriginal people to build their houses at a location of their choice between a half-mile and one mile from the mission as a kind of satellite village (Pilling 1962: 324). Such developments were likely related to the fact that the populations on some of the missions were too large for the mission to manage in terms of rations and work. Before the 1960s, many remote missions had to be relatively self-supporting, as was the case for northern missions, because most bulk supplies came by sea at three or six-monthly intervals. In a few missions, this led to the population being divided into two, with one group staying in the bush and supporting themselves for two weeks and then swapping with the group in the mission, who went bush for two weeks. Such was the case at both Milingimbi in Arnhem Land, Aurukun (see Martin and Martin, this volume) and at Port Keats in the Daly River area (Falkenberg 1962: 18). David Brooks and Vikki Plant (this volume) present the case of probably the most severely constrained mission, at Warburton, and the effects of this on community formations in the contact period.

In 1959, Jeremy Long, then an employee of the Northern Territory Welfare Branch, was reviving proposals for the decentralisation of Pitjantjatjara people at Areyonga. Long explains this proposal was occasioned principally by population pressures, although as he commented there was great enthusiasm for the idea of a community at Docker River in the home area of many of the people there (Long, see Appendix 3.1, this volume). On the basis of Long's and others' concerns about the population issue, in October 1961 the Northern Territory Administrator wrote to the Secretary of the Department of Territories (under which the Territory fell), emphasising the necessity for 'outstations' because of major problems of water supply and settlement hygiene at Yuendumu, Papunya, Haasts Bluff and Areyonga, where communities built to accommodate 350 people at the outside all had populations in excess of this (Appendix 3.1, this volume).

The enormous problems many recently settled people such as the Pintupi faced formed another basis for decentralised communities in Central Australia. Some of them had left an independent existence only between the late 1950s and mid-1960s (Long 1964; Myers 1986) and were traumatised by living in the large community of Papunya. There were extremely high rates of death, illness, conflict and depression. The Pintupi's desire to get a place of their own, combined with the administration's concern about bad publicity, led to several attempts at forming a separate community—beginning in 1967, reattempted in 1970 and finally achieved in 1973 with the establishment of Yayayi, on the basis of a decision made by the people themselves in the face of administrative difficulties, although supported with a $30,000 grant (see Myers, this volume; Cavanagh 1974: 13).

A more ambiguous situation was that of the working populations and their dependants living on cattle stations. Their camps were not called outstations, as most of them were quite close to the homestead, but many of the people living in them were to become outstation dwellers following the change in the pastoral award between 1965 and 1968. Wages and conditions for Aboriginal people on cattle stations became a national issue in 1966 when there was a mass walk-off by Aboriginal people from the Vestey-owned stations in the Victoria River District of the Northern Territory (see Hardy 1968). While most of the stockmen returned to work, one group at Wattie Creek (Dagaragu) held out, and the protest over conditions turned into a claim for return of traditional land (Doolan 1977: 106–13). At the same time, the Australian Workers' Union was pursuing an equal wage case for Aboriginal pastoral workers, which was settled with equal wages being phased in over a three-year period to 1968. Unfortunately, as is now well known, equal wages led to a more or less immediate layoff of virtually all Aboriginal pastoral workers, many of whom left the stations for the towns, as was the case in the east Kimberley region, or for the nearest mission or government settlement in other areas. Both Dagaragu and later Yarralin communities that resulted from these events were much bigger than most outstations from the start and both have evolved into major communities made up of ex-pastoral workers and their families. However, elsewhere in the Northern Territory, the Government approach was different and was:

> [D]irected towards helping Aborigines to maintain themselves in their traditional areas and towards providing them with the advantages of a Western standard of health services and educational system. Policies have been directed towards providing Aborigines with the machinery and the opportunity (in the areas

where they live) to be as independent as possible of the pastoralists and to encourage and create opportunities for education and employment outside the pastoral industry if Aborigines wish to take this advantage. (Gibb 1971: 66)[4]

Yet another impetus to decentralisation was the damage being done to sacred sites by the mining industry through prospecting in Central Australia. In 1971 a group of Aboriginal people from Amata in northern South Australia set up a 'permanent camp' (Coombs 1974: 136–7) to the west of Puta Puta to enable people to care for rock arrangements and other sites in the area. Subsequently, yet another camp was set up at a site where a bore had inadvertently been sunk through a ceremonially important hillock (Coombs 1974: 136–7). The members of the Council for Aboriginal Affairs were particularly struck by the 'contentedness and purposefulness' of some of these outstation groups as contrasted at the time with the unhappiness of the Pintupi at Papunya, and, as early as the council meeting of 8–9 July 1970, it had decided to encourage, initially, the establishment of the outstation at Puta Puta as well as another on Sunday Island off Derby in Western Australia (see Dexter 2015: 153, 155).[5]

A final factor in at least one place, Maningrida, came shortly after a major change in Aboriginal lives in remote Australia. This was the direct payment of social security monies to Aboriginal people in 1969, instead of to a mission or government superintendent on their behalf. At Maningrida, this availability of funds led to the opening of a wet canteen there in the same year. According to some accounts, the availability of alcohol greatly aggravated quarrelling and conflict between members of the nine different resident language groups. In 1970, some people who had left an independent bush life only 12 years earlier started to move away from Maningrida—a move that was greatly facilitated by the superintendent, John Hunter, who was very supportive (Meehan and Jones 1980: 133).[6] The same money that was making the increased consumption of alcohol possible also greatly facilitated the establishment of outstations as it provided the means to purchase items from the store without having to work for wages in the settlement.

---

4   Dexter (2015: 480) indicates that Coombs' membership of this committee was 'unwelcome' but clearly had an important influence on its recommendations.

5   Note that Dexter (2015: 155) has misnamed Puta Puta as Pitti Pitti.

6   There are considerable similarities between Maningrida and Papunya, it should be noted. Both were large, mixed-language government settlements established at the height of the assimilation policy in the 1950s. Both were considered to be 'problematic' by the Welfare Branch, as sites of conflict, and particularly look like the problems Rowley emphasised in his books. It is further of interest, one could argue, that John Hunter had influence at both. His policies at Maningrida in support of decentralisation are a matter of record, but it is less well known that he was the DAA officer who visited Yayayi in 1974 to make recommendations about its future and he was very positive about supporting the community, despite his awareness of the still limited development of local political awareness (Myers, personal communication).

From the foregoing, it is clear that there were a considerable number of groups of Aboriginal people choosing to live or remain living in small groups well before the advent of the so-called outstation movement. For all of these groups, access to a limited range of commodities was fundamental to the possibility of outstation life, as well as to managing relations to the surrounding society's goods and services while retaining some local control over their lives.

The impact of the Whitlam Government

The outstation movement proper, as it is generally thought of, started with the election of the Federal Labor Government in 1972. It came in on a platform of land rights and self-determination, reinforcing the end of the assimilation policy announced by William McMahon at the beginning of that year when, on 26 January, Australia Day, he said:[7]

> [Aboriginal people] should be encouraged and assisted to preserve and develop their own culture, languages, traditions and arts so that these can become living elements in the diverse culture of the Australian society … [and exercise] *effective choice about the degree to which, and the pace at which, they come to identify themselves with … [the wider Australian] society* … [The Government would] (a) encourage and strengthen … [Aboriginal people's] capacity increasingly to manage their own affairs—as individuals, as groups, and as communities at the local level; (b) increase their economic independence. (McMahon 1972: 3–4, emphasis added)

Although this had no immediate effect in the north, what one might call the 'ultimate outstation' sprang up on the lawns outside Parliament House with the establishment of the Aboriginal Tent Embassy, shortly after midnight of the day of McMahon's speech in protest at his failure to address the land rights issue.

McMahon's statement was meant to mitigate the negative decision in the first land rights test case, *Milirrpum and Others v NABALCO and the Commonwealth of Australia*, handed down on 27 April 1971. Mr Justice Blackburn had ruled that while the Yolngu people of Yirrkala had a system of law and customs in relation to land, this system could not be recognised under Australian law. The Yolngu had brought their case because a bauxite mine was to be developed on 'their' land without their consent and threatened a number of sites of religious significance near their community (for example, see Williams 1986).

---

7   The principal focus of the speech was rejecting land rights and proposing only leasing land to Aboriginal people, such as the Yirrkala community, which was to be offered a general purpose lease (see Rowse 2000: 67–8).

There is little doubt that the establishment of the Royal Commission into Aboriginal Land Rights and its inquiries across the Northern Territory in 1973 were a major proximate stimulus for the establishment of outstations (Meehan and Jones 1980: 135).[8] Everywhere the commissioner Mr Justice Woodward went, he asked people how they were going to 'look after' their land and what they were going to do with it. This aligned with the new policy outlined by McMahon, which entailed, in theory, funds being available to support such Aboriginal choice. Together, the two policies of 'self-determination' (choice) and land rights were a very powerful combination. Within the year, a number of people at Yirrkala were moving back into the bush (see Morphy and Morphy, this volume), a response that must have been facilitated by the existing outstations in the region serviced by the Reverend Shepherdson. The speed and rate at which groups of people left the communities across Arnhem Land took policymakers by surprise (Rowse 2000: 84). By the beginning of the wet season of 1974, 25 per cent of the Yirrkala population had moved to outstations and likewise approximately 450 people had left Maningrida for outstations, reducing the population by 35 per cent. It was expected that more people would leave in the immediate future (see Gray 1977: 115). In Central Australia, the movement was generally slower to develop, although the third Pintupi attempt at securing their own outstation was probably among the very first, if not the first, post–Labor Government outstation to be established (see Myers, this volume). The Yayayi location was not itself on their own land, which lay in and around the Kintore Range to the west, where they were to eventually get a fully serviced settlement of their own, first established in 1981. However, their move out from Papunya also led to the local landowners setting up another outstation, at Mount Liebig bore, eventually leading to the emergence of a whole new identity group (see Holcombe, this volume).

Rather than articulating anything like the full range of motivations for moving to outstations, most Aboriginal participants themselves simply emphasised their desire to return to their own country. The primary evidence for other dimensions of these decisions has come from reports by anthropologists. Some of the earliest public formulations of the reasons, however, were synthesised by H. C. ('Nugget') Coombs both on the basis of his own visits to the early outstations in 1973 and from his conversations with anthropologists (see Coombs 1974). His accounts of the movement are particularly relevant because Coombs was at the height of his powers and influence on policymaking in Aboriginal affairs in the period 1967–75. He was at that time the chair of the Council for Aboriginal Affairs and the chief government adviser on Aboriginal policy. In his account of Coombs' legacy in Indigenous affairs, Tim Rowse (2000: 84) reports that the outstation movement

---

8   Peterson makes this point on the basis of having worked as the research officer to the commission and being present at the consultations across the Territory.

cut across his earlier assumption that places like Yirrkala, where the outstation movement got off to a very rapid start, would persist. Coombs subsequently devoted considerable energy to understanding the choice by Aboriginal people to move to outstations (for example, see Coombs 1974, 1978, 1979; Coombs et al. 1982). His initial understanding was in relation to three factors: the special relationship to the land and concern about protecting sacred sites from damage; the desire to regain control over the young and avoid the stress and conflict associated with living in large communities (see Myers; Peterson; Cane, this volume); and a desire to minimise white presence and influence in their lives, including the alcohol they were associated with (Coombs 1974: 141).[9]

More nuanced understandings emerged quite quickly from observers close to the activities. One issue that became clear was the significance of what one might call 'local' or 'inter-group' politics, particularly as it related to the relationship between the landowners on whose land the missions and settlements were originally built and the majority of the population, whose land was elsewhere. Local attachments were clearly more significant than assimilation policy anticipated. This seems likely to have been as significant at Yirrkala, as described by Morphy and Morphy (this volume), as it was at Maningrida (Altman, this volume) and Papunya (Myers, this volume). As a second influence, the financial support available for people on outstations was also attractive. If a group demonstrated that they were committed to living at their outstation for a year, through all the seasons, they would become eligible for a $10,000 grant that provided enough to buy a four-wheel-drive vehicle (typically, a Toyota LandCruiser). Thus, by moving back to the bush, senior men were able to draw the administration into direct negotiations with them, circumventing the domination of their lives by the landowners of the mission or settlement, who often appropriated more than a fair share of the resources at the disposal of the council. Such financial support articulated with long-prevailing Indigenous understandings of senior men's authority and political autonomy as the foundation of Indigenous polity.

Other arrangements followed, it seems necessarily, the establishment of outstations themselves. As early as 1974, the community of Maningrida started to develop a special unit to help service the outstations, which was to turn into the Bawinanga Aboriginal Corporation in 1979 and become the oldest outstation 'resource centre'. By the early 1980s, there were a number of such

---

9   Interestingly, Barrie Dexter (2015: 153) indicates that the report written by Stanner after his visit to Yirrkala, and submitted to the council on 28 November 1969, suggested two additional reasons for people wanting to move out of Yirrkala: to tend to their land and perform ceremonies necessary for its continued health and bounty; and to occupy their land in the forlorn hope of thereby preventing non-Aboriginal people from moving into it and devastating it by exploitation.

outstation resource centres, which consolidated the separation of the resources for outstation populations from those of the local town-dwellers (see Palmer, this volume).

The struggle over resources is important in the understanding of Aboriginal motivation for the formation of outstations, and helps to ground the sometimes romantic views of the public who imagine a disinterested Aboriginal political field and believe Aboriginal people to be community-oriented communalists (see Martin and Martin, this volume). These struggles also can be seen to illuminate the limits of Indigenous polities as self-governing forms, limited by the capacities to share resources and moral identity in larger, sedentary communities. Rolf Gerritsen argued that the entry of the Commonwealth Government into providing funding for outstations (as well as the NT Government), created the opportunity for prominent men to circumvent the power of the dominant male landowners of the mission or settlements by moving to an outstation and securing a highly prized vehicle.[10] In Gerritsen's view, these vehicles were a constant source of tension with the Department of Aboriginal Affairs since they were used for a great deal more than servicing the outstations, leading the Government to start providing tractors instead, which were a major cause of complaint (Gerritsen 1982: 62).

In any case, the struggle over resources—at least that between settlements and outstations—was somewhat reduced with the advent of the Community Development Employment Projects (CDEP) scheme in 1977. This allowed the pooling of all unemployment benefits due to people in any community, together with a 20 per cent add-on for administration and equipment, so that people could work for the dole on a wide range of projects, including those that would not normally be counted as appropriate 'work'. This CDEP money made the proliferation of outstation resource centres possible and contributed greatly to the growth of the Aboriginal art movement in the 1980s. Such money could be used to help fund the art centres that marketed art, which became a major source of income for many in remote Australia, including those on outstations (see Altman; and Thorley, this volume).

The complex history of policies for outstations

The majority of outstations have always been in the Northern Territory. Thus, policy for these has influenced the policy for outstations elsewhere, especially because it directly involved the Commonwealth. Complications began with

---

10   See also the arguments and discussion in Myers (1986) about the centripetal push of Indigenous concerns of autonomy on the formation of dispersed outstations in the Pintupi case.

the granting of self-government to the Northern Territory on 1 July 1978. The resulting self-government divided services to outstations between two jurisdictions. At that time, the Commonwealth Government handed over responsibility for running municipal and local government services for Aboriginal townships, of which there were approximately 70, to the Territory. It retained responsibility, however, for the provision of most services to all other communities—described as 'smaller communities' or 'outstations'—of which there were approximately 500. Calling these smaller communities 'outstations' was very confusing because it included a wide range of settlement types, many much larger and older than outstations as discussed here. This arrangement remained in place until 1 July 2008 when the Commonwealth handed back responsibility for all these smaller communities ('outstations') to the Northern Territory along with a small annual payment of $20 million to fund them. The irony here, as Bob Beadman (2011) points out, is that if full responsibility for 'outstations' had been transferred to the Northern Territory in 1978 the funds would have been factored into baseline funding and indexed forever.

Outstation policy has been a varied story, overseen by many differently acronymed and politically embedded administrative forms. During this 30-year period, 'outstations' were initially under the Department of Aboriginal Affairs (DAA), then the Aboriginal and Torres Strait Islander Commission (ATSIC), then the Department of Immigration and Multicultural and Indigenous Affairs and then the various manifestations of the Department of Families, Housing, Community Services and Indigenous Affairs. Because the Territory has always had responsibility for essential services (water, power, sewerage, roads, airstrips and barge landings) for townships, there was constant argument about when an 'outstation' was so big that it was a township. Further, the Territory has also always had responsibility for education, health services and policing on 'outstations'. Housing, on the other hand, was a Commonwealth responsibility, taken on in 1980 by yet another body, the Commonwealth Aboriginal Development Commission. One can imagine the three-way arguments that were occasioned between the commission, the DAA and the NT Government about the provision of what sorts of housing and where. A consequence of these shifting and split administrations was that some conventional houses were built on outstations without power or water. From another perspective, of course, a more positive consequence of this complexity was the small political space it left for outstation communities, either directly or through their local outstation resource centre, to try to play one administration off against another.

Such complexities became a central part of the subsequent histories of outstations. Scott Cane (this volume) and Jon Altman (this volume) both provide searing accounts of the difficulties encountered by Indigenous leaders who sought to establish and maintain their communities in the face of almost endless administrative changes in their 'political environment'—difficulties that led to their exhaustion, depression and decline. One has to wonder at the 'capacities' imagined for 'self-determination' on a scale that included management of infrastructure that few non-Indigenous communities would face. Cane (this volume) considers some of the implications of the change from 'self-determination' to 'self-management'. These have continued to be significant issues in the representation of 'outstations', although there has been little attention to the history of such projects of 'self-determination' in their actual political environment, while failure has often been cast as the result of cultural inadequacy, nepotism or lack of interest.

In July 1985, the House of Representatives Standing Committee on Aboriginal Affairs received a reference on outstations and their futures, eventually reporting in March 1987. Its report, known as the Blanchard Report, listed 588 outstations, with an estimated population of 9,538, and a further 3,921 Aboriginal people in the Northern Territory living on excisions—in effect outstations—from 111 pastoral leases (Blanchard 1987: Appendix 4). Other estimates put the total number of outstations at 625 and the total population at 17,527 in 1985 (see Altman and Taylor 1987: 4). The dynamic nature of the situation is revealed by the Department of Aboriginal Affairs' estimate that in June 1981 there were only 165 outstations, with a total population of 4,200 (Blanchard 1987: 18). Overall, the report was very supportive and made a range of recommendations about service delivery.

The variability in the statistics suggests a dynamic situation but also gives some grounds for caution about them. While there was great variation in the size of the outstation population, the average was 25 people, so it is not surprising that Blanchard recorded 159 outstations (see Altman and Taylor 1987: 5) as having no population, since many outstation populations were not serviced from the local centre but had to go into the local centre to purchase supplies, cash their social security cheques and access medical treatment. These figures underline the fact that outstations are not isolated places but are linked into complex regional social networks with other outstations and one or more regional centres, between which there is a great deal of movement (see Morphy and Morphy, this volume).

The rapid growth of outstations was probably responsible for ATSIC's 1996 moratoriums not only on support for new outstations but also on building more houses at any of them. In the next year, ATSIC arranged a review of outstation resource centres, which estimated, on the basis of official statistics, that there were about 1,000 outstations serviced by approximately 100 funded outstation resource centres with a total population of about 12,000 (see Palmer, this volume). In this study, the reviewers tried to mirror the residential complexity and mobility by providing minimum, maximum, usual and effective population figures. They extrapolate from their sample to suggest an effective population of 19,572 across approximately 1,400 outstations nationally. These figures make it clear that outstations were central to the life of many people in remote regions although their significance varied greatly from outstation to outstation. While many had permanent populations year in and year out, others were more like holiday camps or were just visited at the weekend (for example, Thompson n.d.: Ch. 6, on eastern Cape York).

During the first decade of the twenty-first century, a strong and effective case has been, and is still being, made by Jon Altman and others (for a way into this literature, see Altman and Kerins 2012) for the enormously important role outstation populations could play in looking after what has come to be called the 'Indigenous estate'.[11]

The 'Indigenous estate' includes large areas of some of the most pristine environments left in the country. Looking after it in the national interest, it is argued, could provide employment opportunities for outstation residents who are ideally located to provide a wide range of environmental services. Aboriginal people's interest in these opportunities is shown in the wide adoption of 'Caring for Country' programs, and their preparedness to grant Indigenous Protected Area (IPA) status to large areas of Aboriginal land, covering 260,000 sq km between 50 IPAs in 2012 (see Altman 2012: 13), making this land part of the National Reserve System. Nationwide, 680 Aboriginal people are now employed in ranger positions.[12]

At the same time, however, as the first decade of the twenty-first century passed the halfway mark, there was a hardening of government attitudes to the funding of 'outstations' and some strong voices criticising them. Critics such as Gary Johns (for example, 2009) and Helen Hughes (2007) were receiving a hearing in policy circles. The same people, and others, have also been highly critical of the CDEP scheme, which has been characterised as not providing 'real' work, and indeed in some cases as being no more than an income support program. Such a poor understanding of the nature and complexity of 'outstation' economies and the role of CDEP schemes in them has threatened what informed observers feel is a scheme crucial to many very worthwhile projects. Hughes and other critics view 'outstations' as the ultimate expression of what they regard as a senseless policy of supporting Aboriginal people to maintain separation from the mainstream economy. For Hughes and Johns, there is no justification for the long-term support of even the remote Aboriginal towns. What is needed, they

---

11   This term refers to the totality of the land held under various titles by Aboriginal people, which now amounts to more than 22 per cent of Australia.
12   This allowed large areas of Aboriginal land with high environmental and cultural heritage values to be incorporated into the National Reserve System, which is established according to criteria set out by the International Union for Conservation of Nature (Altman 2012: 13).

maintain, is to get the economic incentives right to motivate people to join the mainstream. Neither author shows any sign of understanding the diversity of life situations in Aboriginal Australia, nor any understanding of the diversity of motivations and cultural orientation present today.[13]

With the transfer of Commonwealth responsibilities for 'outstations' to the Northern Territory in 2008, and the rapid changes of policy after the Intervention in 2007, from 'Closing the Gap' to the 'Working Future' policy issued on 20 May 2009 and then a first ever NT policy for 'outstations/homelands', a new and unsympathetic regime was clearly articulated. There is to be no support for new outstations or building houses on them. The rationale for this is articulated in terms of outstations being on private land and so outside government responsibility for public housing. To secure support, existing outstations must be occupied for at least eight to nine months of the year, each resident can only maintain one principal place of residence, there must be adequate drinkable water as per national guidelines, and the residents must commit to increasing self-sufficiency by making reasonable financial contributions for services.[14]

Conclusion

Writing about malaise in the Central Australian community of Areyonga in 1970, Nugget Coombs (1978: 11) commented that it was a community that appeared to lack the stimulus of achievable aspirations. Much the same could have been said about many such remote communities. The changes to policy in 1972–73, however, provided Aboriginal people across remote Australia with the stimulus of immediately achievable aspirations to which many responded rapidly. It is evident that initially older men led these movements, but by the late 1970s, the population structure in the larger communities had stabilised to approach that in the regional centres (see Young 1982: 73; Blanchard 1987: 32–3). Indeed, the masculinity ratios and age structure suggest that women and children were the anchors in most regions of the Northern Territory (Young 1982: 81). The motivations of the movers to outstations came to be well understood as driven by the desire of people to take charge of their lives, to be on or near the country of the founders of the outstation and to gain access to newly available resources. They were also an immediate response to the growing conflict in the larger communities aggravated by access to cash and alcohol, and loss of control over younger family members. The achievable aspirations were not long-term plans for the future. Likewise, with hindsight, it is evident

---

13   Of course, the future of these orientations and motivations for the younger generations remains to be seen.
14   See policy at: www.aph.gov.au/~/media/wopapub/senate/committee/indig_ctte/hearings/Northern_Territory_Government_b_pdf.ashx (accessed 31 July 2014).

that the policymakers' vision of the place of the outstation movement also did not look to the future or incorporate any long-term view, although somewhere in the recesses of their minds there was a concern about it. Indeed, Charles Perkins, then secretary of the Department of Aboriginal Affairs, described the movement as creating a 'breathing space' from which outstation-dwellers 'can start a number of other things. They can look at what options are available to them; what opportunities are available; what the good and bad things are in white society' (Blanchard 1987: 85).

It is significant that only a small number of outstations have metamorphosed into permanent townships in their own right, reproducing the settlements with the full range of services but at a more manageable scale. In each of these cases, they were originally outstations located at a maximum distance from the regional centre and created by people who were among the last to settle down. As the chapters by Nicolas Peterson, Sutton and David and Bruce Martin suggest, the role of non-Indigenous outsiders was usually important if not crucial in this transformation. The reason seems to be the role they played in ensuring the reliability and predictability of supplies and the working of key infrastructure.

Support from policymakers for the outstation movement initially simply tracked Aboriginal desires in the context of a period of radical reorientation of government attitudes with the Labor Party election that saw the establishment of the National Aboriginal Consultative Committee (in 1973), the Royal Commission into Aboriginal Land Rights (1972–74), the passing of the *Racial Discrimination Act* (1975) and the policy of self-determination. The rhetoric was the right to choose and the obligation of the Government to support Aboriginal people as citizens. With the general shift to the right and now a Liberal Federal Government, land rights are being cast as private property when it suits government, and citizenship is conceived of in terms of an obligation to move towards, if not achieving, self-sufficiency. In November 2014, when it became clear that the limited Commonwealth funding for outstations in the States would not be extended, both Western Australia and South Australia made it clear that they could not support very small communities often with only five people. In Western Australia, up to 150 such communities have been identified as likely to lose all support and it seems clear that virtually all of these are Aboriginal.

While there clearly are significant issues about equitable expenditure in remote areas, the extent of the negative focus on outstations appears as a huge diversion from the real issues. Only a small proportion—about a maximum of 10 per cent at the very most—of the remote Aboriginal population lives in outstations, which by and large provide their residents with satisfactory lives. All of the real policy challenges relate to the large regional centres, where social problems are often considerable and economic activity is limited. All that withdrawing support from outstations will do is to swell the numbers in the regional centres, adding to their immediate problems, such as in the area of housing, and to the number of people without work. When government has resolved the policy issues around the major remote communities, outstations might sensibly feature on the agenda. Meanwhile, outstations provide a more desirable form of long-term dependency for a portion of the remote population who have crafted their life projects around them and it is in the interests of all concerned to find ways to continue to support them.

Reflecting on this history of the early period of the establishment of outstations, it is evident that it was never a simple attempt to turn the clock back to a pre-contact ideal, although key Aboriginal motivations had their basis in pre-existing cultural orientations. Central to the life projects that the founders of the outstations were seeking to realise was the desire for political autonomy, to be in charge of their lives, which drew on a long history of value related to ideas of personal autonomy and authority, with their basis in land ownership. Land ownership determined in most cases where people established their outstations, as in western Cape York, throughout Arnhem Land and in much of Central Australia. This was not always in terms of the primary rights of the founders, as in some situations practical factors such as logistical constraints intervened, as in the case of the Pintupi at Yayayi or the Balgo residents who moved to Yagga Yagga, or in the light of pre-existing infrastructure, as for the Ngaanyatjara, or land title constraints at Ntaria/Hermannsburg. But in these compromise situations, the drive for autonomy by being separate was clearly there, as confirmed by the situation at Hermannsburg, the emergence of satellite outstations from Yagga Yagga and in the way that Pintupi worked their way westwards back to their homeland. In the case of Doyndji and some of the early South Australian outstations, another enduring value was quite explicit: the desire and responsibility to protect key sites on the land.

The varied histories and successes of the many outstations clearly suggest the complexities of the issues around self-determination. The evidence from those outstations that have turned into small sustainable communities, where contentedness and purposefulness are more clearly evident than in some of the larger communities, provides further evidence that such communities are not a disengagement from Australian society. All of them have been established and sustained collaboratively with the help of non-Indigenous people who have been attentive to the life projects of Aboriginal men and women seeking their own solutions to the wicked policy problems around the future of remote communities. Outstations are only one solution, and they are not without some of their own problems, nor are they a solution necessarily attractive to the majority of the remote population, but government needs to recognise their true significance and to find equitable ways to draw them into the array of policies for remote area populations.

References

Altman, J. 2012. People on country as alternate development. In J. Altman and S. Kerins (eds), *People on Country: Vital Landscapes, Indigenous Futures*. Sydney: The Federation Press, pp. 1–25.

Altman, J. and Kerins, S. (eds) 2012. *People on Country: Vital Landscapes, Indigenous Futures*. Sydney: The Federation Press.

Altman, J. and Taylor, L. 1987. *The economic viability of Aboriginal outstations and homeland*. A Report to the Australian Council for Employment and Training. Canberra: AGPS.

Austin-Broos, D. 2006. Working for and working among Western Arrernte in Central Australia. *Oceania* 76(1): 1–15.

Beadman, B. 2011. *Coordinator General for Remote Indigenous Services Six Monthly Report*. Canberra: Commonwealth Government.

Berndt, R. 1962. *An Adjustment Movement in Arnhem Land, Northern Territory of Australia*. Paris: Mouton.

Blanchard, C. A. 1987. *Return to Country: The Aboriginal Homelands Movement in Australia. Report of the House of Representatives Standing Committee on Aboriginal Affairs*. Canberra: AGPS.

Blaser, M. 2004. Life projects: Indigenous people's agency and development. In M. Blaser, H. Feit and G. McRae (eds), *In the Way of Development: Indigenous Peoples, Life Projects and Globalization*. London: Zed Books, pp. 26–44.

Cavanagh, J. L. 1974. *Selected Policy Statements on Aboriginal Affairs 1973–1974*. Canberra: AGPS.

Coombs, H. C. 1974. Decentralization trends among Aboriginal communities. *Search* 5(4): 135–43.

Coombs, H. C. 1978. *Some aspects of development in Aboriginal communities in Central Australia following visits to them in April–May 1978*. CRES Working Paper HCC/5. Canberra: Centre for Resource and Environmental Studies.

Coombs, H. C. 1979. *The Future of the Outstation Movement*. Canberra: Centre for Resource and Environmental Studies.

Coombs, H. C., Dexter, B. and Hiatt, L. 1982. The outstation movement in Aboriginal Australia. In E. Leacock and R. Lee (eds), *Politics and History in Band Societies*. Cambridge: Cambridge University Press, pp. 427–39.

Dexter, B. 2015. *Pandora's Box: The Council for Aboriginal Affairs 1967–1976*. G. Foley and E. Howell eds. Brisbane: Keeira Press.

Doolan, J. 1977. Walk-off (and later return) of various Aboriginal groups from cattle stations: Victoria River district, Northern Territory. In R. M. Berndt (ed.), *Aborigines and Change: Australia in the '70s*. Canberra: Australian Institute of Aboriginal Studies, pp. 106–13.

Eastley, T. 2005. Vanstone says remote Indigenous communities becoming 'cultural museums'. *AM*, ABC Radio, 9 December.

Falkenberg, J. 1962. *Kin and Totem: Group Relations of Australian Aborigines in the Port Keats District*. Oslo: Oslo University Press.

Gerritsen, R. 1982. Outstations: Differing interpretations and policy implications. In P. Loveday (ed.), *Service Delivery to Outstations*. Darwin: North Australia Research Unit, pp. 57–69.

Gibb, C. A. 1971. *The Report of the Committee to Review the Situation of Aborigines on Pastoral Properties in the Northern Territory*. Canberra: Department of the Interior.

Glowczewski, B. 1983. Manifestations Symbolisque d'une Transition Economique: Le Juluru, Culte Intertribal du Cargo (Australie Occidentale et Centrale) [Symbolic manifestations of economic transition: The Juluru intertribal cargo cult (Western and Central Australia)]. *L'Homme* 23(2): 7–35.

Goffman, E. 1961. *Asylums: Essays on the Social Situation of Mental Patients and Other Inmates*. New York: Anchor Books.

Gray, W. 1977. Decentralization trends in Arnhem Land. In R. M. Berndt (ed.), *Aborigines and Change: Australia in the '70s*. Canberra: Australian Institute of Aboriginal Studies, pp. 114–23.

Hardy, F. 1968. *The Unlucky Australia*. Melbourne: Thomas Nelson.

Hughes, H. 2007. *Lands of Shame: Aboriginal and Torres Strait Islander 'Homelands' in Transition*. Sydney: Centre for Independent Studies.

Johns, G. 2009. *No Job, No house: An Economically Strategic Approach to Remote Aboriginal Housing*. Canberra: The Menzies Research Centre.

Kimber, D. 1977. Aboriginal organisation: An examination of some potential problem areas. *Aboriginal Nutrition*: 2–4.

Kolig, E. 1979. Djuluru: Ein Synkretistischer Kult Nordwest Australiens [Djuluru: A syncretic cult in Western Australia]. *Baessler-Archiv* 27: 419–48.

Kowal, E. 2010. Is culture the problem or the solution? Outstation health and the politics of remoteness. In J. Altman and M. Hinkson (eds), *Culture Crisis: Anthropology and Politics in Aboriginal Australia*. Sydney: UNSW Press, pp. 179–94.

Long, J. 1964. The Pintupi patrols: Welfare work with the desert Aborigines—the later phases. *Australian Territories* 4(6): 24–35.

McMahon, W. 1972. *Australian Aborigines. Commonwealth Policy and Achievements*. Canberra: W. G. Murray, Government Printer.

Meehan, B. and Jones, R. 1980. The outstation movement and hints of a white backlash. In R. Jones (ed.), *Northern Australia: Options and Implications*. Canberra: The Australian National University, pp. 131–57.

Myers, F. n.d. *What is the Business of the Balgo Business: A Contemporary Aboriginal Religious Movement*. Canberra: AIATSIS Library.

Myers, F. 1986. *Pintupi Country, Pintupi Self: Sentiment, Place and Politics among Western Desert Aborigines*. Washington, DC: Smithsonian Institution Press.

Peterson, N. 1976. Ethnoarchaeology in the Australian Iron Age: An Arnhem Land perspective on Aboriginal conservatism. In G. De G. Sieveking (ed.), *Problems in Social and Economic Archaeology*. London: Duckworth, pp. 265–75.

Pilling, A. 1962. A historical 'versus' a non-historical approach to social change and continuity among the Tiwi. *Oceania* 32(4): 321–6.

Rowley, C. 1970. *The Destruction of Aboriginal Society*. Canberra: The Australian National University Press.

Rowse. T. 1993. *After Mabo: Interpreting Indigenous Traditions*. Melbourne: Melbourne University Press.

Rowse, T. 2000. *Obliged to be Difficult: Nugget Coombs' Legacy in Indigenous Affairs*. Cambridge: Cambridge University Press.

Rowse, T. 2012. *Rethinking Social Justice: From 'Peoples' to 'Populations'*. Canberra: Aboriginal Studies Press.

Shepherdson, E. 1981. *Half a Century in Arnhem Land*. Adelaide: H. & E. Shepherdson.

Stanner, W. E. H. 2011. The Dreaming. In *The Dreaming and Other Essays*. Melbourne: Black Inc. Agenda.

Taylor, J. and Bell, M. 2004. Continuity and change in Indigenous Australian population mobility. In J. Taylor and M. Bell (eds), *Population Mobility and Indigenous Peoples in Australasia and North America*. London: Routledge, pp. 13–43.

Thompson, D. n.d. Freedom to choose: Responding to change in a mobile environment among Aboriginal people of Lockhart River, Cape York Peninsula, Australia. Unpublished PhD thesis. University of Queensland, Brisbane.

Williams, N. 1986. *The Yolngu and Their Land: A System of Land Tenure and the Fight for its Recognition*. Stanford: Stanford University Press.

Young, E. 1982. Outstations 1981: The wider setting. In P. Loveday (ed.), *Service Delivery to Outstations*. Darwin: North Australia Research Unit, pp. 70–84.

HISTORY AND MEMORY

2

From Coombes to Coombs: Reflections on the Pitjantjatjara outstation movement

Bill Edwards

In September 1957, nearing the end of my studies at the University of Melbourne, I met the Reverend Victor Coombes, general secretary of the Presbyterian Board of Missions, to discuss the possibility of serving on a north Queensland Gulf mission. What motivated my interest in Aboriginal missions in an era when the more exotic overseas missions such as in the New Hebrides (Vanuatu) and Korea received more attention? Growing up in a very small country town in the Wimmera region of Victoria in the 1930s, I had little knowledge of Aboriginal people and their history. Monuments on nearby roads bearing the words 'Major Mitchell passed by here' suggested that this was the beginning of history. A rare meeting with an Aboriginal person was when a 'swagman' passed through my hometown of Lubeck. In return for the food my parents gave him, he cut firewood and gave my father an incised boomerang—now one of my prized possessions.

My studies in arts, education and theology in Melbourne contributed nothing to my knowledge of Aboriginal culture and history. However, in 1954, I visited universities around Australia as a staff worker with a Christian student organisation, the Inter-Varsity Fellowship. A visit to Adelaide in March that year coincided with a visit by the Ernabella Mission Choir. They came to see

Queen Elizabeth II on her Australian tour. I heard them sing in the Teachers College and spent time with them at their accommodation, not imagining that four years later I would assume the role of conducting the choir. The next year, I visited Alice Springs as a member of a work party, and in 1957, I heard Doug Nicholls (later Sir Douglas) speak at the University of Melbourne, after his visit to the Western Desert region of Western Australia to investigate the effects of the Woomera rocket range tests on Aboriginal people. These events contributed to my interest in Aboriginal missions.

When I met Victor Coombes, he had recently visited Ernabella. Two matters arising from that visit led him to invite me to take on a role there as assistant to the superintendent, the Reverend Bruce Edenborough. First, my immediate responsibilities would be to assist him in this multifunctional role. Coombes obviously took note of the fact that I was raised in a country storekeeper's family and had worked as a bank clerk before entering university. These skills were required at Ernabella. Second, Coombes, concerned at the pressure on water and firewood supplies as the Ernabella population increased, proposed that a series of outstations be established to the west to enable some residents to return to their traditional homelands. He suggested that after a period at Ernabella, I would move to open the first of these outstations. After completing a Summer Institute of Linguistics course, I arrived at Ernabella on 2 May 1958. Ernabella is in the Musgrave Ranges in traditional lands of the Yankunytjatjara people, although the majority of residents are Pitjantjatjara. People of these Western Desert dialect groups are often referred to now as Anangu, a term meaning 'person' or 'body'.

Because of health problems, the Edenborough family left Ernabella in September 1958. I was appointed acting superintendent (and later superintendent). Thus, the plan to proceed to an outstation did not eventuate, although in 1961, I supervised the establishment of the first outstation, Fregon, and in later years spent much time visiting the newly established homeland communities of the 1970s. Here I will outline and reflect on the history of the Anangu outstation movement in the light of my own experiences and observations.

Several writers attribute the outstation movement to the influence of Dr H. C. ('Nugget') Coombs, an economist and former governor of the Reserve Bank, who in his retirement became involved in Aboriginal affairs. For example, another economist, Helen Hughes (2007: 11), referred to the 'Coombs socialist "homeland" model'. In this chapter, I will question Hughes' assumptions about this movement and its origins. I will refer to outstation movements in Aboriginal Australia that predated Coombs' involvement. As the term 'outstations' assumes the existence of previous 'stations', reference will be made to the establishment of mission and government settlements in the region and to the motivation for, and development of, the homeland movement in the Anangu region, and will conclude with brief comments on the present state of this movement. I will also question some of the romanticism expressed in some of the earlier writings about homelands.

The terms 'outstation' and 'homeland' are used interchangeably here. Outstation, a term with a long history of usage in Australia, was used in the Anangu area in the early stages of the movement. The term homeland was applied in Arnhem Land, and despite reservations about its use because of its connotations in South Africa during the apartheid era, its usage spread to other regions.

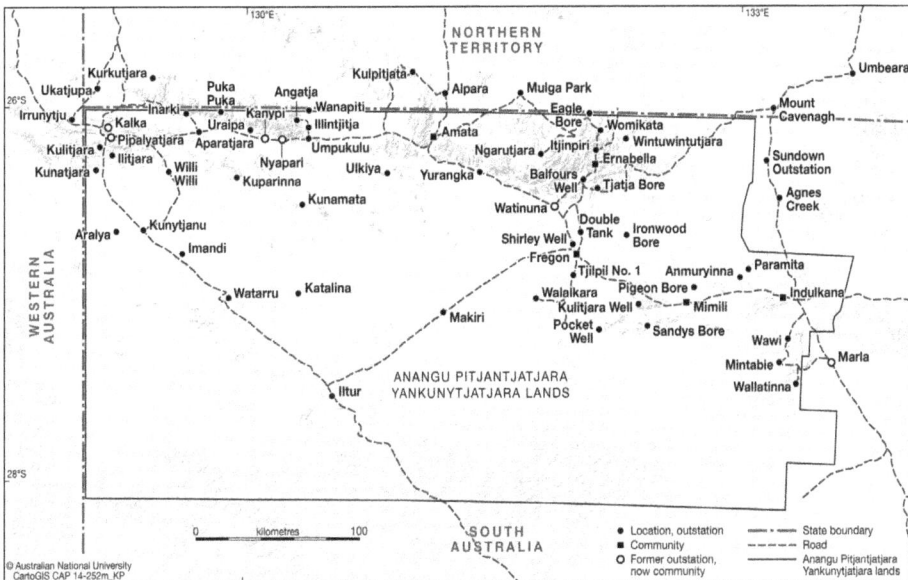

Map 2.1 Ernabella and its Pitjantjatjara outstations.
Source: Karina Pelling, CartoGIS, ANU College of Asia and the Pacific

Literature review

Before embarking on the history of settlements in the Anangu region, some issues raised in the literature associated with the homeland movement will be identified. In 1973, Dr Coombs presented a paper entitled 'Decentralization trends among Aboriginal communities' at the 45th Australian and New Zealand Association for the Advancement of Science (ANZAAS) Congress in Perth. As chairman of the Council of Aboriginal Affairs, he visited communities throughout Australia. He described the movement as 'one response to the complex problems created by contact with our society' (Coombs 1974: 135).

He referred to the problems of institutionalism on settlements and tensions arising when people from different clans and language groups lived together on these stations. According to Coombs:

> [A] growing desire to break away from this was stimulated by land rights campaigning and a desire to demonstrate the reality of these rights, reports of damage to sacred sites, increased access to income such as pensions and child endowment and changes of policy by government officials and missionaries who encouraged groups to assert their own identity. (1974: 136)

An arts administrator, Peter Brokensha, in *The Pitjantjatjara and Their Crafts* (1975), referred to problems associated with some early outstations as rivalry was engendered between groups as they competed for European resources. However, he concluded that the principal motivation for the return to sites was 'what could be termed an act of religious faith' (Brokensha 1975: 15). In an article published in 1977, Brokensha and McGuigan recorded that 200 people had left Amata, Ernabella and Fregon to establish homeland centres. While happy to be back in their lands, some women expressed concerns at the lack of health and education services and there was ambivalence as to the extent to which building development should take place and non-Aboriginal assistants be employed (Brokensha and McGuigan 1977: 120). A report in *The Canberra Times* of 15 November 1977 referred to a submission to establish a homeland health service. It claimed that 1,000 people had moved from the major settlements to 16 outstations (Waterford 1977). From my observation of the outstations at that time, I suggest that this figure was greatly inflated.

Noel Wallace, who undertook research at Amata settlement from the late 1960s and visited several traditional sites with groups of Anangu, wrote a comprehensive report on Pitjantjatjara decentralisation in 1977. While acknowledging that there were several motivations, he emphasised the desire to be near one's country, where spirit ancestors travelled (Wallace 1977: 124).

A report by Heppell and Wigley, also published in 1977, noted differing ideas about the movement between old and young people and suggested that the Coombs' model of simple camps was too restrictive and would frustrate the ambitions of younger people (1977: 4).

In an article in the *Adelaide Preview* in 1979, John Tregenza referred to the homeland movement as 'a rejection of European solutions to Aboriginal problems' (1979: 3). Tregenza, a welfare officer at Amata, moved to one of the first major outstations, at Wingelinna, as community adviser in 1975. He asserted that in earlier decades, Anangu had been encouraged to leave their lands and migrate to missions and government settlements to the east, where a colonial status quo was maintained. However, he overlooked the extent of migration that had taken place as the people themselves moved east because of drought, the attraction of new resources at the encroaching white settlements, the fact that those settlements were homelands to some of their residents, and the encouragement that had been given to Anangu to maintain links with their traditional sites. His assertion that 'white superintendents and their staff made all the decisions on behalf of their subjects' (Tregenza 1979: 3) disregarded the domains of Anangu life in which they continued to make decisions and the consultation that took place between staff and Anangu people.

Tregenza recorded that by 1976, 76 per cent of the Amata population had decentralised and that in 1979 there were 1,500 people in Pitjantjatjara homelands compared with only 500 at European-founded settlements (1979: 3). These figures do not correspond with demographic survey numbers I recorded in the area and appear to have been inflated to support proposals for the establishment of a homelands health centre. Figures I recorded are presented later in this chapter.

A report on the outstation movement published in 1980 by the Institute of Aboriginal Studies contained three papers written by Coombs, Barrie Dexter and Les Hiatt. They interpreted the movement as 'an attempt to select and integrate elements of both Aboriginal and European traditions in a context free from white domination' (Coombs et al. 1980: 19). They observed that while outstations were more peaceful than settlements, an initial euphoria was followed in some places by a degree of frustration and disputes over land ownership, leadership and property.

The most strident critic of the homelands movement was the late Helen Hughes, a Senior Fellow of the Centre for Independent Studies and frequent contributor to *The Australian* newspaper. While she assembled statistics to support her claims about welfare dependency, low educational standards and violence on remote communities, she made broad, unsubstantiated statements and underestimated the role of Anangu in establishing outstations. Her argument was based on a broad distinction between two models of Indigenous development: 1) a liberal model that aims to integrate Indigenous peoples into the economic mainstream; and 2) a socialist model that promotes separatism (Hughes 2007: 11). This dichotomy blurs the intricate nature of the movement. With her focus on Coombs, Hughes overlooked earlier outstation developments.

Earlier Aboriginal outstation movements

Much of the rhetoric associated with the homeland movement assumed that this was a new phenomenon, without precedent. However, Fregon was established as a result of Reverend Coombes' vision of outstation settlements. Much earlier, missions had experimented with similar proposals as they realised that tensions were created when people from several clans lived together in permanent settlements. For example, after the establishment of Mapoon Mission on Cape York Peninsula in north Queensland in 1891, as the population grew to 400, families settled at two outstations, in 1905 and 1906. They were designed to 'develop self-reliance and local energy' (W. Edwards 2007: 272). At these outstations, referred to as 'homesteads', the Aboriginal residents cultivated corn, pumpkins, cassava and other crops.

The Presbyterian Church established Aurukun Mission south of Mapoon in 1898. The Reverend Bill MacKenzie, who served there as superintendent from 1923 to 1965, also encouraged the people to settle on outstations in order to become more self-supporting and independent. A couple, Uki and Archiwald, established an outstation south of Aurukun in 1933 to work with people who lived in that region (B. Edwards 2009: 39; MacKenzie 1981: 140). This was an example of an earlier outstation based largely on Aboriginal initiative. Another outstation was established, at Peret, 25 km south of Aurukun, in the 1960s. Cattle camps, including Titree, were another example of outstations based on Aurukun. Other early examples of outstations in north Queensland were those established near the Church of England's Trebanaman Mission, later renamed Mitchell River, which was founded in 1905. In a 1922 publication, Logan Jack listed Angeram, Koongalara and Daphne as outstations (1922: 680).

Figure 2.1 Aparatjara outstation in 1978.
Source: Bill Edwards

One of the most adventurous efforts to support outstations was that of the Reverend Harold Shepherdson, who was appointed to the Methodist Mission at Milingimbi in Arnhem Land in 1927. In 1942, he established Elcho Island Mission. He and his wife, Ella, remained in Arnhem Land for 50 years. Shepherdson realised that the aeroplane was the answer to isolation and medical emergencies. In 1933 he sent to America for a blueprint for a monoplane, obtained linen from Ireland and an engine from England and constructed his own plane. Over the years he had several planes, which he used to supply outstations. Ella later wrote:

> As many Aborigines wanted to stay in their own areas and not at the Mission Stations, the outstation work was conceived. These places were inaccessible except by aeroplane, so the people set to and cleared airstrips, using only hand tools, axes, shovels and saws. (Shepherdson 1981: 35)

In her memoir, Ella Shepherdson records the establishment of several outstations that her husband serviced by air, the first being at Gattji, 16 km south of Milingimbi (1981: 35–8). Nugget Coombs (1974: 140) referred to Shepherdson's 'courageous and imaginative servicing by air of these communities'.

In Central Australia, the Lutheran missionaries at Hermannsburg established outposts at Haasts Bluff (in 1941), Papunya (1954) and Areyonga (1942), to provide Aboriginal people with food and other resources in an attempt to limit the drift of people from the desert areas west of Hermannsburg towards Alice Springs and other railway settlements. Although missionaries supervised this development, Aboriginal people such as Manasse and Obed Raggett played important roles (Leske 1977: 54–61). These outposts later became government settlements. The above examples indicate that there were several outstations 'BC': Before Coombs.

Mission and government settlements in the Anangu lands

The Presbyterian Board of Missions established Ernabella Mission in 1937 at the instigation of an Adelaide surgeon, Dr Charles Duguid, who, having heard reports of the abuse of Aboriginal people, visited the region in June 1935. Returning to Adelaide, he advocated the establishment of a mission to act as a buffer between 'the white settlers east of it and the Native Reserve west of it' (Kerin 2011: 32). The 1,300 sq km Ernabella pastoral lease was purchased, and three other water permit blocks of the same size were added later. As the focus of this chapter is on homelands, there is no space for an extended outline of the history of the mission. This has been done in my recent monograph published by the Uniting Church Historical Society. Ernabella remained under the administration of the Presbyterian Board of Missions until the end of 1973. From 1 January 1974, control was transferred to the Ernabella Community Council Incorporated (B. Edwards 2012: 43–4).

During Ernabella's 36-plus years as a mission, sheep work was central to the economy and the employment of Anangu residents, as they worked as shepherds, shearers, fencing contractors, well sinkers and boring contractors. Women used a traditional method to spin wool for the making of hooked floor rugs, woven scarves and knee rugs in the craft industry that was established in 1948. A school based on a vernacular education policy was opened in 1940. From 1945, a nursing sister staffed a clinic. Anangu were employed as aides in the school and clinic.

After shearing, most of the people left on an annual spring 'walkabout' holiday, travelling west and south-west on camels, donkeys and on foot to visit traditional totemic areas. As this was the dingo pupping season, they caught pups and some adult dingoes, to exchange them for the government bounty. Staff members drove from Ernabella, taking flour, sugar, tinned food and other supplies to trade for the scalps at prearranged sites. These holidays lasted for approximately six weeks, with the school and craft room reopening when the people returned to Ernabella. A similar holiday was taken after Christmas. These breaks enabled Anangu to maintain contact with traditional sites and the related knowledge and ceremonies.

The SA Government's Aborigines Protection Board rejected Coombes' proposal that the Board of Missions be permitted to establish outstations of Ernabella on the North-West Aboriginal Reserve. Some members, including the secretary, were critical of Ernabella's policies of vernacular education and respect for traditional customs. In their eyes, Ernabella was not assimilating Aborigines quickly enough. The Protection Board decided to open its own settlement on the reserve at Amata.

Stymied by this rejection, the Board of Missions established an outstation of Ernabella on Shirley Well block, one of the three blocks granted as water leases. After discussion with people associated with this sandhill country, a site was selected on the banks of Officer Creek, a normally dry watercourse that ran from the Musgrave Ranges before petering out in the sandhill country further south. This site was approximately 50 km south-west of Ernabella. The new outstation, named Fregon after a benefactor, opened in October 1961 with a staff of four: an overseer, a cattle adviser, a teacher and a nursing sister, who also supervised craft work. Fregon was administered from Ernabella. One hundred cows with calves were purchased from a nearby station. Anangu, including Albert Lennon, Bernard Tjalkuriny, Michael Mitinkiri and Angkuna Tjitayi, played significant roles in Fregon's development. Planned to have a population of approximately 100, this increased to more than 200 in later decades. Fregon became a separate incorporated community in 1974.

In the meantime, the State Government went ahead with its plans for a government settlement on the reserve. This was opened in April 1961 towards the western end of the Musgrave Ranges, with six couples from Ernabella moving there. Two married couples originally staffed it. At first named Musgrave Park, the name was later changed to Amata, the name of a local waterhole. Musgrave Park was planned as a cattle station to provide employment. The cattle industry did not develop to the same extent as at Fregon as the Government found it difficult to recruit cattle overseers who could work cooperatively with Aboriginal people. A nursing sister was later stationed at Amata, and a school opened in 1967. The population grew as people moved from Ernabella and from other settlements and cattle stations.

Another government settlement was established, at Indulkana, approximately 145 km east of Fregon. Several Anangu families had resided on Granite Downs Station, where the men worked as stockmen. As the demand for labour declined with changes in handling cattle, some families moved to a waterhole in the Indulkana Creek. Following a change of ownership of the station, the SA Government negotiated the excision of an area of 30 sq km around the waterhole and gazetted it as an Aboriginal Reserve. Indulkana settlement opened in 1968 with a small staff and approximately 150 residents. A school opened in 1971. Thus, there were at that stage two mission and two government stations in the Anangu region. Indulkana was incorporated as Iwantja community in 1973 and Amata in 1974. Department for Community Welfare offices remained in these two communities with some control until the late 1970s. In 1973, the lease of Everard Park cattle station between Indulkana and Fregon was purchased by the Aboriginal Land Fund Commission and transferred to the local Aboriginal people, who renamed it Mimili. In 1976, a similar process saw the purchase of Kenmore Park Station east of Ernabella. It was renamed Inyarinyi. These, then, were the six stations established in the Anangu lands largely through the initiative of church and government authorities and on which the later establishment of outstations or homelands was predicated.

The North-West Aboriginal Reserve in the 1960s

While some writers on the homelands movement suggest that mission and government authorities had encouraged settlement on their stations and discouraged return to traditional areas, there are several examples of support for such movement. Reference has been made earlier to the assistance given by Ernabella Mission staff for Anangu to engage in the annual 'walkabout' holidays. During the late 1950s, a mining company undertook preliminary surveys of nickel deposits in the Mount Davies (SA) and Wingelinna (WA) areas. Bores were sunk to provide water for their camps. While these mining camps were occupied spasmodically, they provided bases for Anangu to obtain water and supplies.

The *Amata Day Books* contain frequent references to groups of people camping at Mount Davies during the 1960s. While they were largely dependent on bush foods, they were visited by staff from Amata, who provided rations in return for dingo scalps and artefacts. For example, on 12 May 1962, 27 people were taken from Amata to establish a camp in the Tomkinson Ranges. On 19 November, there were approximately 50 people in the Mount Davies camp. While drought conditions limited this development in 1964 and 1965, in the next few years there was considerable interest in mining chrysoprase, a jade-like rock associated with the nickel deposits, although this was done by men who travelled out each week from Amata, leaving their families at Amata.

A camp established in 1971 at Putaputa, 24 km east of Mount Davies, was a bridge between the 1960s camps serviced from Amata and the more independent outstations of the later 1970s. On 8 October 1971, I noted that there were two or three families, with water obtained from a bore equipped with a hand pump. Older men associated with important *Malu* (red kangaroo) Dreaming sites nearby, concerned that these sites might be disturbed by proposed nickel mining in the area, camped there to protect them. By 1976, a windmill and tank had been erected at Putaputa.

The homeland movement of the 1970s

Substantial changes were occurring in the policy, economic, employment and mobility situations relating to Anangu by the early 1970s. The 1967 referendum enabled the expenditure by the Commonwealth Government on Aboriginal programs in the States; Anangu had direct access to pensions and other social service benefits, the assimilation policy had been abandoned, steps were under way towards transferring administration of settlements to local incorporated councils and the number of privately owned motor vehicles had increased. These factors contributed to the development of the homeland movement from the mid-1970s. Another factor, as identified above in regard to Putaputa, was concern that culturally significant sites might be desecrated by prospecting and mining ventures in the region (Toyne and Vachon 1984: 35). The first two major homelands were situated near bores that had been put down to supply mining prospecting camps.

I was able to observe the development of this movement, as, after two years' absence from the region, I returned to live at Amata from 1976 to 1980 as parish minister for the Pitjantjatjara Church—a parish stretching 600 km from east to west. In this role, I regularly visited the newly established outstations. During this period, I acted as interpreter and minute secretary for the newly formed Pitjantjatjara Council in negotiations leading to the granting of land rights. Although I moved to Adelaide in 1981 to lecture in Aboriginal studies, I visited the Anangu lands annually and continued to observe the movement.

The first outstation in this era was settled in 1974 at Wingelinna in Western Australia, near the border with South Australia and close to important *papa* (dingo) totemic sites. Following reports of the likely development of nickel mining, people moved from Amata to protect these sites. An Amata staff member was appointed community adviser, with a caravan provided as a residence. The WA Education Department appointed a teacher, with classes conducted in a brush shelter. As other families moved there from Amata and from Warburton Mission in Western Australia, the population reached approximately 170 by 1982.

The second was established in 1975, at Pipalyatjara near the Mount Davies mining site in South Australia, 40 km from Wingelinna and 200 km west of Amata. It is near important *Malu* Dreaming sites. A government grant enabled the employment of a community adviser. A schoolteacher transferred from Amata to open a school in a brush shelter in 1976. A shed was erected to serve as a store. An airstrip previously used for the mining camp enabled light aircraft to land nearby. By 1982, the population had grown to 130 Anangu and 13 white residents, the latter including five children. Bulldozers were introduced to mine chrysoprase and this provided employment for some men. A garden was developed but had limited productivity. Bricks were made from local earth and a large building erected to house the store, office, school and clinic. Pipalyatjara took on the character of a settlement rather than an outstation and became a service centre for several outstation communities established in the area, as it provided stores and fuel and handled social service payments and communications. Some of these outstations were settled as residents of Pipalyatjara and Wingelinna moved away to avoid the same kind of tensions as had existed on the larger settlements as people from different local groups lived together for long periods.

In 1976, the Commonwealth Department of Aboriginal Affairs offered $10,000 each for the establishment of four outstations: Cave Hill, Kunamata, Lake Wilson and Ilturnga (Coffin Hill). Ilturnga is 200 km south-west of Fregon across sandhill country. A road was graded from Fregon and a windmill and shed were erected. A few people from Fregon moved there, but because of remoteness, residence was spasmodic. In May 1976 a meeting was held at Amata to elect councils for the other three outstations. The budgets were intended to provide for the purchase of a windmill, tank, shed and second-hand Land Rover. These were seen as basic requirements. Cave Hill, 25 km north-east of Amata, is a *Kungkarangkalpa* (Seven Sisters) site. A few families from Ernabella and Amata settled there. Some returned to those larger settlements because of the lack of a school and the failure of a proposal to develop tourism. In the late 1970s, a father and son who had spent many years working on stations far to the south settled there because of matrilineal ties. They developed a garden and maintained housing at a reasonable standard. In 1987, the population was recorded as 20.

Some long-term Ernabella residents were related to important *ili* (native fig tree) sites at Kunamata, approximately 110 km south-west of Amata. They expressed resentment that priority had been given to the *malu* (kangaroo) group by the establishment of Pipalyatjara. Some, having obtained skills at Ernabella by working in the school, hospital and store, felt they could manage these services at Kunamata. However, while older people remained there, younger ones found it difficult to remain away from Ernabella. Water quality was a problem. Another incident that hindered progress was a fatal accident involving their motor vehicle on New Year's Day 1977, which led to tensions and reluctance to live there.

The grant allocated for Lake Wilson, a dry salt lake at the western end of the Mann Ranges, was used for a camp at Yaluyalu, south of Lake Wilson, as a bore was already there and it was on the Amata–Pipalyatjara road. People related to the *Wayuta* (possum) Dreaming moved there from Ernabella and Amata and, later, moved a few kilometres east to Aparatjara, approximately 150 km west of Amata. A few people were camped there in October 1976 and in December there were nine *wiltja* (bush shelters) and a store shed. Although they planned to conduct a store to supply others travelling on the road, the initial capital grant of $10,000 was soon exhausted because of kinship obligations and lack of understanding about store financing. The site was intermittently occupied from 1978 to 1980, but again moved a short distance east. As older people died and there was friction between groups, there was occasional residence in the early 1980s, but the site was then deserted. A few people had moved to camp at Inarki, nearer Lake Wilson, in 1980 and a large area was cleared for a garden. This enterprise was short-lived. Although gardens were regarded as part of the model of an outstation and areas were fenced off and drip piping laid, little success was achieved (Cane and Stanley 1985: 126).

The establishment of the four outstations in 1976 motivated others to move to their traditional sites. In 1977, families associated with the *wanampi* (water serpent) story moved from Fregon and other settlements to camp at Kunytjanu, approximately 50 km south-east of Pipalyatjara. In May 1977, there were 13 brush shelters—two unoccupied—with 25 people living there, including five children. Most of the adults were elderly but one young man said that they would not ask the Government for help but would build the place themselves. They relied on social service payments and bush foods. By October, the population was reduced to three older couples. One couple remained there and in 1983 had a small single-room dwelling. However, the man later expressed sadness that younger people were not helping them and they also returned to Fregon.

Another outstation was established in 1979 at Walytjitjata, 38 km north-east of Pipalyatjara and just across the border in the Northern Territory. This was close to sites of *kutungu* (the first mother) and *kampurarpa* (bush tomato). The innovators in this outstation were two brothers who had lived at Indulkana. One worked for several years on stations further south, attaining skills that enabled them to build sheds, fences and a shower room. Trees were planted to provide shade. This man wanted to look after his father's country. There were approximately 20 people living there in October 1979. There were some tensions as other men resented his return after a long absence and accused him of bringing undesirable people to the area. After a fight, he moved to Alice Springs and the site was deserted until another group moved there by October 1983 and small houses were erected. However, it was again deserted in the late 1980s. Walytjitjata was similar to Cave Hill in that experience gained by men who had worked further south enabled them to construct and maintain infrastructure on the outstation. In 1982, 12 people were camped at Kurkutjara, 27 km north of Walytjitjata.

In March 1978, a group of older people moved to a remote *nyiinyii* (zebra finch) site approximately 40 km south of Wingelinna to establish Kata ala outstation. One reason for the move was the problem of alcohol abuse at Wingelinna. Thus already, as homeland communities were exhibiting some of the features of the older settlements, residents were motivated to leave them to create outstations. In November 1978, there were 15 men, 20 women and 18 children living in basic camp conditions at Kata ala, with water provided by a bore and tank.

In 1978, a Homelands Health Service was established at Kalka, 12 km north of Pipalyatjara. Large caravans accommodated a doctor, sister, administrator and clinic. The site was selected to indicate that it was to service homeland centres in the area and not just one community. However, several Anangu settled there and it became a community.

People camped at two sites near the road from Amata to Pipalyatjara on the southern side of the Mann Ranges in the late 1970s. An old man who was born in the Deering Hills further south camped at Kanpi, near a *kalaya* (emu) site in 1977. A few older women joined him in 1978. They were supplied with drums of water. Complaining of lack of support, they returned to Amata, but moved back to Kanpi in 1979 after the sinking of a bore. Residence was spasmodic until substantial houses and a store were erected by 1987. An innovation was the installation of a solar battery plant that supplied power for a freezer and house lighting. Another site, 10 km east of Kanpi, was occupied in 1979 by a group of people from Fregon but occupation was intermittent until 1987 when, as at Kanpi, houses were erected by the SA Aboriginal Housing Board. These two homelands have been regularly inhabited since then. In 1993, a school named Murputja was erected midway between Kanpi and Nyapari to service both homelands. An art centre, Tjungu Palya, was established at Nyapari to provide materials and retail services for residents of these two communities as well as Watarru homeland.

Figure 2.2 Nyapari outstation from the air, 1980s.
Source: Bill Edwards

Another significant centre was established, at Angatja, in a valley in the north-eastern section of the Mann Ranges, by Charlie Ilyatjari and his wife, Nganyintja, who had been prominent residents at Ernabella and Amata. This was Nganyintja's homeland, but her husband settled there, as he was concerned at the amount of alcohol consumption at his Wingelinna homeland. Angatja became the centre for two significant innovations. First, the couple developed it as a rehabilitation centre for children affected by petrol sniffing at Amata. Second, with the assistance of a white couple, they invited visitors to participate in a cross-cultural tourism experience. Another short-lived outstation in this area where some initiative was shown was Umpukula, 17 km east of Nyapari. As it was on the road, a couple who moved there from Amata had a baker's oven installed and made and sold bread to passers-by.

This brief history of the main homeland centres established to the west of the older settlements indicates that despite the rhetoric of a wholesale move of people from the Ernabella/Amata region, the occupancy of most of these centres was periodic. Several did not survive long but were deserted as older people died or returned to the settlements. Also, these centres were not immune from the tensions and social problems from which Anangu had sought refuge. The following population figures (Table 2.1) for the eastern and western communities in the 1980s refute claims that there was a mass movement of people to homelands. The 1981 and 1986 figures are based on Australian Bureau of Statistics census data. The 1982 figures are estimates provided by staff of settlements and my own count at the smaller homelands.

Table 2.1 Population figures

		1981	1982	1986
Eastern communities	Amata	180	200	277
	Ernabella	322	300+	365
	Fregon	203	200+	268
	Kenmore Park	63	20	66
	Mimili	132	100+	145
	Indulkana	301	250	238
	Mintabie			49
Western communities	Kalka	59	20	69
	Pipalyatjara	64	120	102
	Wingelinna		170	
	Aparatjara		7	
	Angatja		10	
	Kunytjanu		4	
	Putaputa		11	
	Kurkaratjara		12	

As the remote south-western outstation of Ilturnga was short-lived, residents of Fregon later opened a community at Watarru, near an isolated mountain, Mount Lindsay. As there was a fairly settled population there, a school was opened in 1986 and it remained one of the more stable homeland communities. However, as revealed in press reports, the population decreased due to tensions in the community and the school and store were closed in 2012 (Martin 2012: 40).

Satellite communities

Another response to the political, economic and social changes of this period was the establishment of many outstations near the older settlements. Rather than move to distant western homelands, many people who had grown up or been born at Ernabella or nearby centres were attached to these places and desired to remain close to the employment, educational and health services afforded by them. I refer to these outstations, all of which fell within a 35 km radius of Ernabella, as 'satellite communities'. This initiative enabled people to escape from the tensions of the larger settlements and assert their own family identity and some degree of independence.

Several outstations were clustered around Ernabella, based on wells and bores used previously for watering sheep. Their residents belonged to four main categories. Katjikatjitjara, established in 1977, and Wintuwintutjara, both north-east of Ernabella, were established by men with patrilineal ties to sacred sites that they wished to protect. Second, Ngarutjara and Eagle Bore to the north-west of Ernabella were founded by men whose patrilineal ties were far to the west, but as they had lived most of their lives at Ernabella they wished to remain nearby. In the case of Ngarutjara, which is near Mount Woodroffe, the highest point in South Australia, a man whose totemic base was near Wingelinna claimed a right to Ngarutjara as his birthplace. He and his family later allowed visitors to climb Mount Woodroffe for a fee. Third, a man whose ties were with Kunamata, the *ili* (wild fig tree) site south-west of Amata, asserted his claim to Wamikata, a former sheep camp north of Ernabella, on the grounds that the *ili* had begun their Dreaming journey there. Fourth, some people who had been born to Anangu mothers and white fathers and raised in mission homes at Oodnadatta, Quorn and other centres returned to reclaim their heritage and lived at outstations including New Well and Turkey Bore.

This variety of claims and experiences reflected Fred Myers' conclusion concerning the Pintupi people that the limited resources in the Western Desert region necessitated greater flexibility and movement than in Arnhem Land, where the clan groups are more tightly structured and title to land is vested in named groups (Myers 1986: 138).

As funding for such centres increased in the early 1980s, more satellite communities were established with Ernabella as their service centre. In June 1988, informants identified 19 such satellite outstations, with eight reported as unoccupied at the time.

This model of satellite communities was followed at Amata, Fregon, Mimili and Indulkana. In 1981, two families with traditional ties established an outstation at Katjikuta, 4 km east of Amata. Another man who had spent many years working on cattle stations claimed an area around Alpara, 30 km north of Amata, where he ran a cattle enterprise. Other outstations based on Amata were opened at Wintuwatu, Manyirkangka, Ulkiya, Yurangka and Tupul. Residence at most of these places was spasmodic. A man who had one grandparent with a link to the area and who lived in the Flinders Ranges area worked at Amata in the 1970s and his sons later joined him there. One married a local woman and they settled for a time at Tupul, 10 km north of Amata. They later returned to Amata.

As at Amata, cattle bores provided water for satellite outstations based on Fregon and Mimili. Those at Fregon included Shirley Well, Morrison Bore, Double Tank, Officer Creek, West Bore, Puupuu, Tjilpil and Ilitja. Attempts were made to develop small cattle projects at some of these sites. When Mimili was a cattle station, people had been encouraged to camp near cattle bores. When it became an Aboriginal-owned community, this tradition was maintained as people established outstations at Tita bore, Robb's Well, Pocket Well, Kulitjara and other sites. In the mid-1980s there were nine satellite outstations based on Indulkana, including Amaruna, Witjintitja, Ininti and Waawi.

Thus, at the same time as the homeland movement was developing in the western Anangu region, there was a significant movement to establish satellite outstations based on the older settlements in the eastern sector—a movement that was often given little attention as writers tended to focus on the western homeland movement. While there was a great deal of interest in, and effort and financial resources expended on, the development of these outstations in both areas, in the long term, residence has tended to be spasmodic, with several of the sites now unoccupied and others used as weekenders or holiday centres. The larger centres such as Pipalyatjara and Wingelinna have taken on the characteristics of the older settlement-type communities with non-Anangu staff, stores, schools and art centres. The smaller outstations that have survived tend to be ones such as Kanpi, Nyapari and Watarru where stores and schools have been erected and staffed.

Figure 2.3 Pipalayatjara, 1989.
Source: Bill Edwards

Little attention was given in earlier reports to the role of non-Anangu people in supporting and facilitating this movement. Although some reports emphasised the motivation of 'leaving whites behind', several whites and other non-Anangu people were involved in the movement. Some outstation residents found that they needed the assistance of a white staff person to help them with finances, stores and other services. One man in 1976 expressed a motivation for having a white person on staff when he said to an adviser at Amata, 'If there is no white man, who will settle the arguments?' (B. Edwards 1988: 11). One researcher, Gerritsen (1982: 63), referred to 'white wayfarers'. The movement proved attractive to people involved in the alternative society movement in Western society in that era, sometimes referred to as 'hippies', whose values and practices contrasted with those of the more conservative people who had worked in the region previously. Whereas the latter had introduced work programs with sheep, cattle, gardens and building on the basis of 'no work, no food', Anangu were now told that they were owed a living without the discipline of work. Marijuana was introduced to the lands on the grounds that it was less dangerous than alcohol. However, young people began using both, with disastrous results. In recent years, I have interpreted in mental health institutions for people severely affected by marijuana. South American panpipes and yurt buildings were other innovations designed to promote peace and harmony. Another example of the influence of this influx of people associated with the alternative movement was an occasion when I visited Fregon in the late

1970s and the community adviser asked me what he should do about the *nikiti* (naked) white fellows who were camped at, and running around, the Morrison Bore satellite outstation. Anangu whose parents had roamed the bush in a state of nakedness were sometimes bemused when calling at a house to be greeted by a naked white person.

Conclusion

Gerritsen referred to the outstation movement as 'a phenomenon of great complexity' (1982: 69). Some writers have tended to simplify the issues relating to the movement. On one hand, some with a romanticised vision overlooked the past movements of Anangu, stereotyped the role of the earlier established settlements and presented a model of the movement that is too simplistic. For example, Tregenza (1979), Waterford (1977) and others have overstated the extent to which people were forced or encouraged to move from their traditional sites in the earlier period, exaggerated the numbers of people who left the settlements to reside at homelands and largely ignored the tensions and social problems that led to people leaving the homelands, either to return to the settlements or to establish other outstations. The model that was often presented of an earlier mass movement largely forced by mission and government authorities from west to east and the later movement of large numbers from east to west does not take sufficient account of the complexity of the to-and-fro movement that continued throughout both periods.

On the other hand, Helen Hughes has given too little attention to the difficulties that Indigenous people, with their long attachment to land and language and their tradition of kinship obligations, face in adjusting to the dominant mainstream social, political and economic life in contemporary Australia. She assumed that they could have made this transition within a generation or two. Hughes overemphasised the influence of Nugget Coombs in the movement and underestimated the role of Aboriginal people themselves.

Having often camped with older people in these outstations, I have been aware of the comfort they have afforded Anangu who bore the brunt of white intrusion into their lands, made some adjustments to their way of life by working on cattle stations and other settlements but returned to their homelands in their later years. Their presence there contributed to the negotiations that led to the granting of title for these lands to Anangu Pitjantjatjara/Yankunytjatjara Incorporated under the *Land Rights Act* of 1981. It enabled the establishment of significant settled communities at Pipalyatjara and Wingelinna and smaller ones such as at Kanpi and Nyapari. Their occupancy of sites strengthened their case to be involved in negotiations in relation to possible mining and other developments. In places such as Watarru it has enabled them to participate in environmental programs such as the protection of threatened species. It also provided sites, resources and opportunities for people of shared descent who had been removed from the lands in earlier decades, or their descendants, to reclaim their Anangu heritage.

However, as instanced earlier, these communities have not been immune to the recent social problems in the region. My diary for the period contains several references to problems that occurred there when residents of Pipalyatjara and Wingelinna homelands brought alcohol to Amata when returning from liquor outlets on the Stuart Highway. This led to fights and families seeking refuge from men affected by alcohol.

I have sought to demonstrate that the homelands movement of the 1970s and 1980s was a more complex and multifaceted phenomenon than assumed in some writings of the period. Anangu responded to the challenges and opportunities of the era in a variety of ways as they sought relief from the tensions of their communities. However, three decades later, the problems of dependency, limited employment opportunities, substance abuse and occasional violence continue in both the older communities and the homeland outstations.

References

Brokensha, P. 1975. *The Pitjantjatjara and Their Crafts*. Sydney: Aboriginal Arts Board.

Brokensha, P. and McGuigan, C. 1977. Listen to the Dreaming. *Australian Natural History* 19(4).

Cane, S. and Stanley, O. 1985. *Land Use and Resources in Desert Homelands*. Darwin: North Australia Research Unit.

Coombs, H. C. 1974. Decentralization trends among Aboriginal communities. *Search* 5(4) (April).

Coombs, H. C., Dexter, B. G. and Hiatt, L. R. 1980. The outstation movement in Aboriginal Australia. *Australian Institute of Aboriginal Studies* [NS](14) (September).

Edwards, B. 1988. Pitjantjatjara decentralisation. Paper delivered at the Fifth International Conference on Hunting and Gathering Societies, Darwin, August–September.

Edwards, B. 2009. An epic of the ordinary: The Uniting Church and Aboriginal missions. *Uniting Church Studies* 15(1) (June).

Edwards, B. 2012. *Mission in the Musgraves: Ernabella Mission 1937–73, A Place of Relationships*. Adelaide: Uniting Church Historical Society (SA).

Edwards, W. H. 2007. Moravian Aboriginal missions in Australia. PhD thesis. Flinders University of South Australia, Adelaide.

Gerritsen, R. 1982. Outstations, differing interpretations and policy implications. In P. Loveday (ed.), *Service Delivery to Outstations*. Darwin: North Australia Research Unit, pp. 57–69.

Heppell, M. and Wigley, J. J. 1977. *Desert Homeland Centres: Their Physical Environment*. Canberra: Aboriginal and Torres Strait Islander Housing Panel Inc.

Hughes, H. 2007. *Lands of Shame: Aboriginal and Torres Strait Islander 'Homelands' in Transition*. Sydney: Centre for Independent Studies.

Jack, R. L. 1922. *Northmost Australia: Three Centuries of Exploration, Discovery and Adventure in and around the Cape York Peninsula, Queensland*. Melbourne: George Robinson.

Kerin, R. 2011. *Doctor Do-Good: Charles Duguid and Aboriginal Advancement, 1930s–1970s*. Melbourne: Australian Scholarly Publishing.

Leske, E. (ed.) 1977. *Hermannsburg: A Vision and A Mission*. Adelaide: Lutheran Publishing House.

MacKenzie, G. 1981. *Aurukun Diary: Forty Years with the Aborigines*. Melbourne: The Aldersgate Press.

Martin, S. 2012. Outback town abandoned. *The Advertiser*, [Adelaide], 14 January.

Myers, F. R. 1986. *Pintupi Country, Pintupi Self: Sentiment, Place, and Politics among Western Desert Aborigines*. Canberra: Australian Institute of Aboriginal Studies.

Shepherdson, E. 1981. *Half a Century in Arnhem Land*. Adelaide: E. & H. Shepherdson.

Toyne, P. and Vachon, D. 1984. *Growing up the Country: The Pitjantjatjara Struggle for their Land*. Melbourne: Penguin Books.

Tregenza, J. 1979. Pitjantjatjara: Back to the bush. *Adelaide Preview* (November).

Wallace, N. 1977. Pitjantjatjara decentralistion in north-west South Australia: Spiritual and psycho-social motivation. In R. M. Berndt (ed.), *Aborigines and Change: Australia in the '70s*. Canberra: Australian Institute of Aboriginal Studies.

Waterford, J. 1977. Pitjantjatjara seek new health approach in homelands. *The Canberra Times*, 15 November.

3

Returning to country:
The Docker River project

Jeremy Long

A short account of the return to the Petermann Ranges might begin with the stirring of interest in the Welfare Branch of the Northern Territory Administration in Darwin in 1958 and end with the arrival of Max Cartwright, the first manager, at the nascent Docker River outstation in late December 1967. I thought it more interesting to start the story earlier to illustrate how ideas about the use of Aboriginal reserves changed over time. In 1920, when the large South West or Lake Amadeus Reserve was created, it was intended to rule out any alienation of the land as well as allowing the inhabitants to continue in undisturbed occupation. Nevertheless, the Mackay Exploring Expedition, which included Dr Herbert Basedow, was allowed to traverse the range in the winter of 1926 and reported that the country was exceedingly dry but that the party had friendly contact with groups of up to 30 or 40 of the locals.[1]

In 1928, J. W. Bleakley, the Chief Protector of Aborigines in Queensland, was engaged by the Commonwealth Government to report on the 'present status and conditions of aboriginals' in the Territory. In Alice Springs, he learnt that 'two exploring missionaries' had visited the Petermann Ranges that winter and had reported seeing a large number of people in the reserve. Possibly on their advice, he recommended extending the reserve 'north and east' to embrace

---

1   *The Mail*, [Adelaide], 18 September 1926.

country 'containing primitive tribes', and he proposed establishing 'one or more mission stations—Lutheran suggested—to exercise supervision over the conditions and to relieve where privation is evident' (Bleakley 1929: 35). Clearly, his general aim was to preserve some of 'this fast dying race' by encouraging the inhabitants to stay away from the settled areas and even return from those areas.

No action was taken on these recommendations. At that time, and for the next three years, Central Australia was being administered separately from the northern part of the Territory and the small staff was not likely to give any priority to such a scheme. By 1931, when Central Australia was again administered from Darwin, the Chief Protector Dr Cecil Cook likewise had few resources and little chance of gaining more in those Depression years. He did not share Bleakley's enthusiasm for having missions take responsibility for the 'benevolent supervision' of the areas reserved for 'nomadic aborigines', and he regarded the congregations of people that resulted as a health hazard.

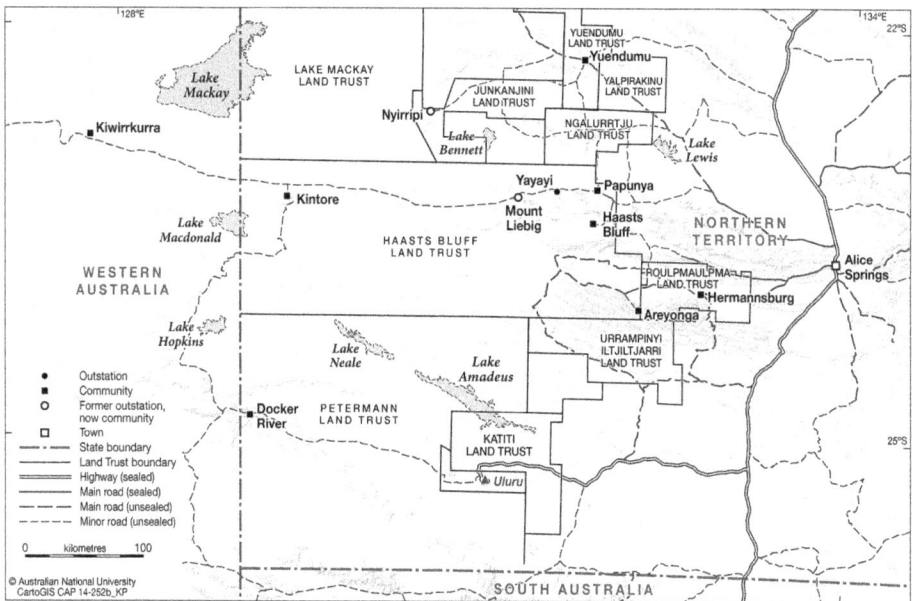

Map 3.1 Docker River in relation to Areyonga and Haasts Bluff.
Source: Karina Pelling, CartoGIS, ANU College of Asia and the Pacific

An inquiry in 1935 into alleged misconduct by police responsible for what was known as the 'South West Patrol' recommended that police patrols should be replaced with patrols by an officer directly responsible to the chief protector and that the reserve should be surveyed to see whether 'a government Aboriginal station and medical depot might usefully be established there' (Long 1992: 16–8). This inquiry did lead to the appointment of T. G. H. Strehlow as a patrol officer in Central Australia. Even before he formally took up duty, he was dispatched with camels in July 1936 to visit the Petermanns and report on stories of a violent encounter there between a prospecting party and the local men. His inquiries indicated that the story was almost certainly a concoction. He reported that game was scarce and the native population sparse; but he did propose that a ration depot be established in the reserve to relieve the situation and ensure that the reserve was not completely evacuated in the next few years.

Again, nothing followed from these proposals, but three years later Dr Cook was replaced with the director of a newly established Native Affairs Branch, E. W. P. Chinnery, who took up duty in February 1939. He was charged with responsibility for implementing a new policy with the long-term aim of raising the status of 'these native Australian people' to 'entitle them by right, and by qualification to the ordinary rights of citizenship'. The policy announced by (later Sir) John McEwen, Minister for the Interior, stated that those 'still living in tribal state' would be protected 'from the intrusion of whites'. It was envisaged that 'missions or district officer stations will be maintained to act as buffers between the tribal natives and the outer civilization' (McEwen 1939: 3). 'Visiting patrols' were to keep in touch with 'even the most backward peoples' and one of the first three 'district stations' was to be 'in the south-west portion of the territory'. The plans for these stations were spelt out at some length: the aim was to prepare 'the aboriginals gradually to develop in their own way, within their own reserves, rather than drift into distant settlements seeking employment or sustenance only to become hangers on, as many of them now are' (McEwen 1939: 4).

It seems that Chinnery was not initially convinced of the need for a district station in the south-west, but conversations with Pastor Friedrich Albrecht, who was in charge at Hermannsburg, persuaded him of the urgent need to provide at least a ration depot in the Haasts Bluff area and to investigate the need for something in the Petermann Ranges. What resulted was a kind of 'joint patrol' involving Albrecht himself, a party from the Ernabella Mission and Strehlow. Early in July, Strehlow first dispatched from Hermannsburg a three-man team with 12 camels to take supplies for the party to Piltadi Rockhole in the Petermanns.[2] Strehlow then set off in his truck for the recently established Ernabella Mission in South Australia, taking with him Pastor Albrecht and Oswald Heinrich, a farmer and supporter of the mission. There they were joined by the Reverend Harry Taylor, superintendent of the mission; Roy Edwards, secretary of the Aborigines Protection League in Adelaide; and Dr Charles Duguid. Duguid had been instrumental in persuading the Presbyterian Church and the State

---

2   Report on Trip to the Petermann Ranges, July–August 1939 (22 pp.), AA CRS A659 34/1/15262, Commonwealth Archives.

Government in 1937 to back his plan to set up at Ernabella the sort of 'buffer' station envisaged in McEwen's policy. With the larger Ernabella truck as fully loaded as Strehlow's, the party set off on a slow and circuitous four-day drive, following existing wheel tracks, to meet the camel party at Piltadi. They then spent 10 days having a close look at the western Petermanns with the camels.

Strehlow's lengthy and detailed account of the journey and of his conclusions told much the same story as his earlier report: the area was still suffering from a run of relatively dry years, the remaining inhabitants were few—the party met just 26 men, women and children—and he thought it likely that altogether only 50 or 60 people remained: 'The "leave 'em alone" policy has done its worst: a chapter in the history of the Petermann Range natives has closed for ever.' But Strehlow saw potential for raising cattle there if wells were sunk in the reserve. If a government ration depot were established, workers could supply their own meat and 'nomads' could earn cash by bringing in dingo scalps. Strehlow's main concern was with 'the hundreds of homeless Petermann natives ... wandering about' in the settled areas, the younger ones 'degenerating into a race of useless wasters'. He hoped that 'the Government will have sufficient humanity to save the aboriginal from extinction while yet there is time'.[3]

Chinnery wrote back to Strehlow on 29 August asking for details of what was needed to establish a depot and an estimate of the costs.[4] Strehlow's relatively brief response, dated 9 September 1939, suggested three likely sites to test for water and again proposed that a road should first be made between Hermannsburg and Ayers Rock (Uluru) and thence to the Petermanns. This could be done by a team of six Aboriginal labourers with a two-tonne truck, under his direction, in about 10 weeks.[5]

The dates of this exchange may serve to explain why no action followed. The scheme was effectively put on hold with the outbreak of war. The civil administration did not disappear in 1940, but military needs took priority. The Army offered work to a few men from Central Australia, but the main emphasis was soon on removing the aged, infirm and unemployed Aboriginal people from Alice Springs—first to Jay Creek, but there the water supply was inadequate to provide for the numbers. The Army then backed a 1940 proposal for a ration depot at Haasts Bluff, paid for by the Administration and supervised by patrol officer Strehlow, but managed by the Hermannsburg Mission. The military authorities were also keen to clear people from the sidings on the

---

3   ibid.
4   AA CRS: F1 38/418: memorandum, 29 August 1939.
5   AA CRS: F1 38/418: memorandum, 9 September 1939.

rail line south of Alice Springs and backed the establishment in 1943 of a similar depot at Areyonga, intended to attract people who had moved east from the Petermann Ranges.

The South West Reserve remained as desolate as Strehlow had feared. In the postwar years, some of the several private expeditions to the ranges were accompanied by an officer from the Native Affairs Branch (latterly the Welfare Branch). Patrol officer John Bray reported on a January 1951 visit by a party interested in the area's mineral potential, and was impressed enough by the country to suggest that it was a suitable place for a settlement. This party met just one group of nine men, women and children (Long 1963: 8). Bray's suggestion was endorsed in 1958 when a joint examination of the South Australian, West Australian and Northern Territory reserves was made by a party including Max Althaus, superintendent at Areyonga, and Clarrie Bartlett from the SA Aboriginal Affairs Department, which was proposing a new government station west of Ernabella (Long 1992: 133). This prompted the Welfare Branch of the Administration to submit a proposal for a settlement in the South West Reserve.

In January 1959, the Department of Territories in Canberra responded, rejecting the idea on the grounds that a settlement would have 'a better chance of fulfilling its purposes … [near] a closely settled area'.[6] It was 'necessary to encourage movement to more settled areas' and if the area in the ranges was 'suitable for pastoral purposes just as much opportunity could be provided by making the land available to private enterprise'.[7] Since Paul Hasluck, the Minister for Territories since 1951, took a very close interest in Territory administration, it is hard to imagine that these comments did not reflect his views. He had agreed in 1958 to the excision of the Mount Olga–Ayers Rock area from the reserve, after being assured that no Aboriginal people had been living there for many years.

Proposals had also been made at this time that a single authority might be set up to administer the adjoining 'Central Reserves' in Western Australia, South Australia and the Northern Territory, which by then were affected by the operations of the Weapons Research Establishment (WRE) based at Woomera. The area of the reserves in WA and the NT was then being greatly extended, after a 1957 patrol to the area near Lake Mackay had confirmed that there were people living outside the reserves. The South West Reserve became part of a much larger one in 1959 with the gazetting of the Lake Mackay Aboriginal Reserve and the WA reserve was extended northward to match the NT expansion. Hasluck rejected the idea of a separate authority, but accepted the need for closer cooperation. When the Commonwealth and State ministers responsible for Aboriginal affairs (the Native Welfare Conference) met in January 1961,

---

6   AA CRS: F1 59/333: minute, 28 March 1961.
7   ibid.

they agreed to set up a consultative committee to exchange information and coordinate practice in the Central Reserves. The first meeting was held in Alice Springs in mid-August 1961, attended by one of the two patrol officers employed by the WRE (Long 1963: 8).

Meanwhile, in late March 1961 (about six months after I started as a research officer with the Welfare Branch), I submitted proposals for research related to the need I saw for accelerated development to meet the needs of the growing populations in the three western settlements, as the records of births and deaths at Yuendumu and Papunya had shown that populations there had been increasing since the mid-1950s.[8] It seemed clear to me that the 'settled areas' in Central Australia were not able to provide work for these people and even less likely to provide for their growing populations. To hope that the settlements might in the short term 'serve their purposes as "staging camps" and "training centres" and disappear' seemed unrealistic. I noted existing plans for sinking bores north-west of Areyonga for a subsistence cattle project and suggested that bores should also be sunk in the Petermann Ranges to provide three or four watering places for a cattle project there. I also suggested that bores should be sunk west of Mount Liebig, to expand the Haasts Bluff cattle project to the Ehrenberg Range, noting that it seemed likely that it would be 'necessary and desirable to establish another Settlement at or west of the Kintore Range within the next ten years'.[9]

I spent a fortnight at Areyonga in August 1961 and submitted a report on 'the movements and rate of growth' of the population there, noting that the people were markedly more mobile than those in the other settlements; that the prospects for development of a cattle project there were severely limited; and that the water supply might be inadequate for a growing population.[10] Developing the Petermann Ranges area offered much better prospects. It would certainly 'arouse real interest and enthusiasm in the Areyonga community'; I was told that the leader of a team making a road to a new bore site had proposed that they next make a road to the Petermanns. I suggested that an 'outpost station' (comparable with the Fregon outstation of Ernabella recently established in the north of South Australia) would be 'a start towards ensuring some future for these people', as well as reducing 'the number of families moving round the stations and sitting down on the Ayers Rock road' and would also 'provide a much needed service for the people of the Rawlinsons who tend to sit down at Giles where they are a constant problem for the Weather Station and the WRE patrol officers'. I suggested that the aim might be to keep the population in the 100 to 150 range and 'to plan for at least two small stations, one towards

8   AA CRS: F1 59/333: minute, 28 March 1961.
9   ibid.
10   AA CRS: F1 61/3022: minute, 12 September 1961.

the eastern end of the ranges and the main settlement near the western end'. I hoped that a patrol officer might visit the Petermann Ranges 'to record the extent of the mulga and grass country there' and its potential for 'development based on pastoral activity'.[11]

This was quickly agreed to, and on 16 September, patrol officer John Hunter and I left Areyonga with two guides: a senior man from the western area and a younger man who had recently been out to the ranges with camels. In a week, we travelled the length of the ranges, including areas on the southern side of the main range. We reported meeting just one group of people, near the WA border, and finding the country very dry, but we had seen kangaroos every day. We were impressed with the potential for cattle grazing in several areas. We endorsed the view, urged by Bartlett and Althaus after the 1958 joint patrol and again by the recent Central Reserves Committee (CRC) meeting in Alice Springs, that 'the Reserves in this area should be developed to provide useful employment, a place to live and prospects of further economic advancement for their original inhabitants, as well as to reverse the drift into pauperism on the stations, in towns and on tourist routes'.[12] We recommended initial test boring for water near the existing well-marked track from Ayers Rock and Mount Olga:

> The Kikingura/Docker River area has the most appeal as a site for the establishment of a first trading-post-cum-cattle station. This is an area with great ceremonial and emotional significance for the Areyonga people; it is handy to the Rawlinson area, Giles and the graded roads of the WRE; it is central to some useful grazing areas and is well situated for the control of entry to this section of the Reserve … Outstations should be established early, south of the Range and towards the eastern end near the Irving Creek.[13]

We also indicated that a community there would provide 'a contact point convenient for the Rawlinson natives and those to the north-west'— an alternative to the Giles Weather Station.

On 28 September 1961, the director of welfare in Darwin, Harry Giese, drafted a four-page memorandum for the Administrator to send to Canberra, headed 'Outstations on Settlements in Central Australia'.[14] He began by mentioning discussion at the August meeting of the CRC in Alice Springs about decentralising activities on the settlements, noting that these communities had been built to accommodate at most 350 people and now had much larger populations. He reported the establishment of small 'village' groups on bores a few miles from Yuendumu and referred to 'sporadic attempts' to establish similar small

---

11   ibid.
12   AA CRS: F1 61/3022: minute, 29 September 1961.
13   ibid.
14   AA CRS: F1 69/1864: memorandum, 9 October 1961. See Appendix 3.1.

groups at bores near Papunya. He mentioned proposals for more bores west of Papunya and made a recommendation that an outstation of the Haasts Bluff cattle operation was needed at the Mount Liebig end of the run. He indicated that this might be an attractive location for perhaps 100 to 150 of the Pintubi group at Papunya and listed the facilities needed at such an outstation. He also outlined plans for the development of a similar outstation from Areyonga, if boring to the north-west was successful, and possibly at least one 'small native village'. Field reports on the Petermann Ranges patrol would be examined before making any recommendation to the minister on development there. Meanwhile, he sought 'clearance in principle' of the proposal for an outstation in the Mount Liebig area.

This message was apparently sent on 9 October and the reply on 25 October reported that the minister had approved the general principle of decentralisation with 'outstations or village areas' and that proposals for the Mount Liebig outstation be developed for the 1962–63 draft estimates. Hasluck had commented that any outstation given 'substantial buildings and facilities' ought to have a prospective life of 20 to 25 years and that careful consideration should be given to the educational policy question of whether children would be better served by one larger central school than by several smaller ones.[15]

My report on the Petermann Ranges patrol was sent to Canberra with a recommendation to approve in principle the establishment of a community and to make provision for test drilling of bores in the area. The minister gave general approval to the suggested development in the Petermann Ranges and approved that 'provision be made in the 1962/63 programme for four bores to be sunk, one of which will be equipped in the areas suggested by Mr Long, subject to further investigation by officers of the Animal Industry Branch' (AIB).[16] In July 1962, Giese asked the director of the AIB to have officers visit the area and comment on carrying capacity, location of water, fencing, annual turn-off and so on.

It was at this point that the 'green' opposition to the proposed introduction of cattle (and horses) into the area was revealed. The AIB botanist had been to the Petermanns with the 1958 party and had then expressed concern about the suggestion that a settlement should be developed there. Now he was supported by the field biologist, who let me know that their concern was that 'the last ungrazed mulga community in Australia is there' (personal communication). We met and agreed that an area should be set aside for scientific purposes as a flora and fauna reserve. In the event, no cattle were grazed in the Petermanns, but that is another story.

---

15   AA CRS: F1 69/1864: memorandum, 25 October 1961.
16   AA CRS: F1 69/1864: memorandum, 27 July 1962.

The next April (1963), with a trainee patrol officer, I picked up two senior men from Areyonga and drove to the Petermanns to join the geologist and the boring contractor, who were selecting seven or more possible drilling sites. The Water Resources Branch provided a 'completion report' in April 1964 on a bore at the Docker River, equipped with a mill and tank, recommending that it should be equipped to pump 4,500 litres an hour. Plans for an outstation were then developed in the Alice Springs office. Initially, it would have a manager and a nursing sister, and, when enough children of school age were present, a teacher. Creed (T. C.) Lovegrove, a senior official first in the Native Affairs division of the Welfare Branch and later in the Department of Aboriginal Affairs, submitting his plans in 1965, noted:

> The manager will have to be very self sufficient during the early developmental period of this outstation. He will need to have some experience with Aborigines, know something about building, and be able to repair his own vehicle and maintain the water supply if necessary. (Cartwright 1994: 78)

An airfield site was chosen. Drought-breaking rain in 1966 and heavy falls in February 1967 caused delays in taking out caravans and a demountable house. The Docker River overflowed and demonstrated that the bore was in a flood-prone area. The building supervisor, who was there at the time, had everything moved to a better site away from the bore. I made a visit to the Petermanns in April 1967, on the way to a CRC meeting at Giles, and another in September 1967, joining the Australian Institute of Aboriginal Studies (AIAS) film unit and a team of 19 men from Areyonga for the filming of rituals relating to the Kikinkurra area. Coincidentally, in April, Neville Harding, one of the most determined seekers of Lasseter's fabled reef of gold, had led a party of 14 men with several four-wheel-drive vehicles and a Cessna aircraft to prospect in the western Petermanns (Cartwright 1994: 72). Harding was still out, camped south of the main range, in September.

In December two patrol officers took out a small party of Areyonga men to begin work on clearing the airstrip. A few days later, Max Cartwright, the first manager of the outpost, arrived with more men from Areyonga. Max has written an excellent account of the first year of the Docker River outpost. Through the heat of January, work on the airstrip remained the priority for him and his team of 14 men working a six-day week. On their day off, he drove them out to visit places of interest to them and to do some hunting, and as a change from the airstrip work, they also laid out some roads in the community, planted trees and made a new road crossing of the Docker River. Cartwright started a 'social club' where the men could spend some of their pay on soft drinks, biscuits, cigarettes and other extras.

By February, he records that the population 'was starting to expand slightly, with a few people arriving by any means possible'. He made his first visit to Giles and a week later returned to pick up a family of 'bush people' who had recently reached Giles in 'destitute condition'. On one of their days off, he and the men visited 'Wanguri', where Harding had camped and found there an abandoned four-wheel-drive truck, which he promptly had 'in running order' as a useful addition to the outstation's equipment. In March, he drove to Ayers Rock to collect some 30 people trucked from Areyonga and brought them on to the outstation; and in April he collected two families who had walked as far as Giles from the Warburton Ranges Mission. In May the Areyonga truck brought another 18 people, along with a DCA roller to improve the airstrip. A journalist who visited in late May reported a population of about 80, including 25 schoolchildren, a teacher having been supplied in late February. In August several families arrived by car from Warburton.

In May the first tourist group arrived and later some VIP travellers visited (Bill and Barbara Wentworth in August; Sid and Cynthia Nolan in October). In the winter months, nursing sisters were sent out to help with influenza outbreaks. Giese and Lovegrove made a visit of inspection in August—the 'whole population were at the airstrip to witness the event'—and attended a council meeting where 'various hopes were expressed for the future'. A few petrol sniffers had made a nuisance early. Cartwright recorded the first big fight in late November. In January, he handed over to his successor as manager, John Smith.

References

Bleakley, J. W. 1929. *The Aboriginals and Half-castes of Central Australia and North Australia*. Commonwealth Parliamentary Paper 21. Canberra: Commonwealth of Australia.

Cartwright, M. 1994. *From Bush Track to Highway*. Wollongong, NSW: Leisure Coast Graphics.

Long, J. P. M. 1963. Preliminary Work in Planning Welfare Development in the Petermann Ranges. *Australian Territories* 3(2): 4–12.

Long, J. P. M. 1992. *The Go Betweens: Patrol Officers in Aboriginal Affairs Administration in the Northern Territory 1936–1974*. Darwin: North Australia Research Unit.

McEwen, J. 1939. *Commonwealth Government's Policy with Respect to Aboriginals*. Canberra: Commonwealth Government Printer.

Appendix 3.1

Outstations on settlements in Central Australia

The Secretary,
Department of Territories,
CANBERRA.

OUT-STATIONS ON SETTLEMENTS IN CENTRAL AUSTRALIA

Following consideration of the question of establishing out-stations on various settlements in Central Australia as discussed at the Conference with representatives of the Western Australian and South Australian Governments in Alice Springs recently, the Director of Welfare has been giving consideration to the whole problem of decentralising activities on these settlements.

2.   You will know that there are large numbers of aborigines con-gregated around settlements like Yuendumu (total population 466), Papunya and Haasts Bluff (603), and Areyonga (357), and that these congregations create major problems of water supply and settlement hygiene and place an undue strain on community facilities which have been built to accommodate at the outside 350 persons. In Central Australia at all these settle-ments, water supply, because of the fact that the water comes from under-ground sources, and settlement hygiene because of the stage of development of personal and community hygiene of the people, present major difficulties and this position must continue for a good many years to come.

3.   The process of decentralisation has already been started in a small way with selected families at Yuendumu where family groups are now resident at Penhall's and White Point Bores. These bores are situated approximately four and nine miles from the Settlement itself. These distances are such that children can walk to school from Penhall's and can be transported from White Point Bore, and the Nursing Sister from the Settlement can make regular visits to the areas to care in particular for the mothers, babies and pre-school children. At the present time, develop-ment at these two places consists of a small market garden, a small citrus grove, and the beginnings of a lucerne area. At both also, some attempt is being made to erect a small native village using local materials of stone and lime. During portion of the year when water is in the creek, the Kerridy area is also used for a similar purpose and plans are being developed to increase the capacity to enable water to be held here for the whole year. As further waters are provided by dams or bores in th Reserve, it is proposed to extend these small out-stations and to deve. some citrus orchards, market gardens and lucerne plots as well.

This development has been proceeding quietly at Yuendumu and has enabled the water supply which is in short supply at the settlement area, to be sufficient for immediate settlement requirements. Because of the diffi-culties of getting underground water, it is planned to establish a large dam at the Settlement and under these circumstances there should be sufficient water to maintain essential Settlement services and a native village but without any large agricultural or orchard development in this area. It must be quite obvious that under these circumstances where the water supply, whether by bore or surface water, will always present difficulties, and where the standards of personal and community hygiene are poor, some such decentralisation as is at present being practised at Yuendumu, is inevitable.

4.   The situation in the Papunya area is being exacerbated by th movement of primitive natives from the western areas in fairly large numbers and in view of this, some decentralisation of activities in

..../2

A handwritten date of 9/10/61 has been omitted from the top of the scan of the document in order to fit the scan on this page.

2.

this area also appears inevitable. Sporadic attempts have been made
to establish small groups at Ekracowra and Allumbra bores but in the
absence of staff and vehicles to supervise and service these areas,
the projects have not been maintained. At the present time the water
supply at Papunya is adequate for present settlement needs and to
enable the maintenance of a small market garden and citrus orchard
in addition to a small lucerne plot. However, with the extension
of the native village with more people reaching a stage where they
can be accommodated in small houses and not wurlies, there will be
increased demand for water on this settlement. There is still a
bore in reserve which will be equipped this year and which will provide
some reserve for the future; however, it seems clear that if possible
the numbers on this settlement should not exceed 350 when the people
are housed in a reasonable village area. At the present time there
are bores at Ekracowra (3 miles east of Papunya), Allumbra (15 miles
west), Leibig (30 miles west) and a further bore ten miles west of
Leibig which has just been equipped. All these bores are on the north
of the Haasts Bluff Range and would offer some possibilities for
decentralisation activities. In addition, a further bore is being
sunk 15 miles southwest of the bore west of Mt. Leibig and another
bore will be sunk south again of this to the west of the Marini Range.
The bores west of Mt. Leibig are on the edge of some good cattle country
which, with the waters, will now be opened up, and as well extends into
the tribal country of the Pintubi group.

At the present time this country is being supervised and managed from
the Haasts Bluff homestead which, as you will appreciate, involves staff
in moving considerable distances for mustering and for inspection of
bores etc. There would be, in these circumstances, considerable advantage in establishing an out-station of the cattle project in this western
area; the Acting Senior Stock Inspector in Alice Springs of the Animal
Industry Branch, following a recent inspection, has recommended that
we consider very strongly the establishment of an out-station in this
area. This, together with the obvious advantages in relieving the population pressure at Papunya, seems to me to lend support to the view
that it would be advisable to decentralise activities from Papunya to
this area. What the Director of Welfare has in mind so far as this
area is concerned, is to have one of the Head Stockmen at present on
this establishment, stationed at one of the bores (Leibig or one of
those to the west or southwest) to control the bores and cattle in this
area under the Cattle Manager, and to move some 100 to 150 natives from
Papunya to this area. This would be right in the Pintubi country and
there would be no difficulty in having this group move to this area.
In addition, at this project the Director of Welfare suggests that there
should be a Manager whose wife is a Nursing Sister and, depending on the
number of children of pre-school and school age, one or two teachers.
If two teachers were required, a teaching couple would be appointed to
this location.

5.   On this basis, the facilities required for such an out-station
would consist of -

    (a) Three staff houses.
    (b) Small native village including latrine/
        ablution and laundry units.
    (c) Small food store (60' x 24' Nissen).
    (d) Small kitchen/mess unit (including cool room).
    (e) Electricity supply.
    (f) Pump, 5,000 gall. overhead tank and reticulation.
    (g) Two classrooms school unit (prefabricated Kingstrand).
    (h) Garage, saddlery and equipment store (96' x 35' Romney).

6.   The men could be employed on stock work (mustering, fence and
yard building, horse breaking etc.), at cutting and carting fence posts,
yard rails etc., making and maintaining roads in the area, under the
supervision of the Head Stockman and Manager. Some would be employed

....../3

3.

2/

on hygiene, cooking and other duties in the homestead area. Employment could also be found for the majority of the able-bodied women without young children in the area.

Equipment required for this project would include a landrover for the Head Stockman, a 30 cwt. truck for general settlement duties (hygiene, servicing road gangs, fence gangs etc.) and 3/5 ton truck for use of the gangs in carting fence posts, yard building etc. The out-station would need, of course, to have a fixed transceiver for contact with Papunya and Alice Springs; an airstrip would of course be essential and would be one of the first tasks undertaken by the natives in the area.

7.   I would like to plan the development of such an out-station in the Mt. Leibig area at this stage to relieve the population, hygiene, and water supply pressures at Papunya and at the same time, enable the more effective control and management of the cattle project in this area.

8.   Further development of out-stations in this area could be looked at then against the development of further waters in the western area and on the basis of the development of this proposed out-station.

9.   At Areyonga where the water supply position quite obviously, is always going to present difficulties, I believe we will have to consider two possible means of decentralisation, one in the old Haasts Bluff Reserve area and the other in the Petermann Ranges area depending on the results which we obtain from the patrols and surveys which are at present being undertaken in this area.

10.   Boring is at present going on at the Areyonga Settlement area and it is proposed then to move into the next valley near the airstrip and bore there. A further site has been selected at Amilda, some 5 miles along the road back to Alice Springs where there are extensive springs, and boring will take place at this location as soon as funds can be provided for this purpose. It is proposed also, to look at the question of erecting a dam at Tent Hill where there is already some permanent water. Planning is now proceeding to construct a road, to build a holding paddock and yards (including killing pen) at this site so that instead of carting beef by open truck to Areyonga from Haasts Bluff, cattle will be moved on the hoof to Tent Hill, held there and killed as required for Areyonga. It should be possible, based on our present knowledge of the area, to hold up to 150 head of cattle in this area. If the proposed dam to be erected in this area is successful and sufficient water can be found, this appears one of the logical places for an out-station at Areyonga. Again, it would be proposed to move from 100 to 150 of the natives from Areyonga and in this case, commence ir'-tially with a Manager, Nurse and Schoolteacher, leaving development of a cattle out-station to the future.

Having regard to the fact that Adolf Inkamala and at least one other of the part-coloured pastoralists from Hermannsburg, have run cattle in this area over many years, it is reasonable to assume that the area south of the Marinis and east to the Gosses is suitable for cattle. In the future consideration could be given to appointing a Head Stockman, here again under the supervision of the Cattle Manager at Haasts Bluff. On this basis the run could be divided into three main areas with the Head Stockman from Haasts Bluff controlling the country between the Bluff and the Marinis under the general supervision of the Cattle Manager. The appointment of this extra Head Stockman at this location would, in my view, enable a much more efficient operation of a substantial piece of good cattle country and would provide a means of obtaining regular supplies of beef in good condition for Areyonga Settlement.

11.   If water were located in the aerodrome valley or at Amilda, the same development as is now in operation at Yuendumu would be followed, i.e. a small native village would be established with natives operating a small market garden, citrus orchard and lucerne plots. These would be close enough as at Yuendumu, to have the children walk to school or be transferred by truck.

..../4

4.

12.   So far as the Petermann Range area is concerned, I would propose to examine the field reports from the Patrol Officer and Senior Research Officer of the Welfare Branch, and from the technical officers of the Animal Industry Branch and Water Resources Branch before placing any recommendation before the Minister concerning development in that area.

13.   I have developed this proposal particularly at this stage so that the Minister may see what the thinking is here in overcoming some of the obvious problems which face us at these settlements in Central Australia. I believe very strongly that some such decentralisation programme as this is necessary to enable more effective control of the population moving from west and south of this reserve, to provide a better means for employment, to relieve population, hygiene and water supply pressures on the main settlement areas, and to provide better management and control of the cattle herd on the reserve.

14.   Because of the numbers at Papunya at the present time, the fact that we have bores in the Mt. Leibig area with a good supply of potable water to maintain a population of this order, and the need for control and management of cattle in this area, I would propose to commence the first of these out-stations in this area. At the same time, I would propose to continue with the development of the small village areas only at bores close to the settlement at Yuendumu and at Areyonga (when available).

15.   I whould be glad, therefore, if this proposal could be placed before the Minister for his clearance in principle and I will then, as I can, include provision on the draft estimates for these projects.

(ROGER NOTT)
Administrator.

4

'Shifting': The Western Arrernte's outstation movement

Diane Austin-Broos[1]

Gustav Malbangka (Malbunka) and his family lived at the Hermannsburg Mission in central Australia. Like many other people, they wish to leave the social problems of the congested settlement behind them and return to their traditional land at Gilbert Springs … to carve out a more satisfactory life for themselves, drawing strength from being in the homeland again.

… Encouraged by the 'out-station movement', many people like Gustav left the mission to return to their traditional country, leaving Hermannsburg looking 'like a ghost town'.

Life at Gilbert Springs is not easy: until bore water is provided, everyone has to live close to the Springs in bush shelters. Gustav, however, has plans to build houses with running water, and to establish a viable station with a church and

---

1   I would like to thank all the Western Arrernte people who offered me information and insights on their outstation movement during discussions throughout the 1990s and early 2000s. I would also like to thank a small group of Lutherans who, as erstwhile residents of Hermannsburg, also contributed to my understanding. John von Sturmer assisted my entry into the milieu of Ntaria/Hermannsburg. I remain indebted to him. Shortcomings in this account are my own.

a school, growing produce and raising cattle. [For the moment they depend] on a weekly visit from a travelling 'store truck' and have their financial affairs managed by the truck's operator, Murray Pearce. (Levy 1975)[2]

This passage is part of the cover note to a film made in 1975 by the Australian Institute of Aboriginal Studies (AIAS), directed and produced by filmmaker Curtis Levy with anthropologist John von Sturmer acting in the role of associate producer. The film was narrated by the late Gus Williams, a Western Arrernte man. Members of the Malbunka group first moved out of Hermannsburg Lutheran Mission in the Northern Territory in 1974 as part of a larger group that camped along Ellery Creek. Soon they began to move again, this time west to their ancestral land, which soon harboured numerous camps. These initiatives east and west of the mission were, to the east, close to an ephemeral creek that allowed soakages and wells used in the past both by Aboriginal people and by pastoralists. To the west, the camps were close to ancient underground springs that fed permanent waterholes. In a desert region, both the creek and the underground springs held ritual as well as practical significance. Other sites that became outstations posed greater problems concerning potable water. Nonetheless, these initial shifts presaged a major move by Arrernte and some Luritja and Luritja-Pintupi people also resident at the mission, which was established in 1877. By mid-1976 there were 17 outstations, with an Aboriginal population of about 450. Eight more camps would be added by the end of the year. Outstations were located at distances up to 60 km from Hermannsburg, which, at the time, retained little more than 100 people.

Nine years after the shift began, in 1983, the Western Arrernte outstation movement numbered 33 sites. Prior to this year, the movement had been resourced by grants to the mission for the management of a Western Arrernte outstation project. In 1983 Hermannsburg, now known as Ntaria, became an incorporated Aboriginal community, and early in 1984 Tjuwanpa Outstation Resource Centre (TORC) was also incorporated under the Federal *Incorporations Act 1983*. Thereafter funding for the outstation movement, which grew to 40 outstations before it began to contract in the mid-1990s, was channelled through TORC, which, under the Aboriginal and Torres Strait Islander Commission (ATSIC), became the hub of a major Community Development Employment Projects (CDEP) program. Although today there are significantly fewer than 40 outstation sites with continuous residence, the movement left an enduring legacy: it involved a significant step away from both settlement life as manifest in the Hermannsburg mission and a pre-settlement life reflected

---

2   *Malbangka Country* was directed and produced by Curtis Levy, with photography by Geoff Burton, edited by Stewart Young, sound by Fred Pickering, liaison by Murray Pearce, narrated by Gus Williams and anthropologist and associate producer John von Sturmer. The film is available today through Ronin Films, Canberra.

in the central role that ceremony and foraging played in linking people across a region. Western Arrernte life today is neither simply settled nor traditional. It commonly involves regular movement on a weekly basis between outstations, the community hub of Ntaria/Hermannsburg and the regional centre of Alice Springs—a new life foreshadowed in the initial phases of the outstation movement. The Arrernte, like other Aboriginal people, would cease to be wards of the state and become citizens with specific Indigenous rights that made it feasible for them to pursue this life.

In addition to the aspirations of Arrernte people and some mission staff who assisted them, this legacy rested on at least three factors. In part, it was due to the land rights movement and the fact that the erstwhile mission lease became five land trusts of the Western Arrernte people under the *Aboriginal Land Rights (Northern Territory) Act 1976* (*ALRA*). In part, the move back to country was made feasible by improved resourcing, first under the Department of Aboriginal Affairs (DAA) and then under ATSIC. Finally, the period of very rapid outstation growth also coincided with the 1970s take-up of unemployment benefits by many Central Australian Aboriginal people. Similarly, the transition to CDEP payments at the end of the 1980s once more stabilised incomes to residents and made feasible the maintenance of numerous outstation camps.

The following discussion has three sections. The first juxtaposes two types of event. One was created by developments of national significance in the 1960s and 1970s that set the stage for outstation movements—understood as self-determination for Aboriginal people. The other was local change at Hermannsburg responsive to national developments, but also largely controlled by the mission. At both the national and the local levels, those involved understood these developments as a move away from assimilation practices. Nonetheless, the first such initiatives at Hermannsburg failed. Consequently, at least some mission staff looked in a different direction that beckoned towards outstation development. As events clearly show, Western Arrernte people grasped the moment. The second section of this discussion considers the local experience of Western Arrernte people and the developments that oriented them towards outstations. For a time, their interest coalesced with that of some missionaries. While the latter saw outstations as a way to sustain a Christian Arrernte community, Arrernte themselves saw outstations as a way to realise an autonomous life that could accommodate both some Indigenous ways and some settlement activities they valued. From the beginning of the outstation movement, Arrernte people sought to use it as a medium to reconcile a range of institutions—some drawn from the mission settlement and some from their Indigenous domain. Their movement actually conformed to the original sense that anthropologist Anthony Wallace gave to the notion of a 'revitalisation' movement: a 'deliberate, organized attempt by some members of a society to construct a more satisfying culture by rapid acceptance of a pattern of multiple innovations' (Wallace 1956: 265). In fact, although the Western Arrernte did retrieve substantial forms of tradition, their movement was also a new initiative in life-ways. The second section of this chapter draws on recorded comments of the time and the film *Malbangka Country* in order to typify the innovation that the return to country involved. The final section of the discussion considers a retrospective view of the outstation movement offered mainly by older Arrernte women between 1998 and 2000. Their view is a touchstone for remarks on three different notions of self-determination found in contemporary literature. A short conclusion follows.

The context for an outstation movement

Perhaps the most general backdrop to the Arrernte's outstation movement came in the postwar years of the late 1940s and the 1950s when first the Federal Government and then the states and territories began to move via legislation away from the notion of 'Aboriginal natives' outside an Australian nation, first to citizens without rights and then to citizens with rights that ultimately would include at least some Indigenous rights (Chesterman and Galligan 1967). After the 1967 referendum, Aboriginal Australians were not only 'counted' in censuses but also included in national population tables. Moreover, increasingly, they received benefits previously denied them. In Central Australia, for example, Aboriginal access to unemployment benefits was only secured in the 1970s, after the 1966 Gurindji stockmen's strike against the Vestey Company at Wave Hill (Hardy 1968). In sustaining a claim for equal wages, the Federal Government paved the way for Aboriginal people to receive unemployment benefits. The Wave Hill strike, precipitated by attempts to delay the implementation of equal wages, also involved a land claim component. Strikers withdrew their labour and sought land beyond both station and reserves on which they might reside and work independently. This dialogue about traditional Aboriginal land usurped by the state had already received national prominence due to the Yolngu people of Yirrkala. Their protest over land in the form of the Yirrkala Bark Petitions presented to the Federal Parliament in 1963 became a *cause célèbre*, especially among some Labor opposition politicians (see Williams 1986). Like the diffident extension of equal wages to Gurindji, the fact that negotiations over reserve land between the Federal Government and the North Australian Bauxite and Alumina Company (Nabalco) had not included Yolngu Traditional Owners demonstrated the enduring assumption, even in the midst of assimilation, that 'Aboriginal natives' were perhaps permanently beyond the nation. Creeping along through the 1950s and 1960s, and reaching a culmination in the *ALRA*, these developments began to shape a different view of Aboriginal people among many non-Indigenous Australians. This process also informed life at Hermannsburg, though possibly in a peripheral way before the late 1960s.

It is important to juxtapose an account of these momentous events with those offered by Gary Stoll, Paul Albrecht and Elizabeth Sommerlad regarding social change at Hermannsburg in the 1960s and early 1970s. Stoll was mission superintendent during this period and Albrecht was the Lutherans' pastoral field superintendent for Central Australia. Sommerlad, based at The Australian National University, produced a report in 1973 regarding 'community development' at the mission station. Of the three, Albrecht has been most explicit in noting retrospectively the larger context in which local events unfolded (see Albrecht 2002: 33–4). However, reports at the time, mainly to the Lutheran Synod or to the church's Finke River Mission Board in Adelaide, as well as Sommerlad's ANU Continuing Education Report, focused mainly on issues of conflict, social order and social control. Stoll and Albrecht traced these matters back to unanticipated or unwanted 'consequences' of the *Nationality and Citizenship Act 1948*, followed by the Commonwealth's confirmation of voting rights in 1962. The latter facilitated the Northern Territory Aboriginal enfranchisement but also anticipated the demise in 1964 of restrictions on the sale of alcohol to Aboriginal people. The Lutherans identified three such consequences: growing drunkenness even among male elders, increased petty theft and lawlessness among male youth, and heightened conflict between families often manifested in schoolroom and schoolyard spats. This conduct was described in terms of the failure of assimilation policy, 'as it was being implemented', and the need for Arrernte people to take more 'responsibility' for the changes in their lives brought by the postwar legislation (Albrecht 2002: 40–2; Austin-Broos 2009: 185–6). There was a keen view among those involved at the mission that these eventualities were undermining the authority of the mission and the Lutheran Church overall (Albrecht 2002: 46).

The Village Council, established in 1963, was the first of three all-Aboriginal elected councils to be formed at Hermannsburg. The council was conceived as a local law and order body not unlike the 'night patrols' still common at Ntaria/Hermannsburg in the 1990s and 2000s. Village councillors could appear as witnesses in the courts held periodically at Hermannsburg by an Alice Springs-based magistrate (Sommerlad 1973: 37). The council had no legal status, though, and did not fill the 'authority vacuum' that Albrecht and Stoll saw emerging at Hermannsburg as federal legislation began to redefine the mission milieu. On Albrecht's recommendation, an elected Town Council with governance roles was established in 1970. The mission sought to instigate and maintain a system of elections based on family groups, which, to a degree, coincided with the residents of regionally identified camps around the mission at the time: east camp and west camp. From the outset, not every family group elected a representative to the council and some groups elected more representatives than others. In short, there were differing degrees of engagement with the project among the groups at Hermannsburg. One of the council's initial roles concerned 'booking up' at the mission store—an activity the Lutherans felt demanded oversight as a cash economy expanded. The council supervised the new beer garden and the ingress and egress of drinkers to and from Hermannsburg. It also had some responsibility for the hiring and firing of Aboriginal people employed in the mission's various divisions such as maintenance and housing, the store and the garage (Sommerlad 1973: 36). This role did not extend to the hiring and firing of non-Indigenous mission employees, although this was foreshadowed by the chair of the Town Council, Jeffrey Wheeler, in 1973 (Albrecht 2002: 50–2). Perhaps its most ambitious act was the incorporation of an Ntaria Housing Society, although the initiative did not flourish. Once Federal Labor came to power in 1972, the mission's intent was to see the Town Council evolve into the settlement's governing body. Its initial roles, however, largely involved low-level policing of the Aboriginal population. Before too long, it was overtaken by events.

The School Council, dating from 1971, was the third council to be established and involved the most interesting dynamic, pointing towards a 'decentralisation' of mission activity that would dovetail with an outstation movement. A significant decrease in school attendance was concurrent with the increase in alcohol consumption and a more rebellious spirit throughout the community. Albrecht's view was that the decoupling of school attendance and child endowment payments—a system previously controlled by the mission—caused the decline in attendance, especially among 'more traditional' Arrernte (Albrecht 2002: 102). At the end of the 1960s, the school principal, Rex Ziersch, and an Arrernte assistant, Nahasson Ungwanaka, consulted on the issue. Ziersch proposed a school council and Ungwanaka observed that such a council should comprise a representative from each 'skin-group family' that had children at the school. The council played roles similar to those of the other two councils: following-up absent kids, keeping the schoolyard clean and securing school buildings (Ungwanaka 1973). However, it also had a more ambitious agenda. The council was in charge of both hiring and firing Aboriginal teaching assistants financed by the Federal Government's newly introduced training allowances. These allowances were intended as an interim measure between the 1950s cash-and-kind payments to Northern Territory Aboriginal state wards and the payment of equal wages and benefits to Indigenous Australian citizens foreshadowed in the Wave Hill strike. The council, it was proposed, also would be involved in the selection of non-Indigenous teaching staff. It promoted the teaching of 'full English', or idiomatic spoken English, as well as textbook written English. In a rapidly evolving regional circumstance, some parents called the former 'inside' English—a secret language that in the future their children would need to know. A suggestion from the council was that this type of English be taught in a family environment, and thereby involve senior generations as well as the school kids (Sommerlad 1973: 39). Families should be assigned one teacher as their 'own' and the authority structure of the classroom in fact would be a kinship structure.

Heightened conflict at Hermannsburg recommended this kinship-oriented approach to some Arrernte and missionaries alike. By 1972, the conflict was evident in the Town Council, which, Gary Stoll reported, was 'strongly divided between two family groups', the one 'trying to move into a position of overall control and another, larger group trying to prevent them' (Stoll 1972a, 1972b, 1973). This kin-based struggle over new forms of resources and authority, also informed by the respective ritual standings of those involved, ramified in the classroom where children saw each other on a daily basis. Some families asked for children to be separated in different rooms. In 1973, both the specific issue of family conflict in the classroom and the more general one of family and regional conflicts in the community sent Rex Ziersch to study Aboriginal social organisation with anthropologist John von Sturmer at the University of Queensland. Thereafter, up to and including 1975 when the film *Malbangka Country* was made, von Sturmer had an intimate association with Lutheran mission staff, informing their evolving view of Arrernte kinship and relatedness, as well as mapping with various Aboriginal men much of the mission lease that would be scheduled as Aboriginal land under the *ALRA*. On Ziersch's return to Hermannsburg, the view rapidly evolved among missionaries that safeguarding of 'the Christian families', as they were known among Arrernte, and the protection of the church's standing, as well as the promotion of relevant forms of governance, rested on pursuing a 'decentralisation' of family groups from the mission settlement on to their traditional lands. This process, the mission hoped, would create a network of nexus between kin and country that would provide a framework for governance. Thus, a new way forward was identified in preference to the previous one that merely sought to indigenise imposed 'European' structures such as elected councils. While this might be a very particular understanding of Arrernte social organisation, this changed direction on the mission's part brought its support for some evolving Western

Arrernte aspirations. (The mission stance did not entail support for the advent of a Central Land Council (CLC) or, even entirely, support for an Aboriginal community council, which was established at Ntaria/Hermannsburg in 1983.)[3]

Western Arrernte outstation life

In February 1973, the Finke River Mission Board resolved that discussions should be 'instigated whereby the way is opened for the disposal of the assets and lease at Hermannsburg to the Aboriginals' (Leske 1977: 115). This decision and the local events that led to it were preceded by a regional event that likely prompted some Luritja, Arrernte and Luritja-Pintupi people to look to life beyond the mission. In 1963, gas and oil reserves were discovered at Mereenie in the Amadeus Basin, about 150 km west of Hermannsburg. In 1965, gas reserves also were discovered in Palm Valley, proximate to Hermannsburg. Through 1970 and 1971, discussions were taking place between the miners and involved Aboriginal people, including some based at Hermannsburg. This was the initial stage of negotiations that ultimately would see gas royalties and rental for a gas pipeline to Alice Springs come to Western Arrernte people. Relatively speaking, the payments would be modest. Nonetheless, their advent offered a new source of power and dignity to regional Aboriginal people. These negotiations also provided a different frame in which to reflect on local governance issues at the mission—a frame possibly linked to developments in Yirrkala and Wave Hill. In a milieu where the Mission Board proved reluctant to give Aboriginal people a role in hiring and firing non-Indigenous staff, Gary Stoll reported of the Mereenie negotiations:

---

3   In 1975, Paul Albrecht, with the cooperation of a number of Lutheran mission staff, organised a petition of some 250 foolscap typescript pages that contained the recorded and translated statements of land owners and their managers regarding countries in and around what had been the Hermannsburg Mission lease. The submission was presented to the Australian Prime Minister, the Federal Minister for Aboriginal Affairs and to all members of the Federal Parliament (see Albrecht et al. 1976). As Albrecht would later summarise, the thrust of the submission was that the Aboriginal landowners involved did not wish to be bound by land trusts or other elements of the legal apparatus of the Australian state. In Albrecht's terms, Aboriginal people had their own 'imperium' or legal-moral order quite independent of the state and its legal and administrative apparatus (see Albrecht 2002: 69–74, 93–108). Clearly, this position derived in part from the mission's failed experiment with councils and its staff's newfound insights derived from anthropology and especially the study of kinship. The engagement with anthropology was a commendable one but also naive to the extent that it hid from the missionaries their own engagement for generations in roles pertaining to the state. In short, the Aboriginal 'imperium' had already been much trammelled and the outstation movement would require a range of measures beyond the return to tradition (with Christianity in train) that Albrecht and his associates hoped for. Possibly the Hermannsburg mission also felt some regret at the prospect of the transition from a Hermannsburg mission to a secular Ntaria. Tensions between the Ntaria Council and lay Lutherans at TORC extended for many years. See Eames (1983) for a critique of the mission's procedures in the early land rights years. Unfortunately, his account, although politically correct, is impoverished by his misplaced certitudes and moralising. Ironically, the Hermannsburg submission remains a fascinating record of the way in which missionised Arrernte deployed managers with more extensive knowledge to keep substantial links with their country. It is a moving document despite its background politics.

The thing that all [Aboriginal participants] felt very strongly about was that whether the mining operation be small or large, they want to own it and where possible work it. In the event of it being necessary for Europeans to be involved, they do not want them to become partners but rather employees. The last people they want interfering in their business are government personnel. They also felt they want Europeans kept off the reserve as this was the place they can call their own. (Stoll 1970, 1971; also cited in Austin-Broos 2009: 187)

Talk between Arrernte and missionaries began in 1973, and by early 1974 one large group had decamped to Kwatjinmarra on Ellery Creek (Austin-Broos 2009: 214–5). As one missionary reported:

Suddenly people began to pack up and move out from Hermannsburg to settle as kinship or clan groups on their own chosen area … It was a spontaneous migration … The people simply left the conveniences and opportunities provided at Hermannsburg, to start off again at the grass-roots of their culture. (Leske 1977: 115)

In 1999–2000, people at Ntaria/Hermannsburg estimated that the original camp attracted up to 60 people. Lack of water and shelter became a problem and soon there were further, smaller relocations determined as appropriate by senior men—to Pmokaputa (Old Station), Tnawurta, Ilbal' Alkngarrintja (Red Sandhill) and Arrkapa, among other places. Before too long a riff of outstations was established along the northern edge of the James Range and in proximity to Ellery Creek (see Map 4.1). It was in this milieu that ceremony also began again, led by men, some of whom were guests of the Arrernte from the south, north and west. Often the guests had forged connections with Hermannsburg men through cattle work on Tempe Downs and Henbury stations in the south or on the mission lease itself. Contacts were also made via the cattle camp at Undandita that drew in men from the Glen Helen Station in the West Macdonnell Ranges.

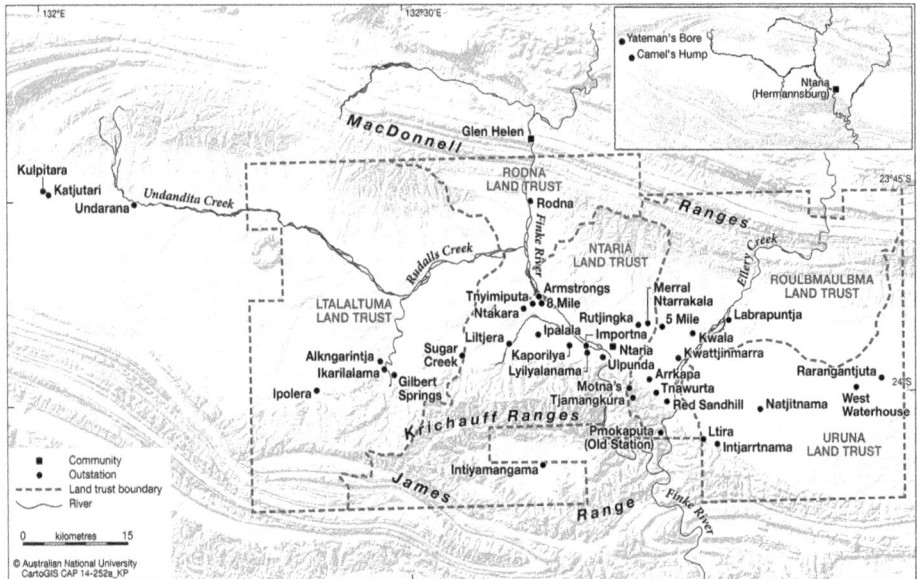

Map 4.1 Arrernte outstations.

Source: Karina Pelling, CartoGIS, ANU College of Asia and the Pacific

Kevin Coulthard, a man whose father, Jack, was central to events, described it this way:

> Well, that mob from Hermannsburg. Too much drinking, fighting. They want family to stop separate, away from trouble. Then they had ceremony. Lotta ceremony. All those old bloke pass away now ... Kwatjinmarra first outstation. Then Ungwanaka mob talking about Apma Kapurta [Old Station]—that's southern Arrernte language. Then we build big fence around here. Gardening. And after that my father and uncle talkin' with Nahassan to get outstation for my father. Maybe Illamurta, then Tnawurta was better. (cited in Austin-Broos 2009: 219)

Lutheran Gary Stoll, invited as a mediator between the men and the 'Government', provided this moving account of:

> [T]wo complete ceremonies involving many days and quite a few nights of singing and re-enacting the travels and exploits of various 'ancestors' ... The impression ... this has made on me is hard to describe. I was staggered by the extent and intactness of knowledge and skills still retained by men ranging in age from their late twenties to mid-seventies, many of whom grew up in the Mission and among whom I would have confidently predicted little of this kind of traditional knowledge remained. The efficiency of the organisation was also impressive as was its complete independence of any European assistance ... Another revelation was seeing men one has known for 18 years and many of whom have not impressed one as being other than mediocre, playing a very significant role and being very important in this situation. (Stoll 1976; also cited in Austin-Broos 2009: 192)

It was from this milieu that a group led by Traugott Malbunka broke away to move west of the mission and locate at Liltjera in April 1974. Soon thereafter, in December of the same year, Traugott's eldest brother, Gustav, established his camp at Ltalaltuma or Gilbert Springs. In the next year, the youngest of these siblings, Colin Malbunka, would establish his own outstation north of the Gilbert Springs at a place called Alkngarrintja. Colin Malbunka was already an ordained pastor with the Lutheran Church, while Gustav and Traugott were evangelists, the latter to be subsequently ordained. At the time of the initial outstation shift in 1973–74, Pastor Colin Malbunka held a missionary position in the distant location of Neutral Junction, north-east of Hermannsburg. He was granted an assignment home in order to participate in the outstation movement and thereby occupy his 'block'. It seems unlikely that the Malbunkas maintained an Indigenous ritual milieu as rich as that at Ellery Creek in the early days. Nonetheless, the Malbunkas' actions showed something else: that even Arrernte people close to the mission as a family could maintain some knowledge 'all round', as they described it and as Gary Stoll had found. Moreover, the order of priorities reflected in Colin Malbunka's return simply reflects the order of priorities among mission residents in general when they moved to Kwatjinmarra. As resources became available, even modest ones, and as the values of assimilation flagged, Western Arrernte became engaged in an outstation movement that they saw in significant part as a pursuit of autonomy.

Yet, even the resurgence of rites near Ellery Creek, and the strong preference expressed for domestic units and authority structures based on kinship and locality did not make this outstation movement simply a return to tradition. The human technologies that the mission brought had fundamental ontological impacts. These included the persuasions towards a sedentary life provided by domestication and processed foods as well as bore water accessed in places where previously Western Arrernte generally would not have had more than ephemeral camps. Again, space–time coordinates were rearranged first by horseback travel and then by motor vehicles, which were being used increasingly by the 1970s. Even when vehicles were driven across country or on ungraded tracks sometimes etched previously by stockmen and cattle on their way to soakages, the duration of a trip between two camps could become some hours rather than two or more days. All these changes would affect expectations regarding the activities that occurred each day in camp, the frequency with which near and more distant relatives were engaged, and the types of regional connection that could be maintained. Both processed food and greater ease of travel would affect the intensity with which Arrernte in camp would engage their immediate environment and the micro-ecologies through which they regularly passed. Where many family groups were concerned, two or three previous generations in the mission brought a relativising of cosmology. A Lutheran Christian view of the world had to be located and, initially at least, bounded in relation to another world that became specifically an Arrernte or 'blackfella' one. Eric Kolig (1972) suggests that Aboriginal people held the new European presence on the very edge or 'horizon' of their world. Where the Western Arrernte were concerned, over time they seemed to locate Lutheran 'law' at Ntaria/Hermannsburg and along that section of the Finke River that passed by the mission. Missionaries came to that site because they brought a law that had been forgotten for that place. In this way, Arrernte sought to accommodate the missionaries quite some time before women would say, in the late 1990s, that though ancestral stories were not 'true', Arrernte kept them for their country.[4]

Finally, the actual pattern of outstation settlement reflected a significant reconfiguration of people on land due to the impact of settlement. Gustav Malbunka could claim his country as the country of his great grandfather Mangina. However, most of the relations to country on the basis of which Western Arrernte took up outstations were negotiated by groups of men, some of whom retained ritual knowledge and some of whom were prominent as leaders in the mission. In fact, these negotiations of locality reveal the ingenuity of the Western Arrernte in their drive to reproduce a system significantly disturbed by European settlement. Outstation leaders could in fact be 'mother's side', 'occupying mother's father's country'; more immediate affines of owners, 'occupation negotiated through wife' or 'occupation negotiated through son-in-law'; or guests with knowledge, 'occupation negotiated with traditional owners', some of whom took over sites 'occupying land that is part of their dreaming [where] traditional owners may have died out' (Haeusler 1976). Such negotiations would have occurred in pre-settlement times due to drought or prolonged feud, or even according to aptitude. In this instance though, the negotiations were extensive and laid the grounds for petty and more serious conflicts later on.

Malbangka Country provides some insight into daily life circa 1975. Gustav Malbunka's camp was constructed of a number of shelters made from native brush, canvas, corrugated iron and blankets. Careful scrutiny of the film indicates different locales for older women, among them Gustav's father's second wife, Della, and young men, some of them in cowboy gear and presenting a lively demeanour in contrast to old Gustav's restraint. The film's introduction invites Malbunka to name his conception site and to stipulate the origins of both his father and his Luritja mother from further west. He also indicates that his father was mission-raised while his mother was not. She came 'naked' from Mereenie to Hermannsburg. As these matters are discussed, Gustav helps a small

---

4   Although his discussion fails to address the Western Arrernte, Peterson (2000) gives an excellent account of the general manner in which ritual knowledge and practice might attenuate with the types of changes cited here—especially the attenuation of diverse and specific regional rites that rested on uses and knowledge of the land that new technologies and social practices have rendered obsolete or nearly so.

grandchild play a cassette of country and western music that pervades the camp. A young man carries a charred bullock head, which he places on a wire bed. He splits the skull with an axe to obtain the roasted offal. This source of food is juxtaposed with another. The store truck arrives, driven by the stock manager from the mission, Murray Pearce. He brings meat, drinks and various fruits and vegetables. He also brings pension cheques and child endowment payments—all to be signed for. The commentary notes that this Malbunka station also has a government grant to pay for fencing materials and for the wages of the young men. Does the family still hunt for food? Though the film will later show women and children bringing home a rabbit and perentie caught from one hole, Gustav Malbunka observes that hunting is 'stranger for us now'—'too long' with sugar and flour. The other form of foraging shown is by women searching for bush tobacco, which remains a perennial of Arrernte life.

Pearce also discusses with the elder Malbunka and his wife, Eileen Ungwanaka, father's sister to Nahassan, the task of sinking a bore that, he suggests, might be done by the younger men. The film cuts to the nearby springs and a women's ritual site and camp located at a distance from Ltalaltuma, a 'big place' for men. The women's site and camp is used as a water source, but men are still reluctant to use it though it has been 'freed'—a common Lutheran term for conversion.

As evening nears, the elder Malbunka calls his group together for devotional hymns and prayer—a daily ritual still maintained in the 1990s by surviving Malbunkas of the last mission generation. In turn, this practice is juxtaposed with another form of ritual concern as Malbunka on another day inspects the caves that hold some of his stone *tywerrenge* (*tjurunga*). The cave is near collapse and another one must be found as a storehouse. Gustav Malbunka consults a *kwertengerle* (*kutungurla*) on a new location for the ritual objects. Another day and two trucks head for Areyonga to visit other *kwertengerle* of Gustav Malbunka, who are managers for sites in that locale. Malbunka relates that the entire country down to and including Areyonga is Malbunka country that harbours many significant sites. Areyonga was established as a government ration depot in the 1920s as drought-affected Pitjantjatjara to the south moved north (see Long, this volume). In 1943, the Hermannsburg Mission assumed the depot's administration and also offered some social welfare services. Neither measure, Gustav underlines, involved significant consultation with the Malbunkas whose land it was. With his managers, Malbunka inspects one particular site of great significance.

Malbungka Country begins and ends with Gustav Malbunka's hopes for the future. His remarks are notable for the fact that he projects patterns of settlement that mirror Hermannsburg but in a context that evokes a specifically Indigenous life: Malbunka envisages 'proper' houses with running water and his own church and school. Asked about outstation income, he suggests that the family might grow vegetables and fruit, perhaps to be sold to other settlements. He notes that, on its closure, the mission will probably distribute some cattle (it did), which would be the foundation for a Malbunka breeding herd, and also a source of fresh meat. In the years to come, services, employment, cash and ritual coherence along with intergenerational authority relations and debates between families about where 'the boundaries' of countries are, would produce frustrations both for the Malbunkas and for other groups. Numerous such issues would impinge on well-being. Nonetheless, the outstation movement did realise new life-ways in which family camps in various locales—on country and 'in town'—allowed space for Arrernte people to modify but also maintain very dense fields of relatedness. Paradoxically perhaps, a sedentary life, motorised transport, lower levels of infant mortality and cash incomes had encouraged relatedness even in the midst of change. As the Lutheran mission withdrew and as land rights were secured, Arrernte people strove to realise a revitalised life.

Self-determination and the Western Arrernte

Discussions with Western Arrernte around the end of the 1990s underlined a thought-provoking point: in the view of these elderly women and men, there always had been outstations linked to settlements. Asked to list outstations, most did not confine themselves simply to the Western Arrernte outstation movement. Various initiatives, often associated with the mission, were described as 'outstations'. Some accounts began with Jay Creek and the Lutheran Church in Alice Springs. The latter, established in 1938 and also known as the 'mission block', had acted as a refuge for 'full-bloods' whose visits to Alice Springs at the time were illegal.[5] The block had also served as an old people's camp and had provided some accommodation for Aboriginal people visiting relatives in hospital. As an extension of the Hermannsburg Mission, it was indeed an outstation. Less often, Jay Creek was cited. Established as a camp for 'half-castes' in 1937, it seemed to earn the name 'outstation' because T. G. H. Strehlow, son of the missionary Carl Strehlow, resided there as a patrol officer between the late 1930s and early 1940s. Other outstations commonly mentioned were the ration depots at Haasts Bluff and Areyonga. Haasts Bluff had a long prior history as a site for trade in artefacts, skins and dingo scalps between Aboriginal and European people. Resourced by the Government from 1939, the depot was staffed by the mission beginning in 1942. Because it also had a missionary role, it was commonly called 'Old Albrecht's Station', referring to Paul Albrecht's father, Pastor Friedrich Albrecht. Areyonga, as discussed above, had multiple

---

5   This circumstance was integral to the laws that regulated residence in and around Alice Springs for different, racialised categories of Aboriginal and non-Aboriginal people.

links with the Malbunka family. In addition, for many years the driver of the truck that supplied Areyonga was Colin Malbunka's father-in-law—like the Ungwanakas, a Southern Arrernte.

Other places commonly cited were Pmokaputa (Old Station) and Undandita, which long before the Western Arrernte's outstation movement had been cattle camps. The former was attached to Henbury Station in the south and the latter to Glen Helen Station, north of Hermannsburg. Of this stock-camp type, the earliest outstation cited was one from Hermannsburg itself: the goat camp at Labrapuntja on Ellery Creek, established by the mission in the early 1880s. More recent outstations from Hermannsburg included Albert Namatjira's artists' camp at Tjuwanpa, established in 1945, and another on the Finke River north of the mission. The latter was provided for Manasse Armstrong on his retirement in 1959. He was Hermannsburg's Aboriginal works manager and senior tanner for many years.

In short, Western Arrernte saw outstations as a perennial of settlement. Therefore it is not surprising that many described the more recent outstation movement simply in terms of 'shifting' from one site to another: to avoid 'noise'; to move from a Hermannsburg in which there were 'too many family'; and to leave a camp where there was now 'no room' and where people quarrelled 'for anything' and 'all the time' (see Austin-Broos 2009: 220). Yet this shift was also different from previous ones both before and after the mission settlement. This move was to a place or 'block' where a form of authority was reclaimed; a return to a particular milieu in which one or another group was acknowledged as 'boss' for a place with ritual significance. Moreover, this time the Arrernte shifted because they wished to and because now they could—due to changed legal status and an increasing access to resources denied them for generations.

These factors bear on two different notions of 'self-determination' at large in Australian society and in some academic writing. One identifies self-determination with the outstation movement as such, as a return to country by residential groups seeking a local Indigenous autonomy. Another view is that self-determination involves building an 'Indigenous sector' in the wake of land rights and the outstation movement; Aboriginal administrative control of a new social formation consisting of outstation systems and regional administrations linked to various state centres of governance. This account has argued that, for the Western Arrernte, their distance from foraging and the attenuation of their ritual life would mean that outstations also retained major dimensions of settlement life—and life within the state. For this reason, the second notion of self-determination is a necessary adjunct to the first. Within the bounds of the Australian state and with all the legacies of settlement, there could be no resumption of simply local practices. But neither, in Arrernte experience, was the outstation movement only or principally an exercise in a state-related politics. It was also a statement about the mission's social-moral limitations and, as well, its faltering power. When the Western Arrernte began to shift, they did so to preserve and reinvigorate a valued kin-based life on ritually significant country that seemed to facilitate autonomy—'same but different' from the past. The outstation movement sought a new way and realised some initial steps towards it. This path has brought some particular challenges as Arrernte struggle to incorporate in it livelihoods and forms of education compatible with their desired milieu (Austin-Broos 2010, 2011, 2012). These are parts of any culture, old or revitalised, and call on further dimensions of self-determination (Austin-Broos 2013a, 2013b). Notwithstanding, the outstation movement was and remains the first successful step in a journey away from the forced dependency of mission life—which the Arrernte themselves deemed unacceptable.

Conclusion

This discussion has focused principally on the early years of the Western Arrernte outstation movement. It has not addressed the tangled and instructive history of TORC, especially during the 1990s as it evolved from a mission-derived organisation into a secular one answerable to the state in the form of Federal and Territory administrations and their changing policies shaped by the politics of Aboriginal issues nationwide (see Austin-Broos 2001; 2009: 229–37). A notable document linked to that history is a letter written in 1985 that begins 'Dear Charlie'. The letter was addressed to Charles Perkins, then secretary in the Department of Aboriginal Affairs. It carried a direct request for more resources to support the 600 people living at the time on outstations located on one or other of the Western Arrernte's five land trusts. Among the letter's signatories was Jack Coulthard, a leader of the Western Arrernte's ritual revival, who, like some others involved, signed with a cross. They had not been mission schooled. The letter was also signed by sons of Gustav, Traugott and Colin Malbunka who had taken over as leaders of their fathers' outstations, along with a youthful Herman Malbunka, whose father, Jeremiah, had died in 1975. The document presaged the struggle that unfolded to maintain the outstation system as it was initially conceived. Like the film *Malbungka Country*, the letter is a symbol of the Western Arrernte's engagement with revitalisation: the 'deliberate, organised attempt by some members of a society to construct a more satisfying culture by rapid acceptance of a pattern of multiple innovations'. This was and remains the significance of the Western Arrernte's outstation movement.

References

Albrecht, P. 2002. *From Mission to Church 1877–2002, Finke River Mission*. Adelaide: Openbook Publishers.

Albrecht, P., Pfitzner, J., Stoll, G., Ziersch, R. and Fargher, R. K. (eds) 1976. Objections of traditional Aboriginal land owners to the proposed Aboriginal land rights legislation, submission to the Prime Minister. Typescript.

Austin-Broos, D. 2001. Outstations and CDEP: The Western Arrernte in Central Australia. In F. Morphy and W. Sanders (eds), *The Indigenous Welfare Economy and the CDEP Scheme*. Canberra: Centre for Aboriginal Economic Policy Research, pp. 167–76.

Austin-Broos, D. 2009. *Arrernte Present, Arrernte Past: Invasion, Violence and Imagination in Indigenous Central Australia*. Chicago and London: University of Chicago Press.

Austin-Broos, D. 2010. Quarantining violence: How anthropology does it. In J. Altman and M. Hinkson (eds), *Culture Crisis: Anthropology and Politics in Aboriginal Australia*. Sydney: UNSW Press, pp. 136–49.

Austin-Broos, D. 2011. *A Different Inequality: The Politics of Debate about Remote Aboriginal Australia*. Sydney: Allen & Unwin.

Austin-Broos, D. 2012. Keeping faith with self-determination: Economy and cultural difference. *Indigenous Law Bulletin* 7(29): 18–23.

Austin-Broos, D. 2013a. Economy, change and self-determination: A Central Australian case. In L. Ford and T. Rowse (eds), *Between Indigenous and Settler Governance*. Abingdon, UK: Routledge, pp. 108–20.

Austin-Broos, D. 2013b. Livin' this way: Freedom and Aboriginal self-determination. Paper presented to Freedoms and Liberties in Anthropological Perspective Conference, University of St Andrews, 31 May – 2 June.

Chesterman, J. and Galligan, B. 1967. *Citizens without Rights: Aborigines and Australian Citizenship*. Cambridge: Cambridge University Press.

Eames, G. 1983. The Central Land Council: The politics of change. In N. Peterson and M. Langton (eds), *Aborigines, Land and Land Rights*. Canberra: Australian Institute of Aboriginal Studies, pp. 268–77.

Haeusler, M. 1976. *Report on a visit to Hermannsburg, 23–26 August*. Document 69/166. Department of Aboriginal Affairs, Central Australia.

Hardy, F. 1968. *The Unlucky Australians*. Melbourne: Thomas Nelson.

Kolig, E. 1972. Bi:n and Gadeja: An Aboriginal model of European society as a guide to change. *Oceania* 43(1): 1–18.

Leske, L. H. 1977. *Hermannsburg: A Vision and a Mission*. Adelaide: Lutheran Publishing House.

Levy, C. (dir.) 1975. *Malbangka Country*. [Film]. Canberra: Australian Institute of Aboriginal Studies Film Unit.

Myers, F. 2011. Foreword. In *A Different Inequality: The Politics of Debate about Remote Aboriginal Australia*. Sydney: Allen & Unwin, pp. ix–xx.

Peterson, N. 2000. An expanding Aboriginal domain: Mobility and the initiation journey. *Oceania* 70(3): 205–14.

Sommerlad, E. 1973. *Community Development at Hermannsburg*. Canberra: Centre for Continuing Education.

Stoll, G. 1970. *Hermannsburg Mission superintendent's report to the Finke River Mission Board*, October.

Stoll, G. 1971. *Hermannsburg Mission superintendent's report to the Finke River Mission Board*, February.

Stoll, G. 1972a. *Hermannsburg Mission superintendent's report to the Finke River Mission Board*, March.

Stoll, G. 1972b. *Hermannsburg Mission superintendent's report to the Finke River Mission Board*, August.

Stoll, G. 1973. *Hermannsburg Mission superintendent's report to the Finke River Mission Board*, November.

Stoll, G. 1976. *Hermannsburg Mission superintendent's report to the Finke River Mission Board*, April.

Ungwanaka, N. 1973. The development of the Hermannsburg School Council. In *Community Development at Hermannsburg*. Canberra: Centre for Continuing Education, pp. xvi–xix.

Wallace, A. 1956. Revitalization movements. *American Anthropologist* 58(2): 264–81.

Williams, N. 1986. *The Yolngu and the Land: A System of Land Tenure and the Fight for its Recognition*. Canberra: Australian Institute of Aboriginal Studies.

WESTERN DESERT COMPLEXITIES

5

History, memory and the politics of self-determination at an early outstation

Fred Myers[1]

Looking back at the experience of the Pintupi outstation of Yayayi[2] over the initial period 1973–75, when I was a PhD student doing field research there, I am divided between nostalgia and ambivalence. One can hardly ignore the memory of Pintupi people's excitement to be away from the tensions and density of the large government settlement of Papunya, or the distinctive embrace of the resurgent civil rights movement expressed at Yayayi in a language of 'Black Power'. Yayayi was one of the very first 'outstation communities' in the Northern Territory under the umbrella of changes articulated by the Whitlam Government's embrace of

1   This research was supported by a research grant from the Australian Institute of Aboriginal and Torres Strait Islander Studies (G09/7478) and an Australian Research Council (ARC) Linkage Grant, 'Pintupi Dialogues: Reconstructing Memories of Art, Land and Community through the Visual Record' (2010–13). I want to thank my collaborators on the project, Pip Deveson, Peter Thorley, Ian Dunlop and Nic Peterson, for their help and insight. I would like to acknowledge the contribution of our Pintupi consultants on this project: Irene Nangala, Monica Robinson Nangala, Bobby West Tjupurrula, Jimmy Brown Tjampitjinpa and Marlene Spencer Nampitjinpa.
2   There have been many spellings in the literature to refer to this place, depending on how non-Indigenous speakers heard the name, and we have included them as they occurred in archival materials. The spelling of 'Yayayi' represents the orthography and phonology currently used in literacy materials.

something we call 'Aboriginal self-determination'. A powerful notion at the time, as Peter Sutton (2009) has testified, this phrase needs to be kept in quotation marks, as we should, I suggest, explore what this political slogan meant.

The exuberance of Pintupi returning to Yayayi, 40 km west of Papunya, was palpable. Their enthusiasm was matched by indeterminate expectations, by inchoate ideas of a future. Nonetheless, for me to have been there, as a young man with an equally un-nuanced progressive view of a possible future, is the source of my nostalgia, which, I suspect, is shared by many who lived or worked on the early outstations.

Let me consider for a moment, then, what I mean by 'ambivalence'. What did Yayayi amount to? I want to think about this because in recent years, the political screw has turned and one routinely now hears that the project or policy of 'Aboriginal self-determination' was a failure, the source of a perceived current severe dysfunction in many remote communities (see, for example, Hughes 2007; Johns 2001; Howson 2000). Many of us who did research in remote communities in the 1970s were strong supporters of an Aboriginal right to self-determination, as Peter Sutton has (again) pointed out, and in that sense, we may feel implicated in these results. What went wrong? It is important to say here that these policies were not really the consequence of the sympathies of anthropologists. The movement for Aboriginal self-determination was embedded in and catalysed by international movements of national liberation, civil rights and human rights.

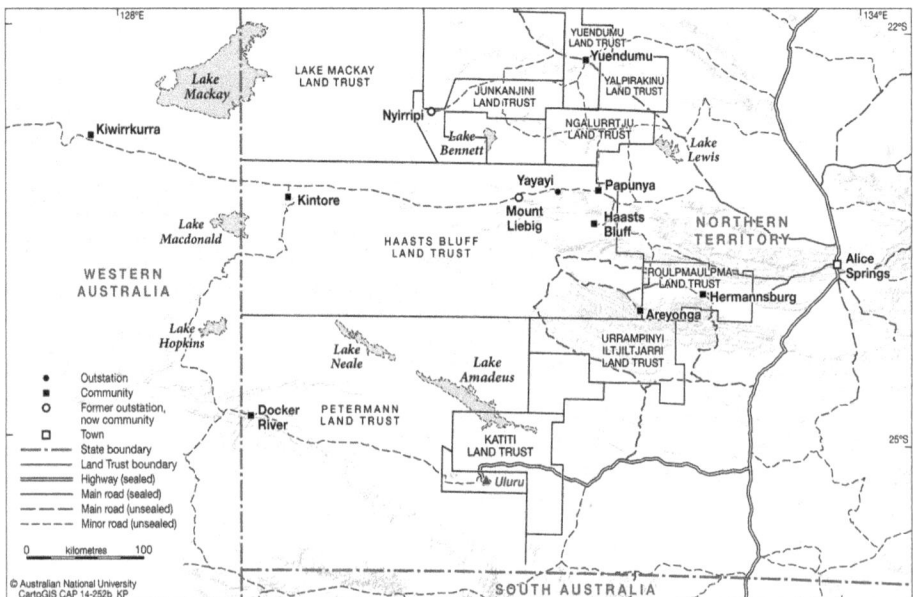

Map 5.1 Yayayi in relation to Papunya and Kintore.
Source: Karina Pelling, CartoGIS, ANU College of Asia and the Pacific

In my initial imaginings of this essay, I was expecting to go back to the experiences of everyday life at Yayayi, through my notes, government documents and the film footage that Ian Dunlop shot there in 1974.[3] To explain briefly, Dunlop came to Yayayi in 1974 to follow up with Pintupi people he had met with Jeremy Long on one of the last 'Pintupi patrols', at a time when people were leaving their homelands for Papunya and other government settlements. Dunlop was thinking of making a film that would explore what had happened to people who had so much impressed him. He shot 12 hours of 16 mm colour sound-synchronised footage, but he never made it into a film. In 1975, with the help of two Pintupi consultants, I translated and further documented the footage. Thirty-two years later, after it had been deposited in the National Film and Sound Archive and been transferred to tape and then digitised, I took the footage back to the Pintupi communities of Kiwirrkura and Kintore as part of a project of repatriation. Based on the enthusiastic reception of the footage in those communities, this footage and Pintupi responses to it have provided the instigation for the project of which this essay is a part—namely, a re-examination of the early moment of self-determination in a remote outstation.

Figure 5.1 Minyina Tjampitjinpa's camp at Yayayi, 1974.
Source: Fred Myers

---

3 My original monograph based on this fieldwork, and later research, was published in 1986 (see Myers 1986).

Figure 5.2 Pintupi watching archival footage, Kintore, 2006.
Source: Fred Myers

In asking 'What was Yayayi? What did it amount to?', I have come to realise that how it looks varies according to different subjects, with a range of social imaginaries. In the research undertaken with the Yayayi film footage, Pip Deveson, Peter Thorley and I interviewed a range of people involved in Yayayi—including most of the non-Indigenous participants who were there and five Pintupi consultants who had lived, as young people, at the outstation. Our research sought to understand what Pintupi people found interesting or important in the film material and, relatedly, what the experience or memory of Yayayi—as well as of self-determination—might be.

The most immediate responses to seeing the old footage, as I learned from a nursing sister who was living at Kiwirrkura in 2006, concerned the apparent 'health' of the folks living at Yayayi. 'We were so healthy then', many of the Pintupi viewers remarked, according to this report. In contrast, certainly, to the more common obesity of the present, the fitter bodies of the men and women in 1974 were quite noticeable and meaningfully so in the context of the severe challenges to health of the present, with high rates of renal failure and diabetes.

Let me explain why one might regard these comments with some ambivalence, perhaps even 'irony'.

Despite the celebration of the outstation movement in many accounts of the early 1970s, its inauguration at Yayayi was considerably more fraught. The movement of Pintupi to Yayayi was part of a series of attempts to allow Pintupi to separate themselves from the larger complex of Papunya. Jeremy Long, who has an essay in this volume, had proposed such decentralisation westward as early as 1962. As the latest (even last) people to migrate from the Western Desert, many Pintupi arrived at Papunya in the 1960s under the somewhat negative characterisation of 'myalls'; they were seen as ignorant and less civilised by their more knowledgeable brethren who had experienced contact earlier. Additionally, the movement in from the bush exposed them to disease and infection that resulted in a substantial series of deaths—a rate of dying some officials suggested was compounded by a lack of will to live in the new circumstances. When they first went to Papunya (in 1966), the linguist Lesley Hansen remarked in one of our interviews, 'You'd hear crying and we'd say, "Why are they crying?" And they'd say, "All the Pintupi are going to die. They're going to finish up"' (interview with Lesley Hansen, 2011). The mounting death toll and illness seemed overwhelming. These are among the specificities of the Pintupi history as it relates to self-determination and to outstations.

The desire to live independently

These circumstances were a worry, indeed a problem, for the Welfare Branch of the NT Administration and later the Department of Aboriginal Affairs—fearing the bad publicity but also out of genuine concern. To alleviate the problems— illness, morbidity, conflict and depression—an initial outstation was founded at a bore away from Papunya called Waruwiya, where Pintupi moved in 1967. When this water source was found to be a health problem, with high levels of nitrates, it had to be abandoned and the Pintupi returned to Papunya. In 1970, another outstation community was established, at Alumbara Bore, about 30 km west of Papunya. Life here was, apparently, very satisfactory for the Pintupi who moved there, but a conflict with police and the difficulties of administering this location again forced the Pintupi back. During this time, various officials of the regional Welfare Branch (and later Department of Aboriginal Affairs, DAA) continued to look for locations to allow the Pintupi to hive off from the larger settlement. At the time, movement back into their own traditional country— much further west near the NT border—was considered impossible: there were no bores out there and the difficulties of servicing such a remote location were regarded as insurmountable.

Nonetheless, the accounts suggest that Pintupi leaders continued to agitate for the establishment of a separate community, and this became possible in early 1973. Indeed, as soon as the location of Yayayi—at a place also called Kakali Bore—in Luritja territory[4] became possible, they moved out with some support from the DAA.

T. C. (Creed) Lovegrove's[5] account of the situation to the next Minister of Aboriginal Affairs, James Cavanagh, written in January 1974, is clear:

> When the group moved to Yai Yaia on 4th June 1973 it was a decision that the Pintubi group *itself made* because they were fed up with being discouraged from moving because of administrative difficulties. The departmental representatives at Papunya assisted them with transport, but it would have been more convenient to the Departments of Aboriginal Affairs Health and Education if the group had not insisted on moving at that stage as none of these departments were geared to provide a satisfactory service to the community. However, the Department of Aboriginal Affairs recognized *a right of self-determination* in this decision of the community. [Emphasis added][6]

It was the end of what those who still remember call 'Welfare Time'. In an interview I had with Marlene Spencer Nampitjinpa (in June 2013), a Pintupi woman who was a teenager in 1974, Marlene delineated the period as one of governmental supervision: of settlement officials coming to camps to make sure children went to school, for example, or even showing them how to take showers. These were hallmarks of an earlier policy of paternalism or training, in which the government settlements had kitchens providing food for residents, especially older people and children. 'Welfare time,' she remarked in remembering school, 'not allowed to stay in camp'. Others remember a time of dependency on white institutions 'like the kitchen coming in, three meals a day. They were just sitting there, waiting for the next meal. It was very debilitating' (Ken Hansen, interview, 2012). These are the circumstances about which C. D. Rowley (1971b) wrote so devastatingly against 'total social institutions'.

The government support of local aspirations to move out of large, mixed settlements sounds like a good story. Consider the following statement by the Minister for Aboriginal Affairs, Gordon Bryant, offered shortly after the Pintupi move:

> The Federal Government has made an urgent grant to a group of 250 Pintubi Aborigines in the Northern Territory to help them *establish their own community*.

---

4   The 'Luritja people' here refers to the speakers of a different dialect of the general Western Desert language, who lived to the east of those known as Pintupi. See Tindale (1974).
5   Lovegrove was a senior official of the Department of Aboriginal Affairs, based in the Northern Territory.
6   National Archives of Australia [hereinafter NAA], Canberra: F1, 1973/6202 Pintupi Outstation Yai Yaia, p. 29, Letter of 17 January 1974.

The Minister for Aboriginal Affairs, Mr. Gordon Bryant, announced today that he had approved a grant of $30,000 to cover the cost of items requested by the group.

The Pintubi group had decided earlier this month to move from Papunya, where they had been living with other tribes, to their new site at Yai Yaia, 24 miles [19 km] away.

The only facility at the new site was a stock water bore …

'Their move is an expression of their desire to live independently,' he said. [Emphasis added][7]

The controversial move: Political ironies of self-determination

Apparently, this movement did not enjoy universal support. For reasons I cannot trace effectively, this Pintupi outstation move came under substantial criticism— from unlikely sources, indeed, from those with a deep concern for Aboriginal well-being. The well-known advocate for Aboriginal health Dr Archie Kalokerinos is featured in a segment of the Australian Broadcasting Corporation (ABC) program *This Day Tonight* aired on 26 June 1973. Along with the then young Indigenous political activist Neville Perkins (nephew of Charlie), Kalokerinos appears in this segment and expresses his deep concern about the health situation of Papunya and, secondarily, of Yayayi. In what I find to be a very disturbing scene, Kalokerinos asks the Pintupi medical aide, Pinny Tjapaltjarri, to demonstrate how he gives eyedrops. Talking to the camera as if Pinny Tjapaltjarri—a Ngangkari trained by the health service as part of an attempt to give responsibility to local people—is either not present or incapable of understanding, Kalokerinos is critical of Pinny's knowledge. After the narrator explains that Pinny had only an hour's training in preparation to become 'the guardian of health' for the community, Kalokerinos watches Pinny use an eyedropper and comments: 'It's quite obvious that in Benny's [Pinny] untrained hands, infection is really spread from one eye to another.' Such comments suggest to the viewer that the health situation at Yayayi is unmanageable without white presence—although the Pintupi themselves were determined to be there. The implication of the broadcast, therefore, subsequently articulated in a letter sent to the Minister of Aboriginal Affairs by a viewer, is that the movement to the outstation was a government project taken without consideration of Aboriginal well-being. If, in the end, this challenge helped persuade the Health Department to agree to send

---

7   NAA: F133, 1977/66 Part 1 Yai Yai Bore, p. 261, 20 June 1973.

a nursing sister on a regular basis, it also threatened the entire Pintupi project and imposed a Euro-Australian set of values and judgments against those of the community.

Subsequent to the broadcast, Bryant reiterated the Labor Government's policy in a response to a disturbing letter from a citizen of Adelaide who had seen the segment. Aileen Thompson had written a letter to *The Advertiser*.[8] In reply, Bryant wrote:

> First of all, let me assure you that it is in the intention of the present government to do everything that is possible to improve the quality of life of this group of people, but we will be governed to a large extent by the expressed wishes of the people themselves and will not impress upon them those values through which we as Europeans judge to be important to a quality of life.
>
> You will probably be interested to know that this group of Pintubi Aboriginal came to Papunya several years ago and have in the last few years been anxious to establish their own community. The decision that brought about their move from Papunya to Yai Yaia was one that they made entirely on their own and since moving the morale of the group has lifted considerably …
>
> An officer of my Department is working in close liaison with the community and they are expressing great interest and initiative as a result of the opportunity which is being given to them to become more closely involved in their own future welfare and a responsibility for decision making on their own behalf.
>
> Much has to be done to assist these people and other Aboriginals in Australia, and you can be assured that while the present Government is in power we will be working towards this end but will continue to have as our guiding principle the self-determination of Aboriginal communities themselves.[9]

There was also a furious exchange of telegrams between the DAA officials and Neville Perkins about Perkins' claim that it was *his* personal intervention that resulted in the grant of vehicles and other resources to Yayayi.[10] The DAA had put these requests into play before his arrival, they insisted; they sought to deny the implication that they had failed to help these people appropriately. I relate these tensions to indicate the complex field of responsibilities and goals invested in the outstation. If one extends the interpretation of Kalokerinos's intervention, and

---

8   The letter in *The Advertiser* [Adelaide] was published on 5 July 1973. See NAA: F133, 1968/60 Papunya Outstation, p. 11. She also wrote a letter directly to Bryant. NAA: F1, 1973/6202 Pintupi Outstation Yai Yaia, p. 128, Letter 10 July 1973.

9   NAA: Gordon Bryant, 9 August 1973, F1, 1973/6202 Pintupi Outstation Yai Yaia, p. 105.

10   NAA: Folder 53883095, Pintupi Outstation Yai Yaia. Indeed, R. McHenry, the senior DAA officer in Darwin, wrote in response to this claim: 'Initial $30,000 grant based on reports of Owens following consultation with Pintubi people. The visit by your group and particularly those comments offered by Mr. Bruno helpful in confirming assessment of initial needs. I will not have it inferred that anyone other than the department and its agent Owens which commenced a special study on this matter two months ago was responsible for the grant.' NAA: F1, 1973/6202 Pintupi Outstation Yai Yaia, p.144.

that of Perkins, one can see the outlines of a continued paternalism (concern for Aboriginal health defined in Western terms) arrayed against local Indigenous desires to move to outstations—their version of 'self-determination'.

I do not offer this history in order to take a side in this contest, the stakes of which seem to resemble the concerns that Peter Sutton (2001, 2009) defined for himself some years ago about what ethical responsibilities one might have in regards to people's well-being. I have pursued this account because it highlights, very exactly, the ironies of 'self-determination' at Yayayi, with those who ordinarily advocated Aboriginal self-determination impeding a determined Indigenous decision and seemingly doing so in terms of a Western health rationality.

I have to put my own cards on the table. I identified with and supported the Pintupi desire to determine their own trajectories and values. I do not believe it could have been different. The privilege of doing research at Yayayi during this emergent administrative period of self-determination required local permission. The Pintupi at Yayayi said they were happy for me to be there, but they made it clear that I was expected 'to help Aboriginal people'. One could hardly, in those circumstances, strongly question or challenge their decisions or judgments. To do so was seen as a return to the pattern of the previous welfare regime—a pattern they rejected in claiming what they took to be their rights to self-determination. This commitment—and commitment it was—was nonetheless sometimes in tension with my subjective experience and also my cultural position as a Western person. For example, motor vehicles were an endless problem at Yayayi (see Myers 1988), as I have described elsewhere. According to the dictates of Aboriginal self-determination, the vehicles (trucks) granted to Yayayi from the DAA (and elsewhere)—its most valuable capital items—were provided to serve the community for work and for getting food stores from Papunya. Not surprisingly, these vehicles were frequently taken on hunting trips and taken off road, with rather bad mechanical outcomes (ranging from broken axles and stripped transmission to total wreckage). If the mobility and opportunity to get out into the country were a huge boost to morale, there was also very clearly a conflict between Indigenous values (the vehicle in the service of relatedness, kinship obligations, hunting as a valued activity and mobility) and Euro-Australian values (use only for assigned purposes, accountability to grant provisions, contracts, and so on). Moreover, the local leaders in charge of the vehicles could hardly refuse the requests of their relatives to help them, lest they forfeit their authority under the requirement to help.

Figure 5.3 All aboard the 'red truck' at Yayayi, 1973.
Source: Fred Myers

One must remember, this was a particular political moment—in Australia and the world. At Yayayi, although teenagers wore denim jackets decorated with the words 'Make Love, Not War', the talk was of 'Black Power'. 'Black Power', as it was articulated, was not nuanced, but it was largely understood as a change in the relationships of whites and blacks. Rumours about the content of 'self-determination' abounded: some thought all the resources and assets of Papunya were to be turned over to the Aboriginal people. The reach of 'Aboriginal self-determination' was not itself evident. Restrictions on their 'autonomy', to use a word that I have clarified elsewhere (Myers 1986), were difficult to reconcile with what they were told in countless meetings with Euro-Australians (officials as well as political activists) about 'self-determination'.

Black and white

The field of Indigenous/Euro-Australian relations at Yayayi and Papunya was quite unstable—as I learned very quickly. After getting permission to conduct research at Yayayi in July 1973, I still had to return to Alice Springs and get the equipment for a long stay. Within a few days of returning to Papunya, passing through the so-called 'European' area that was spatially segregated, with the 'Europeans'[11] living in more substantial houses and the Aboriginal people in transitional houses or tents, I wrote in my journal about hearing the white workers—'old hands' (former Welfare Branch employees, now part of the DAA) who *did* seem to 'like' Aborigines and to care about them—discuss what they referred to as the 'half-caste problem'. They questioned Gordon Bryant's new administration of the DAA and the 'new-made Aboriginal experts' of the emerging era. In a time of transition in Aboriginal affairs, marked by the change in title and administrative location from the Welfare Branch to the DAA, the local public servants were not entirely happy; their remarks made it clear that they intended me to be addressed as a 'European'. They expressed their concern with the way money was 'thrown around' and the change towards a policy of 'Aboriginal self-determination' that meant superintendents could only give advice. 'The Yayayi council truck is used like a taxi', my field notes record one Papunya administrator as telling me in a critical tone. For these men, settlement life was spinning out of control.

There were hints that the situation at Yayayi was tense when I got there. Paul Bruno, an English-speaking Pintupi boy whom I met on my first drive to Yayayi, made a point of informing me on that very day that Neville Perkins, then known as a radical Aboriginal activist, had been at Yayayi and that he had struck a memorable chord. 'Laurie Owens doesn't help the Pintupi,' Paul told me, 'but Neville does.'[12] Neville had arrived with news of a truck delivered from a government grant, which local people saw as his doing; by other accounts, he was delivering one supplied by DAA. This was the occasion for the furious exchange of telegrams and accusations. Laurie Owens was the DAA officer who had become the community adviser for the Yayayi community, and he was known to be hugely supportive of this move for independence. Neville and Laurie had an argument, Paul told me. He reiterated that Laurie 'doesn't do anything for the Pintupi, but Neville does'.[13] The idiom of 'helping', of course, was a crucial moral discourse, as vital in Pintupi cultural understandings as it was for activist criticism. The 'old men' (that is, the authoritative senior figures), according to Paul, were thinking of kicking Laurie out and putting Neville in as community adviser. I realised something political was going on, and I could see a reorganisation of alliances—with Perkins' shared Aboriginal

---

11   The category 'European' was used particularly by whites to refer to themselves, as distinct from 'Aboriginal' people, and in that sense it's primary referent was white Australians. The local Aboriginal English referred to 'walypalas', as distinct from 'blakpalas' and (sometimes) 'yellafellas' or 'half-castes'.
12   Neville Perkins, nephew of the well-known Aboriginal activist and leader Charles Perkins, had family origins in the Alice Springs area, but had grown up 'down south' and was a student at the University of Sydney.
13   Telegrams in the archive show how heated their encounter must have been. Perkins wrote to Laurie Owens, shortly after the visit: 'In discussion with [R. W.] McHenry Darwin Tuesday Shorty Bruno, Helmut Pareroultja and I secured a $30,000 immediate grant but the issue of your role and credibility is still at stake. Representations will be made to Bryant. It would be foolish to intimidate [sic] anyone else.' NAA: F1, 1973/6202 Pintupi Outstation Yai Yaia, p. 145.

identity challenging Pintupi confidence in Owens, the significance of his local knowledge and the good faith of the DAA.[14] Settlement workers' jarring (to me) characterisation of Neville Perkins as 'half-caste', implying for them a lesser Aboriginality, and as an interloper (lacking real knowledge) traced this anxiety. I felt very uncomfortable myself, a possible target of activist anger as a white interloper and also someone who had received some help from the actual target of Perkins' accusations.

My concern was probably not unwarranted in those days—for example, Perkins had even threatened to have the popular Summer Institute of Linguistics (SIL) linguist Ken Hansen sent away! While Hansen's regard for the Pintupi should have been beyond question because of his long dedication to their concerns (as clearly indicated in the various reports I have seen in the National Archives of Australia files),[15] Perkins was suspicious of him and questioned whether Hansen was accurately translating what Pintupi leaders said about their desires to live at Yayayi.[16] It says something about the confusion of the time, and the uncertainties of race politics, that some Pintupi may have doubted Hansen's commitments.

Beyond these intricate complexities, people spoke enthusiastically that there was a 'new government', and now whites must 'help' Aborigines. For the Pintupi who were living at Yayayi when I arrived in 1973, such ideas no doubt informed the view that I should 'help Aborigines'. This concept elided easily as well with the understanding of me as becoming a 'one-countryman', so that the politics of self-determination made sense in the culture of Pintupi politics (see Myers 2006). Nonetheless, I understood this obligation as a serious practical condition, and an ethical one that I accepted, as someone who came of age on the politicised North American campuses of the 1960s.

There was a lot going on here, especially concerning the shifting frameworks to define relationships between various kinds of people. Here I want to note especially the framework of Aboriginal *power*, desperately sought, but also the contradictions: while strong supporters of Aboriginal power such as Kalokarinos

---

14   Another level of complexity or conflicting interests, depending on one's point of view, is that Owens seems to have had considerable support from and connection to very senior people leading the self-determination policy, such as Barry Dexter in Canberra. Dexter wrote to R. W. McHenry, the senior DAA officer in Darwin, copying to him what he wrote to Owens: 'We at head office are pleased that there has been quick response to Pintubi group's decision to move to Yaiyaia. We understand their anxiety to move from Papunya without further delay … We consider any attempt to delay or hinder free movement of the group as a whole or individuals would be indefensible. This applies equally if as result of boring program in reserve groups later wish to move to places farther west.' NAA: F1, 1973/6202 Pintupi Outstation Yai Yaia, p. 132, 25 June 1973.

15   NAA: F1, 1973/6202 Pintupi Outstation Yai Yaia, pp. 73–4.

16   Owens writes in a report about the discussions at Yayayi, on 7 June 1973, 'I was somewhat surprised to be informed by Mr. Perkins that last night he had rethought things after discussion with Sister Livingstone and that he felt that Mr. Hansen had not competently interpreted for him and that he had not conveyed the point of the questions he had asked.' NAA: F1, 1973/6202 Pintupi Outstation Yai Yaia, p. 160.

and Perkins were, at least initially, *opposing* the Pintupi initiative to move out of Papunya, to seek their own autonomy and community, the DAA, ostensible object of their criticism and certainly not lacking some doubters, was *supporting* the local Aboriginal decisions and refusing to impress on this community the values through which Europeans might judge the quality of life.[17] At the same time, the various government agencies were in disagreement. Owens' response as a DAA officer to the Pintupi impatience about moving was resisted by the head nursing sister at Papunya, who, representing the Department of Health, felt that arrangements for health and also for visiting nurses' safety were inadequate. It was this nursing sister, partly representing her view of the potential health challenges for small children against the wishes and desires of their kin, who apparently drew Perkins and Kalokerinos into the drama.

From black and white to colour

I now turn to the theme of a 'healthy' Yayayi provoked by the Pintupi engagement with the archival footage. The attribution of 'health' or 'well-being' has been a comment from nearly every Pintupi viewer. How does it look from the outside? As I have now had the opportunity to screen the footage to others unfamiliar with Yayayi or even Aboriginal realities as many of us have come to know them, the claim of 'healthy people' does not square with what they see.

Some American viewers see dogs licking at meat being butchered, for example, just as Kalokerinos saw the eye infections and dangers of diarrhoea. They see a food supply, discussed by one of our consultants, Marlene Spencer Nampitjinpa, that is not really 'healthy': white bread, self-raising flour, cold drinks, sugar and tea. Indeed, in our interview with Marlene Nampitjinpa, my fellow filmmaker Pip Deveson honed in on exactly this issue, asking Marlene if she thought the food they ate at the time was good food. Marlene found this question confounding. Although she has been a leader in the Pintupi Homeland Health Service and an advocate of a healthy lifestyle, my impression is that knowledge about nutrition is not informing her evaluation of what she sees and what she thinks about the past at Yayayi. For her, health is something broader.

The health theme is illustrative of a general orientation to the Yayayi experience and to the film record. Pintupi consultants emphasised four significant themes in what they saw. These themes were: *health, sharing, family and people being*

---

17   Indeed, Owens expressed precisely this view to the director of the DAA in Darwin: 'He [Perkins] feels that responsibility is being placed too quickly on the Pintubis and he said that he was concerned that the pace for change was too great. I feel that this is a contradiction when in fact he wanted facilities to be placed at Yai Yaia before any movement took place. I think that needs have been adequately expressed and time scales appropriately expressed also. To me it seems that Mr. Perkins is still very paternalistic—a thing I thought he was against.' NAA: F1, 1973/6202 Pintupi Outstation Yai Yaia, p. 159, Letter from Laurie Owens.

happy, and *the strength and commitment of the leaders, elders*. These themes recurred in all of the commentaries of our consultants, but are equally evident in the meetings that were filmed at Yayayi in 1974.

It seems as if the major arenas of 'self-determination' at Yayayi in 1973–75 were 'health' (with a local Ngangkari as the health worker), 'language' (with bilingual education and the development of materials in Pintupi), the local Aboriginal 'council', and the increased ability to hunt and gather food for themselves through access to 'vehicles'. The themes offered by the Pintupi consultants are all very positive, supporting a view of this period as a happy one, a healthier one, with people speaking for their community. As a corollary, indeed, my friend and our consultant Bobby West Tjupurrula, in particular, emphasised himself as taking a lead from these older people in becoming a leader and speaking for his community. Monica and Irene, similarly, saw a commitment to looking after the community that they regard as lacking in the present (and probably especially so with the creation of the shires that have evacuated local governance). In viewing the film footage from 1974, Marlene commented on how these older people 'worked for us'. She also identified herself as continuing this commitment, as a health worker and leader: 'I try to help my people' (Marlene, interview, Alice Springs, June 2013).

Most of the non-Indigenous interviews we have undertaken in relation to the archival footage have had a decidedly different cast, viewing the outstation more as a dysfunctional failure. I have to say some of these opinions surprised me. But I would cite Ian Dunlop and also Terry Parry,[18] the schoolteacher at Yayayi, as sharing a disappointment in what they saw and experienced. I believe Ian was disturbed by the violence he observed, especially during a particularly extended period of alcohol consumption while he was there. Both Parry and Dunlop had things stolen from their camps or caravans—events that turn up in the film footage. In Parry's case, what were stolen were the headphones he used as a schoolteacher for the hard-of-hearing children, as well as his own property. His disappointment was surely exacerbated by the fact that the destruction had its effect on other members of the community itself—a rather sad statement about Pintupi community spirit or concern for others. Dunlop felt that the theft was so out of tune with his experience in other Aboriginal communities and in Papua New Guinea—where no one, he maintained, had ever taken anything—that it was a sign of moral decay. He did not recognise in Yayayi the people he had met on patrol with Jeremy Long ten years earlier. Yayayi, for him, seemed fundamentally and sadly different from Pintupi life in the bush. Finally, both men were also disappointed at the inability of the community council to address this problem.

---

18   The interview with Terry Parry took place on 6 June 2012.

In contrast, the Pintupi consultants spoke with great respect for what they saw in the meetings held by the men of the community, with what they saw as 'speaking strong' and as actually demonstrating concern. They found this to be a striking difference from the present (of 2009–12), where there is insufficient concern and taking of responsibility for communal well-being.

These perceptions raise the question, in fact, of what Yayayi was. I have used the word 'community', which was more or less how it was understood by the DAA and others. The people living at Yayayi were still subjects of the Australian state, and the Northern Territory, but no longer wards, as they might have been some years before. The formal organisation or leadership of Yayayi was established through an elected council that administered (signed, and so on) the budget and resources that belonged to the incorporated council, but—as I have written elsewhere—was not really recognised by other Pintupi to have the authority to punish wrongdoing or to legislate rules.[19] The council members, who were supposed to represent the voice of the 'community' of which they were the leaders, tried to break up fights and they went to meetings with government officials and others on matters of community business. They were 'bosses' of a sort, but they were expected to 'look after' the community, to help them. And if they refused the material requested, this was typically viewed as a failure of care. They were, nonetheless, the agents in whom 'self-determination' was located.

In retrospect, perhaps too much was expected of the council, and also of the community's capacity for self-determination. They exercised this strongly in many ways, however, and often successfully, in their view. To me, the most successful exercise of their rights lay in their insistence that no one could visit without their permission (they had to be asked) and no one should/could be permitted to travel to Pintupi country without asking. 'That's our country', councillors would say, 'not just anyone's. Not allowed to travel there without asking.'

Others spoke with muted anger about the appropriation of their stories and the theft of sacred objects (Jeremy Long, in one of his reports in the 1960s, noted the concern about listing Tjitururrnga as a sacred site, with significant objects, and the decision not to make note of its location in order to prevent looting or desecration). And, as a consequence of filming trips made to record ceremonies in their own country, they were attempting to work out a framework in which their custodianship responsibilities and privileges were acknowledged and respected by outsiders.[20] This was part and parcel of 'Aboriginal self-determination' in which *Yarnangu* (Aboriginal people) would

---

19   For discussion of Pintupi ideas about local politics and authority, see Myers (1985, 1986).
20   An account of the changing attitudes towards and the projects of salvage filming of Pintupi (and Warlpiri) rituals can be found in Ian Bryson (2002).

be able to decide, even to refuse or reject, the requests of white people—refusals that were sometimes accompanied by such a notable anxiety that one could reckon the reversal it reflected: Black Power.

If they felt that their authority was being disregarded, local leaders—or even other Pintupi in the community—might evoke the threat of going to the institutions that they thought defended their rights: Aboriginal Legal Aid, in those days, or even Neville Perkins. How often did I hear that Neville would send these interlopers packing! If a mechanic would not fix your car, one heard, Legal Aid would get rid of him. Of course, in those early days, the extent of these powers was sometimes imagined excessively, indicating the uncertainty of it all and, to some old hands no doubt, a still humorous lack of 'real' knowledge.

At Yayayi, at least according to the initial government reports, the rise in morale was hugely important, and a recognition that Pintupi were on the way to making their own decisions was highly lauded and defended. At the same time, and as government officials changed and the much loved 'Minister Bryant' was replaced with the more pragmatic Cavanagh as Minister of Aboriginal Affairs, accountability began to be expected of the local council and its plans. Officials asked what projects were they actually going to do in order to have wages? What economy would they propose for the future of living at Yayayi? As a 'self-determining community', they now had some responsibility to set a plan—and when I met (as interpreter) with Yayayi leaders and Cavanagh, I saw how disconcerted they were when he asked them exactly what they were going to do if they were allowed to run cattle on their land or muster horses.

Here, then, I want to add the perspective offered by Jeffrey Stead, community adviser to Yayayi in 1974:

> One of the things I always remember about Yayayi was how it taught me something about community development. Like essentially it is a failure …

> Remember … when there was … football and we used to cart them around on the back of that trailer, take them to all the football matches … You know, I'd been trained at ASOPA [Australian School of Pacific Administration], 'you got to do something that people were interested in.' So we graded that football oval, and we put the fence up so we knocked all those desert oaks down, we put a fence up? Then, the first cold day, remember? They knocked all the fence down and burned the fence for firewood. I said to myself, 'you have to learn a lesson here, Jeff.' [Hearty laugh] … Firewood is much more important than football, that's for sure. (Interview with Jeff Stead, Melbourne, 7 June 2011)

Perhaps one can summarise here to draw things together in considering these different perspectives. What horizons do they—and I—bring to these judgments? I have already mentioned the disappointments of Ian Dunlop and Terry Parry, which I would characterise as failures to live up to the romantic image, as a fall from a purer past.

Reflecting on his time as community adviser, Jeff Stead also had doubts about the success of Yayayi, which were related to the scale of violence there and the inabilities he experienced to do more than simply provision the place. However, his views—now of a lifelong experience with Aboriginal communities—were more nuanced. He remembered, for example, that the level of violence was particularly high during the time of Ian's filming: 'six weeks in when everyone was on the grog.' And he remembered the Yayayi Council meeting at that time trying to establish rules about grog—'but … '. At this point, he shrugged, implying 'nothing'. His experience included inadequate support from the DAA in town. But he recognised that probably too much was expected of the council and the community's capacity for self-determination. Yayayi, as far as he remembers, was barely able to keep going.

Stead's point of view is very instructive—both in highlighting the failure of these unrealistic development projects that were the price, so to speak, of continued funding and in the lessons he learned. People may have different values and needs than are supposed in the plans for self-determination. Their actual needs may be so great that the capacity for development is undercut. Were the plans or expectations of self-determination unrealistic? Were they met?

I want to conclude by turning to the interview undertaken with Ken and Lesley Hansen, linguists from SIL who spent many, many years with the Pintupi— in Papunya and almost all of their various community formations in outstations, dating from the late 1960s.[21] The Hansens had been living and working with Pintupi people since 1965 and 1966, beginning at Papunya and following them to various community locations. This perspective has provided them particular insight, a sense of Yayayi as a juncture in Pintupi history. They described, in the interview, a range of dramatic changes in Aboriginal policy that were occurring at the time. What happened at Yayayi in 1973 and 1974 was, for them, based on the election of the Whitlam Labor Government, with its policy of 'self-determination', and the more or less concomitant 'outstation movement'. These changes were reversals of the much disliked assimilation program associated with Harry Giese's former administration of the Welfare Branch in the Northern Territory. Giese, Lesley Hansen remembered, 'was full-on social engineering, for assimilation'. As Ken elaborated, '[t]hat involved putting everybody

---

21 This interview was done by grant partners Peter Thorley and Pip Deveson, at the Hansens' home in New South Wales.

together in large communities, forget all your backgrounds, everybody is all the same'. This had not served Aboriginal people well at Papunya—a view clearly articulated by C. D. Rowley's (1970, 1971a, 1971b) three-volume study of Aboriginal policy and its criticism of Aboriginal settlements as debilitating total institutions that robbed residents of their initiative and agency.

Lesley offered a moving example of the assimilation policy in action, a story that she told me when we all lived at Yayayi in 1973. This example involved a woman I knew as Murmuya, a recent migrant from the bush (in 1963), the wife of my close friend Freddy West Tjakamarra and mother of Bobby West, one of our consultants on this project. According to Lesley, the Welfare Branch officials were:

> Insisting on the feeding of babies from six weeks on solids (which now nobody would do), and she [Murmuya] was angry. She'd say, 'I know how to look after my babies.' And she boycotted and wouldn't take her children there, so they slashed her meals. She couldn't get meals from the kitchen. You know, there was all that sort of thing going on. (Lesley Hansen, interview, 2012)

When they went out to Yayayi, moving along with the Pintupi, Lesley continued, 'with this new thing, *they* had control over what they ate, *they* had control over where they were living and how they were living'. Ken's conclusion to this part of the discussion is a precise articulation of what 'self-determination' meant then:

> They could organise their own living patterns rather than being put into one of the Giese houses that were in line. They could organise their own cultural way of having relatives close that they interacted with and other people would have other areas. So, it gave them an opportunity to do things more their way. (Ken Hansen, interview, 2012)

Indeed, Ken's interpretation of what many regarded as the 'motorcar problem' is especially illuminating. As I have already said, with the move to Yayayi, shortly after, the government organised for the community to buy two trucks. Each was under the charge of a different local leader. Ken remembers that they would get petrol from Papunya and go out west from Yayayi, further away from human settlement, hunting with those trucks and a whole lot of men, and bring back meat. While this was certainly not the Government's aim, as Hansen notes, '[t]hat was another stage where people were learning to run their own things'. 'These were the first two vehicles that Pintupi people had in that area', and 'even at Papunya most of the vehicles were government-controlled and Aboriginal people were not able to use them, on the whole. But the two trucks were a landmark' (Ken Hansen, interview, 2012).

The Hansens, among the very few people who could speak to Pintupi people in their own language, had seen the morbidity and misery of Pintupi in Papunya. They judged the Yayayi experience both from that perspective and based on their continuing intensive conversations with Pintupi. I believe that they, like me, identified with the local values and trajectories expressed by Pintupi people—and especially articulated a view expressed in Lovegrove's articulation of 'self-determination'—namely, that administration should 'be governed to a large extent by the expressed wishes of the people themselves and will not impress upon them those values through which we as Europeans judge to be important to a quality of life'.[22] Living in tents and/or bough shelters, having neither toilets nor ablution blocks, having no refrigeration or food storage, no doctors or nurses living there—these were not as important as having the basic ability to organise their own affairs.

It is not that Pintupi did not want these amenities of Anglo-Australian society; rather, their value paled before the possibility of independent living, freedom from the constraints of the large and competing groups at Papunya and the pressures of white administration. Was this not 'self-determination'? But was it a 'self-determination' with which administrators or government officials or anthropologists could live?

As a final note, or perhaps simply a postscript to this discussion, one must mention the early development of the successful cooperative Papunya Tula Artists at Yayayi. In the archival footage, the presence of this activity is illustrated by the filmed visit of Bob Edwards, head of the Aboriginal Arts Board (AAB), to Yayayi in June 1974. The existence of the AAB is an expression of the very same governmental direction envisioned in 'self-determination' by Nugget Coombs and the Office of Aboriginal Affairs, but here in the form of support for Indigenous art-making as cultural maintenance—a value on Aboriginal culture itself. If Yayayi has become only a memory, if a recorded one, of Pintupi assertion of their own direction, Papunya Tula Artists has continued into the present as a link to that past.

---

22   Lovegrove wrote about the connection between self-determination, initiative and confidence as fundamental to the move to Yayayi: 'The decision by this community in what it sees as its best interests, whilst causing some anxieties to this and other government departments as well as other interested and well meaning people is applauded as a display of initiative which it is hoped and expected will help to re-establish more self-reliance and self confidence in the group and it is recommended that this department respond with funds and resources to those requests put forward by the community which will enable their decision to be sustained.' NAA: F1, 1973/6202 Pintupi Outstation Yai Yaia, p. 149.

Conclusion

I began this chapter with an expression of my sense of both nostalgia and ambivalence about the Pintupi project of self-determination at Yayayi. It is clear that there are bases for both sensibilities in the history of the outstation. But it is interesting that Pintupi who talk about the Yayayi period, through the film, do not regard it as the failure or dysfunction that some of the outside participants have.

I tried to engage with this bifurcation previously, in the second of two connected essays I published in the journal previously known as *Mankind*. In that article, pointedly titled 'A broken code: Pintupi political theory and contemporary social life' (Myers 1980), I argued that Pintupi at Yayayi did not really come to experience their unfortunate destruction of trucks (through lack of control in their use) as enough of a problem to force them to change their use (for hunting, and so on). On the one hand, they had their own theory, as I showed, that the Government owed them 'help' (as Neville Perkins maintained and as they also believed because the Government was their 'boss'). On the other hand, the Government could not—I came to realise—refuse to provide that help, which would have caused them to suffer unacceptably. In this way, I concluded at the time that the Pintupi people I knew had a better understanding of their world than I did, reflecting that I was imposing my own moralistic models of proper behaviour, in which self-determination means that you take care of your own affairs completely and also that a truck given for food transport should not be used for other purposes. Over time, I have also understood that Pintupi and perhaps more widely Indigenous models of personhood and sociality dictate a different hierarchy of responsibility. Some models of self-determination seem to require a particular response to modernity, a particular mode of selfhood and moral boundaries of the self. This is not necessarily a form of selfhood that Pintupi have embraced, at least not in the short time we have witnessed. Rather, what has prevailed is the form of sociality I sketched in the first article I published (Myers 1979) and which is evident in everyday life at Yayayi.

So what, then, of the model of difficult experiences and personal suffering motivating a change in cultural practice and values, in accord with local histories, as a path of self-determination? The history of the outstation at Yayayi is one of these histories, of course. But as I trace the path, leading eventually to Kintore and Kiwirrkura and the restoration of life in Pintupi homelands, it is far more complicated and bureaucratically involute than I would have anticipated. The withdrawal of the DAA, with its trained officers with knowledge of local communities and reach into support services, was, I would argue, a step too far. This left local communities such as Yayayi in charge of basic services such as water, mechanical help, medical services and, later, power. As self-determination, this exceeded the expectation of Pintupi people, who wanted to determine who came to do these services, but not necessarily to take them over completely. Later struggles in Papunya over housing and power, as services were switched from the Federal Government to Territory supervision, display what seems to be an almost constant change in sources of support, systems of support, personnel and regulations. What small community, with limited literacy, could easily surmount these obstacles?

Who is to say, then, that the outstation experiment has been or is a failure or a success? Indeed, from what point of view are we to take such a view? What sort of discourse permits one to stand outside the local cultural life and impose judgments of failure or success? When would or should this occur?

Postscript

Yayayi ended gradually in the period after 1976. It had slowly eroded in population from the initial high point of 300 people, as interpersonal conflicts and new opportunities led people to move to other communities—and also to establish other 'outstation' communities in the Papunya area. When I returned to Yayayi for a visit in the winter of 1979, only one extended family was still living there, under the leadership of Ronnie Tjampitjinpa. His elderly father and mother, his sister Yuyuya and her children, and his brother Kantjatjarra Tjampitjinpa and his family lived there together in a closely cooperating group. Ronnie remained, he told me, to hold custodianship of the storehouse of sacred objects the men had established at Yayayi. Other relatives from Yayayi had relocated some 30 km further west to the new community of Yinyalinkgi, where a bore had been drilled. This community incorporated a number of older Pintupi men: Shorty Lungkarta, Uta Uta Tjangala, Charley Tarawa and Ginger Tjakamarra, with his brother-in-law Hilary Tjapaltjarri. This move was made possible by the provision of more vehicles and water sources, and, as I argued in my monograph (Myers 1986), a devolution in size as Pintupi groups began to approximate smaller collections of kin groups who shared resources among themselves and had fewer conflicts of leadership. At the same time, deaths—including a murder—strained the relationships among people who had been living together, leading to relocations and reorganisations of community life. Other communities were being established in the area, outposts from Papunya and Haasts Bluff, and teachers were travelling to visit and teach at these communities from the resource centre of Papunya. Their finances were, at this time, managed under the rubric of an 'outstation centre' at Papunya, but control over these resources and their allocations proved to be an issue of conflict until Pintupi from these outstations officially separated themselves from Papunya in moving further west to their own country at Kintore in 1981. These movements themselves were expressive of greater mobility through control of vehicles and the attempt of many people to re-establish relationships with long-separated relatives at Balgo Hills Mission (in the north) and then Tjulyurunya and Warakurna in the south. That is, these movements rehearsed former patterns of kinship connection and visiting in the context of self-determination.

To understand these changes, and the devolution of Yayayi, one does not need to posit a failure of self-determination. In fact, the pursuit of smaller communities and eventually the establishment of Kintore should be understood as exercises in the quest for some kind of autonomy and self-direction. For Pintupi people as I have known them, these movements are unexceptional, temporary accommodations to personal circumstances and ongoing political projects. What might have appeared as failure to those imagining sedentary communities of permanent residence was an assimilation of changing circumstances and options to Pintupi political projects.

References

Bryson, I. 2002. *Bringing to Light: A History of Ethnographic Filmmaking at the Australian Institute of Aboriginal and Torres Strait Islander Studies*. Canberra: Aboriginal Studies Press.

Howson, P. 2000. Reality and fantasy: The abject failure of Aboriginal policy. *Quadrant* 44(4): 20–4.

Hughes, H. 2007. *Lands of Shame: Aboriginal and Torres Strait Islander 'Homelands' in Transition*. Sydney: Centre for Independent Studies.

Johns, G. 2001. *Waking up to Dreamtime: The Illusion of Aboriginal Self-Determination*. Singapore: Media Masters.

Myers, F. 1979. Emotions and the self: A theory of personhood and political order among the Pintupi. *Ethos* 7: 343–70.

Myers, F. 1980. A broken code: Pintupi political theory and contemporary social life. *Mankind* 12: 311–26.

Myers, F. 1985. Illusion and reality: Aboriginal self determination in Central Australia. In C. Schrire and R. Gordon (eds), *The Future of Former Foragers*. Cambridge: Cultural Survival, pp. 109–21.

Myers, F. 1986. *Pintupi Country, Pintupi Self: Sentiment, Place and Politics among Western Desert Aborigines*. Canberra & Washington, DC: Australian Institute of Aboriginal Studies & Smithsonian Institution Press.

Myers, F. 1988. Burning the truck and holding the country: Property, time and the negotiation of identity among Pintupi Aborigines. In T. Ingold, D. Riches and J. Woodburn (eds), *Hunter-Gatherers. Volume II: Property, Power and Ideology*. Oxford: Berg, pp. 52–74.

Myers, F. 2006. We are not alone: Anthropology in a world of others. *Ethnos* 71(2): 233–64.

Rowley, C. D. 1970. *The Destruction of Aboriginal Society: Aboriginal Policy and Practice. Volume 1*. Canberra: The Australian National University Press.

Rowley, C. D. 1971a. *Outcasts in White Australia: Aboriginal Policy and Practice. Volume 2*. Canberra: The Australian National University Press.

Rowley, C. D. 1971b. *The Remote Aborigines: Aboriginal Policy and Practice. Volume 3*. Canberra: The Australian National University Press.

Spencer, B. and Gillen, F. 1899. *The Native Tribes of Central Australia*. London: Macmillan.

Sutton, P. 2001. The politics of suffering: Indigenous policy in Australia since the 1970s. *Anthropological Forum* 11(2): 125–73.

Sutton, P. 2009. *The Politics of Suffering: Indigenous Australia and the End of the Liberal Consensus*. Melbourne: Melbourne University Press.

Tindale, N. 1974. *Aboriginal Tribes of Australia*. Berkeley: University of California Press.

6

The interwoven histories of Mount Liebig and Papunya-Luritja

Sarah Holcombe

Mount Liebig, known by Anangu as Amunturrngu and referred to by the regional shire as Watiyawanu, is part of the regional constellation of Pintupi-Luritja settlements that also includes Haasts Bluff, Papunya and at least 16 outstations, the majority of which are still inhabited.[1] The 2011 census recorded Mount Liebig with a population of 156 people,[2] while the Mount Liebig and Outstations *Quickstats* showed a slightly higher population of 184 people.[3] Note that both of these figures also include non-Indigenous people. Mount Liebig—though now regarded as a 'state suburb' for the purposes of the census—itself began as an outstation. This chapter will trace the emergence of this place as it became the focus of both Pintupi-Luritja sentiment and respite from the earlier days of Haasts Bluff and the later coercive assimilationist vision of Papunya. That its relatively informal and incremental development into a substantial settlement has been led by Anangu, rather than the state, also has implications for the ways in which the place has emerged as a community, rather than merely a settlement. Unlike Papunya, which has been described as 'mixed up', Mount Liebig has

---

1   *Anangu* is the Western Desert term for person, Pintupi-Luritja being a Western Desert language, on the north-eastern edge.
2   That is: 69 male, 87 female, with a median age of 31. See the Australian Bureau of Statistics (ABS) *QuickStats* website: www.censusdata.abs.gov.au/census_services/getproduct/census/2011/quickstat/SSC7013 5?opendocument&navpos=220
3   Average people per household: 4.6.

an internal coherence that was led by succession processes and subsequent re-territorialisation. The reconfiguring of people at this place has been enabled by the new Indigenous language of Pintupi-Luritja; residents who chose to remain after the 1980s actively identified with this new language, referred to by linguists as a communilect. By foregrounding endogenous political processes, this essay conceptualises self-determination as a process in relation to other Aboriginal people *as well as* in relation to the State. The emergence of the Luritja language in this region, and its consolidation at Mount Liebig and surrounding outstations, was an expression of the need to regroup and reformulate a local identity after unprecedented historical interventions.

From stock bore to community

Mount Liebig Bore was a camp in the days when Haasts Bluff was a ration station for Aboriginal people west of Hermannsburg in the 1940s. Many of the people who had early come in to the Lutheran ration depot used it only as a convenience; they traded dingo scalps for food and returned to the bush. There is a series of permanent springs west of Haasts Bluff in the Amunturrngu and Kartilka ranges that makes for plenty of bush foods, even in the dry. The springs of Amunturrngu, Impimpi, Arlkngilkinti, Irantji, Putati and the numerous semi-permanent waters and rockholes were places for 'holiday camps' and remain so for many community members today. These waters gave people the autonomy to live without any absolute reliance on rations and supported a series of families. Many of these families were originally enticed into the area by the Hermannsburg missionaries, from the period of the establishment of Hermannsburg in 1877 through to the establishment of Haasts Bluff in 1941 and the few ration depots at surrounding springs (see Long 1989: 22–3).

Mount Liebig first became an 'official' outstation service centre in 1982, when the Central Desert Store was established. It provided a convenient location for provisioning the surrounding outstations of Warren Creek, New Bore and Inyilingi. The original Mount Liebig Bore was sunk as a stock bore in 1946, followed by Warren Creek, also as a stock bore, in 1961. Nearby Inyilingi Bore was sunk in 1975 and New Bore in 1980, both as community-purpose bores to encourage the Pintupi movement west, homewards, from Papunya. Kakali Bore, originally sunk for the Haasts Bluff cattle project but then the foundation for the Yayayi outstation, was the first of these community-purpose bores and the closest to Papunya. Unlike these others, however, Yayayi was not further consolidated as an outstation, and other than the derelict bore by the main east–west road, no other infrastructure remains (see Myers, this volume).

Mount Liebig, and later Inyilingi, was originally conceived in terms of the government policy of encouraging the Pintupi to shift away from Papunya, where life was proving so traumatic for them, and the Pintupi themselves were keen to move westward in the direction of their country. In Papunya, there was conflict between the more latterly arrived Pintupi and the more established Luritja and Warlpiri. Kimber sums up the sentiment surrounding this policy era in the region: the assimilation '[p]olicy and its implementation both west of Papunya and at Papunya can best be summarised as a white disaster, an Aboriginal tragedy' (1981: 23). There were a significant number of deaths among the newly arrived Pintupi, many of which were blamed on sorcery and related antagonisms (cf. Myers 1976; Kimber 1981). The official medical point of view was that 'more disastrous (than fighting and adjustment to rations) were the infections, largely pneumonia or viral (measles), that destroyed more than half the population, which came with low levels of immunity to close contact with reservoirs of disease' (Kimber 1981: 26). Of the 72 people who came into Papunya in 1963 and 1964, 29 had died by August 1964 (Nathan and Japanangka 1983: 79–80).

With this high mortality rate, questions were raised in Parliament. This led to an unofficial policy change in 1964, so that centralisation was replaced with dispersal (Nathan and Japanangka 1983: 79–80). However, as Long notes, this policy was not activated until the late 1960s and early 1970s. This delay was due to the centralised focus of the food disbursement, among other things. In Papunya, Aborigines who wanted to eat had to attend the communal dining room—'because it made it easier to organise and to supervise the settlement work programs' (Kimber 1981: 24; and see Myers, this volume). The, at times, militaristic demands made on people to 'learn European manners' caused newly arrived people to be ridiculed by both insensitive white staff and the more sophisticated Aboriginal people, primarily the Luritja. Kimber states that 'I have been told that almost the entirety of one newly arrived Pintupi group were made to feel so ashamed that they stayed away or refused to eat' (1981: 24).

The Pintupi were thus keen to establish their own outstation/community that was not only closer to their country, but was also independent of the strictures of settlement life and these other groups, with Yayayi outstation the first formal expression of government support for this. And with the sinking of the Ilypili Bore in the Ehrenburg Range and soon after the series of Kintore bores, the Pintupi continued the move west via Mount Liebig to their own country, establishing Warlungurru (Kintore) as a community in the early 1980s.

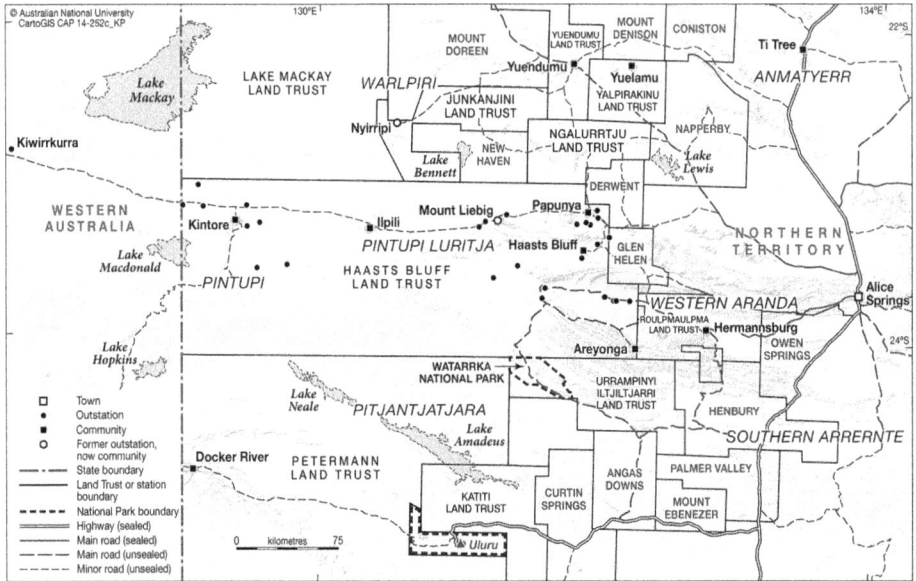

Map 6.1 Luritja-Pintupi outstations.

Source: Karina Pelling, CartoGIS, ANU College of Asia and the Pacific

Nathan and Japanangka state:

> [The Luritja] people reoccupied the [Mount Liebig] site [from the Pintupi] in 1981. There were 39 people comprising 17 women, 4 men and 18 children. Some of the men were absent because they were engaged in stock-work elsewhere ... there are 12 temporary shelters including bough shades and half tanks turned upside down ... there is one tap about 120 metres from the main camp site. The camp is provided with a radio. There is no council truck but a number of private vehicles, some of which are broken down. A health worker and an Aboriginal assistant for the mobile school are employed. The school which operates on a four day a week basis, consists of a shady tree and a quarter moon shaped corrugated iron windbreak. Today, there is no evidence of the temporary resource Centre which was built in 1979. This Centre was to have been used as a store and garage, and to house horticultural equipment. (Nathan and Japanangka 1982: 132)

Although it seems that the early service provisions at Mount Liebig were originally established for the Pintupi, the Luritja did not suddenly reoccupy the site when the Pintupi left in 1981, as suggested above. The Luritja who were recorded there in 1981 had also been intermittent residents, but more long term than the Pintupi. They had been mustering cattle in the area since the 1950s, making use of the Mount Liebig and Warren Creek stockyards. Cattle were herded south to Haasts Bluff through Berry Pass and Irantji Spring. Others, who were elderly when I interviewed them in the mid-1990s, were recorded at Putati and Mount Liebig during the 1932 joint Adelaide University and South Australian Museum expedition (Holcombe 1998). However, in 1981, Mount Liebig became a family outstation similar in size to the surrounding outstations, after the Pintupi left to return to their country. And it was then that the small Central Desert Store was established. It became an Aboriginal corporation in August 1988 and effectively a major settlement, attracting several other Luritja families from Papunya.

This expansion brought with it increased services. Today, these include a school, clinic, store, the council (now shire) office, an aged care centre, a preschool, a Lutheran church and approximately 30 Aboriginal houses and six non-Aboriginal service-worker houses. More recently, a large demountable complex was also established for the temporary influx of service provider staff from the various government agencies after the 2007 NT Emergency Response (NTER).[4] While the NTER set of legislation and policies was an unequivocal rejection of self-determination, as it ushered in the current neo-assimilationist era, the years during which I undertook field research in the mid-1990s were the final ones of the official policy of self-determination and a period of considerable autonomy for Anangu. Engagement with the apparatus of the state, such as the education and employment systems, was not mandated. Indeed, it has been noted during this period that there was a structural disengagement by government (Dillon and Westbury 2007), not only in Mount Liebig but also across remote communities. So while, on the one hand, there were very active customary and ritual economies practised at Mount Liebig and surrounding outstations, there were also significant social issues with youth petrol sniffing in this region, as in other Western Desert communities. Thus, this government disengagement at that time, while extremely positive in some ways, also impacted as limited recognition of the emergence of the petrol-sniffing problem (see Brady 1992). Indeed, researchers like myself were also unaware of the scale and long-term debilitating effects of the petrol sniffing at that time.

Early 'contact' and movement towards settlement

The pattern of movement for the majority of middle-aged and elderly members of the Mount Liebig community, almost without exception, has been from Haasts Bluff to Papunya and finally to Mount Liebig or surrounding outstations. Their parents and several elderly women and men who only passed away within the past 10 years first migrated to the settlement of Haasts Bluff in the early 1940s. Many of the people who initially moved to the settlement had been

---

4   The NTER was a suite of measures implemented through legislation and policy designed to run for five years to 'stabilise and normalise' remote NT communities on Aboriginal land and in town camps. It included strongly interventionist measures to ensure that parents sent their children to school, welfare reforms, income quarantining and increased policing levels (see Altman and Hinkson 2007).

living in the outlying areas. On an annual visit in 1936 from Hermannsburg, Pastor Friedrich Albrecht estimated that his party had contacted groups totalling nearly 300 people in the area between Haasts Bluff, Mount Wedge and Mount Liebig (Long 1989: 21). The rationale for establishing the Haasts Bluff settlement was government concern over the eastward drift of 'western people' towards Alice Springs and, in particular, towards pastoral leases such as Glen Helen and Tempe Downs. These western people were, at this stage, the Eastern Pintupi and the Ngaliya Warlpiri.

In the period from 1930 to 1932, the eastern reaches of Pintupi country had been visited by several prospecting parties and missionaries and probably by a police party—more visitors than in the preceding 60 years since explorer Ernest Giles first reached the Ehrenburg Range (known by Anangu as Ilypili) from a spring within the range (Long 1989: 29). As the Pintupi and Ngaliya from Ilypili had moved east, by 1942 a wide expanse of uninhabited country had opened up between Haasts Bluff/Mount Liebig and the WA border. This not only had implications for those Anangu who remained further west, as they were growing increasingly isolated, but it also reflected a broader pattern of migration and a demographic pulsing (see below).

It seems that as these western and northern peoples were travelling east, those who were principally affiliated with the country affected by this migration had themselves migrated east and south considerably earlier. Long indicates that by the time the Haasts Bluff settlement was established, the Aboriginal population of the area proper had 'largely disappeared ... having died out or become absorbed into the population of ... Hermannsburg ... and other places to the east' (1970: 321). While there are historical disagreements and elements of conjecture about who these peoples were, the language labels of Mayutjarra and Kukatja were provided to me in the mid-1990s by elderly residents of Mount Liebig, while the Lutheran linguist John Heffernan also recorded these names for the same area. Although some of us find this movement of language frontiers intrinsically interesting—and I have written about this history in detail elsewhere (Holcombe 1998, 2005)—the point to be made here is the correlation between the emergence of the communilect of Pintupi-Luritja, the succession to this land and the consolidation of Mount Liebig as an articulation of self-determination. This self-determination was in relation to both other Aboriginal and non-Aboriginal people. Thus, it was an attempt to reform the internal relations of the Aboriginal polity, to return it to the land/people relationships that were either 'traditional' or idealised as such. This reconstitution or reclamation of an Aboriginal polity was just as relevant a discursive act in the decentralisation process as the desire to live independently of government interference and control.

Pintupi-Luritja is categorised as a communilect, rather than a dialect, according to Heffernan (1984). This is because the language developed as a lingua franca for the various family groups who first moved to Haasts Bluff in the 1940s who spoke various languages, such as Western Desert 'multi-group dialects'[5] that are now conflated as Pintupi, various Arandic dialects, Warlpiri dialects such as Ngaliya, and Anmayterr—especially after the massacre of Aboriginal families at Coniston Station, as people fled south.[6] Because the language first emerged in these communities, linguists originally referred it to as Papunya-Luritja. So although this is an Indigenous language, it is not a pre-settlement language. It also has different features to the Luritja that is spoken from Areyonga south to Finke and Oodnadatta. However, as the Mount Liebig and Papunya residents refer to their language simply as 'Luritja', I also will from now on.

Luritja as a process of re-territorialisation

The Mount Liebig community and outstation members identify themselves as Luritja and the country they are living on as Luritja country. The configuration of people in this community and the identity they share today developed as a result of movement towards settlement. They came together primarily from neighbouring areas on to country that had been apparently 'vacated'. They adopted this country, the country of the Mayutjarra, and its name, Amunturrngu. The dynamics of re-territorialisation are considered in the light of this history. The term 'Luritja' can usefully be interpreted as a trope. The meaning of the original word is not only indicative of the regional history, it also signals the value of the term in contemporary usage, as I will discuss.[7]

As the history and pattern of movement indicate, the country within which the communities of Haasts Bluff, Papunya and Mount Liebig are today situated became the focus of several groups as they moved towards settlement. But as these groups were more or less neighbours, how discrete as 'groups' were they? Tindale recorded that the 'Pintupi made their first modern contact with the Jumu [Yumu] and Ngaliya in 1932 … at Mount Liebig where they were studied' (1974: 138). It seems unlikely, however, that they had not encountered each other before this.[8] Heffernan (1984: 2) indicates that 'in pre-contact days the *Ilypili*

---

5   See Ken Hansen (1984) for a discussion of the Western Desert 'multi-group' dialects.
6   Occurring in 1928, this massacre claimed the lives of between 17 (the 'official toll') (Cribben 1984: 75), 31 (the number the board of inquiry found) and 100 Aboriginal men, women and children, depending on which texts are consulted. Fred Brooks, the non-Aboriginal dingo hunter who was killed by Aboriginal people, would never have been at the same soak with the group of Ngalia Warlpiri if mutual desperation for water and the Aboriginal need for non-native foods had not been high. The massacre, led by police, was an official reprisal party.
7   See also Holcombe (2004a) for further analysis.
8   Note that Mackay recorded both Pintupi and Yumu living at Ilypili Spring in 1930.

people intermarried with the Ngaliya Warlpiri from *Kunatjarrayi*, a significant Ngaliya site to the north of *Ilypili*. Almost without exception, the descendants from the *Ilypili* people are both of "Pintupi" and "Warlpiri" parentage.[9] He also found that the eastern neighbours of the Pintupi are the Mayutjarra (Kukatja). Like myself, Heffernan appears to have found no evidence of the 'Yumu', the name that Tindale gave to the peoples of the Mount Liebig, Haasts Bluff and Papunya region.

So Luritja identity is an articulation of the shared heritage of the otherwise disparate people who moved east and south and remained. So why Luritja, and not some other language appellation? The term 'Luritja' is itself a derivative of a general term for Western Desert people. Strehlow indicates that:

> Loritja [Luritja] is the name applied by the Aranda to all Western Desert speech groups. Loritja languages are spoken from the Western MacDonnells to Mount Margaret, in Western Australia, and from the Granites in the north to Ooldea on the Trans-continental railway. None of these Western groups speak of themselves as 'Loritja'. They call themselves Kukatja, Pintupi, Ngalia, Ilpara, Andekerinja, etc. (Strehlow 1947: 177–8)

Tindale emphasised that the name Luritja was considered derogatory and that Strehlow referred to the Kukatja from the Arrernte perspective. He stated that 'in 1929 [he] was asked by the old men of this tribe to refrain from using the term imposed on them by the [Arrernte] and to record their "true" name—Kukatja' (Tindale 1974: 229). And understandably so, given that the term was an insult. Strehlow (1947: 52) indicates that the term Luritja is 'suggestive of everything that is barbarian, crude, savage and generally speaking non-Aranda'.[10] This Arrernte ethnocentrism was earlier recorded by Elkin, who noted that 'Loritja is an Aranda word meaning stranger' (1938: 424, in Doohan 1992: 36). Thus, historically, the term was not self-definitional.

However, over the settlement period in Haasts Bluff and Papunya, the meaning of the term Luritja shifted dramatically. It was the dynamic of this period through which the Luritja became self-identified as a group in terms of language and predisposition. This identification was, of course, oppositional, in relation to non-Luritja. Heffernan (1984: 3) 'guesses' that the wholehearted adoption of the term Luritja was not made until the most recent arrivals from the desert

---

9   According to my 'informants', Ilypili formed the eastern boundary of the Pintupi. Interestingly, Heffernan has the eastern neighbours of the Pintupi as the Kukatja/Mayutjarra, rather than the Luritja. He has also suggested that 'Papunya Luritja could in fact be a true description of the Eastern Pintupi dialect as it existed prior to European contact. Whereas this is partly true there is good evidence from text material to show that speakers east of Warlungurru [where the Kintore community is situated] spoke much the same as the description given by Hansen and Hansen [for Warlungurru or Western Pintupi]' (Heffernan 1984: 3).

10   In fact, Strehlow wrote this in relation to a statement made by a Northern Arrernte man, who referred to the Western Arrernte as 'half-breed Loritja'.

occurred in the late 1950s and early 1960s—a perspective also supported by the linguists Hansen and Hansen (1978). It was initially this construction of difference between the Luritja as the people 'from the east', in relation to the (western) Pintupi, that contributed to Luritja becoming a positive group label. Those who had been in the settlements the longest and had become accustomed to the new ways of interacting in this context were differentiating themselves from those newly arrived from the west. This distinction between newcomers and residents, notably in Papunya, became so marked that to be called 'Pintupi' was an insult, like the term Luritja before it. This term was comparable with the poor country cousins, the unsophisticated. Clearly government policy during the Papunya period played a key role in ostracising the Pintupi, so that the adoption of the term Luritja is deeply implicated in this period of assimilation. As Myers notes in his chapter in this volume, the latterly arriving Pintupi with whom he worked at Yayayi were determined to leave the 'illness, morbidity, conflict and depression' of Papunya.

Earlier I noted:

> The adoption of the Luritja language is an implicit rejection of the multiple genealogies represented in the communities, as expressed in the languages of the previous generation. The language of Luritja, contemporary as it is, places the past in abeyance (cf Jackson 1996). As a communilect, Luritja is representative of what Clastres defines as a people without history, a people concerned more with today than yesterday. By emplacing the individual speaker, the term holds within it an identity that conjures up the surrounding land and its settlement history. (Holcombe 2004a: 267)

Although being a member of a speech community is relative, as being a member of any group is relational, it is the element of choice that informs a political position. For instance, the now deceased Ginger Tjakamarra of New Bore outstation, one of Fred Myers' informants, was during Myers' fieldwork identifying as Pintupi (Myers 1986: 8, 264). When I conducted my field research some 20 years later, Tjakamarra and his family from New Bore identified as Luritja. After living on this outstation on Luritja country for more than 20 years, this long-term post-migration residence has encouraged a shift towards an identity that marks not only a shared history, but also a distinctive label that tells of the need for grosser, community-based distinctions.[11] Likewise, Whisky Tjapaltjarri (also recently deceased), the male head of the family from Yinyilingki outstation, was historically Pitjantjatjara. However, after a comparable history of long-term residence and the conception of children and grandchildren at the outstation, a reconfiguration of social identity emerged. Likewise, these two

---

11   This lability of identification also speaks of the context and historical moment in which the researcher is operating.

men, along with their spouses and residential classificatory female kin, have been especially active in the performance of *inma kuwaritja* (new ritual derived from dreams) that situates them sentimentally and politically within the landscape of their residence (Holcombe 2004b: 267).

Although not all Luritja are landholders, there is a correlation between language territory and land ownership. The pulsating heart analogy offered by Sutton is useful here, as it connotes the propensity of a people to fill a void—perhaps akin to a type of human osmosis—in the drive to reach a demographic equilibrium (see Sutton 1990: 74). This striving towards integration, out of possible disintegration, is invoked in this history of movement from the west that many now deceased, elderly Luritja in Mount Liebig spoke of when questioned. This migration to the better-watered country of the relatively fecund fringes of the West MacDonnell Ranges could be understood as part of the general tendency of desert dwellers towards expansionism and opportunism, given the ecological constraints of the area (see Hamilton 1982: 103; Peterson 1975 Sutton 1990). The logical progression of this line of argument suggests that when constraints are lifted, when the environmental limitations on food and water are radically diminished by the new welfare apparatus then so too are there possibilities to 'stabilise' local organisation. I found such stability in the land tenure of Mount Liebig during the mid-1990s where the concept of re-territorialisation was appropriate.[12] This concept evoked the processes of succession or 'tenurial migration', to borrow Sutton's (1997) term, *as well as* the imaginative processes that are involved in long-term post-migration residence. The term 're-territorialisation' offers a more generous and less hierarchical approach than that of the concepts of primary and secondary succession (per Peterson) when considering community member attachment to the community country. Clearly, this is a big topic; what I can say here is that for Mount Liebig, the constellation of the social technologies such as the 'company relationship' for Dreamings and social groupings—as these were locally long term and included the site of conception—was such that succession processes were fairly seamless and relatively un-politicised. This was not the case in Papunya.

Tod Woenne (1977: 56) indicates that the 'self-conscious reconstruction and assertion of local pre-settlement conditions was a conspicuous and much engaged in activity at Docker River in the early years of its establishment', in 1968. The situation in Mount Liebig has differed from this in that it is the reconstruction of *early settlement* conditions that is a primary means through which people negotiated affiliation rights in Mount Liebig in the mid-1990s. Those Luritja families who first established themselves at the Mount Liebig

---

12   I am not using this term here in the manner of Deleuze and Guattari (1987), although their employment of this term (and its opposite) also has clear implications in geopolitical terms.

Bore became the definable core of the community. The families who arrived in the late 1980s, after the increased services, also had a right to settle on the basis not only of identifying as Luritja, but also of sharing a history of holiday camping in the Mount Liebig area as far back as the Haasts Bluff days, the 1940s. As these immigrants to this land have remained, deep attachments have formed. Their knowing of the land, by travelling over it, utilising its resources and learning its law, has translated into various forms of 'ownership'. This 'ownership' can only be considered in terms of the 'emplacement' of the community members and the processes whereby they have become locals. The land of the community is, in many respects, the land of their learning.

The rights of residents are, however, based not only on this shared settlement history. There are a number of other factors—some alluded to earlier. There is, for example, the question of what the impetus was for the second major wave of migration from Papunya. An 'original' resident, the now-deceased Maudie Nungurrayi, phrased it as 'they only came after the store. We lived here with nothing.' Maudie consistently stressed the role that she and her family played in establishing the community. They created a resource base that then allowed others to move there in numbers. Her emphasis on the community as a recently built environment is contrasted with the days when there was 'nothing'—only the bore, bullocks and bush. This contrast can be read as suggesting that the establishment of locality begins with dwelling; the stress is on the *place* prior to its occupation as a resource centre. Thus, the recent influx of others—after the resource allocation—is perceived as having less legitimacy. Yet, it was after this provision of resources that the place gained permanence and a sense of recognition. Heidegger's notion of 'gathering' and the construction of location through building and therefore 'dwelling' is relevant to perceptions of the built community, as opposed to the pre-community bush.[13]

So a major incentive for the new residents was increased access to services and, concomitantly, less competition for these services, relative to Papunya. The ways in which these families negotiated access to resources, such as houses and store profits (from which vehicles were purchased), offered a lens, during this late period of self-determination, through which to view processes of community membership (see Holcombe 2005).

---

13   Heidegger's focus, however, is European and accordingly the notion of people without dwellings—such as in pre-contact Aboriginal culture—is not considered. As a result, his argument is relevant to change and the creation of locations of permanence, yet the subtleties of considering the construction of locations through the imagination (as in the case of the *tjukurrpa*, Dreaming) seems to elude him (cf. Heidegger 1978).

Conclusion

My research focus in the mid-1990s was on the various mechanisms that crafted a community from a settlement and the ways in which this 'community' was the medium through which contemporary forms of cultural authenticity were constructed, and so how the 'Aboriginal power of imagination' (Stanner 1966: 52) was brought to bear on this new home. In doing this, Mount Liebig was understood in terms that specified its power to direct and stabilise its residents, 'to memorialise and identify [them] by considering who and what [they] are in terms of where they are' (Casey 1993: Preface). As Geertz (1983) and Casey (1996) have both noted: to live is to live locally and to know is first of all to know the place one is in. The cultural imagination in Mount Liebig derived from the stimulus of Amunturrngu as a location that has been doubly colonised in recent history: by non-Aboriginals, followed by neighbouring Aboriginal groups. The fact that the country was apparently vacant enabled this reimagining of various forms of ownership, which the communilect of Pintupi-Luritja effectively facilitated. Self-determination in this context applies as much to the endogenous processes of re-establishing an Aboriginal polity as it does to escaping the grip of the colonial masters through decentralisation. Mount Liebig and neighbouring outstations were expressions of reformulated social groupings after the enforced settlement of Papunya. This period, in the mid-1990s, was one in which Anangu in Mount Liebig practised considerable autonomy from the state. The neighbouring outstations were all active, and while cultural activity (such as hunting and ceremony) were thriving, petrol sniffing was also a significant emerging issue that took another 20 years to be brought under control in Central Australia (see d'Abbs and MacLean 2011).

References

Altman, J. C. and Hinkson, M. (eds) 2007. *Coercive Reconciliation: Stabilise, Normalise and Exit Aboriginal Australia.* Melbourne: Arena Publications.

Brady, M. 1992. *Heavy Metal: The Social Meaning of Petrol Sniffing in Australia.* Canberra: Aboriginal Studies Press.

Casey, E. S. 1993. *Getting Back into Place: Toward a Renewed Understanding of the Place-World.* Bloomington & Indianapolis: Indiana University Press,

Casey, E. S. 1996. How to get from space to place in a fairly short stretch of time: Phenonemological prolegomena. In S. Feld and K. H. Basso (eds), *Senses of Place.* Santa Fe, NM: School of American Research Press, pp. 13–52.

Clastres, P. 1987 [1974]. *Society against the State*. New York: Zone Books.

Cribben, J. 1984. *The Killing Times: The Coniston Massacre 1928*. Sydney: Fontana Books.

d'Abbs, P. and MacLean, S. 2011. Petrol sniffing interventions among Australian Indigenous communities through product substitution: From skunk juice to Opal. *Substance Use and Misuse* 46: 99–106.

Deleuze, G. and Guattari, F. 1987. *A Thousand Plateaus: Capitalism and Schizophrenia*. B. Massumi trans. New York: Continuum.

Dillon, M. C. and Westbury, N. D. 2007. *Beyond Humbug: Transforming Government Engagement with Indigenous Australia*. Adelaide: Seaview Press.

Doohan, K. 1992. *One Family, Different Country*. Oceania Monograph 42. Sydney: University of Sydney.

Geertz, C. 1983. *Local Knowledge: Further Essays in Interpretive Anthropology*. New York: Basic Books.

Hamilton, A. 1982. Descended from father, belonging to country: Rights to land in the Australian Western Desert. In E. Leacock and R. Lee (eds), *Politics and History in Australian Band Societies*. Cambridge: Cambridge University Press, pp. 85–108.

Hansen, K. C. 1984. Communicability of some Western Desert communilects. In J. Hudson and N. Pym (eds), *Language survey*. Work Papers of SIL–AAB, Series B, Vol. 11. Darwin: Summer Institute of Linguistics, Australian Studies Branch.

Hansen, K. C. and Hansen, L. 1978. *The Core of Pintupi Grammar*. Alice Springs, NT: Summer Institute of Linguistics, Australian Aborigines Branch.

Heffernan, J. A. 1984. *Papunya Luritja Language Notes*. Papunya, NT: Papunya Literature Production Centre.

Heidegger, M. 1978. *Basic Writings: From 'Being and Time' (1927) to 'The Task of Thinking' (1964)*. London: Routledge & Kegan Paul.

Holcombe, S. 1998. Amunturrgu: An emergent community in Central Australia. Unpublished PhD thesis. University of Newcastle, NSW.

Holcombe, S. 2004a. The politico-historical construction of the Pintupi-Luritja and the concept of tribe. *Oceania* 74(4): 257–75.

Holcombe, S. 2004b. The sentimental community: A site of belonging. A case study from Central Australia. *The Australian Journal of Anthropology* 15(2): 163–84.

Holcombe, S. 2005. Luritja management of the state. In M. Hinkson and B. Smith (eds), Figuring the intercultural in Aboriginal Australia. *Oceania* 75(3): 222–33.

Jackson, M. 1996. Introduction: Phenomenology, radical empricism, and anthropological critique. In M. Jackson (ed.), *Things As They Are: New Directions in Phenomenological Anthropology*. Bloomington and Indianapolis: Indiana University Press, pp. 1–50.

Kimber, R. G. 1981. The Pintupi of the Kintore Range. Unpublished report for the Department of Aboriginal Affairs.

Long, J. 1970. Change in an Aboriginal community in Central Australia. In A. R. Pilling and R. A. Waterman (eds), *Diprotodon to Detribalisation: Studies of Change among Australian Aborigines*. East Lansing, Mich.: Michigan State University Press, pp. 318–32.

Long, J. 1971. Arid region Aborigines: The Pintupi. In D. J Mulvaney and J. Golson (eds), *Aboriginal Man and Environment in Australia*. Canberra: The Australian National University Press, pp. 262–70.

Long, J. 1989. Leaving the desert: Actors and sufferers in the Aboriginal exodus from the Western Desert. *Aboriginal History* 13(1): 9–43.

Myers, F. 1976. To have and to hold: A study of persistence and change in Pintupi social life. PhD thesis. Bryn Mawr College, Pennsylvania.

Myers, F. 1986. *Pintupi Country, Pintupi Self: Sentiment, Place and Politics among Western Desert Aborigines*. Washington, DC and Canberra: Smithsonian Institution Press & Australian Institute of Aboriginal Studies.

Nathan, P. and Leichleitner Japanangka, D. 1983. *Settle Down Country: Pmere Arlaltyewele*. Alice Springs, NT, and Melbourne: Central Australian Aboriginal Congress and Kibble Books.

Peterson, N. 1975. Hunter-gatherer territorality: The perspective from Australia. *American Anthropologist* 77: 53–61.

Stanner, W. E. H. 1966. *On Aboriginal Religion*. Oceania Monograph 11. Sydney: Sydney University Press.

Strehlow, T. G. H. 1947. *Aranda Traditions*. Melbourne: Melbourne University Press.

Sutton, P. 1990. The pulsating heart: Large scale cultural and demographic processes in Aboriginal Australia. In B. Meehan and N. White (eds), *Hunter-Gatherer Demography: Past and Present*. Oceania Monograph 39. Sydney: Sydney University Press, pp. 71–80.

Sutton, P. 1997. University of Adelaide Summer School notes on Aboriginal land tenure. Unpublished ms.

Tindale, N. B. 1932. Journal of a visit to Mt. Liebig, Central Australia. August 1932. Unpublished ms, South Australian Museum, Adelaide.

Tindale, N. B. 1974. *Aboriginal Tribes of Australia: Their Terrain, Environmental Controls, Distribution, Limits, and Proper Names*. Canberra: The Australian National University Press.

Tod Woenne, S. 1977. Old country, new territory: Some implications of the settlement process. In R. M. Berndt (ed.), *Aborigines and Change: Australia in the '70s*. Canberra: Australian Institute of Aboriginal Studies, pp. 54–64.

7

Out of sight, out of mind, but making the best of it: How outstations have worked in the Ngaanyatjarra Lands

David Brooks and Vikki Plant

This chapter discusses an exceptionally remote region of the Western Desert in which outstations have played a significant role. Outstations have not, however, necessarily or always been linked with self-determination here in the way suggested by the title of this volume, giving us one matter to disentangle from the start. But another question also immediately follows: was the arrival of self-determination necessarily such a watershed moment, as the premise of this volume's title seems to suggest? That is, was there one basic trajectory that applied throughout remote Australia, within which at a certain point self-determination provided the compelling response? We do not suggest that self-determination did not make a big impact in the Ngaanyatjarra region, as elsewhere, and bring with it many gains, but we do wish to problematise the historical part that it played.

We begin by considering some manifestations of outstation phenomena that came well before the self-determination era and accompanying outstation movement 'proper' of the 1970s. We will sometimes refer to the latter as the 'winds of change' movement, alluding to the national political associations and flavour that it had.

We identify the first local manifestation of phenomena generically classifiable as outstations to have been the 'summer holiday camps' or 'Christmas camps' that are associated with Warburton Mission history from the 1950s through to 1972. Virtually the whole Aboriginal population of the mission, which was the centre at which most Ngaanyatjarra people settled, would go to stay temporarily at one of several camp areas out from Warburton, remaining for up to three months, while the mission itself went into 'stand-down' mode for the summer. A degree of mission support would be provided, but other than this, the people would live off the country and do whatever they wished. In effect, these were 'intermittent' outstations. They did represent at least partially a 'return to country' and a return to a life less influenced by the mission, but the people would go back in between times, and for stays of much longer duration, to the centralised mission world. Also, of course, such camps did not represent a decentralisation of the population as such, and a winding down of the influence of the mission as a place of colonial congregation, in ways that are associated with the outstation movement proper and with the accompanying notion of self-determination. In fact, during the heyday of the summer camps, the mission was increasing in size and to some extent in influence. The summer camps developed out of, and as a consequence of, the people's increasing involvement with the mission, and in one sense, it could be argued, were a means of facilitating their increasing incorporation into the European world by softening what might otherwise have appeared as too drastic a step to take. But it could equally be argued—and this is much truer to the general Ngaanyatjarra view on the matter—that the people actively chose, for a long time, to become only partially involved in the mission environment, and that the summer camps represented one of the compromises that they negotiated with the mission to retain some autonomy while engaging in a gradual adaptation to a more sedentary, incorporated life. To better appreciate these and other matters pertaining not only to the summer camps but also to the subsequent period of the outstations proper, it is necessary to go back further in time to the beginnings of Ngaanyatjarra interaction with the 'whitefella'[1] world.

---

1   This is an Aboriginal English term for non-Aboriginal people.

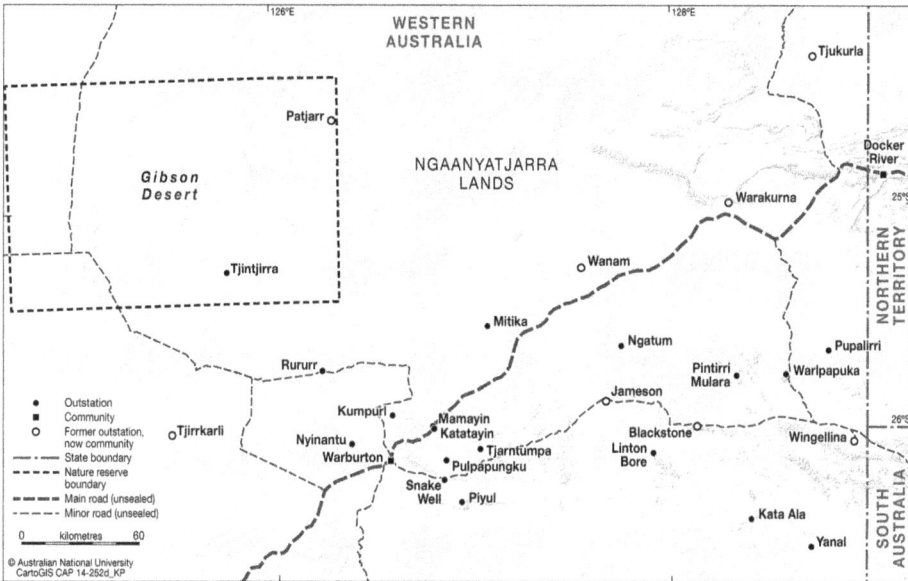

Map 7.1 Ngaanyatjara outstations.
Source: Karina Pelling, CartoGIS, ANU College of Asia and the Pacific

Warburton Mission history

The Warburton Mission, established in 1934 by the United Aborigines Mission (UAM), was, until its relinquishment of control of the settlement in 1973, by far the biggest factor in the encounter between the Ngaanyatjarra people and the European world. Not only was it the first point of contact, and a very lasting one, for most of the people, but also it has indelibly shaped the history of the region. Because of the area's extreme remoteness and lack of attractions for Europeans, the involvement of, or impact arising from, other external influences has been very limited and may be summarised quickly. The gold rush around Kalgoorlie and Laverton in the 1890s was the first impact, but it was an indirect one, instigating an outward 'drift' of some people from their desert homelands towards those centres—a phenomenon that has continued at a low level right up to the present, though it has been counterbalanced by returns made by many of the people concerned. After the gold rush itself, small parties of prospectors, explorers and 'doggers' came through the area, but their impact was minimal. No significant impacts of a direct kind, other than the mission, arose until the 1950s. In this decade, the WA State Government permitted access by several mining companies to areas around Wingellina and Blackstone in the Central Ranges, while in 1956 the Commonwealth Government built the Giles Weather Station in the Rawlinson Range. A little later, another mining company explored in the Jameson area. Vehicular roads appeared for the first time in the Ngaanyatjarra Lands in connection with these initiatives, and the developments affected the area in a number of ways, although the mineral exploration activities were unsuccessful and temporary in nature. Overall, the external impacts other than those associated with the mission could not be considered transformative of the area, although the extent of the impact may be measured by the fact that the first four settlements of the outstation movement proper were sited at Wingellina, Blackstone, Warakurna and Jameson—all places singled out by whitefellas in and through the developments just mentioned.

But while the Warburton Mission was the key whitefella institution in 40 years of Ngaanyatjarra history—and in the founding period when many of the lasting patterns of black/white interaction were created—a crucial fact about the mission from an analytical point of view is that it was essentially a very powerless institution. For virtually the whole time of its presence at Warburton, it teetered on the verge of collapse through lack of finance. Mainly as a result of this precariousness in its position, the missionaries' powers vis-à-vis the Ngaanytatjarra people were in most respects very limited. It is truer to say that the missionaries lived in fear that the people would withdraw from them than that they exercised control over any kind of captive audience. The carrot was necessarily the weapon of choice for them, rather than the stick. Yet in spite of this powerlessness and their frequent ineffectuality, some of them—notably, the founder, Will Wade—achieved a strong rapport with the people through demonstrations of commitment, humility and openness, giving rise to the universally fond regard in which the mission continues to be held. Thus, they were not without influence and even authority; it was just that other factors served to limit their capacities severely.

The tentativeness of the mission was founded mainly on the effects of that same remoteness that discouraged other parties from coming to the region. The significance of this remoteness in so many ways cannot be overstated. Even in the 1950s, it could take three weeks for the mission truck to get back and forth from civilisation as represented by the mining town of Laverton, itself more of an outpost than a centre. But coming on top of the difficulties arising from the remoteness was the consistent and debilitating neglect displayed by the State Government of Western Australia. In part, the Government's disregard probably sheets back, yet again, to how remote and 'out of sight, out of mind' the area was and is, but the Government was also always hostile to the mission and refused to assist it in any way for almost the first 20 years of its existence.[2]

---

2   It is perhaps worth noting for comparative purposes that unlike their counterparts at Ernabella, the Warburton missionaries had no middle or upper-class links into metropolitan society, and government correspondence shows that as people they were viewed by many bureaucrats almost with contempt, and certainly with none of the respect that someone like Dr Duguid of Ernabella commanded in Adelaide circles.

The financial survival of the mission, meagrely realised as this was, is a critical matter, in that it points to a marked interdependence that developed between mission and people. A powerful mutuality arose in intentions, desires and strategies, intertwining the very destinies of the respective parties. It is present in the way that the mission responded to its impoverished situation. Apart from the small income from the donations of church supporters, it had few options available, but it managed to find *one*. Though the subject is rarely mentioned in the missionaries' own records, their survival came to depend on the dingo-scalp trading in which they engaged with Ngaanyatjarra people. The dynamics of this trade are significant. The basic facts were that scalps brought in by the desert people, and repaid with food and clothing items, were used by the missionaries to claim the bounty that governments across several jurisdictions had instituted to lessen the impact of the dingo on the pastoral industry.[3] In many regions, the collection activity was monopolised by non-Indigenous 'doggers', but not so many of these made their way to the Ngaanyatjarra Lands, which were apparently too remote even for them. Doggers were far more prevalent in the Pitjantjatjara Lands, which were significantly closer to settled areas.

The new activity was taken up almost universally by the Ngaanyatjarra desert-dwellers at a very early point in their interaction with the mission. The pattern that developed represented in effect the first form of engagement with the whitefella for most Ngaanyatjarra people and the characteristic one for many years to come.

An important aspect of the dynamic arose from the logical fact that the best way for the desert people to get the most scalps was by spending their time mostly *not at the mission* but out in the bush, preferably distributed as widely as possible. In other words, the ideal from a dingo collection point of view was that the people should maintain close to their pre-contact way of life and territorial distribution, with one difference: that they would make periodical visits to the mission to hand in their scalps. This was, in fact, basically what happened for the first 20 years or more of the mission's presence. It was a scenario that worked for the mission, at least from the financial point of view, which was the most critical issue for them. And it also worked for the people, who by this means were able to obtain the whitefella foods they quickly came to like, primarily flour and sugar items. Whether or not it was intentional, this situation also meant that the people were able to pace their rate of adaptation to the whitefella world as represented by the mission. It appears that most of them were quite happy to do this, and to remain basically as band-dwellers in

---

3   There was an agreement with the Government that the mission could return half the value of the scalps to the people in goods, and put the other half towards the running of the mission.

the bush. To a considerable extent, however, it was not an option for them to move into the mission even had they so desired, as there would generally be no food awaiting them there.

In time, for a range of mutually reinforcing reasons that in general terms were repeated over and over around Australia, the degree of ability, and perhaps inclination, of the Ngaanyatjarra desert bands to maintain their old pattern of territorial organisation and way of life decreased, and they became centred more and more on the mission. If the engagement in dingo-scalp collection represents the first phase in the transition to incorporation into the whitefella world, the second phase was heralded by this increased centring on the mission. This occurred as they became more accustomed to and then burdened by whitefella food, clothing and other possessions, while their previous levels of good health and fitness—essential to living the mobile desert life—declined. Overall, the forces driving longer stays at Warburton multiplied. By the 1960s, the population at the mission was well into the hundreds and rising, with more and more people staying there on a semi-permanent or permanent basis. The dingo-scalp trade was now dying, with an accompanying decline in finance to the mission from this source, while no new source had arisen. Overcrowding and the associated pressures were becoming dire and were to remain so until 1975, which was when the 'winds of change' reached the region, and government funding in a sufficient quantity to make a difference arrived for the first time. This was Commonwealth money for the purpose of establishing major outstations at four well-spaced sites across the region, in the process changing the entire complexion of the Ngaanyatjarra Lands.

Summer holiday camps

Well before this time, however—in fact, right back in the early 1950s—a solution to the gradual centralisation at Warburton emerged that again worked for everybody, as had the dingo-scalping symbiosis in its time. This was the phenomenon of the summer holiday camp alluded to above. An early precursor of the camps occurred in the dingo-scalp days as some groups whose country was far out from the mission, instead of returning entirely to the desert ways when their stint at the mission was over, began basing themselves closer in, and taking some of the desired whitefella foods with them back out bush. The closer proximity meant that in turn it became feasible for the mission to service them as they started to need this. As more groups went down this track, however, such servicing became increasingly onerous for the mission. Hence further compromises were made, resulting in a smaller number of serviced locations, each of which would be occupied by two or more groupings that would previously have lived separately. Thus, the very composition of the groups as bands was changing even as the reasons for them to remain constituted *as* bands were evaporating. The distinction between living in one way (at the mission) or living in another (in the bush) was collapsing. It was no longer, or not only, a matter of the mission temporarily accommodating groups that were essentially still desert-dwellers, but about dealing with the situation of people who had effectively become sedentarised at the mission, or one could say incorporated within a world constituted by the state. But even as this was all happening, and groups were descending in numbers on Warburton or close by, there arose a push from the people themselves to find a way back, if in modified form, to where they had come from. For the mission's part, with the numbers and the pressure rising, there was a complementary imperative to alleviate its own increasingly unsustainable burden in whatever way it could. Getting some of the people out from the immediate mission area at least for some part of the year helped, as long as the servicing costs could be contained. Thus emerged the summer camps, at locations that soon came down to about three in total, sited along the better roads and about 30 km from the mission, and eventually equipped with bores and water tanks. The orientation of the campsites from the mission was determined in a rough manner by the country of origin of the occupants. Thus, two were located to the north and one or sometimes two to the east, these being the directions from which most of the mission residents came. The most well used of these were Mamayin, Katatayin and Snake Well. These can still be seen in varying states of repair today, and are remembered as the outstations of the mission time.

In summary, there are two features to emphasise about the mission time scenario. One is the interwoven character of the story, in terms of the actions and orientations of those involved. This interweaving was not present in the same way in the dynamics of the following period, that of the outstation movement proper. The second feature concerns the way in which this very interwoven character of relations starts to disintegrate towards the end. Once the dingo scalping was over, the people were left with little of a concrete nature that could allow them to either maintain some independence or negotiate an arrangement with the representatives of the state, as they had effectively done to this point. The interactions and the reasons behind them become more clouded and complex to decipher, though the inexorable decline in autonomy is apparent enough. It was not necessarily a matter of the state *wanting* to control them—although in certain respects this was undoubtedly a factor—but the situation arose ultimately as the consequence of the loss by a people of the ability to provide for themselves. The Ngaanyatjarras delayed this loss, but could not stave it off forever.

Outstations

In the case of the outstations of both the mission and the self-determination eras, association with a particular country was a major priority for the people. In the mission period, there was a countervailing pressure to centralise. In the case of the 'winds of change' movement, one of the major points was to do away with this kind of pressure and free people up to live in their country and away from the centres established by white agencies; but in fact, of course, wherever there are budgetary limitations a pressure to centralise will exist, and such limitations are never absent for long.

The outstation enterprises of either period could minimally be described as activities involving a person or group that wants to be able to live, if not full-time at least part-time, at or near a place remembered from or associated with the past. In explanation of their motives—and this material relates to more recent times, because we have no record of the contemporary ideas of the summer camp participants—many have described themselves as having been preoccupied by thoughts of the country concerned. This preoccupation is often expressed in English as 'worrying for' a place, although interestingly the Ngaanyatjarra term is simply *kulilpayi*, which is a broadly used term meaning listening or understanding. The connotation of a thought nagging away at someone, which is captured in the English term 'worrying for', is not necessarily present in the Ngaanyatjarra term. In some cases, the motivation may be more specifically explained as a matter of a desire or need to fulfil obligations associated with a place, obligations that are likely to involve the protection of or care for *tjukurrpa* (Dreaming) sites, or other considerations based in desert culture. There are many other possibilities here, including cases where a person is seeking recognition for or wishes to gain possession of a place for the political advantage that this could bring. Whatever the case, the proponent will always have significant prior associations. It should be noted though that while the summer camp locations were always oriented to places whose associations were located in the pre-contact past, the locational choices made in the later movement were often oriented to an 'intermediate' past, one lived out during the decades of the preceding mission era.

The 'winds of change' might have been blowing for some years in parts of Australia, but they did not reach the Ngaanyatjarra backwater until 1975. Meanwhile, the decline in autonomy that began with the end of the dingo-scalp trade and progressed slowly through the remainder of the mission period had long since reached its nadir. By the early 1970s, the people were all in Warburton and even the summer camps had been discontinued. The missionaries had bowed out, limiting their activities to what was now called 'Christian fellowship', and to linguistic work. There were no successors to the centralising and leadership role that they had once played. Government—that is, State Government—was slow to arrive, and when it did come its manifestations were confused, and divided, while the money available to assist the people seemed no more plentiful than ever. It seems fair to describe these as years of hiatus in Warburton. In 1975, missionary Wilf Douglas, now visiting as an observer, wrote:

> As well as the advisor supplied by W. D. Scott and Co, the Federal Government was represented by a Department of Aboriginal Affairs Advisor. The State was represented by officers from Community Welfare, Medical Department, Community Health, State Housing Commission, Education Department, Kindergarten Union, and now also the Police Department. Then the Australian Inland Mission is represented in the hospital, there are the UAM linguists and one other missionary, also represented are C. P. Bird and Co, the Cooper and Oxley Construction Company, plus the Aboriginal Lands Trust, the Aboriginal Affairs Coordinating Committee, the National Aboriginal Consultative Council, and the Warburton Community Council. (See Douglas 1978: 118–9)

In the same paper, Douglas refers to a visit by a Commonwealth politician to Warburton in 1972 during which he promised houses within six months. Two years later, when another Commonwealth politician visited, the people 'pointed to a disarray of used car bodies and stated, "Your predecessor promised us houses—do you see those old bombs? They are our houses now."' At the same time, before the eyes of the senator there was a large settlement of airconditioned houses that had been built for the departmental staff and advisers.

This was written in 1975, well down the track in terms of the adoption of the new polices of self-determination and support for outstations introduced by the Whitlam Government. Yet there is no mention whatsoever of outstations in Douglas's report.

As it happened though, and perhaps there was a connection, it was to be in that same year that funding did arrive for the implementation of the outstation movement, and the four major outstations alluded to above were established.[4]

It should be mentioned that these four initial outstations cannot be considered as having begun life uniformly as outward movements from Warburton, though they did ultimately come to be seen as dispersed around that site as a centre of sorts. The difference is most notable in the case of Wingellina, which was initially settled by a group that had been living for many years at Amata in

---

4   There was one development that at a crucial time functioned as a pressure-release for Warburton, and this was the Docker River settlement. Many Warburton people went there for stints of two or three years or more after 1968 and especially after 1970 to share in the greater income-related money that circulated there. Many of these people were originally from the Rawlinson Range or country to the north of there, so that when they left Docker River, rather than returning to Warburton they moved on to Warakurna, especially after that community received its outstation funding in 1975.

South Australia. Many of the Blackstone settlers also had a recent background in SA centres, though there were also many who arrived there from Warburton, and the impetus came from the latter place. Jameson and Warakurna were more clearly outshoots from Warburton. Overall, it is definitely Warburton that we are looking at in terms of the role played by the 1970s outstation movement in the departure of a sizeable proportion of a centralised population and the concomitant release of prevailing pressures. Internal conflict associated with the prolonged co-presence of large numbers had been brewing for years at Warburton, but by now it had reached the point where the physical and verbal threats and abuse were sometimes so extreme that they are still remembered today, 40 years later.

The four new settlements, when they did come, were modest affairs at first. John Tregenza, who accompanied the people from Amata to take the first community service officer position at Wingellina in 1975, described how he went to Perth to report for his job and brought out a truck, generator and caravan. They had one water tank, and two power cords running off the generator—one to John's family's caravan and one to the store. Tregenza was one of the new breed of 'believers' of the winds of change era, of which there have been many on the Pitjantjatjara Lands, but fewer on the Ngaanyatjarra side.[5] The big difference in political terms between the new settlements and those of previous eras was that governance (not called that at the time) was by community councils of Aboriginal members, directly funded by the Department of Aboriginal Affairs (DAA). This arrangement was intended to provide for 'self-determination' of local Aboriginal groups vis-à-vis the staff around them, who were now in *their* employ, and to cut out many other *interests* at various levels, such as accountancy firms, which had been exerting de facto control in often complex and opaque arrangements. The citation from Douglas above indicates that these intentions, which were to apply to a centre like Warburton as much as to outstations, were not always or easily realised.

While the actual benefits of the new era were slow to arrive, some Ngaanyatjarra people had come to know early on about the new ideas and the developments that were happening in other places. Some Ngaanyatjarra men, notably Tommy Simms and Fred Forbes, identified from an early point with the self-determination and land rights ideology and imagery, and later were in the thick of trips to Parliament House in Canberra, in company with Pitjantjatjara Council lawyers and anthropologists and the like. The delay in fulfilment of the promises that sounded so alluring added to the many frustrations and pressures of the time.

---

5   This new breed tended to wear red headbands, have strong commitments to land rights and self-determination, speak the desert language and have close domestic associations with the desert people.

Apart from the matter of getting out from Warburton, what were the circumstances and atmosphere surrounding the actual mobilisation of individuals and outstation groups and the choice of the particular four sites chosen? Some of it involved the hopes and dreams given shape in the winds of change ideology, as illustrated in the following account by Jim Downing, a Presbyterian minister and later activist. Downing refers to the Woodward Commission into land rights. One of its meetings with Aboriginal people in Alice Springs was attended by Fred Forbes, who lived at Warburton, though his country of identification was Blackstone. The ideas of land rights were strongly linked in many minds with those of self-determination and outstation development, and such meetings might be attended by people, like Fred, who would not be part of the specific case of the NT legislative push. Downing says:

> Those discussions greatly stimulated the hopes of … Fred Forbes, a middle-age man of considerable authority [who] told me 'The men asked me to go to that meeting in Alice Springs to speak for them.' He spoke so well in his own language, Ngaatjatjarra, that I overheard a Queen's Counsel on the Commission say to a colleague, 'I don't know what he is saying, but what wouldn't you give for that eloquence and that kind of presence in court?'
>
> Fred said of that meeting, 'I told them, "It is Aboriginal men's land and rocks and hills, and White men came later." So I took a map back to Warburton and showed them.' (Downing 1988: 61)

Downing goes on to relate how Fred told him how he got assistance to fill in a form to apply for incorporation, and a few weeks later was told he could go out and sit in his country. It is common local history that he and his group lived under bough shades at a site named Warutjarra, a few kilometres from the Blackstone site, for several months, with stores being trucked out to them from Warburton while they waited for the bore-drillers and builders to arrive.

Downing concludes: 'It is my firm belief that the quiet dynamic enthusiasm of Fred Forbes, his response to the Woodward Commission and his full reporting to the people … [at Warburton] stimulated the establishment of … [Jameson] and Warakurna also' (1988: 61).

A somewhat more humble perspective comes from Herbert Howell, a missionary who at the time had been in the Ngaanyatjarra Lands for 10 years and who not only witnessed events first hand, but also lived close to the people of Warakurna both before and after the establishment of the community in 1975. After describing how these people had found it very difficult to stay in the Warakurna locality since the mid-1950s because of the attitude of the Giles Weather Station administration, he relates how:

> In 1973–74 the Government began to encourage Aboriginal groups to return to their original homelands, providing funds to sink bores and erect basic facilities. There was great rejoicing among those from the Rawlinson Range. They happily returned to camp on the doorstep of the Weather Station. (Howell n.d.)

A point noted earlier was that the four initial outstation sites were 'well spaced'. This in itself was important and must certainly have been a factor in the decisions. There would have been pressure from government and others to ensure that the initiative brought about a fair and even dispersal of the population across the available land. But the map shows that the four sites were not by any means distributed equidistantly across the surface area. They are in fact located close to the main ranges of hills in the Ngaanyatjarra Lands, which are in broad terms the most fertile areas. It could be correctly assumed that these were places where the classical population was particularly concentrated, but other factors were at play as well. All the sites were places where whitefella activities had produced concentrations of Ngaanyatjarra population in the not too distant past. Thus, to some extent, the choice of locations was not a manifestation purely of the 'voice of the people', but was a more straightforward and practical matter of the existence of some significant infrastructure—bores, roads and the like—associated with the mining industry and the weather station.

The location of outstations

It can be taken for granted that every outstation that is built has a group that is pushing for it, and that the desire for outstations exceeds the number that can be funded. Whatever the politics was and whoever the players were, when the situation was being looked at in the lead-up to the 1975 deployment of funds to the Ngaanyatjarra region, Wingellina and Warakurna did virtually pick themselves, down to the actual location, within a range of a few kilometres. In addition to possessing the practical assets that have been mentioned, both had large numbers of potential residents who were keen to move in. They had strong Ngaanyatjarra proponents. And, though this is not a subject that we have so far flagged in this chapter, there were major sites of cultural significance very close by. The same is essentially true of Blackstone, though there was less prior specification here about the location of the community. It could probably have been placed at a number of spots within a radius of 30 or 40 km. Jameson had to win out against other competitors.

There were to be no more major outstation developments in the Ngaanyatjarra Lands until the late 1980s, when Tjukurla, Patjarr, Tjirrkarli and Wanarn were established under somewhat different arrangements, with heavy support from the Ngaanyatjarra Council, a non-governmental body that had emerged more recently. These four, together with the initial four, became known as 'communities' and all are still running today. But in the aftermath of 1975 there were many individuals and groups whose aspirations were not catered for by the framework of the first four. In following years, small amounts of funds were made available for the establishment of mini outstations at about 20 places. Each of these survived for varying periods but none has stood the test of time.

Conclusion

We have concentrated here on providing some underlying insights about the outstation movement by contextualising it within the broad narrative of Ngaanyatjarra interaction with the outside world and its local representatives. We have seen how at first the engagement had a collaborative character, which for three decades or so worked in a way that could be judged successful for the Ngaanyatjarra, at least in terms of issues of maintaining autonomy, until that particular dynamic died away, and the people were left effectively stranded at Warburton and cut off from the land that had continued to sustain them until very recently. And we have seen how the hiatus that set in at Warburton was broken when the outstation funding arrived—funding that came out of the new mindset of 1970s Australia—allowing a new direction to be pursued that again involved the occupation and the use, albeit in a somewhat different way, of the land. What of the new interactional field that developed along with the outstations of 1975 and later? While there was never quite the same sort of collaborative character, the same interweaving that had characterised the mission time, the influence of the early experience of those kinds of relations persisted. At no time have the Ngaanyatjarra been inclined to espouse anti-white sentiments, or to be preoccupied with demanding control of all the affairs of the region. It seems fair to say that they did not 'need' many of the ingredients of self-determination as a policy, but they had certainly come by the 1970s—or earlier—to need government support. The support was needed both to create outstations away from Warburton and to improve conditions at Warburton itself. But given the conditions of the time, support was going to come as part of the self-determination package, whether or not the package as a whole was wanted. And it is in the nature of the notion of self-determination that a distance between white and black will exist—a distance conceptualised by proponents not as a negative but precisely as a positive. It was seen that a space is necessary, for restorative and maybe developmental purposes: the whitefellas needed to 'back off'. But for a group whose history did not really contain a sense of oppression or domination, the distant stance of the new crop of whitefellas that came with the new funding has often been perplexing for the Ngaanytjarra. Bearing in mind that the more recent staff who have come their way have not tended to be in the activist mode, but rather politically and personally conservative, the Ngaanyatjarra have not been quite sure why they have come, other than to get a paid job. They have not got to know most of these staff well as people, but partly because the Ngaanyatjarra attitude to whites is mostly benign, the staff tend to stay on for long periods, and everybody gets on amiably enough. The Ngaanyatjarra attitude may be summed up as, 'You do your job helping us, and we'll live our lives'. All well and good. The missing elements, though, have been in the area of leadership and in the development of an increased—and necessary—engagement with the outside world. The Ngaanyatjarra relationship with this outside world, via the missionaries, began felicitously, but against this background, and to some extent because of it, what came next—self-determination—was not the ideal progression. For Aboriginal groups that had something to fight back against it probably allowed for the development of leadership and a sense of forward movement, but for the Ngaanyatjarra it created not so much a space as a vacuum.

Interestingly, the Ngaanyatjarra have done quite well in some respects. The stability associated with their working accommodation with their staff has resulted in them having come to own a number of valuable assets that have provided some services and income independently of government. These assets have included a set of elaborate and effective goods, services and transport provision companies, as well as businesses in Alice Springs. By these means, the region is at the time of writing one of the few places that has been able to retain self-determination as a working reality within its communities, some seven years after the Commonwealth moved away from policies of this kind to more authoritarian, centralised approaches.

References

Douglas, W. 1978. Evolution of a rampage of destruction at Warburton Ranges. In M. C. Howard (ed.), *Whitefella Business: Aborigines in Australian Politics*. Philadelphia: Institute for the Study of Human Issues, pp. 105–24.

Downing, J. 1988. *Ngurra Walytja: Country of My Spirit*. Darwin: North Australia Research Unit.

Howell, H. n.d. Why move to Warakurna? Unpublished report.

8

Outstations through art: Acrylic painting, self-determination and the history of the homelands movement in the Pintupi-Ngaanyatjarra Lands

Peter Thorley[1]

Australia in the 1970s saw sweeping changes in Indigenous policy. In its first year of what was to become a famously short term in office, the Whitlam Government began to undertake a range of initiatives to implement its new policy agenda, which became known as 'self-determination'. The broad aim of the policy was to allow Indigenous Australians to exercise greater choice over their lives. One of the new measures was the decentralisation of government-run settlements in favour of smaller, less aggregated Indigenous-run communities or outstations. Under the previous policy of 'assimilation', living arrangements in government settlements in the Northern Territory were strictly managed

---

1   I would like to acknowledge the people of the communities of Kintore, Kiwirrkura and Warakurna for their assistance and guidance. I am especially grateful to Monica Nangala Robinson and Irene Nangala, with whom I have worked closely over a number of years and who provided insights and helped facilitate consultations. I have particularly enjoyed the camaraderie of my fellow researchers Fred Myers and Pip Deveson since we began working on an edited version of Ian Dunlop's 1974 Yayayi footage for the National Museum of Australia's *Papunya Painting* exhibition in 2007. Staff of Papunya Tula Artists, Warakurna Artists, Warlungurru School and the Western Desert Nganampa Walytja Palyantjaku Tutaku (Purple House) have been welcoming and have given generously of their time and resources. This chapter has benefited from discussion with Bob Edwards, Vivien Johnson and Kate Khan.

with the aim of integration into a mainstream Australian way of life. Under the new policy ideal, Indigenous Australians would, in principle at least, be given greater freedom to live in the manner of their own choosing.

Outstations were not the only policy area in which the revitalisation of Indigenous cultures and the restoration of people's power to control their own destiny were seen to be mutually beneficial. Reform of the arts was also high on the new government's agenda. In 1973, the Australia Council for the Arts took over responsibility for Indigenous arts and crafts from the Aboriginal Arts Advisory Committee, which was formed in 1970. The Aboriginal Arts Board (AAB) was established as one of seven boards within the restructured Australia Council, under the auspices of its Chair, H. C. ('Nugget') Coombs, who had been an adviser to the Government on the arts and Indigenous policy since 1968 (Rowse 2000). In keeping with the Government's broader agenda, the board gave advisory and decision-making powers to its 14 Aboriginal and Torres Strait Islander members, providing Indigenous representation in the arts at a national level for the first time.

The National Museum of Australia (NMA) Aboriginal Arts Board collection was a product of the AAB and its operations from 1973 to 1981. The NMA's holdings from the Western Desert include paintings from Warakurna (Giles) and Yayayi, two outstations established in 1973 and operating under the new policies of the Whitlam Government. Yayayi (see Myers, this volume) was then home to Pintupi people who had moved from the government settlement of Papunya. Two years earlier, while living at Papunya, the Pintupi artists had been instrumental in the beginnings of the acrylic painting movement.

In 1971, Pintupi along with other groups, including Anmatyerre and Warlpiri who were living together in the confines of the government settlement, began to reproduce traditional designs using Western art materials, creating vibrant works that were to become internationally acclaimed. What began as a singular painting community at Papunya in 1971 has in the past two decades proliferated into a number of enterprises spread across the Western Desert and beyond. The Ngaanyatjarra artists living at Warburton and Warakurna were not directly involved in the formative years of the acrylic painting movement in and around Papunya, yet remained in contact with the artistic developments through relatives living at Yayayi. Many Pintupi who were among the original painting group in the 1970s identified with Warakurna and before European contact were neighbours of Ngaanyatjarra, with whom they shared a common language and ceremonial links.

Since its inception, acrylic painting has contributed to the fabric of Western Desert communities in many ways. As has been well documented elsewhere (for example, Altman 1988), art and craft have played a central role in the economic development of outstations and have continued to provide income support through sales and government grants. My emphasis here is on the role of art in the construction of narratives. Narrative can powerfully influence how a community perceives itself and what it hopes to achieve as a collective. By extension, art can be a force for exercising the collective will of the community. Once confined to *Tjukurrpa* (creation) paintings, Western Desert acrylic painting has expanded to include new forms, styles and subjects, yet the primacy of narrative has remained a constant throughout its history. As such, the body of acrylic works produced in the Western Desert provides a unique record of outstations from 1971, when the painting movement began, to the present day.

The formal incorporation of Papunya Tula Artists in 1972 as an independent, Aboriginal-owned enterprise was a landmark in the development of Indigenous art in Australia, in many ways foreshadowing the new era of government policy in the 1970s (Johnson 2008). The emergence of painting as a commodity based on traditional practices tapped into the artists' attachment to country and aspirations to live a lifestyle of choice—principles that resonated with the Whitlam Government's policies on outstations and self-determination. In Papunya Tula, the artists were able to form their own enterprise in which they were actively involved in a decision-making capacity. The spate of new art centres that have arisen in the Western Desert region in recent decades, driven by the success of Papunya Tula, is a lasting legacy of this period.

Many of these new art centres have battled financially, as did Papunya Tula in its first decade. Yet art enterprises perform a vital role in the community beyond producing works for sale. The key painters are often the storytellers and shapers of oral history. Their paintings are the products of shared narratives of what is important in their lives and their hopes for the future. In this way, the act of painting and the discussions that take place around it have helped to sustain outstations in difficult times.

In this chapter, I argue that the production of paintings of country, under the patronage of the AAB, affected both the possibility and the desirability of Pintupi decentralisation. AAB funding supported the vision of Pintupi artists to return to country, which they expressed through the medium of acrylic painting. I then go on to look at the Warakurna paintings and how the construction of history orients Western Desert communities towards the future. The current generation of leaders, artists and schoolteachers is bringing the past to life through their desire to engage with historical images and narratives (cf. Thorley 2002). Reflecting on their struggles and achievements in the face of adversity, Western Desert communities are laying a foundation to imagine a desired future and move forward with confidence amid significant challenges posed by increasing government control and the threat of outstation closures.

The emergence of acrylic painting

The acrylic painting movement that sprang up at the Papunya settlement in the early 1970s was reflective of wider political currents, emerging on the cusp of the transition from 'assimilation' to 'self-determination'. Opposition to assimilation had been mounting for some time when the 1972 change of government in Canberra brought about an end to the policy, as Bob Edwards (2004: viii) recalled: 'When Geoffrey Bardon arrived in Central Australia the winds of change were already beginning to blow, through Aboriginal societies. The destructive impact of the long applied policy of assimilation was being challenged.'

While the first painting boards were being produced in Papunya, the settlement was continuing to function as an instrument of assimilation policy. Bardon, a schoolteacher, was operating to a degree in defiance of the Government in encouraging artists to take up acrylic painting at the time (Perkins 2009: 12). His efforts attracted unwanted attention from settlement administrators who he claims felt he had 'become too close to the Aboriginal people' (Bardon and Bardon 2004: 38).

By 1971, Pintupi were back living in Papunya after two attempts to establish separate communities (see Myers, this volume). The second such attempt was the short-lived Alumbra (Lampara) Bore, which ended in September 1970 after a brawl with police (Coombs 1974: 11). After the closure of Alumbra, Pintupi took up residence in a separate camp on the western side of Papunya. The NMA's holdings from this period include pencil and watercolour works on paper by Uta Uta Tjangala produced on the verandah of Bardon's house in Papunya in September 1971. These roughly executed works did not come with any accompanying documentation from Bardon, although the design of one of the drawings closely resembles a 1973 painting in the NMA's collection recorded by Myers (2002: 112) of Tjangala's conception site, Ngurrapalangu.

What Tjangala and the other Pintupi artists were expressing in their paintings may not have been entirely clear to Bardon at the time. Bardon was not a fluent Pintupi speaker and the artists were not fluent in English. Placenames rarely appear in the title of the paintings recorded by Bardon and his renderings of the early painting boards from 1971–72 suggest he struggled with the depth of knowledge and multilayered meanings embedded in the works. Bardon also had pressing personal issues to contend with while living in Papunya. By his own admission, he felt like an outsider in the white community and fell out with the Welfare Branch administrators over the Aboriginal management of Papunya Tula, which, he claimed, they opposed. This was the final straw that led to his departure in August 1972 (Bardon and Bardon 2004: 38–9).

Self-determination and the arts

The establishment of a separate Indigenous board for the arts within the larger Australia Council, with powers to make decisions and distribute funds, was one of the pillars of the Federal Government's Aboriginal self-determination policy. Whitlam expressed his vision for the AAB in the introduction to the catalogue for one of its first major international initiatives, known as the 'Rothmans Exhibition': 'The Aboriginal Arts Board exemplifies the Australian Government's policy of restoring to Aboriginal people the power of decision about their way of life within a community that honours and respects their contribution' (*Art of Aboriginal Australia* 1974).

The 14 board members were drawn from communities across Australia and were intended to be representative of both sexes and urban and remote areas, providing a national platform for Indigenous involvement in decision-making.

Robert ('Bob') Edwards, the founding director of the AAB, was a close follower of the Papunya painting movement from the outset (see also Johnson 2007; Myers 2002). As curator of anthropology at the South Australian Museum (1965–73), Edwards organised private exhibitions of Papunya paintings in Adelaide in 1972. Later, while he was director, the AAB subsidised Bardon's films and documentation projects about the painting movement at Papunya.[2] The Papunya painting enterprise strongly aligned with Edwards' background in cultural heritage and marketing (before becoming a heritage professional, he had worked for many years in the family fruit-growing business). Edwards' view of self-determination drew strongly on his cultural heritage background:

> It's a pivotal thing because ... to say, forget your culture because if you want to get anywhere your kids have got to be educated and the more you cling to the past the less opportunity you've got for the future. We took another line that was if you've got your language and you've got pride in your culture you've got a confidence and you're more able to do it. (Bob Edwards, interview, 16 November 2010)

Minutes of AAB meetings, held in the NMA's archive, provide a fascinating record of the board's operation during its first decade. In its formation, structure and practice, the AAB explicitly recognised Indigenous protocols. Meetings were often held on country and local forms of decision-making were respected. In this way, the retention of culture was seen to be consistent with the goals of self-determination (on which outstation policy was also based).

---

2   National Museum of Australia (hereinafter NMA) Archive: Minutes of the third AAB meeting, 11–13 August 1973.

A key topic in the board's early deliberations was the promotion of Indigenous art through international exhibitions and commissions. These lucrative commissions were to become highly sought after by the painters, who rated them as equivalent to vehicles. A single large painting, such as those commissioned by the AAB for overseas exhibitions and international diplomatic efforts, could alone raise enough money to purchase a four-wheel-drive vehicle. The desire for vehicles thus fed competition between communities to secure the best AAB commissions.

In 1973, the AAB acquired 17 works from Papunya and Yayayi for *Art of Aboriginal Australia*, an international touring exhibition sponsored by the tobacco giant Rothmans Stuyvesant. The Rothmans Exhibition, as it became known, toured 13 Canadian venues between 1974 and 1976 and was the first international exhibition of its kind. The works from Papunya and Yayayi featured alongside a selection of Hermannsburg watercolours, bark paintings, boomerangs and Tiwi sculptures. Around the time the AAB was acquiring works for the exhibition, the original Papunya painting group had recently been split by the Pintupi move to Yayayi (see Myers, this volume) and tensions increased as the two communities vied for access to the AAB commissions.

Artists from Papunya produced the majority of the acrylic works in the Rothmans Exhibition, and the two largest paintings. The two large collaborative works were painted by Long Jack Phillipus (assisted by Old Mick Walankari) and Kaapa Mbitjana and Billy Stockman (assisted by Dinny Nolan and Eddie Etamintja). Smaller individual works were painted by Yayayi artists John Tjakamarra, Shorty Lungkarta, Yanyatjarri Tjakamarra, Watuma Tjungurrayi (Charley Tjaruru) and Uta Uta Tjangala.

The two large works stood out from the rest of the exhibition. At 204 x 173 cm, both were much larger in size than any acrylic paintings previously produced. Kate Khan, senior project officer with the AAB from 1974 to 1980, recalls that all of the paintings were on wooden board, which made them extremely heavy and expensive to transport by air to Canada (canvas later became the standard medium).[3] The large paintings and most of the smaller works were gifted to Canadian institutions at the culmination of the tour.[4] Although Yayayi artists were well represented in the exhibition, they were overlooked for the two largest collaborative works painted by Papunya artists. These were the first of

---

3   Kate Khan, personal communication, 2011. Khan recalls discussing the advantages of using canvas as a medium with Peter Fannin at a milk bar in Alice Springs in 1974.

4   One painting by Yanyatjarri Tjakamarra, titled '*Story of the Women's Camp and the Origin of the Damper*', was credited in the catalogue as belonging to Machmoud Mackay, the general manager of Aboriginal Arts and Crafts Pty Ltd, the commercial and sales arm of the AAB. Mackay, a Scotsman who became a Muslim, is acknowledged in the catalogue for his assistance. NMA acquired Tjakamarra's painting at auction in 2010.

many spectacular large paintings (mostly on canvas) commissioned for overseas venues, which became the hallmark of the AAB's promotional strategy during the late 1970s and early 1980s (Berrell 2009; Johnson 2007).

Yayayi's lack of representation on the AAB may have further aggravated the rift between the two communities. The artists who represented Papunya Tula on the board in the first decade of the painting movement—Tim Leura, Long Jack Phillipus and Billy Stockman—were all residents of Papunya. The Pintupi, whose country was further west and who had recently moved to Yayayi outstation, were not appointed to represent Papunya Tula on the AAB. The discrepancies between the two communities were a source of tension that became apparent when the board's director, Bob Edwards, attended a meeting at Yayayi in June 1974, the same month the Rothmans Exhibition opened in Stratford, Ontario.

Self-determination in practice: Yayayi, June 1974

While the AAB was empowered to make decisions over the allocation of resources, its limited funds were stretched by the needs of artists living in remote communities, particularly in regard to vehicles. Archival footage shot by Ian Dunlop (for Film Australia) at Yayayi in 1974 provides insight into how these pressures played out on the ground in a newly established outstation.[5]

On 6 June 1974, Edwards, accompanied by Long Jack Phillipus, visited the artists at Yayayi. Other key participants at the meeting were Jeff Stead (community adviser employed by DAA), Peter Fannin (art adviser for Papunya Tula) and Chris McGuigan (DAA). Dunlop's footage shows Bob Edwards mingling with male artists in the painting camp with Long Jack Phillipus and Fannin alongside. Phillipus was to become Papunya Tula's next representative on the AAB.

The following passages have been extracted from Dunlop's footage. Watuma Tjungurrayi, a prominent Yayayi councillor and important painter, is worried that the *mayutju* from the Government have not delivered the vehicles—the 'two big ones'—as anticipated. *Mayutju* means 'boss', a term the Pintupi men are using to refer to Bob Edwards.

'We got no truck,' Watuma says, '*Council-la tjurta* [all you councillors] *nyaampa kulirnin* [what are you thinking]?'

5 Ian Dunlop's footage from Yayayi has been the subject of research undertaken by the author with Fred Myers and Pip Deveson. Assistance has been provided by an Australian Institute of Aboriginal and Torres Straits Islander Studies Research Grant and an Australian Research Council Linkage Project Grant (LP100200359) (in a partnership between The Australian National University, the National Museum of Australia and Papunya Tula Artists).

Some of the artists continue to paint while Watuma speaks.

Fannin and Edwards talk among themselves, seemingly oblivious to Watuma's concerns. Jeff Stead, the young community adviser at Yayayi, from the DAA, then appears and approaches Fannin.

'They're worried about the car, Papunya's car,' Stead says. 'I told them that you're going to get one and that's going to be used at Papunya and come out here one or two days. Billy Stockman [the current AAB member] and Jack Tjakamarra's gonna be in charge of it, right?'

'That's what we thought,' Fannin replies, 'but they're [the artists from Yayayi] directors [of Papunya Tula], too.'

'I think you better have a talk to them and explain, because I think they want to hear it from you,' Stead suggests.

Fannin then explains to the men that the AAB has promised a truck for Papunya Tula to be based at Papunya. As a consolation, he suggests that Yayayi apply for a vehicle in the next round of grants. Jack Phillipus, looking in the direction of Edwards, says, 'He might help. Canberra. He might help 'im with painting car. Might be next round [of funding]. I dunno.'[6]

At a later meeting at Yayayi, also filmed by Dunlop, Shorty Bruno (Yayayi councillor) talks about topping up money from the Yayayi Community Council (YCC) 'for that motorcar'. These additional funds were to include $200 being paid to the community by the film crew—payment for their part in the film.

The YCC's request for assistance with funding of a vehicle was raised at the AAB's seventh meeting, on 22–24 July: 'Mr McGuigan (DAA) reported that a very vigorous bush community existed at Yai yai [sic]. The artists were happy and a number were painting on a full-time basis. The community required a vehicle and had applied to the board for a subsidy.'[7]

The YCC, the minutes go on to say, had applied for $3,500 'for the subsidisation of vehicle costs and running expenses. The vehicle was to be used for gathering materials and transport of paintings and craftwork.' The application was approved. This vehicle was subsequently used by a group of Pintupi men in late 1974 to visit and engage with a distant Emu Dreaming ritual site in Western Australia (Myers, personal communication, 2015).

6   For another account of this meeting, from Fred Myers, who was present, see Myers (2007).
7   NMA: AAB Minutes, NMA Library.

As well as providing commissions, the AAB supported the struggling Papunya Tula Artists company through provision of grants. The board considered Papunya Tula's application for $12,000 to cover operational expenses for a year, the art adviser's salary for six months and provision of a four-wheel-drive vehicle and running costs.

The minutes of the fourth meeting, on 28–29 April 1974, reveal the pressure placed on the board by applications for vehicle funding. The board sought to deflect the issue by highlighting the responsibility of the DAA: 'Mr McGuigan reported that the Department [of Aboriginal Affairs] had rejected the Arts Board's recommendation for the purchase of vehicles for communities at Yirrkala and Papunya.' The onus for vehicle funding was placed back onto the DAA, and the notes continue that 'the Board was concerned the Department of Aboriginal Affairs was failing to accept responsibility for assisting with the purchase and maintenance of vehicles'.

The day after returning from Yayayi, on 7 June 1974, Bob Edwards wrote a gloomy letter to Nugget Coombs. His letter records that 'I returned today from an all too brief visit to Ernabella, Amata, Papunya, Yayayi and Yuendumu. At the moment I can only relate my feelings of sadness and frustration at the situation existing in these communities.'[8] The letter also refers to Yayayi and the general issue of vehicle funding, in regard to which Edwards states: 'At Yayayi a few miles distant [from Papunya], where one sees some hope for a new future, the community is frustrated by lack of transport as their few vehicles have fallen into disrepair.'[9]

Edwards and Coombs shared a very similar perspective in approaching the development of Indigenous art and the maintenance of cultural heritage within the broader framework of service delivery to remote outstations, to which vehicles were integral. As Edwards further states in the letter:

> The Board will have to tackle this problem as vehicles are essential to viable art and craft enterprises. They provide access to vast timber resources and obviate the necessity to devastate the limited supplies near settlements. We will have to grasp the nettle in the near future.[10]

Yet the practicalities of supplying and maintaining vehicles in remote settings remained a challenge that had to be balanced with other board priorities. Constant requests for vehicles placed a strain on the board's attempt to carry out its functions as a national Aboriginal and Torres Strait Islander arts body empowered to make decisions and to manage the funds at its disposal.

8   NMA: Letter from Robert Edwards to Dr H. C. Coombs, 7 June 1974, File 11/387.

9   ibid.

10   ibid.

Ultimately, the decision-making powers of the board were to be tested on a number of fronts. The obligation of members to family, kin and community and the balancing of remote and urban interests weighed heavily on the board's decisions. In the director's role, Edwards was essential to the smooth operation of the board and the success of many of its initiatives. In the meeting at Yayayi on 6 June, it is clear that Pintupi saw Edwards as a *mayutju* (boss) and representative of 'the Government' and 'Canberra', and their attempts to win him over suggested they regarded him, rather than an Indigenous-controlled board, as crucial to their objectives—a view that did not entirely conform with Whitlam's vision for the board as one of 'restoring to Aboriginal people the power of decision'.

As demonstrated by the 6 June meeting, the principles on which the board was founded did not always align with local priorities. At the local level, the tensions between Yayayi and Papunya were a mobilising force for Pintupi, who were intent on securing resources for themselves as a separate group. By their own accounts, Pintupi believed they were not well treated while living at Papunya and look back on this period in their lives as a 'sad' time. The rift that developed with Papunya around resourcing issues only reinforced their belief in the need for an independent community.

Since resettling on their own land in the 1980s, Pintupi have developed a reputation for self-funding projects with the proceeds of art sales. When unable to convince the Government to support their own ventures, Pintupi have taken it on themselves to find a way. Notable examples include the pioneering of dialysis for renal patients in the bush and a communal swimming pool at Kintore, both financed through charity auctions of Pintupi paintings. Historically, there is a pattern of Pintupi artists securing resources through art proceeds to make their vision a reality, the seeds of which were sown in earlier periods when they were able to utilise the AAB's grants and commissions.

Moving back to country

Pintupi painting remained dependent on AAB support throughout 1970s. Many large canvases were produced during this period and these commissions helped keep the struggling Papunya Tula Artists company afloat. As well as generating income for the artists, the production of paintings, both large and small, connected the artists with their country—still far from where they lived— through the visualised imaginary. Paintings expressed what the artists hoped to achieve in terms of getting back on country. For the Pintupi artists, the act of painting was anticipatory.

While the desire to establish communities on Pintupi soil remained foremost in the minds of the artists, Pintupi country lay hundreds of kilometres west of Papunya and was, for the most part, physically inaccessible. Before establishing a permanent settlement at Warlungurru (Kintore) in 1981, Pintupi made irregular forays to visit sacred sites in their remote homeland areas. For example, the Australian Institute of Aboriginal Studies (AIAS) sponsored filming trips to record ceremonies at Yumari (in 1969), Yarru Yarru (1970), Mitukatjirri (1972) and Yawalyurru (1974).[11]

Yawalyurru and sites linked to it by the Native Cat (*Kurninka*) story held special significance for Yanyatjarri Tjakamarra, who left the desert in 1966, joining his fellow countrymen at Papunya. A series of 31 paintings, recorded and analysed by Myers (2002) from 1973 to 1975, reveals the importance of Yawalyurru and its associated sites as a source of inspiration in the artist's imaginary. His paintings express a longing to visit Yawalyurru and his heartfelt desire to establish an outstation at nearby Kulkurta. However, the inaccessibility of the terrain has been a major obstacle to the development of a viable community in the area. Before the 1974 trip filmed by Dunlop, Yanyatjarri can be seen trying to convince Long that it would be possible to reach Yawalyurru without numerous sandhill crossings. With the journey under way, vehicles are seen floundering in deep sand while cresting high dunes. The group of men reached Yawalyurru and performed the ceremony, but because of the restricted nature of the place and ceremony, filming was suspended before they got there. In 1987, another AIAS-sponsored expedition mounted from Kintore took six days with four fully equipped vehicles. Yanyatjarri moved a step closer to Yawalyurru after the passing of the *Aboriginal Land Rights (Northern Territory) Act 1976* enabled him to shift to Kintore in 1981, where he lived for a short period before moving to Tjukurla (WA). Sadly, however, he passed away in 1992 without ever resettling on his own country.

In July 1981, Uta Uta Tjangala began work on the giant *Yumari* canvas while living at Papunya, five years after the passing of the *Aboriginal Land Rights (Northern Territory) Act 1976*. *Yumari* is the most celebrated of all the large AAB-commissioned canvases held by the NMA. The title of the work, it could be said, is wrongly attributed to the nearby ceremonially related rockhole site of Yumari, part of the same Dreaming. The giant anthropomorphic being that dominates the canvas, however, is the artist's conception totem, *Tjurntamutu*, who resides in a cave at Ngurrapalangu, several kilometres to the east of Yumari. In July 1981, Myers recorded the artist's hopes to return to Ngurrapalangu, in a four-wheel-drive LandCruiser funded by the proceeds of the painting (Myers 2002: xv).

---

11   Initially, it was intended to record a ceremony at Yawalyurru but by 1974 the Pintupi men decided it was no longer acceptable to do such filming. Jeremy Long took the men on the trip anyway, honouring the obligation to allow them to return. Filming of the journey, but not the ceremony or the sacred site, was permitted to Dunlop in exchange for providing additional vehicles. Myers, personal communication, 2015.

In the late 1980s, working as a teacher-linguist at Kintore (NT), I accompanied Uta Uta several times to Ngurrapalangu and the nearby outstation of Muyin (WA) where he occasionally lived. By then, Kintore had become a homeland resource centre, servicing a network of outstations (or bores) within the surrounding area. The DAA outstation coordinator based at Kintore appointed a full-time mechanic just to maintain the Aboriginal Benefit Trust Account (ABTA) vehicles used by a small population who were intermittently living on outstations. A track was graded to each bore that was equipped with a hand pump. In the late 1980s and early 1990s, dwellings and other infrastructure were added. Despite these improvements, none of the outstations became continuously occupied and in the past two decades they have largely fallen into disrepair. While some groups have moved further afield to Kiwirrkura and Tjukurla in Western Australia, Pintupi at Kintore, now close to their country, have shown little interest in permanently occupying smaller outstations. Nonetheless, outstations continued to be visited and used as a base for hunting trips and to access nearby sacred sites, and vehicles remained essential to these activities.

While at Ngurrapalangu in 1989, Uta Uta spoke to me passionately about his conception site as *Tjuntamurtuku ngurra* (Place of *Tjuntamurtu*). He wanted people to know that *Tjuntamurtuku ngurra* is an important place (*purlkanya*). He hoped that, in taking me there, he would get two Toyota four-wheel-drive vehicles, 'two really big ones' ('*Mutukayi kutjarra mantjilku purlkanya* Toyota'). He talked about how he had brought other whitefellas to the site and told them this important story but they had not been forthcoming with the money and vehicles he wanted ('*Wiyarni yungu mani mutukayi*').

Uta Uta's concerns as related to me in 1989 were remarkably similar to those he conveyed to Myers at Papunya in 1981 and those expressed by Watuma Tjungurrayi at the vehicle meeting filmed by Ian Dunlop at Yayayi in 1974. For the senior Pintupi men, sacred sites, vehicles and money dovetailed into how they understood their situation and what they wanted to achieve from their art in terms of providing funds and communicating their ambitions among themselves and to a wider network of potential supporters.

Warakurna

The artists of Warakurna (formerly referred to as Giles), a Ngaanyatjarra outstation established in the same year as Yayayi, began to paint as a collective in 2004. The first works produced by the Warakurna Artists enterprise were *Tjukurrpa* (Dreaming) paintings with affinities to early Papunya works. In 2011, Warakurna Artists embarked on a project to document their history visually, producing a set of highly figurative works that combined traditional and

Western forms of representing landscape. These 'history paintings', as they became known, specifically reference the arrival of Europeans and subsequent events as they impacted on the development of the community.

Figure 8.1 *Giles Weather Station*, 2011, by Dorcas Tinamayi Bennett. Courtesy of Warakurna Artists.

Photo: Katie Shanahan, National Museum of Australia, nma.img-ci20122838-030

The history of Warakurna has been influenced by its close proximity to Giles Weather Station, a facility set up by the Department of the Interior in 1956 under the Anglo-Australian weapons program. The consequences of weapons research on local populations—Aboriginal and European—came under scrutiny in press reports at the time and have been examined in histories produced by the Department of Defence and the Bureau of Meteorology (Day 2007; Morton 1987). In 1965, the anthropologist Donald Thomson, who had been working in the area, wrote to the Secretary of the Department of the Interior: 'It appears to me a tremendous pity that the Government of Western Australia, aided by the Native Affairs people employed by the Commonwealth on the rocket range and under direction from the Weapons Research Establishment, have concentrated on depopulating the desert.'[12]

---

12   NMA: Letter from D. Thomson to R. Kingsland, File 30/2736, Part 2—Liaison Correspondence on Departmental Policy with Secretary Department of Interior.

A series of paintings by artists Jean Burke, Judith Chambers and Eunice Porter provides another perspective on the relationship between *Yarnangu* (the Western Desert word for 'person', especially an Aboriginal person)[13] and defence personnel. The painting *Macaulay and MacDougall* by Jean Burke shows rations being delivered by these two well-known patrol officers in yellow trucks. 'We were all happy to see them', says Burke in her oral testimony supplied with the painting. 'People would get in the truck and go with them to the mission camp', Judith Chambers recalls in the artist statement accompanying her painting *Mr MacDougall and Tommy Dodd*.

Figure 8.2 *Macaulay and MacDougall*, 2011, by Jean Inyalanka Burke. Courtesy of Warakurna Artists.
Photo: Katie Shanahan, National Museum of Australia, nma.img-ci20122838-020

13   This is a variant of the word *Anangu*, as the Pitjantjatjara pronounce it.

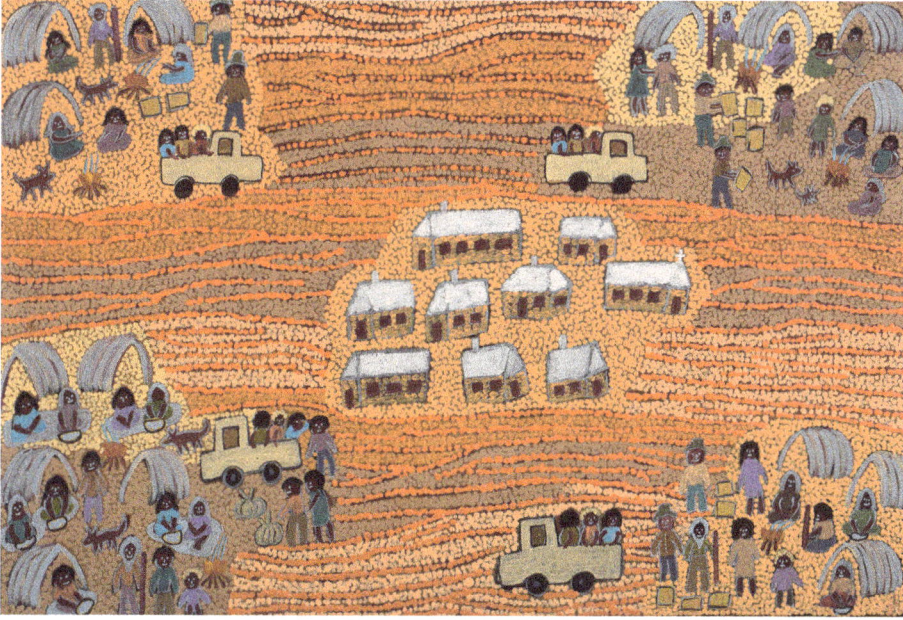

Figure 8.3 *Mr MacDougall and Tommy Dodd*, 2011, by Judith Yinyika Chambers. Courtesy of Warakurna Artists.
Photo: Katie Shanahan, National Museum of Australia, nma.img-ci20122838-016

Rather than the instruments of an anonymous 'Weapons Research Establishment', patrol officers were viewed as people with whom Yarnangu had real engagements. Early contact history is seen through the lens of interpersonal relationships with known individuals. Yarnangu regard themselves as active agents in their resettlement history, rather than passively responding to changes in external circumstances.

People from the Warakurna area eventually took up residence at Warburton, 250 km to the south-west, where the United Aborigines Mission (UAM) established a settlement in 1934. At Warburton, children lived in the dormitory and were looked after by missionaries while attending school. Despite the mission's intervention, children continued to maintain a connection with families and country. In Eunice Porter's paintings, the close proximity of children and parents can be seen in *Waiting for Shop*, in which children are depicted lining up for school as parents wait outside the nearby shop. Adults exchanged dingo skins for rations, which were used to supplement a traditional diet. The related painting, titled *Holiday Time*, shows children returning home during the school holidays to be with parents who were living on country, where they would engage in a range of traditional activities (see Brooks and Plant, this volume). Porter remembers fondly these times spent with family on country. 'At night the children went to sleep. The mothers and fathers would dance and sing. It was a good time.'

Figure 8.4 *Waiting for Shop*, 2011, by Eunice Yunurupa Porter. Courtesy of Warakurna Artists.

Photo: Katie Shanahan, National Museum of Australia, nma.img-ci20122838-023

Figure 8.5 *Holiday Time*, 2011, by Eunice Yunurupa Porter. Courtesy of Warakurna Artists.

Photo: Katie Shanahan, National Museum of Australia, nma.img-ci20122838-022

When a settlement for Aboriginal people was established at Docker River in 1968 (see Long, this volume), Yarnangu with affiliations to the Warakurna area moved there to be closer to their homelands. *Warburton Mission Leaving Time* by Judith Chambers shows people packing up and leaving Warburton for Docker River.

'People heard about the new settlement starting up at Docker River. That was near our Ngurra [country] in the east so my family went there,' the artist recalls.

Figure 8.6 *Warburton Mission Leaving Time*, 2011, by Judith Yinyika Chambers. Courtesy of Warakurna Artists.
Photo: Katie Shanahan, National Museum of Australia, nma.img-ci20122838-024

After 1969, as part of changing policies, Aboriginal people were paid their own social security benefits individually. The ability to manage their own cash increased their capacity to purchase and manage their own vehicles. A graded road between Giles and Docker River made Warakurna accessible by car. The road and amenities available to staff at Giles Meteorological Station attracted increasing numbers of Ngaanyatjarra people back to their country. By 1973, a reasonably stable population was established near the weather station, which then attracted support from the Department of Aboriginal Affairs (Coombs 1974: 10). Limited assistance could be provided by the weather station, although as the population increased to more than 200 people, the relationship with station personnel was tested (Day 2007: 393).

The entangled history of the weather station and the Warakurna community can be read as simulacra of wider political shifts taking place federally. Formerly run by the Department of Supply, Giles was taken over by the Bureau of Meteorology in 1972. Significantly, the change of management took place within a milieu of growing support for Indigenous people's aspirations to live in a manner of their own choosing. According to Day's (2007) account, the bureau's more relaxed approach and the growing assertiveness of the local Aboriginal community were factors contributing to an uneasy relationship. He writes:

> Previously, there had been strict rules regarding the relations between station staff and the indigenous inhabitants, with a view to protecting the latter's traditional lifestyle. But the increased contact as a result of the missions and the station's presence inevitably eroded that lifestyle. By the 1970s, Aboriginal people around Giles were living radically different lives. In one way they were more independent, controlling their own communities, but they were also increasingly dependent on European foodstuffs and other material goods. (Day 2007: 393)

Day goes on to describe these as 'testing times', yet the weather station continued to operate, because its value 'was too great for it to be lightly abandoned' (Day 2007: 394). Amee Glass, a linguist with the Summer Institute of Linguistics working for the Warburton Bible Project, saw the weather station as critical in the history of the outstation: 'As I recall their first community adviser was someone who had been a weather station employee and left that job to become the community adviser.'[14]

As Warakurna developed, other groups living at Docker River and Warburton were planning moves back to the Blackstone and Cavenagh ranges. The painting *Going Home* by Eunice Porter captures the process of decentralisation as it unfolded in the Ngaanyatjarra Lands in 1973. She tells of a 'big meeting' with the Government at Warburton, after which people went their separate ways. In the bottom right-hand corner, the painting depicts groups of people having a meeting. Moving clockwise, distinct groups are shown rolling swags and loading trucks to go back to their separate homelands. Lines in the centre represent the roads on which they travelled.

---

14   Email from Amee Glass to the author, 15 June 2012.

Figure 8.7 *Going Home*, 2011, by Eunice Yunurupa Porter. Courtesy of Warakurna Artists.

Photo: Katie Shanahan, National Museum of Australia, nma.img-ci20122838-026

The implementation of the Commonwealth's self-determination policy is the subject of the collaborative painting *Cutline, Warakurna to Warburton* by Judith Chambers, Dorcas Bennett and Martha Ward. Under the Commonwealth's new policy, the Warakurna community was able to initiate its own projects with government backing. The priority for the newly formed Warakurna Council was the construction of a road to Warburton to replace the existing route that had been graded by Len Beadell of Gunbarrel Highway fame. 'The Commonwealth paid people a wage at Warakurna—that was how it was started' (Amee Glass, interview, 22 February 2013).

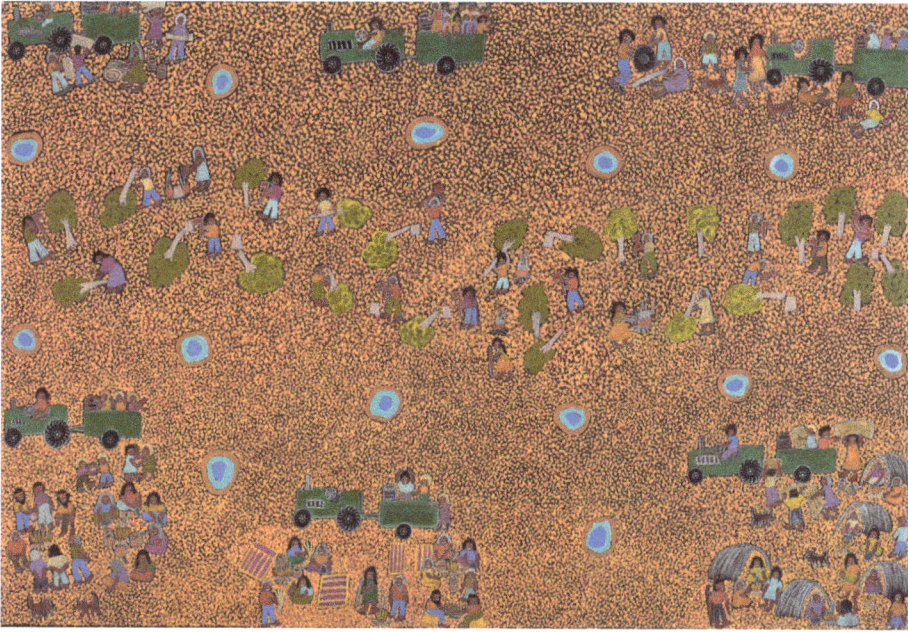

Figure 8.8 *Cutline, Warakurna to Warburton*, 2011, by Judith Yinyika Chambers, Martha Ward and Dorcas Tinamayi Bennett. Courtesy of Warakurna Artists.

Photo: Katie Shanahan, National Museum of Australia, nma.img-ci20122838-042

The new road was cleared by hand, depicted as a ribbon of activity running through the centre of the painting. The route followed a series of rockholes between Warburton and Warakurna, which are shown on either side. Teams from Warakurna and Warburton worked on the route from both ends, using axes. People who remember the road have differing points of view—rough road or signal achievement: 'It was extremely rough to drive over because of the ant bed', according to Glass:

> [I]n those days they had no money. The problem was the roads were the responsibility of the Shire and no Yarnangu were represented on the Council. When universal suffrage came in, Ian Newberry's father was the first person on the Council. That was probably when they first graded the road. (Amee Glass, interview, 22 February 2013)

Although the condition of the road was poor by current standards, Ngaanyatjarra accounts focus on the collaborative project of building the road and what it meant to be working on projects they had conceived themselves. *Cutline, Warakurna to Warburton* celebrates the achievements of the fledgling community as a collective. 'All the families helped', recalled Judith Chambers, 'even the kids came along'.

Building a future

The views of outstation history depicted in the Warakurna paintings are similar in many respects to the comments made by Pintupi respondents when interviewed about Yayayi (Myers, this volume)—comments that emphasised self-reliance and their own agency in separating from Papunya. The Warakurna paintings convey a sense of pride in what people were able to achieve as a collective by returning to country and working together to build their future in the 1970s.

Maisie Nungurrayi, one of a younger generation who paints for Warakurna Artists, has spoken of the importance of art to Western Desert communities: '*Tjukurrpa watjalku paintingmara, ngurra nyuntupa Countrytjarra. And yanku malaku nyaku mularrpa ngaanya* [When you paint you are telling stories about your country. Then you will go back and see those actual places] (Nungurrayi Ward 2011).[15]

For Yarnangu artists, paintings and their stories are grounded in the physicality of place. The act of painting connects the artist with their country through their imaginations, yet this is not enough. The paintings and the stories *oblige* the artist to reconnect physically with those places. 'You *will* go back', in the words of Maisie.

Painting, in this sense, has a role to play in reaffirming values and shaping future action. In the process of painting, certain narratives tend to reoccur and become dominant as they are communicated and consensually validated. Narratives are resources that can be drawn on to imagine how an ideal future would look (Elliott 1999). Acrylic paintings complement deeply held values and compelling narratives, conveying to others a sense of the world as it is and should be. The sharing of stories through paintings thus helps strengthen the resolve of the community and provides direction for people to move forward in accordance with their values.

Given the way in which painting may serve to orient people towards a future of their own conception, the AAB's marrying of art and self-determination was, in principle, well conceived. While the board's decisions were constrained by competing interests and priorities, its financial support was critical to the success of the acrylic painting movement in the first decade. In their dealings with the AAB, Pintupi were able to formulate their own goals and saw the potential of art sales to generate income for their own projects. At the meeting attended by Bob Edwards at Yayayi, Pintupi leaders were clear about what they wanted

---

15   Maisie lives at Warnarn, an outstation south-west of Warakurna and paints for Warakurna Artists. Her father, Yunmul Tjapaltjarri (known to many as 'Doctor George'), worked as the *ngangkari* (traditional healer) for the Pintupi medical service in the 1980s and was a painter for Papunya Tula in the 1970s.

to achieve and the resources required to make it happen. Emboldened by past achievements, Pintupi have been able to approach the future at each turn with a renewed sense of confidence.

Stories of success are popular among Western Desert people today—how they established their own outstations, art centres and health services, how they did not need to wait for government, and so on. The incorporation of these kinds of stories into contemporary discourse has potential to mobilise people to work together towards a future of their own choice and to make it a reality. There is a link between positive affirmation of the desire for particular outcomes and the likelihood of those outcomes occurring. Western Desert communities are now at a critical juncture. Those who experienced a significant part of their life in the bush have all but passed on. The current generation of artists is aware of the challenge of sustaining homeland communities in the face of dwindling knowledge of country, and visual imagery is increasingly being used to convey a sense of how people got to be where they are today.

The shift to documentary forms of painting and increased interest in archival film and photography suggest a greater self-consciousness among Western Desert communities in how the past is viewed and linked to the future.[16] Art is being used not only to record history but also to provide commentary on what is happening now, as witnessed in the form of paintings that document the process of art-making itself and other contemporary issues such as land management and governance. It is unclear whether works based on these types of narratives will prove to be commercially viable, yet the intention of this emerging practice appears to be directed as much inwardly as to engage or appease an external market. Western Desert people today, it seems, are commenting on their own practice and reflecting on their past more often and in different ways, as the need to understand and communicate where they have come from becomes increasingly vital to the well-being and longevity of their communities.

References

Altman, J. 1988. The economic domain. In M. West (ed.), *The Inspired Dream*. Brisbane: Queensland Art Gallery.

Art of Aboriginal Australia 1974. Exhibition Catalogue. Canada: Rothmans of Pall Mall.

---

16 The significance attached to photographic images seems to be shifting in the Western Desert along with understandings of history and the desire to engage with the past (cf. Thorley 2002). The emergence of new painting forms may be linked to the way Western Desert people are viewing themselves in film and other visual media. The relaxing of restrictions on photographic materials appears to be a related phenomenon.

Bardon, G. and Bardon J. 2004. *Papunya: A Place Made after the Story*. Melbourne: Miegunyah Press.

Berrell, N. 2009. Inroads offshore: The international exhibition program of the Aboriginal Arts Board, 1973–1980. *ReCollections* 4(1).

Coombs, H. C. 1974. Decentralisation trends among Aboriginal communities. *Department of Aboriginal Affairs Western Australia Newsletter* 1(8): 4–25.

Day, D. 2007. *The Weather Watchers: 100 Years of the Bureau of Meteorology*. Melbourne: Melbourne University Publishing.

Edwards, R. 2004. Foreword. In G. Bardon and J. Bardon (eds), *Papunya: A Place Made after the Story*. Melbourne: Miegunyah Press.

Elliot, C. 1999. *Locating the Energy for Change: An Introduction to Appreciative Inquiry*. Winnipeg: International Institute for Sustainable Development.

Johnson, V. 2007. When Papunya paintings became art. In V. Johnson (ed.), *Papunya Painting: Out of the Desert*. Exhibition Catalogue. Canberra: National Museum of Australia.

Johnson, V. 2008. *Lives of the Papunya Tula Artists*. Alice Springs, NT: Institute for Aboriginal Development.

Morton, P. 1987. *Fire across the Desert: Woomera and the Anglo-Australian Joint Project 1946–1980*. Canberra: Australian Government Publishing Service.

Myers, F. R. 2002. *Painting Culture: The Making of an Aboriginal High Art*. Durham, NC: Duke University Press.

Myers, F. R. 2007. A day in the life: Painting at Yayayi 1974. In V. Johnson (ed.), *Papunya Painting: Out of the Desert*. Exhibition Catalogue. Canberra: National Museum of Australia.

Nungurrayi Ward, M. 2011. *In Yurliya Gallery*. [Film]. Wingellina, WA: Ngaanyatjarra Media.

Perkins, H. 2009. Preface. In R. Benjamin with A. Weislogel (eds), *Icons of the Desert: Early Aboriginal Paintings from Papunya*. Ithaca, NY: Herbert F. Johnson Museum of Art/Cornell University.

Rowse, T. 2000. *Obliged to be Difficult: Nugget Coombs' Legacy in Indigenous Affairs*. Melbourne: Cambridge University Press.

Thorley, P. 2002. Current realities, idealised pasts: Archaeology, values and Indigenous heritage management in Central Australia. *Oceania* 73(2): 110–25.

POLICY VISIONS AND
THEIR REALISATION

9

What was Dr Coombs thinking? Nyirrpi, policy and the future

Nicolas Peterson[1]

On 5 May 1972, I set out from Yuendumu with six older Warlpiri men on my first bush trip to visit the Waite Creek area on the southern portion of Mount Doreen Station, more than 400 km west of Alice Springs. We visited a number of sites, including the important sacred site of Warntungurru, belonging to people of the J/Nampijinpa-J/Nangala patricouple, marked by a metre-high vertical stone 100 m or so from the creek. We drove south alongside the creek on a station track, stopping off to see various soakages in the creek bed. One of these places was Nyirrpi,[2] a soakage at the edge of the creek adjacent to a clump of trees that formed a very small island in the middle of it, approximately 125 km from Yuendumu as the crow flies. It was remote, the nearest occupied place being the station homestead 40 km to the north.

1   I would like to acknowledge many stimulating conversations with Maggie Brady, Paul Burke, Francoise Dussart, Julie Finlayson, Robert Graham, Anna Kenny, Dick Kimber, Mary Laughren, Francesca Merlan, Yasmine Musharbash, Fred Myers and David Nash about issues relating directly to this chapter. I would also like to thank Frank Baarda and Wendy Baarda for their comments and assistance, and to acknowledge how welcoming and helpful they have always been over so many years. Thanks too to Ormay Gallagher for sharing her history of Nyirrpi.
2   Nyirrpi is the correct spelling of the place name. However, when registered with the Government, it was spelt Nyirripi and that is now the name that appears on some maps.

Warntungurru was the conception site of Jilijanka Jampijinpa, which lay at the heart of his patrilineal estate. I did not spend long there but left Jilijanka and Wanyu Jampijinpa to cut slabs from mulga trees in the vicinity from which to make sacred boards. I travelled a bit further south with four other men to a large clay pan, Walyka, still full of water and covered in emu tracks, and then to Kurdjinyungu, which was created by a pair of kangaroos, one a plains kangaroo and the other a hill kangaroo that are celebrated in some versions of the male circumcision rites. As far as I am aware, there was no talk of an outstation at Nyirrpi or elsewhere at the time, although in the following months Jilijanka and his brother indicated that they would like to live there.

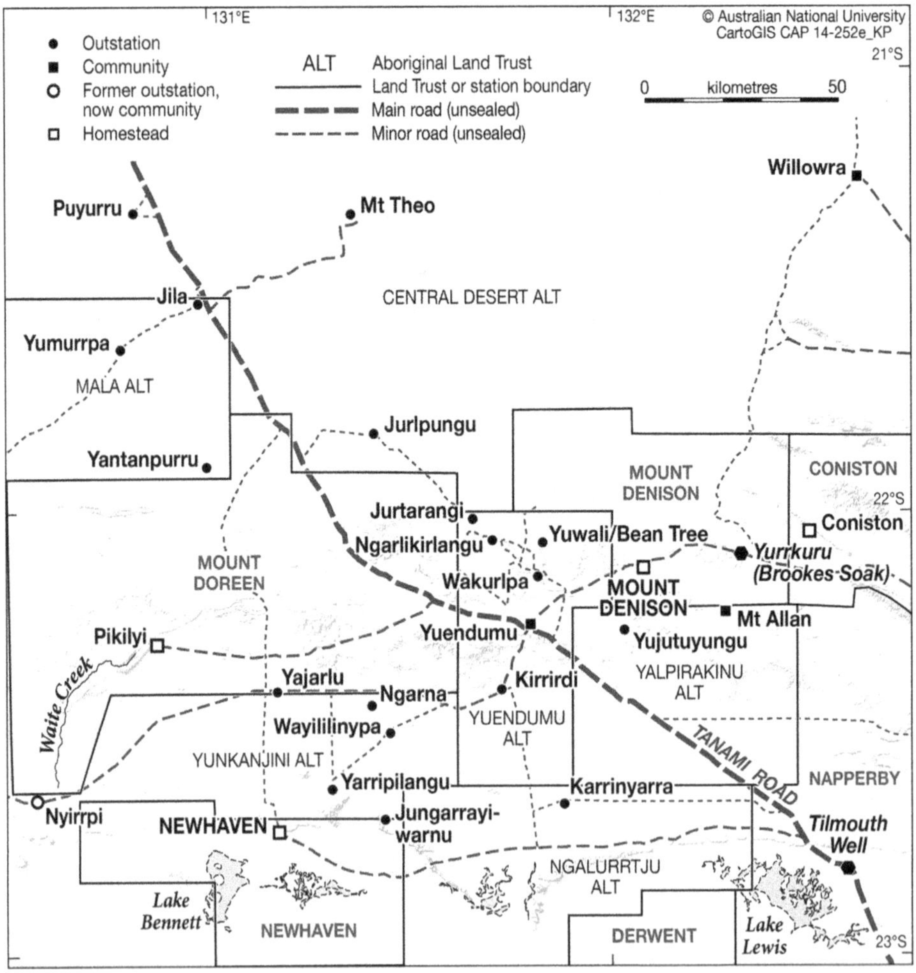

Map 9.1 Nyirrpi in relation to Yuendumu and outstations with infrastructure, although none were currently occupied other than Mount Theo, to which petrol sniffers were taken for rehabilitation at the time of writing.

Source: Karina Pelling, CartoGIS, ANU College of Asia and the Pacific

Amazingly (that is the correct word), by the 1980s Nyirrpi had become a flourishing small community that is now a quite independent village of about 250 people. Just how this came about and what it says about the envisioned future for and by Warlpiri people, and by extension other remote Aboriginal populations, are what I want to explore.

Nyirrpi would never have happened, of course, if Jilijanka and his relatives were not deeply desirous of and committed to living there, but they had none of the obviously needed formal skills required to marshal government monies and support to get a settlement off the ground. So what was the thinking that put government policy into reverse, that switched from a century of concentrating people into settlements closer to urban centres where they were to learn the skills that would eventually help them take a place in mainstream Australian society?[3] How did it seem sensible to encourage people to live 125 km more remotely than the already remote community of Yuendumu, 300 km north-west of Alice Springs? Nyirrpi raises these questions in a particularly apt way, because Dr H. C. ('Nugget') Coombs was not only influential in Aboriginal policymaking at this time, but together with the anthropologist W. E. H. Stanner, he also made a visit to Yuendumu and wrote a report (Coombs and Stanner 1974) on the visit, which, among other things, dealt with the emergent outstation issue in the area.

Although the focus here is on the policymakers, I would, of course, like to know more of the Aboriginal protagonists' views. Even though I made a number of visits to Yuendumu after 1973, my focus was always to the north and it was not until the 1990s that I discovered that a township had grown up at Nyirrpi. As a result, I never did ask any of the original Aboriginal proponents their views, and all are now dead. So the principal sources I have for understanding the Aboriginal perspective are the same departmental records that I am drawing on to get an insight into the thinking and visions of the policymakers and administrators.

---

3   See Long (this volume). Reacting to the proposal for a depot in the Petermann Ranges in January 1959, the Department of Territories in Canberra responded that it was 'necessary to encourage movement to more settled areas' and if the area in the ranges was 'suitable for pastoral purposes just as much opportunity could be provided by making the land available to private enterprise'. Long says that since Paul Hasluck was the Minister for Territories and took a very close interest in Territory affairs, he was probably responsible for the reply, which is really entailed by the policy of assimilation that he strongly espoused.

Figure 9.1 Lunch near Nyirrpi on 5 May 1972.

From left to right: Yarrijarriji Jampijinpa, Wanyu Jampijinpa, Jack Japanangga, Jilijanka Jampijinpa, Long Paddy Jangala and Jack Jampijinpa.

Photo: Nicolas Peterson

Initial moves

Unbeknown to me, in 1970, a close countryman of Jilijanka's and a number of other men had been driven out beyond Nyirrpi to the even more remote location of Ethel Creek, to the north-west, by the superintendent of Yuendumu to leave petrol, water and some food there for a future outstation. The departmental files offer no evidence for the stimulation for the 1970 trip. This was before the Gibb Committee report '[t]o review the situation of Aborigines on pastoral properties in the Northern Territory' (in December 1971), in which recently reformulated government policy was quoted: 'The Government recognises the rights of individual Aborigines to effective choice about the degree to which and the pace at which they come to identify themselves with … [mainstream] society' (Gibb 1971: 4). And before the 1972 Australia Day speech of Prime Minister William McMahon in which he announced the end of assimilation in very similar terms (Griffiths 1995: 119)—perhaps not surprisingly given that Nugget Coombs was a member of the Gibb Committee and also of the Council for Aboriginal Affairs, which was advising the Liberal–National Party Coalition Government on policy issues in this area.

There were, however, hints of the outstation movement further north in Arnhem Land, where the development of the North Australian Bauxite and Alumina Company (Nabalco) mine was causing tensions, as Stanner, anthropologist and member of the Council for Aboriginal Affairs, found during his visit to Yirrkala from 18 to 25 November 1969 (Rowse 2000: 81). Other precursors to the outstation movement had existed in north-east Arnhem Land since the late 1940s, where small, bush-living groups were serviced by plane by the Reverend Harold Shepherdson. Djurrpum of the Marapai-Guyula clan became the recognised authority on making outstation airstrips. In 1959, he and his team cleared one on the Koolatong River where the soil was excellent for gardening and there were many crocodiles available in the river to be hunted for their skins. Later in the same year, the team went to Mirrngadja to clear an airstrip, with the first flight in August 1960. There were strips at Caledon Bay, Matta Matta and elsewhere on the coast so that the news Stanner brought back from Yirrkala that people were thinking of moving back to their country late in 1969 because of the mining developments made complete sense locally even if it caught members of the Council for Aboriginal Affairs by surprise (Rowse 2000: 83–84; 2012: 184). The question of whether there was any connection through the administration of what was threatened in Arnhem Land and the readiness of the Yuendumu superintendent a few months later to take people to a remote area to establish an outstation is unanswered.

On 5 February 1973, the Warlpiri man who had been a key party in the 1970 trip approached me to write to the Minister for Aboriginal Affairs asking for a bore to be put down in his Ethel Creek country (see Appendix 9.1). By the end of the year, this man, Jungarrayi, had had assistance, presumably from the community adviser at Yuendumu, to put in for a grant for a vehicle in relation to the desire 'of himself plus 20 other men and their families [for] … an outstation to be established at Ngarapula [Ngarapalya]'.[4] A year later, in March 1974, the people in the Ethel Creek group, who also had a connection to Nyirrpi, formed their own separate group as even they felt Ethel Creek was too far away.[5]

By 1974 the funding for outstations was well established. This was a direct consequence of McMahon's 1972 Australia Day speech about the right to choice of lifestyle, and stimulated in Arnhem Land at least by the questioning associated with the visits of the Royal Commission into Aboriginal Land Rights (the Woodward Commission) to communities, when people were asked about the use they would make of the land once they had it back.

---

4   National Archives of Australia (hereinafter NAA): F1, 1973/9595, Movement of Wailbri Sub Group (Banjo Jungarai) to Ngarapula west of Yuendumu (Ethel Ck) (Walwuma): 92. NAA can be accessed online.
5   ibid.: 4: 155.

In January 1974, the criteria for funding of such resettlement were:

1. number of people
2. extent of organisation shown by group
   a. voluntary action
   b. non-voluntary action
3. identification of felt needs and priorities as expressed by the community
4. extent to which group proposes to be self-sustaining (cash inflow, food and satisfaction of other basic needs)
5. potential of project to be self-sustaining
6. infrastructure of communication links available to community
7. social visibility.[6]

The Department of Aboriginal Affairs (DAA) office in Alice Springs had received instructions to support such groups from Canberra, provided they met these criteria.[7]

Things moved quite quickly for the members of the Nyirrpi group. They formed their own committee, the Nyirrpi Town Council,[8] but as a newly formed group in March 1974 it seems clear that their ideas about the outstations were very vague as far as the DAA was concerned, especially in relation to how they would support themselves.[9] But by May people were much clearer about what they would do at Nyirrpi. They indicated they would run some cattle and so would need materials for fencing, a truck and a shed. They would also establish a vegetable garden and probably build an airstrip.[10] Some people would live there permanently and others would use it as a holiday spot.

The Coombs–Stanner report on Yuendumu

At this point, Coombs' ideas on policy as they relate to the Warlpiri become quite explicit. He decided in the light of the 'tensions and apparent breakdown in social control' in some remote communities under self-determination (Rowse 2000: 138) that he would visit Yuendumu and Hooker Creek, subsequently renamed Lajamanu, to find out what was going on. Stanner joined him on the trip and together they wrote and published their *Report on Visit to Yuendumu and Hooker Creek* (Coombs and Stanner 1974). A dual concern runs through

---

6   ibid.: 92.
7   ibid.: 90.
8   NAA: E460, 1979/700, Movement of Aborigines from Yuendumu to Waite Creek—Nirrpi: 91.
9   NAA: F133, 1977/222 Part 1A, Yuendumu Outstations, File No. 74/9: 155.
10   NAA: E460, 1979/700: 90, 87.

the report. On the one hand, they were concerned that Warlpiri people had the option of preserving their 'traditional Aboriginal life style' (Coombs and Stanner 1974: 3), but on the other, the more dominant concern was with issues of development, the management of alcohol and improving Warlpiri involvement in the running of the new community council.

In respect of preserving the option of the traditional lifestyle, they recommend that:

> Policy be directed to ensuring that Aborigines are not forced by economic and social pressures to accept a European style of life if they would prefer a simpler more traditional style: i.e. that Aborigines be allowed and helped to adapt freely to their own requirements and circumstances [and] such white Australian practices as they consider to be of value to them. To this end—
>
> a. decentralisation moves initiated by Aborigines should be assisted and efforts made to keep the new groupings small and closer in style to the traditional Aboriginal way;
> b. even when European style housing is available there should be the choice of a camp which is simple and traditional but sanitary and visually pleasant;
> c. offers of employment should be made which do not necessarily require full entry into the work force—e.g. for a shorter working week, for periods of some weeks or months interrupted by periods of unpaid leisure, by contracts let to groups or communities;
> d. efforts should be made to develop sources of income for Aborigines compatible with the chosen life style and if possible deriving impetus from it (e.g. traditional artefacts or crafts based on a traditional skill or design). (Coombs and Stanner 1974: 3–4)

Stanner's surprise at just how intact local traditions were in Yirrkala in November 1969 (Rowse 2000: 81) was probably mirrored at Yuendumu, although nothing is said explicitly about this in the report. However, the report speaks of the 'vigorous' ceremonial life and ground paintings of 'great beauty' still being created and used for the instruction of the young men; that generally the influence of Aboriginal tradition appears to remain strong; and that almost all of the decentralisation moves contemplated are concerned at least in part with protection of, and opportunities to visit, sites of importance (Coombs and Stanner 1974: 14, see also p. 22).

This all suggests that they were impressed with the strength of Warlpiri culture, which I can certainly vouch for at that period, but it also suggests that like many outsiders at that time they were talking to the older men and women in the community and probably more influenced by helping them realise visions of the future that were heavily influenced by the past, rather than thinking of the younger generations and the future that was facing them. Indeed, one of the weakest features of the report is the information under demography that presents no analysis of the structure of the population other than providing the gender ratio, rather than looking at age cohorts and what they might suggest about population growth.

I think this reflects the thinking behind much policy formation coming out of the Council for Aboriginal Affairs: catering to the needs of the older generation who would never need to face a lifetime dealing with the market economy post de-institutionalisation—that is, since the creation of community councils in the 1972–75 period. The thinking behind the report is gradualist, its most forward-looking element being the concern with making the councils work better. The issue of what the growing population would be doing in 10 or 20 years is nowhere explicitly addressed, nor is there any anthropological insight into the social and cultural dynamics of the situation, or thought given to Aboriginal motivation. It is assumed that in getting the political structure, Warlpiri would be enabled to choose their path into the future.

Two paragraphs are particularly revealing:

> Some see this acquisition of more and more sophisticated and complex needs and demands as wholly desirable and as evidence of Aborigines achieving a higher level of civilisation integrating more completely into our society and being motivated more strongly to accept the obligation and the discipline of work.

> But it cannot be denied that it progressively tends to impose on the Aborigines concerned a way of life which in some respects is distasteful to many of them, which brings them together in larger communities than their traditional social disciplines can readily manage. (Coombs and Stanner 1974: 19–20)

There is an extensive discussion of a number of sensible and practical economic possibilities in respect to craft, environmental management, cattle work, mining, getting the majority of young people into paid employment and the involvement of Aboriginal people in the provision of community services, building infrastructure and maintenance (Coombs and Stanner 1974: 5, 11). This manifests a clear concern with young men in particular (Coombs and Stanner 1974: 19), in relation to providing training and work that generated income for the community. Even so, decentralisation also receives considerable attention, and they comment:

> It is our view that policy should be directed to facilitating this movement for those Aborigines who wish to take part in it. This is necessary if Aborigines are to have effective choice as to whether and at what pace they wish to accept the European way of life. (Coombs and Stanner 1974: 20)

The establishment of Nyirrpi

A major issue facing the group was the actual location of Nyirrpi. The problem was that Nyirrpi, chosen for its enduring soakage water, was on Mount Doreen Station, owned by W. Braitling, who did not want an outstation on his land. So either there had to be an excision from the station area or the location of the outstation would have to be moved beyond the southern boundary to an area of vacant Crown land.[11] A related issue was the location of the access road to Nyirrpi, which Braitling wanted to be off the station area as well.

The Yuendumu community adviser at the time, Graham Castine, was diligent in helping the Nyirrpi leaders write letters, and on 8 May 1974, named the 21 men who were involved in wanting to set up the outstation and indicated that between them these men had 35 wives and 53 children. By July 1974, the demand to establish new outstations among the people at Yuendumu was developing momentum and two more groups, in addition to the Ethel Creek group, were seeking money for vehicles. Coombs and Stanner mentioned that there were about 130 people who wished to move 90 km north of Yuendumu to Mount Theo in the heart of the Tanami Desert: as they comment, 'the Tanami desert is extremely arid' and the 'project seems difficult' (Coombs and Stanner 1974: 21), and then there was the Nyirrpi group, said to number approximately 60 people.[12]

Vehicles for all three groups were approved in October 1974 but they were quickly a source of problems because in the first five months they were used continuously for 'flagon runs' and only once for a trip to an outstation location. Use of the Nyirrpi vehicle was brought to an end when it was impounded for being involved in a fatal accident.[13] The then community adviser, Roger Styles, indicated that he had made it clear that it was not his role to control the use of the vehicle, as he was being asked to, but that the leaders of the groups had to be prepared to take on the responsibilities that went with running an outstation.[14] Further, it was a requirement that people showed they were prepared to stay at their outstation. It was recognised that an obstacle to the appropriate use of the vehicles was that there were no appropriate roads and that many Yuendumu residents had been tied up fighting bushfires, preventing them either building roads or occupying the outstation. Later, when it emerged that sales tax was

---

11   ibid.: 87.
12   NAA: F1, 1973/9595: 80.
13   ibid.: 24, 12; 7: 37.
14   NAA: E460, 1979/700: 57.

owing on the vehicle, it was required that each group contribute at least $200 of their own income to pay this to show that they were committed to their outstations.[15]

On 8 and 9 April 1975, the new community adviser, Paul Ashe, took the men out to Nyirrpi using the Museum Society's vehicle, as he had not been allocated one as part of his job.[16] The purpose of the meeting was to speak with Braitling, the Mount Doreen Station owner, to see if it was possible to have the outstation at Nyirrpi, but Braitling made it absolutely clear that he was not keen on the idea.

April was a turning point for many older people at Yuendumu. There had been a lot of breaking and entering.[17] Pressure was brought to bear on the council to do something about it, particularly by the school. A range of methods was tried:

> Including seeing the parent of the children, payment of compensation by parents, chastising the children in front of their parents, patrols around the Settlement etc. etc., all of which had very little effect. Finally it was decided that the offenders, if caught on two consecutive occasions for breaking and entering, would be taken bush for a period of time, preferably in their own tribal country. It was therefore resolved that initially three children who were second offenders would be taken bush accompanied by a handful of old men.[18]

Much to the surprise of the community adviser, at a council meeting on 11 April, the council had a list of 27 children, both first and second offenders, whom they wanted to take bush. It seems that most were accompanied by their parents because of the latters' concern about their welfare there. Because the community adviser's job did not come with a vehicle, he was unable to check what was going on at the outstations as a consequence of this decision, but he had reports shortly after the move that about 100 people were camped at Julpungu, the closest of the outstations to Yuendumu, under the leadership of Jimija Jungarrayi. On Saturday, 12 April, the day after the council meeting, about 60 people set off for Nyirrpi, but their transport broke down at Cusacks Bore.[19]

The party got no further than the bore, but in June 1975, men from the group were cutting a new line of road just to the south of the Mount Doreen Station boundary on vacant Crown land and had completed the first 25 km of the total 125 km required. By the end of July, the men had completed 70 km.[20] In reporting this work, the community adviser commented that the Nyirrpi

15 ibid.: 15.
16 ibid.: 36–34.
17 NAA: F1, 1973/4638, Yuendumu Disturbances: 10, 7, 9, 16.
18 NAA: F133, 1977/222 Part 1A: 106
19 ibid.: 105.
20 ibid.: 4, 77, 60–62.

group 'is the only group that has shown any real initiative in trying to establish an outstation'. He also pointed out that without a vehicle it was difficult for him to monitor the outstation movement.[21]

Reflecting on how the outstation movement could be better managed on 30 October 1975, the community adviser commented that it was a vital mistake to supply vehicles and trailers to the groups before they had indicated any physical move to outstation areas. This was because it created the impression that the setting up of outstations was the responsibility of the Government and virtually the only responsibility that the people had was to move to the area.[22] He was of the opinion that groups might still move even when they realised no more supportive resources would be forthcoming until they left Yuendumu. Indeed, in December 1975, it was reported that the Nyirrpi men were spending up to six weeks at a time out at Nyirrpi but that they rarely took their wives or children because until the bore drilling for a long-term supply of water had taken place there could be no permanent population.[23]

In August 1976, the regional director of Aboriginal Affairs wrote a curt file note saying he was 'somewhat staggered to be told when visiting Yuendumu on the 29th July that groups had moved out to two outstations', Ethel Creek and Mount Theo, because he had heard nothing from the community adviser about this in the previous nine months.[24] This prompted a four-page report from the community adviser, which indicated that the regional director's understanding was wrong. No one was at the places mentioned and the only people beyond Yuendumu were the 30–50 people living at Nyirrpi. Things were looking good for them because not only had adequate water been found at a depth of about 140 m to the south of the Mount Doreen Station boundary, but also Braitling had no objection to them camping at the Nyirrpi soakage on the station, where they had been since mid-May, until they could move to the new location. Further, the Yuendumu Social Club was providing financial support and the group was existing on a grant of $40 per fortnight on top of their own pensions and child endowment payments.[25]

At this date the community adviser estimated that the numbers of people who would live at the various outstations would be: Nyirrpi, 50–70; Julpungu (Djulpung), 30–40; Nyinyiriplangu, 30–40(?); Wanuyaka (that is, Mount Theo), 30–40(?).[26]

---

21 ibid.: 60–62.
22 ibid.: 42.
23 ibid.: 34.
24 ibid.: c25.
25 ibid.: 21c–d.
26 ibid.: 21d.

By October 1977, people had been living at Nyirrpi for two years and it was the most stable of all the outstations,[27] and in that same month a bore was equipped 11 km to the south of the Nyirrpi soakage outside the southern boundary of Mount Doreen Station.[28] It is not clear when the Nyirrpi people moved from Nyirrpi to Jitilparnta, but it was probably sometime in late 1977 or early 1978, and by October 1977, they were back at the original Nyirrpi because of the unserviceability of the windmill at Jitilparnta.[29] Because the outstation was known to everybody as Nyirrpi, the decision was made to keeping calling the permanent outstation at Jitilparnta, Nyirrpi, which I will occasionally call Nyirrpi 2 if clarification is needed.

Roy Fry Jangala spelt out the list of needs to make Nyirrpi 2 viable. These included the grading of the road from Kerridi to Nyirrpi, an airstrip, a new vehicle to replace the four-year-old one and a small tractor. Gardens had been established there but the dwellings were only of natural materials and tarpaulins. At that time, 10 members were receiving unemployment benefits;[30] however, the population was still only 20 at Nyirrpi, but the need for tents was spelt out.

In July 1978, Susan Kesteven visited Yuendumu, at which time there were just two outstations, one at Julpungu and the other at Nyirrpi, but three more were established four months later (Kesteven 1978: 49): these were at Jila, Yarripilangu and Ngana. Elspeth Young also recorded an outstation at Kunajarrayi in 1981 (see Young 1981: 73–74). When Kesteven (1978: 51) visited the outstation, the bore at Nyirrpi 2 was broken and the people had moved back to the soak water at the original Nyirrpi site, where there were eight humpies. There were 40 people there: 13 men, 18 women and nine children, but no one between the ages of five and 25 other than two young wives (Kesteven 1978: 52). Roy Fry produced a map showing how he envisaged Nyirrpi, including with a vegetable garden. In September a new store manager at Yuendumu started store runs to Nyirrpi funded by social security. At that time there were six people receiving child endowment totalling $292 per fortnight, three old-age pensioners, one invalid pensioner and nine receiving unemployment payments. Elspeth Young also visited Nyirrpi in 1978 and records that the fortnightly income at the time of her visit was $1,900, with the per capita income working out at $90 (1981: 73). There were 21 people there at the time she visited. Both Young (1981: 73) and Kesteven (1978: 66) report that the men spent much of their time hunting. On the basis of her quite short visit, Kesteven makes two observations. First, the emphasis on including vegetable gardens in outstation applications for funding

---

27   ibid.: 112.
28   ibid.: 112.
29   ibid.: 86.
30   ibid.: 86–85.

was because people had the impression that the Government wanted outstations to have an economic base. Her implication is that the actual commitment to running gardens was slight. The other observation was about women's attitudes to outstations. She felt that women were slightly less enthusiastic about moving out, especially the younger ones and those who had jobs at Yuendumu. However, what they liked about the outstations was that they were quiet, there was no drinking and they were a good place to mourn—widows having to live separately and observe silence for extended periods (Kesteven 1978: 70–71).

A crucial development took place in April 1979. Dennis Jacobsen of the United Pentecostal Church (UPC) contacted the Department of Aboriginal Affairs about the possibility of establishing a mission at Nyirrpi. He claimed that he had been approached by Edwin Ross and Norman, who had invited him to visit Nyirrpi.[31] The Yuendumu Council took exception to the representative of the UPC going to Yuendumu and Nyirrpi without permission and 'chastised' the Nyirrpi people for not observing the proper procedures, but they relented and asked the Central Land Council (CLC) to issue a permit for four months to allow a mission to be established at Nyirrpi, which would be supported by resources from the metropolitan areas.

A meeting was held in Alice Springs at the Department of Aboriginal Affairs office on 10 May 1979 to explore the issue further. Present were Harry Nelson, the Reverend Dennis Jacobsen of Alice Springs, the Reverend Peter Hargraves from Canberra, John Harwood of Alice Springs, Brailsford from the DAA and Charlie (Jilijanka?) and Tiger Japaljarri from Nyirrpi.[32]

The arrival of Brother John, as he became known, to take up residence there was key to Nyirrpi's success as it provided the community with a scribe and advocate who not only could deal effectively and persistently with the Government but who also had a considerable degree of independence because of his church funding. His effectiveness was clearly seen as a threat by the Baptist missionary at Yuendumu (see Eller 1992). In August, the Reverend Kingston launched a personal attack on Brother John whom he said was not fit to live in a remote community. However, the community adviser believed that the people at Nyirrpi wanted him to stay, and there seems no doubt about this.[33] Indeed, by the end of the year, he had baptised about 18 people[34] and was later that year elected to the Yuendumu Outstation Council over the concerns of the DAA officer, and his superior, who indicated that the Government would have to wait until the Aborigines concerned 'see the light'.[35] The UPC had provided Henwood with

---

31   NAA: F133, 1977/222 Part 1, Hooker Creek and Yuendumu Outstations: 28.
32   ibid.: 27–24.
33   NAA: F133, 1977/222 Part 2, Hooker Creek and Yuendumu Outstations: 178.
34   ibid.: 148.
35   ibid.: 93, 92.

funds for a 5.5 m caravan and a substantial shed. While the visiting DAA officer felt the camp was not 'particularly clean',[36] he noted that the bore and equipment were well maintained and clean, and that Henwood was away hunting with the men. This hints, I think, at the foundations of Nyirrpi's success. With Henwood there, people could be certain that there would be water, equipment would work and that he would ensure the flow of supplies. This seems to be indirectly confirmed in a note from Jeremy Long, then deputy secretary to the DAA, on a visit to Nyirrpi in August 1981, who learnt from Henwood that he, Henwood, had been in touch with various government departments on issues ranging from seeking a solar pump for the water supply and obtaining a radio frequency for outstations to applying for Nyirrpi to be dry (that is, a no-alcohol area). There was also the matter of progressing the building of an airstrip there.[37] By November 1981, the Outstation Council had agreed to fund a shed as a shop at Nyirrpi, which was run by Ormay Gallagher for a period (Gallagher n.d.). Significantly, the note asking for the DAA to organise the purchase of the shed is signed by three Aboriginal men but the postal address is 'Rev J. R. Henwood, P.M.B. 16, Waite Creek, Via Yuendumu, NT 5751'.[38] Brother John became the storekeeper and took responsibility for supplies and transportation (Eller 1992: 9). Such a store was essential as there were more than 100 people living at Nyirrpi by January 1982 and the DAA was finding it difficult to continue to insist that emergency evacuations could be carried out via the Vaughan Springs airstrip 65 km to the north because the road was so bad that it was quicker to go to Yuendumu, two hours away.[39]

In 1984, the DAA was persuaded to erect five two-bedroom sheds there, and in 1985 the Centre for Appropriate Technology (see Mayne 2014) erected six pit lavatories. In the same year, the Department of Education started funding an outstation teacher because there were more than the minimum number of schoolchildren living at Nyirrpi permanently. This position was taken by Wendy Baarda from Yuendumu, who would teach at Nyirrpi on Mondays and Tuesdays, return to Yuendumu on Wednesdays to prepare lessons and then drive back to Nyirrpi on Thursdays before returning to Yuendumu on Fridays. Wendy was a pillar of the bilingual program and the first year of her teaching beneath a tree was dedicated to Warlpiri literacy. She was assisted by Nyirrpi residents Pauline Gallagher and Fiona Dixon. After two years, some of the older children could read and write Warlpiri very well and were also reading in English. Two years later, a permanent building had been erected for the school (Gallagher n.d.). Nyirrpi was clearly on the way to becoming a permanent settlement. Although specific evidence has not yet been found to show Brother John's hand in the

---

36 ibid.: 178.
37 ibid.: 58, 60.
38 ibid.: 25.
39 ibid.: 19.

housing, it seems highly likely that he had a key role. Also important was the support from the Outstation Council and its employee Peter Bartlett for the building of the first houses, and in 1985–86 the first two substantial houses were built (Morel and Ross 1993: 39). With the Government now providing housing and education, the servicing of the community, and its future, took on a life of its own.

Plans for outstations at Yampiri, Yaripilung, Mount Theo in the Tanami Desert proper, and at Ngalikirlungu, although being seriously considered in the late 1970s, never resulted in the establishment of long-term settlements, even though it was estimated that more than 100 people might move to Mount Theo and more than 50 to Ngalikirlungu Bore.[40]

Conclusion

Without doubt Nugget Coombs was the key influence in policy formation in the period 1967–76 when he chaired the Council for Aboriginal Affairs, although both Stanner and Dexter were clearly also important influences on his thinking. This period saw the development of the land rights, self-determination and outstation policies, all of which have been pejoratively characterised by the right as the Coombs socialist experiment (see Rowse 2012: Ch. 10) and responsible for segregating remote Aboriginal Australians from the mainstream. In the views of people like Peter Howson, Geoffrey Partington, Gary Johns and more recently Helen Hughes, it was only in 1996 with the election of the Howard Government that policy began to get back on track, with its biggest achievement being the abolition of the Aboriginal and Torres Strait Islander Commission (ATSIC) in 2004 and the Intervention in 2007. In their view, this marked the end of the separatist policies, fuelled by a romantic desire to preserve tradition, that were stopping people being integrated into the mainstream. In the extreme views of Helen Hughes, all that was required was getting the economic incentives right, including withdrawing support for the ambiguously described homeland communities to encourage people into the urban centres.

Tim Rowse, in his analysis of Nugget Coombs' legacy in Indigenous affairs, presents a much more complex and nuanced picture. His key point that all policies in Aboriginal affairs are experiments, including those of the right, is very well taken (Rowse 2012: 187), as is the evidence for Coombs being open-minded, leading him occasionally to adopt some strange ideas (for example, ethology; see Rowse 2012: 180–3). The overarching element of his approach was that Aboriginal people should have a choice (Rowse 2012: 187), and under the

---

40   ibid.: 48, 51.

anthropologically conservative views of Stanner, Coombs was a strong advocate for continuity, as reflected in the view that the retreat of the people of Yirrkala back to their homelands was a 'wise passivity' (pp. 186, 187). It also seems clear that both men underestimated the rate at which things would change in the future.

While the strong emphasis placed on Aboriginal choice by Coombs seems entirely admirable, it does come with a downside. It relieved policymakers of direct responsibility for facing up to what might happen in the future while assuming that the people themselves were in a position to choose realistically about the degree to which and the pace at which they came to identify themselves with mainstream society. It gives no consideration as to exactly what the choices were between or how they might appear from the point of view of people like those at Yuendumu or Nyirrpi, to whom the world clearly looked, and still looks, quite different from how it seemed from a national policy perspective. In some ways, it was a policy position that shares something with that famously recommended by Donald Thomson and Olive Pink, who both argued for leaving people to pursue their own life on their own terms: in all three cases it was a policy of deferral motivated by deep humanistic concerns.

In Donald Thomson's case, writing in 1937 (Thomson 1939), he recognised change as inevitable but optimistically thought that the science of anthropology and its understanding of change would, in the future, provide a much smoother and pleasanter transition for Aboriginal people than in the past. But, by 1974, not only had even the remotest-dwelling Aboriginal people developed a certain consumer dependency, but there had also been a quantum change in the attitude to Indigenous people and their rights in the community at large. There was much greater interest in the lot of remote Aboriginal people and pressure from many quarters, both national and international, to improve the material circumstances of their lives.

So why would people developing social policy for Aboriginal people want to postpone facing inevitable issues? One possibility was that Coombs saw the outstations as refuges for the older generations and more conservatively oriented Aboriginal people whose 'social disciplines', as he put it, could not easily handle life in the large communities. Indeed, Young (1981: 71–2) reports that 20 per cent of outstation residents in the Yuendumu area in 1978 were aged over 60, whereas people in this age bracket made up only 6 per cent of the Yuendumu population. However, it is not clear if he believed that once the older generation had died, most outstations would disappear. Another possibility is that there was no clear and acceptable policy to suggest that addressed the long-term issues: they were just too difficult, especially in the changed social and political situation that gave Aboriginal people more voice in the policies that affected them. Indeed, one might even suggest that policymakers more generally found it difficult to envisage the future for Aboriginal people in remote desert Australia.

Nevertheless, it is surprising that the long-term future of the population in the Yuendumu area was not canvassed in the Coombs–Stanner report. Although there is an explicit concern with younger people learning the discipline of work expected in a market economy, and a concern with projects that could generate some income, there is no evidence to suggest that Coombs and Stanner thought they were setting up Yuendumu as an economically viable outback town, especially given the emphasis on decentralisation. The most forward-looking aspect of the report is the concern with turning the council into an effective instrument for the self-administration of the community—something that was proving more difficult than they had expected (Coombs and Stanner 1974: 23), in particular because the council was not adequately addressing the difficulties around alcohol. Indeed, it seems clear that the council had neither taken on the responsibilities previously exercised by the superintendent nor internalised the role and functions of the superintendent more generally as now its own.

I would suggest that policymakers still face this problem, which is a manifestation of an emergent problem at a world scale: the issue of populations that are surplus to the labour requirements of their national economies. In Australia, this does not just apply to Aboriginal people, but also, for example, to other workers such as those in the Holden car plants and other areas of manufacturing. This in turn raises the question of whether life in an outstation or remote Aboriginal community can provide a desirable long-term form of dependency in the twenty-first century. If so, Nyirrpi has a long if unclear future. Policymakers, it appears, are still faced with the same problem that faced Coombs in 1974 but now the difficulties are more explicitly on the agenda.

References

Coombs, H. C. and Stanner, W. E. H. 1974. *Report on Visit to Yuendumu and Hooker Creek*. Canberra: Australian Government Publishing Service.

Eller, J. 1992. Pentecostalism and its relation to traditional and contemporary social organization in Warlpiri society. Unpublished paper. Australian Institute of Aboriginal and Torres Strait Islander Studies, Canberra.

Gallagher, O. n.d. Nyirrpi-kirli. Unpublished typescript. Yuendumu School, Yuendumu, NT.

Gibb, C. A. 1971. *The Report of the Committee to Review the Situation of Aborigines on Pastoral Properties in the Northern Territory*. Canberra: Government Printer.

Griffiths, M. 1995. *Aboriginal Affairs: A Short History 1788–1995*. Sydney: Kangaroo Press.

Kesteven, S. 1978. A sketch of Yuendumu and its outstations. Unpublished MA thesis. The Australian National University, Canberra.

Mayne, A. 2014. *Alternative Interventions: Aboriginal Homelands. Outback Australia and the Centre for Appropriate Technology*. Adelaide: Wakefield Press.

Morel, P. and Ross, H. 1993. *Housing Design Assessment for Bush Communities*. Alice Springs, NT: Tangentyere Council & NT Department of Lands, Housing and Local Government.

Rowse, T. 2000. *Obliged to be Difficult: Nugget Coombs' Legacy in Indigenous Affairs*. Cambridge: Cambridge University Press.

Rowse, T. 2012. *Rethinking Social Justice: From 'Peoples' to 'Population'*. Canberra: Aboriginal Studies Press.

Thomson, D. 1939. *Report on Expedition to Arnhem Land 1936–7*. Canberra: Government Printer.

Young, E. 1981. *Tribal Communities in Rural Areas: The Aboriginal Component in the Australian Economy*. Canberra: Development Studies Centre, The Australian National University.

Appendix 9.1

The letter with explanatory notes written with my help and sent from Yuendumu to the Minister of Aboriginal Affairs in February 1973.

> Yuendumu
> Via Alice Springs
> NT5750
> The Minister
> Dept of Aboriginal Affairs Canberra
> ACT * February 1973
>
> Dear Sir
>
> We want to sit down in our country where our fathers' fathers came from. Those men were Pupuwana, Panmawarnu, Mantarkunya, Wararipatu and Raparinyinwana.
>
> We went to our country with Bill Frazier and left drum water and petrol. He want to make new settlement there for we. Too many people in Yuendumu and we get sick all the time.
>
> We want a bore at Yinyiripalangu. We like to go there for holiday and to work there if you help us.
>
> Yours sincerely
> Banjo Jungarrayi.
>
> Explanatory note: Yinyiripalangu is 47 miles [76 km] west of Vaughan Springs on Ethel Creek in the Lake Mackay Reserve (Lake Mackay sheet 5152-11 301233). In 1970 a government patrol led by the then superintendent of Yuendumu, Bill Frazier, chose Yinyiripalangu as a possible site for an outstation. Supplies of food, water and petrol were left there by the patrol.
>
> Yinyiripalangu is in the heart of Walpiri country and a bore here would make it possible for many people to return to their own country for both short visits and more permanent stays.

* Dated 5 February in the copy in my field notes, but dated 7 February 1973 according to the letter that Banjo received on 17 May 1973 from the minister in reply to the original letter and a follow-up telegram sent on 14 March because nothing had been heard for six weeks.[41]

---

41   NAA: F1, 1973/9595: 86.

10

Homelands as outstations of public policy

Kingsley Palmer

This chapter is about the rise and fall of outstations in Aboriginal Australia. In the 1970s, governments, both State and Federal, were at first enthusiastic about these settlements, encouraged by an ideology that promoted outstations as beneficial—in terms of health, social well-being, cultural maintenance and the preservation of links to country, which were generally recognised as being of singular importance for Aboriginal Australians. But funding outstations proved to be expensive, and progressively, funding responsibility was devolved to the States, which in turn showed a developing reluctance to spend money on often isolated and costly support services. Moreover, as ideologies shifted, outstations were seen as too often wasteful of scarce resources and generally did not provide much needed health services. Training and employment—seen by many as the way forward for Indigenous Australians—were conspicuously absent from most outstations.

This chapter tells something of the history of program support for outstations by reference to both a national evaluation of funding for outstations and a case study drawn from the author's own fieldwork. The future of outstations as settlements for Australia's Indigenous people is uncertain since governments are unable (or unwilling) to justify the considerable expense involved. However, there are indications that Aboriginal Australians in some circumstances are diverting their own resources to facilitate choice in their place and mode of residence, although this is an option available to only a privileged few.

Homelands and outstations

Aboriginal Australia in the 1970s saw an unprecedented shift from centralised community living to what has been labelled 'decentralisation'—a process particularly apparent in remoter parts of the continent. Decentralisation was typified by a return to the country with which participant groups had a traditional affiliation. It was a movement away from larger communities that were under the control of the Australian Government or church missions. The newly established settlements were commonly called 'outstations' or sometimes 'homelands' in acknowledgement of the autochthonal relationship between residents and the country of the new settlement. The movement was noted by many commentators and anthropologists at the time (for example, Gray 1977; Coombs et al. 1982). But it was a change in living arrangements that was part of other factors too—in particular, the advent of legislated land rights for Indigenous Australians (Peterson 1982) and an advance in the policy of self-determination for Australia's Aboriginal people. In stark contrast with past practice, Indigenous Australians could live where they chose and have some opportunity to determine their own way forward.

The outstation movement was much vaunted as a solution to the many ills that dogged the administration of public policy in relation to Australia's Indigenous minority. Apart from the social justice issues and recognition of rights for native peoples—part of a wider movement in postcolonial administrations across the globe—outstations were praised as offering better health, living conditions and social harmony than the crowded and sometimes dysfunctional settlements where alcohol and substance abuse were regularly endemic. The Federal Government was prepared to fund these arrangements (Coombs et al. 1982: 428–30). While some voiced reservations about the policy (Coombs et al. 1982: 430), overall the outlook was optimistic. Outstations represented a significant paradigm shift in the administration of Aboriginal affairs. It was a bold new endeavour that only required that funding be provided by the Federal Government to make it a success.

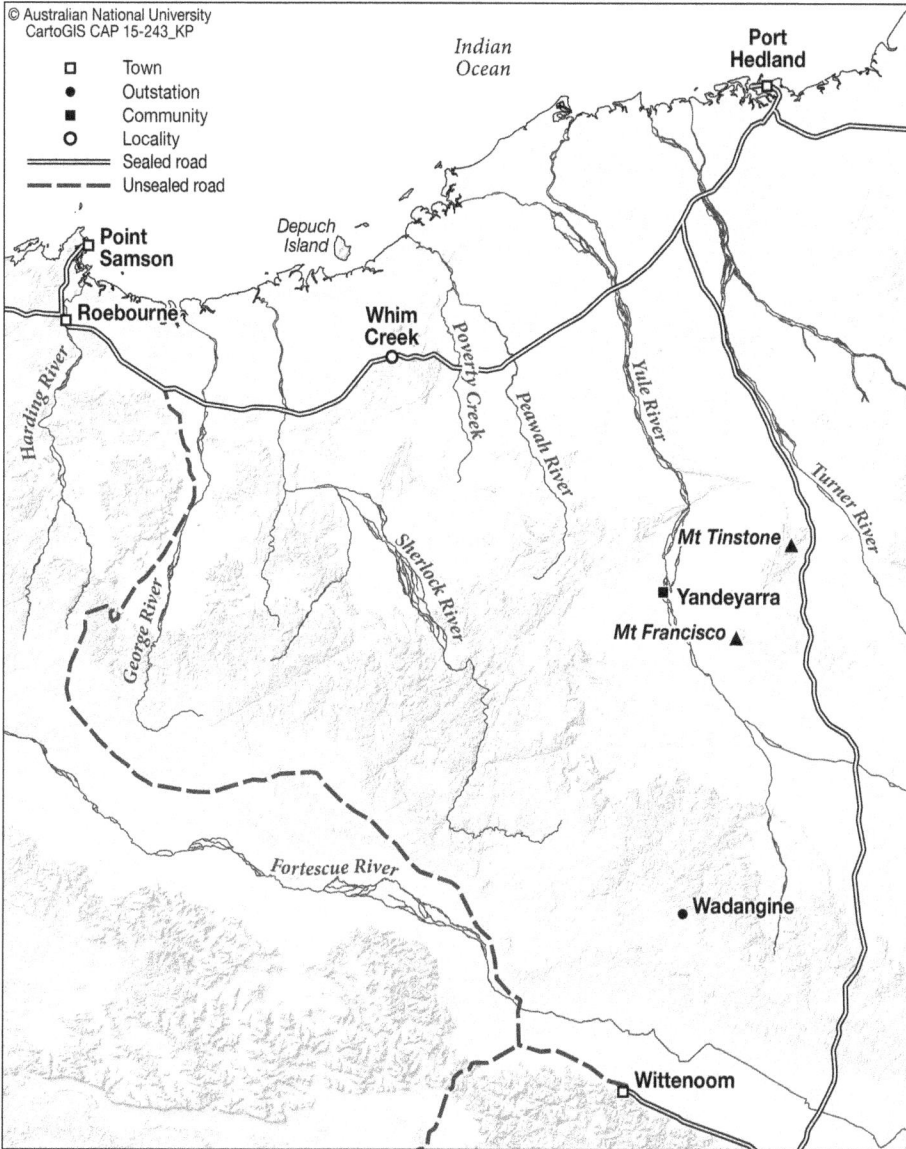

Map 10.1 Wadangine in relation to Yandeyarra.
Source: Karina Pelling, CartoGIS, ANU College of Asia and the Pacific

What might be termed the golden era of outstations was to be short-lived. By the mid-1990s, there were serious problems emerging with the decentralisation process. Health care was difficult to deliver to many outstations while other services like education and training were either impractical to offer or were prohibitively expensive. Transport and provision of power, safe drinking water and sanitation added to the host of difficulties that were intrinsic to maintaining multiple small communities in out-of-the-way places with no real employment opportunities and limited economic possibilities. There were allegations of waste, assets unused, and houses never occupied.

Here I review some data that was developed in the context of a review of outstations across Australia in 1998. Commissioned by the now defunct Aboriginal and Torres Strait Islander Commission (ATSIC), the review sought to provide data that would alleviate problems of perceived waste in resource centres and the outstations they serviced. Such an endeavour was consistent with an increase in funding restraints, a desire to mainstream and demands for greater public accountability. It was, however, also tempered by an ideology that saw outstations as examples of self-determination, independence and a return to the land, supported by the commissioners who allocated funding. With the benefit of hindsight, it is now possible to see that such aspirations were doomed, particularly once ATSIC was abolished. One reading of these materials is to understand the homelands movement and its supporting bureaucracy in the late 1990s as itself an outstation of public policy.

Wadangine, 1972 and 2013

Wadangine is an outstation approximately 40 km south-south-east of Yandeearra (Yandeyarra), an Aboriginal community in the Pilbara region of Western Australia. I first visited Wadangine in 1972 on a familiarisation trip as part of an introduction to my work in the Pilbara region for the Western Australian Museum. At this time, Wadangine was a working cattle camp—always known as 'The Outcamp' rather than an outstation, in the cattlemen's parlance of the time. Over the next few years, Yandeearra, which had been subject to much neglect, was re-established as a community and Wadangine became the bush camp for the cattle business where a few families lived and worked. The majority of those associated with the group with whom I worked lived at Yandeearra, which was progressively developed as a community.

Over my many years of association with Yandeearra, I saw the settlement at Wadangine develop slowly. It offered limited facilities: a makeshift shelter that functioned as a workshop and only one house. Most people who chose to live there occupied small tin sheds or camped under tarps or other makeshift shelters. Despite these limitations, residents of both Yandeearra and Wadangine were marked by their resilience, self-reliance and desire for self-determination. The residents had engaged in a radical struggle that had seen them strike for better wages and conditions in 1946 on the pastoral properties in the region that provided their main employment. Many left the white-owned cattle stations to set up their own enterprises, including mining, shelling and feral goat shooting as well as the Yandeearra pastoral business.

Wadangine was not then an outstation in the sense often applied to places where people have moved away from a central settlement to live on their own country. Most Yandeearra residents (but by no means all) were immigrants to the area, with their country further to the east in the desert regions beyond the De Grey River. Wadangine was not then for most residents a 'homeland'. However, in terms of self-determination, Wadangine was an expression of the desire of its residents to live on country, generate an income through employment and have as complete a management of their own affairs as was possible, given the funding constraints and bureaucratic requirements that went with them.

Returning to country

Outstations and 'outcamps' of the sort I came to know at Wadangine have a long and complex history in the administration of Indigenous affairs in Australia. In public policy terms, they were regarded as positive arrangements that might alleviate all manner of social and economic ills.

> Apart from the strong desire of Aboriginal people to return to traditional land to meet their responsibilities in relation to their land, the [outstation] movement has also been a reaction to the stresses of living in settlements, reserves and missions and to the practice of bringing diverse groups of Aboriginals together to live in these artificial communities. There was widespread dissatisfaction with the institutionalised nature of settlements and missions and a recognition that they had huge social problems ... By contrast, outstation life offered a return to a 'healthy social and physical environment' away from the tensions and trouble associated with large communities and mixed groups. (Blanchard 1987: 14)

The Report of the House of Representatives Standing Committee on Aboriginal Affairs of March 1987, *Return to Country: The Aboriginal Homelands Movement in Australia* (Blanchard 1987), gave formal recognition of the importance of outstations in remote Australia. In fact, the political will to advance the cause of outstations was already well established. The Standing Committee itself identified that there was an urgent need for 'a detailed investigation' into homelands (Blanchard 1987: xxxi) and invited the minister to refer to it an inquiry into homeland centres. The terms of reference for the inquiry were very broad as the committee was asked to report on '[t]he social and economic circumstances of Aboriginal people living in homeland centres or outstations, and the development of policies and programs to meet their future needs' (Blanchard 1987: xxxi).

The inquiry received 44 written submissions comprising more than 2,100 pages of evidence. It examined 111 witnesses at public hearings held around the nation, the transcripts comprising 1,250 pages. The inquiry also considered 17 exhibits and visited approximately 70 communities or settlements (Blanchard 1987: xxxi–xxxii, Appendices 1–4). The 58 recommendations were directed to the then Minister for Aboriginal Affairs, Clyde Holding. The conclusions, recommendations and the arguments for them were the most authoritative expression of the pro-outstation wisdom of the time and were highly influential in framing both the Department of Aboriginal Affairs' and subsequently ATSIC's programs as they related to rural and remote community development.

The 'Blanchard Report', as it was called after the chairman of the committee, made its 58 recommendations with the clear intention of improving the economic security and viability of outstations and increasing the level of services available to outstation residents. At this time the future of outstations was secure: the committee recognised the contribution outstations had in furthering the aspirations of Indigenous Australians and in improving their quality of life.

Before 2004 outstations were sustained by funding, for the most part through the agency of ATSIC, which had programs devoted to outstation resource delivery and housing. Typically, outstations were serviced by small organisations based in a parent community known as an Outstation Resource Centre (ORA). These centres received funding based on the requirements of the outstations they looked after. Broadly, funding for outstations was channelled through ATSIC's State and regional offices to the ORAs, which had responsibility for allocating funds to the outstations for which they were responsible and provided services. The funds were deployed under the auspices of the Community Housing and Infrastructure Program (CHIP) and the Community Development Employment Projects (CDEP) scheme. Other sources of funding from within ATSIC were generally small and specific to a particular activity such as arts or cultural activities. Other Federal Government department programs were also represented, but actual amounts of money varied enormously. Some agencies received funding from State or Territory bodies and government programs, but again absolute amounts varied greatly and grants were often of short-term duration (Altman et al. 1998: 3.1–3.4). ATSIC was responsible for the majority of the funds allocated and ATSIC and its CHIP and CDEP programs facilitated the development and perpetuation of outstations. Outstations were, then, in this environment 'viable', but of course only for as long as the ATSIC (or other) funding continued.

While this funding environment reflected the persistence of the conventional ideology that underpinned the Blanchard Report, by the late 1990s within what was already a somewhat beleaguered bureaucracy, the question of outstation funding and the economic wisdom of the programs had already been subject to substantial criticism. This resulted from cited instances of waste, often noted by Liberal politicians, with tales of generators left to rust in remote locations in their unopened crates, solar panels stolen by passers-by and new houses erected in places where no one had ever lived. Those of us who visited numerous outstations in the course of several national and regional reviews can attest to these stories. However, there were other examples of thriving communities and well-managed resources. Plans to review resource centre funding to make them more accountable and to implement management techniques (regional outstation policy, strategic plans, performance indicators, formula funding) were all steps to stem the waste and make the system more efficient and effective. It was hoped thereby to secure the elements of the program that many Aboriginal people as well as non-Indigenous employees in communities and resource agencies considered to be a sustainable and positive alternative to living in larger communities with their attendant antisocial behaviour, drinking, drugs and alienating living conditions. However, by the time ATSIC commissioned a national review in 1997, the cost of funding outstations, the criticisms of their ability to advance the economic situation of Aboriginal people and accompanying lack of political will meant that the situation was probably beyond redemption for at least many of the outstation resource centres.

The 1997 review

The review proposed by ATSIC in 1997 canvassed a wide-ranging agenda that was to include definitional issues, funding levels, accountability as well as the governance and structures of the ORAs themselves. It also asked for a strategy for the future and an implementation timetable. The consultancy was managed by a consortium of three parties from the Australian Institute of Aboriginal and Torres Strait Islander Studies (myself), the Centre for Aboriginal Economic Policy Research (Jon Altman) and a private company, Tallagalla Consultants (Dan Gillespie). Additional researchers were David Martin, Bill Arthur, Richard Davis, Jerry Schwab and Diana Hafner. These researchers came from an anthropological background and many had extensive experience working in remote Aboriginal Australia while some had hands-on experience working at outstations and with ORAs. It was a strong team.

The review was based on field studies of 25 ORAs.[1] Subsequently, one ORA in Queensland was found to have only marginal involvement in servicing outstations so was excluded from the survey results. We estimated that the six

---

1   South Australia = three; Queensland = five; Northern Territory = 12; and Western Australia = five.

researchers spent more than 100 days in the field so it was an empirically based study that used a mixture of questionnaires and a field observation manual to guide researchers as to the issues that required attention.

The review was not focused on the specifics of the 24 case studies and the many outstations they represented. It was designed to provide an overview of the national situation. In this regard some statistics are significant as they provide an indication of the state of outstations during the last half of the 1990s.

We claimed that the review represented 'the most comprehensive survey of ORAs undertaken to date' (Altman et al. 1998: 6.13). ATSIC data provided to us suggested that at the time of the review there were approximately 12,000 Indigenous Australians living at about 1,000 outstations serviced by approximately 100 ATSIC-funded ORAs. Assuming that the ATSIC figures were correct and that our sample was broadly representative, the review sampled about 25 per cent of ORAs Australia-wide. The 24 ORAs the review visited serviced 340 outstations, indicating that there were possibly 1,400 outstations in Australia (Altman et al. 1998: 6.14–6.15)—somewhat more than the official ATSIC figures. We estimated the populations of the outstations and projected them to provide Australia-wide figures, using a range of population figures from maxima to minima, median and 'effective', which took into account the period an outstation might be vacant. These data are shown in Table 10.1.

Table 10.1 Some estimates of outstation populations at 24 ORAs and Australia-wide, 1997

	Sampled ORAs	Australia-wide
Minimum population	3,381	13,524
Maximum population	8,129	32,516
Usual population	5,770	23,080
Effective population	4,893	19,572

The survey also reported on the numbers of houses, vehicles and funding, which I have extracted for interest in Table 10.2.

Table 10.2 Some estimates of outstation costs and resources, 1997

Item	Total in survey	Total across Australia
Houses	964	'Several thousand'; $200 m minimum
Vehicles	196	800
Budget	$54 m	$200 m
CDEP contribution	$24 m	25–39% of total CDEP channelled via ORAs

The ORAs ranged in size from those that serviced just three outstations to those that had responsibility for 44. Budgets showed enormous variation, ranging from as low as $140,000 per annum to a high of $11.5 million. Sources of funding were variable, with CDEP and the ATSIC-administered CHIP providing the bulk of funds. Outstation populations ranged from two to 770 and staff of the ORAs from 0.5 to 39.

Gaining reliable figures was complex, particularly with respect to outstation populations, which generally showed great variation. Figures were developed through a sophisticated set of measures that attempted to take into account fluctuation and gain some idea of what might be the 'usual' population. The range of the organisations reviewed and the implications this had for similar bodies across Australia made generalising hazardous.

One example of the data retrieved is shown in Table 10.3, which shows not only the range of funding and numbers of outstations for each ORA, but also the average calculated costs of outstations in each case. It is notable that while the average cost per outstation was a little more than $23,000, the median cost was more than $56,000. It is apparent from this that there was a huge variation in costs.

Figures for per capita expenditure were equally diverse. The review found that there was an average of $4,462 per capita but a median of $2,547. Some per capita figures were as high as $15,000, while others fell below the $1,000 mark.

The use of assets, particularly houses, which represented for the most part the most expensive infrastructure on outstations, was subject to review, although statistical data in this regard proved difficult to present as reliable. We concluded:

> Generally, the standard of housing was well below that expected of public or private housing. In some cases, houses are little better than tin sheds, unlined, with no windows and inadequate services or no services at all. (Altman et al. 1998: 5.46)

Table 10.3 Agency funding, outstation numbers and average costs per outstation, 1997

No.	Funding	O/s nos	Annual cost
1	$1,712,000	30	$57,067
2	$2,500,000	10	$250,000
3	$465,000	13	$35,769
4	$413,476	44	$9,397
5	$285,086	3	$95,029
6	$445,258	19	$23,435

No.	Funding	O/s nos	Annual cost
7	$138,000	7	$19,714
8	$156,471	14	$11,177
9	$238,105	19	$12,532
10	$497,213	16	$31,076
11	$281,420	12	$23,452
12	$108,014	6	$18,002
13	$193,933	20	$9,697
14	$154,058	9	$17,118
15	$1,192,000	23	$51,826
16	$1,953,546	11	$177,595
17	$1,282,000	7	$183,143
18	$883,770	20	$44,189
19	$1,836,779	11	$166,980
20	$70,000	3	$23,333
21	$441,621	6	$73,604
22	$198,000	14	$14,143
23	$70,000	7	$10,000
24	$70,000	16	$4,375
Average	$649,406	14.17	$56,777
Median	$349,281	12.50	$23,443
Range	$2,430,000	41.00	$245,625

We also reported:

> Overall, house vacancy rates are, at least in some areas, substantial. However, it should be borne in mind that some dwellings classified as houses are uninhabitable by wider community standards. Nevertheless, there is a general view, supported by the data collected, that vacant houses, some representing a substantial investment of money, are a problem in that substantial resources and infrastructure are under-utilised or, in extreme cases, wasted. Houses on vacant outstations are often subject to vandalism and the Review noted many instances of theft of equipment like stoves and solar panels. (Altman et al. 1998: 5.48)

In a sample of 14 ORAs, the range of unoccupied houses at outstations was 0 per cent (one case) to 91 per cent (one case). The median rate of unoccupied houses was 45 per cent and the mean 33 per cent (Altman et al. 1998: Appendix 5, p. 189). It is evident from these figures that a substantial proportion of houses—expensive assets on outstations—were either not utilised or underutilised.

Home ownership was not considered in the review, as it would have been, for the majority of outstation residents, well beyond their economic means. However, we did suggest that rental agreements might assist in stemming waste, which was clearly evident in the comments we made.

Discussion of cost recovery and user pays was circumspect. We reported:

> It is evident that the introduction of a partial user pays system may go some way toward rebutting myths that Indigenous Australians are entirely welfare dependent. However, if the source of the payment is itself a welfare benefit, then it is hard to understand the logic that drives this reasoning, unless the partial user pays system is designed to be somehow educative. (Altman et al. 1998: 5.33)

The limitations of the cost-recovery process in a community of people who are, for the most part, highly welfare dependent and poor must be understood from the outset. Concerns were expressed about the capacity of some to meet the costs of services, and agencies need to have the flexibility to administer cost-recovery processes to ensure that economic hardship is not a direct consequence (Altman et al. 1998: 5.35).

We ended the review by stressing that it was our opinion that outstations were likely to endure and rather than diminish might in time increase in numbers and importance:

> Indeed there is likelihood that in the native title era, outstation populations will expand. Outstations are a valid lifestyle choice for Indigenous people, especially those who are owners of considerable tracts of land in rural and remote parts of Australia. (Altman et al. 1998: 6.3)

We also stated that there were longer-term cost benefits:

> The longer-term costs and benefits to government of outstations: While it is very difficult to quantify the net cost/benefits of outstations, there seems little doubt that rigorous costing, taking into account documented cultural, economic and health benefits, would indicate a positive net benefit. (Altman et al. 1998: 6.7)

Post-review policy

While it is tempting to assume that the report of the outstation review languished on dusty bookshelves in the offices of ATSIC in Canberra, there is evidence that some of the recommendations were implemented—or attempts were made to do so. For example, the recommendations of the review relating to setting funding for individual outstations against national benchmarks, population and geographic variables such as distance and access from the ORA (Altman et al. 1998: Recommendations 1, 12 and 13, p. 18) were implemented by at least one regional council. Two of us (Palmer and Gillespie) went on to undertake reviews of several regional councils and their outstations in an attempt to establish policy directions through the development of homeland policies, plans and procedures, which was another recommendation of the review (Altman et al. 1998: Recommendation 17, p. 19). These plans included the development of funding formulae that could be used in relation to each outstation managed by an ORA, designed to bring a greater level of accountability and uniformity to the funding and management mix.

The development of these plans and funding tools was a positive step. It perhaps helped to make the process more equitable and the system more efficient. However, the fundamentals of the problems raised by outstations for policymakers, politicians and bureaucrats remained unresolved. Outstations were expensive places to run, tended by their nature to highlight waste and could generally not provide health care, some essential services, training and employment—all of which were seen by many as essential for the social and economic betterment of Indigenous Australians.

Endemic problems

The recommendations of the review were made on the assumption that ATSIC funding would continue—or at least be replaced with a similar arrangement. There was then a prophetic ring to the following, which warned against a loss of federal funding:

> There are growing trends to mainstreaming in Indigenous affairs in particular, and prospects of greater fiscal devolution to the States, partly associated with the proposed division of GST revenue, in general. This indicates that the Federal Government and ATSIC will need to ensure diligently that mainline departments and State/Territory governments meet their obligations to outstation residents as Australian citizens. The data presented in this Review on relative State/Territory contributions to ORAs do not augur well in this regard. (Altman et al. 1998: 6.10)

There are three issues raised in the review that are of particular relevance to this prospect of a changed policy environment. The first is the outstation population. It was not that most outstations were not used—although some were certainly vacant. Our data (see Table 10.1) showed that there was a very large range in outstation populations (approximately 13,500 to 32,500 nationally). The implication of these data was that outstation residents also lived in places other than their outstation, and most likely at the parent community. One inference to be drawn from this is that the services and facilities of the outstation replicated in whole or in part those provided in the parent community. At the time of the review, this duplication of expenditure on essential services, shops, health, education and infrastructure was not a matter for inquiry. However, the 'part-time' characterisation of many outstations—notably, represented by the house vacancies—made the funding vulnerable on the grounds that in a fiscal environment where there was a lack of financial resources, duplication could not be afforded.

The second issue of note relates to the failure of the system to recover costs or implement cost recovery. The outstation review was, I think, realistic in identifying the practical problems evident in this regard since outstation residents lacked the capacity to pay. Moreover, since funds flowing to outstation residents were almost exclusively some form of welfare payment (including CDEP), we questioned the benefits of collecting by way of user payment from what amounted to a subsistence income. Figures on cost recovery reflected a disinclination to follow this path (Altman et al. 1998: Appendix 5, p. 191). The 24 ORAs in the study raised only 2.33 per cent of their annual budget through cost recovery (Altman et al. 1998: Table 'Summary of Data', Appendix 2). Outstations were by this account a fully subsidised welfare benefit vulnerable to the criticism that they were a luxury that the Indigenous budget could ill afford.

There is a third factor, which we did flag in our report: the move towards mainstreaming. There was a growing view that economic futures lay with centralised communities where there might be some possibility of meaningful employment and training. Given demands for uniform and acceptable service provision, health care and education, outstations were again vulnerable to those who saw them as retarding economic development and maintaining unacceptable levels of impoverishment and denial of basic services.

Leaving the country?

Since 2004 there has been a major shift in both State and Federal policies regarding the funding of outstations. John Howard announced ATSIC's abolition on 15 April 2004, saying that 'the experiment in elected representation for indigenous people has been a failure' (SMH 2004). On 28 May 2004, the Howard Government introduced legislation into the Federal Parliament to abolish the commission. After a delay, the Bill finally passed both houses of Parliament in 2005. ATSIC was formally abolished at midnight on 24 March 2005.[2] In 2007 the Federal Government transferred outstation funding for the Northern Territory to the NT Government and ceased direct funding of outstations, ending a 20-year commitment to support homelands following the Blanchard review

---

2   en.wikipedia.org/wiki/Aboriginal_and_Torres_Strait_Islander_Commission (accessed 17 April 2015).

(Altman et al. 2008: 9). This followed the NT Emergency Response intervention of June 2007, which gave the Commonwealth powers to intervene in the affairs of Indigenous Territorians at a level, according to one commentator, 'unmatched by any other policy declaration in Aboriginal affairs in the last forty years' (Hinkson 2007: 1). While the 'Intervention', as it became known, did not directly target outstations, it set administrative arrangements in place that would facilitate the further development and control of larger communities or hubs for the provision of all services, rather than encouraging peripheral development in remote homelands and the aspirations for self-determination that had accompanied such endeavours.[3]

While ATSIC provided policy direction, the ideology that lent principal support to outstations outweighed these vulnerabilities and inherent weaknesses. The outstation review I have discussed above was reporting on a system that was sustained by ideology engendered by ATSIC, which was probably at the time of the review already doomed. ATSIC policy was itself an outstation of mainstream government policy and, as subsequent events have shown, doomed to suffer a withering death to most of its parts. Indeed not only did the funding through ATSIC cease because of the organisation's demise, but also Federal funding for outstations was not a part of the new arrangements, while State and Territory governments provided minimal funds in this regard. Funding for housing and infrastructure was mainstreamed or directed towards building houses in centralised communities, not, as had been the case with the CHIP, in a manner that was designed to assist outstations. At the same time, the Federal Government started winding back the CDEP scheme, which was transferred in 2004 to the Commonwealth Department of Employment and Workplace Relations, rendering it less accessible and sympathetic to the needs of outstation residents (Saunders 2004: 6). Without the funding, many of the outstations we reviewed ceased to be financially viable and the resource centres were either closed or struggled to stay afloat by seeking funding from elsewhere.

While much may have changed since Blanchard, it would appear that for some politicians at least, elements of the ATSIC ideology remain intact. The Northern Territory Indigenous MLA Alison Anderson's policy statement on homelands of February 2013 (Anderson 2013) rings with the rhetoric of times gone by. This rhetoric is part of the ideology that holds that outstations are, echoing Blanchard, 'a good thing'—usually for reasons of cultural continuity and attachment to country and perhaps too because it is asserted that they provide for better health outcomes. The data to support such statements are notoriously

---

3   The 2007 *Memorandum of Understanding between the Australian and Northern Territory Governments on Indigenous Housing, Accommodation and Related Services* precluded the Northern Territory from constructing new housing on outstations with the funds the Commonwealth provided under the Memorandum. (Indigenous Affairs Forum of the NT n.d.: 1.)

hard to find, and the political will to expend funds proportionately lacking. Anderson tells us that in the Territory today there are 10,000 people living on homelands, representing some 25 per cent of the remote Indigenous population of the Northern Territory. She reports that there are 2,400 dwellings on 520 homelands (Anderson 2013). She asserts:

> Our spiritual connection to the land is unique, and today I seek to explain that and to celebrate it, and to describe what this government proposes to do to maintain it through the homelands.
>
> But our indigenous connection is a matter of history, deep history. It goes back well over 40,000 years. Even those of us who have accepted Christianity still feel that connection intensely; it is part of who we are. How we go about keeping that connection alive is crucial to our wellbeing, and homelands are vital to that. They are our ancestral places, where through ceremonies and other means we can fulfil our obligations to our inherited country and its Law. They are safe places where we feel secure, places where we can achieve physical and spiritual health.
>
> We're aware it could be more expensive to have people living in hundreds of small communities scattered around the Territory than restricted to a few dozen towns. But the benefits are potentially great, benefits in health and wellbeing and social harmony. So on behalf of the government, I reaffirm the integral role of the homelands in the Territory. I commit us to providing the residents of the homelands with the same services as other Territorians, within reason and accepting that in many cases they are starting from a low base. (Anderson 2013)

Anderson, then, recognises that homelands are expensive, a cost she considers to be offset by the benefits to health, well-being and social harmony. Services will be provided to the same standard as those available to other Territorians, *'within reason'*—a limitation that is not defined. Anderson tackles a principal problem with the implementation of this policy (lack of funding for houses) by suggesting that home ownership is the answer, and this comprises much of the thrust of her policy. Although the NT Government committed to spend some money on infrastructure on outstations, Altman (2012) has noted that in per capita terms this does not amount to very much. While the thrust of Anderson's statement is encouraging to those who support outstation development and sustainability, it remains unclear how services and housing will actually be provided and to what extent.[4]

---

4   Alison Anderson resigned from the Country Liberal Party (CLP) in 2014 and became an independent briefly before joining the Palmer United Party (PUP). She resigned from the PUP in November 2014 and rejoined the CLP in February 2015. (en.wikipedia.org/wiki/Alison_Anderson; accessed 21 April 2015).

The reality of the situation now with respect to outstations is expressed in a paper prepared by the Indigenous Affairs Forum of the Northern Territory, which cites the Council of Australian Governments' (COAG) *National Partnership Agreement on Remote Service Delivery*, which speaks of 'investment decisions' rather than funding and specifically has it that:

> [P]riority for enhanced infrastructure support and service provision should be to larger and more economically sustainable communities where secure land tenure exists, allowing for services outreach to and access by smaller surrounding communities, including:
>
> - recognising Indigenous peoples' cultural connections to homelands (whether on a visiting or permanent basis) but avoiding expectations of major investment in service provision where there are few economic or educational opportunities; and
> - facilitating voluntary mobility by individuals and families to areas where better education and job opportunities exist, with higher standards of services. (COAG 2008: A-1)

In short, investment must be economically viable to be condoned.

The other major policy principle outlined in the forum's paper is that housing and provision of basic services are a State or Territory responsibility. The paper states that the 'Australian Government recognises the cultural, environmental and strategic importance of homelands across Australia as well as the importance of homelands for their linguistic diversity and Indigenous Knowledge and is committed to sustaining this diversity and knowledge' (Indigenous Affairs Forum of the NT n.d.: 1). However, paying for this asset is not contemplated. It remains, then, an ideal rather than a prospective reality.

More recently (in December 2014), the conservative Barnett Government in Western Australia announced that it would cease funding 150 remote communities in that State because it lacked the funds to do so. *The Monthly* reported that Premier Colin Barnett had stated that 'his state can't afford to keep the outstation communities going, because the money he received from the feds to do so isn't enough' (Marks 2014).

Wadangine revisited

My visit to Wadangine in 2013 highlighted for me the rise and fall of outstations. I observed during this visit that there were signs of a time where the facilities lacking in the early 1970s had been provided: additional housing, reticulated water, power and toilet blocks. However, these were now defunct or unserviceable and I was told that no one lived at Wadangine, although several families would like to do so but could not for the lack of basic facilities. Moreover, no one knew whom to ask or where to go to seek these things. I suspect this is because there is in fact nowhere to go. Yandeearra, the parent community, is planning (so I am told) additional houses and upgraded facilities because it is regarded as a focal community or a 'hub'. However, my brief discussions with the community manager at Yandeearra led me to the conclusion that servicing Wadangine was not on his agenda. Expenditure is to be directed to a community where at least some basic services can be concentrated, building on existing infrastructure and services that are already provided: a school, a visiting clinic, a swimming pool and reasonable road access.

An end to outstation dependency

The rhetoric continues to ring in the political and ideological prose of those who wish to advocate outstations as providing a better way of life and a solution to many of the social ills that we observe all too often on our travels round Indigenous communities and on the edges of remote towns. However, outstations as public policy have long had funding implications that make them unattractive to planners and bureaucrats and difficult for politicians to balance against the other many competing demands of their electorates. This is, of course, no new phenomenon. The outstation review I have outlined above shows dramatically that the outstation system as we reported on it was flawed in its administration by imbalance, inequities and high costs. While it may have been possible to argue that these costs were offset against the social benefits, these advantages could never be properly documented. Moreover, the prevailing ethic of mainstreaming and centralising Australia's Indigenous minorities so that they could be provided with conventional services (at whatever cost) seemed, I think, more appealing and achievable than funding the outstation program.

I hold that not all is doom and gloom in this regard. While I find Alison Anderson's account of outstations in the Northern Territory overly optimistic and the policy statement fenced with qualifications, I am aware from my travels that individual small communities continue to exist. Generally, residents or bureaucrats do not describe these small communities as 'outstations' because they are not part of a national or regional program that advocates the homeland ideal. Rather they survive on the little funding that can be found from one-off grants for such things as Indigenous business enterprise, environmental protection or the private contributions of their residents. In resource-rich areas, people may choose to allocate their royalty payments or other funds to maintaining an outstation. I have come across some settlements (former outstations) that are sustained solely by the income of the residents, often derived through full-time employment in neighbouring towns. Such arrangements are limited and highly dependent on the dedication, ability and resources of one or two principal players. In my experience, Australia's Indigenous minority continues to vote with their feet. It is a matter of regret, given the undoubted benefits of outstation living compared with those of urban fringe camps and suburban ghettos, that for most moving to an outstation (or what was an outstation) and sustaining a life there are well beyond their financial reach.

References

Altman, J. 2012. Another decade for homelands policy debacle. *Tracker* (May): 22–3.

Altman, J., Gillespie, D. and Palmer, K. 1998. *National Review of Resource Agencies Servicing Indigenous Communities, 1998*. Canberra: Aboriginal and Torres Strait Islander Commission.

Altman, J., Kerins, S., Fogarty, B. and Webb, K. 2008. *Why the Northern Territory Government needs to support outstations/homelands in the Aboriginal Northern Territory and national interest*. CAEPR Topical Issue No. 17/2008. Canberra: Centre for Aboriginal Policy Research.

Anderson, A. 2013. Homelands/outstation policy. Ministerial Statement. NT Legislative Assembly, Darwin. www.alisonanderson.com.au/ministerial-statement-homelandsoutstations-policy (accessed 5 December 2013).

Blanchard, C. A. 1987. *Return to Country: The Aboriginal Homelands Movement in Australia*. Report of the House of Representatives Standing Committee on Aboriginal Affairs. Canberra: Commonwealth of Australia.

Coombs, H. C., Dexter, B. G. and Hiatt, L. R. 1982. The outstation movement in Aboriginal Australia. In E. Leacock and R. Lee (eds), *Politics and History in Band Societies*. Cambridge: Cambridge University Press, pp. 427–40.

Council of Australian Governments (COAG) 2008. *National Partnership Agreement on Remote Service Delivery*. Canberra: COAG.

Gray, W. J. 1977. Decentralisation trends in Arnhem Land. In R. M. Berndt (ed.), *Aborigines and Change: Australia in the '70s*. Canberra: Australian Institute of Aboriginal Studies, pp. 114–23.

Hinkson, M. 2007. Introduction: In the name of the child. In J. Altman and M. Hinkson (eds), *Coercive Reconciliation: Stabilise, Normalise, Exit Aboriginal Australia*. Melbourne: Arena Publications, pp. 1–12.

Indigenous Affairs Forum of the Northern Territory n.d. *Outstations/homelands discussion paper*. Status of Australian Government Outstations/Homelands Policy and Current Principles for Investment. Canberra: Department of Families, Community Services and Indigenous Affairs.

Marks, R. 2014. Gathering storm: The assault on self-determination in the West. [Blog]. *The Monthly*, 4 December. www.themonthly.com.au/blog/russell-marks/2014/04/2014/1417667971/gathering-storm (accessed 17 April 2015).

Peterson, N. 1982. Aboriginal land rights in the Northern Territory of Australia. In E. Leacock and R. Lee (eds), *Politics and History in Band Societies*. Cambridge: Cambridge University Press, pp. 441–62.

Saunders, W. 2004. Indigenous centres in the policy margins: The CDEP scheme over 30 years. Paper for the ACOSS Annual Congress 2004, Alice Springs, NT.

Sydney Morning Herald (SMH) 2004. Clark vows to fight as ATSIC scrapped. *Sydney Morning Herald*, 15 April. www.smh.com.au/articles/2004/04/15/1081998279884.html (accessed 18 January 2012).

11

Challenging simplistic notions of outstations as manifestations of Aboriginal self-determination: Wik strategic engagement and disengagement over the past four decades

David F. Martin and Bruce F. Martin[1]

This is a practitioners' chapter, focusing on outstations in the Aurukun region of western Cape York Peninsula, and based on our experience spanning nearly four decades. We are father and son: David Martin, now an anthropologist, who established and coordinated an outstation support organisation in Aurukun for some eight years from the mid-1970s; and Bruce Martin, whose mother is a Wik woman from Aurukun, and who in 2011 worked with his community to establish a community-based organisation, Aak Puul Ngantam (APN), focused particularly on developing productive livelihoods on country. The key aims of this chapter are to outline and critically evaluate the principles and practices

1   We wish to thank the anonymous reviewers of this chapter, and also Robert Levitus and David Hinchley, for their insightful comments and suggestions. We have incorporated them where in our view they lay within the scope and aims of this chapter, and where they went beyond that, set them aside for further consideration in future work.

of the original outstation project against the concept of 'self-determination', and to contrast these principles and practices with what is being attempted now in a profoundly different Indigenous policy environment. The chapter has arisen as part of a long-term and ongoing engagement and dialogue on such matters between us. However, the first sections on the original outstation movement are largely written by David Martin, and those on APN's work by Bruce Martin. The concluding section of the chapter is jointly written.

Initial involvement: Co-option into Wik life projects

It was 1975, the reforming Whitlam Government was still in power and along with so many of my (David Martin's) generation, I had been exposed to and deeply involved in political movements such as opposition to the war in Vietnam. I was raised in Brisbane, still a very white town, but in a Quaker family who enjoyed a close friendship with an Aboriginal family in the community of Cherbourg north-west of the city and visited them there. Johannes Bjelke-Petersen was still Premier of Queensland and P. J. Killoran was the all-powerful director of the Department of Aboriginal and Islander Advancement, and such informal interracial visitation ostensibly still required the approval of the Cherbourg manager. It is perhaps unsurprising that in 1975 I took what was to be a year of absence from my research and teaching as a chemical engineer at the University of Queensland in order to spend the better part of a year travelling around remote Aboriginal Australia with like-minded companions, and that this resulted in a profound change of personal and professional direction.

In July 1975, towards the end of three months spent in Cape York Aboriginal communities as part of this trip, my companions and I arrived in Aurukun. I already had contacts here, including Jonathan Korkaktain, a young man who had previously come to Brisbane for a six-week welding course and who had ended up spending a year living in a house that I shared with a close Quaker friend and others (not altogether inappropriately referred to in the neighbourhood as 'Hippie Hollow'). We camped under big old mango trees near the old Aurukun airstrip, and had a constant stream of Wik visitors, including members of the Korkaktain and other Kendall River families whose traditional lands lay at the very south of the then Aurukun Reserve. The Wik people we met were welcoming, very engaged with and interested in us, and I remember they struck me at the time as politically feisty, assertive, upfront and confident of their rightful place in the world. All around us Aboriginal language was being spoken, and I took tentative steps in learning some basic Wik Mungkan vocabulary. Before the end of our stay, I was told that I had been 'adopted' into the Korkaktain family, and was immediately exposed to the practical and moral implications of the Wik kinship system (albeit without, at that point, understanding anything much of its systematic, classificatory and performative character). They, along with other Kendall River families, expressed their desire to move out to their traditional lands—and suggested that I help them do so. More broadly, I was approached to support Aurukun people's opposition to a bauxite mining lease recently issued over a substantial area of the northern part of the Aurukun Reserve by the Bjelke-Petersen Government, without consultation with them or the mission authorities.

It was an intoxicating time for a well-intentioned but naive young Brisbane suburbanite and I had few of the intellectual resources needed to understand the processes by which Wik people were seeking to incorporate me into their own life projects. I knew nothing of Aurukun's history, or of 'classical' Aboriginal cultures, and I had few bush skills to speak of. Moreover, having been born and educated in Queensland, I knew next to nothing about the history of Aboriginal affairs in that State or beyond it, and after all, I was an engineer. But I did think that my engineering education might be useful in conveying the technical implications of bauxite mining to Aurukun people and, with hindsight, I was looking for challenges in life that engineering could not meet. It was a dangerous combination, and I returned to Aurukun after the wet season in 1976 to work on the bauxite mining issue. However, I was soon recruited by Kendall River families to move with them out bush, initially to their staging post of Ti-tree outstation some 15 km or so north of the Kendall River, where we spent the wet season alongside Ti-tree families (in my case under a tent fly), before we eventually moved in the dry season of 1977 to Kuchenteypenh, a few kilometres upstream from the mouth of the Kendall River (see Map 11.1).

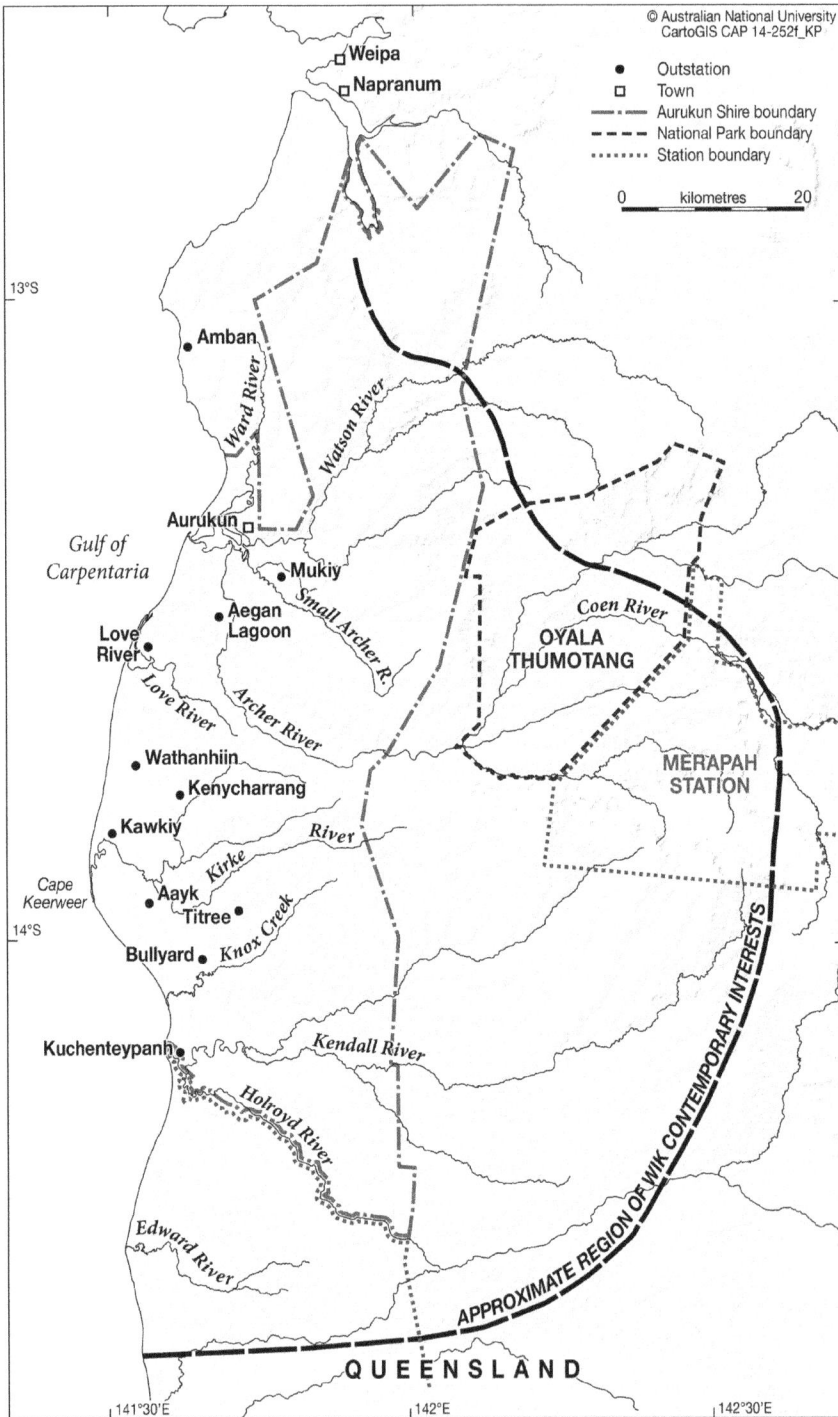

Map 11.1 Aurukun outstations.

Source: Karina Pelling, CartoGIS, ANU College of Asia and the Pacific

I lived at Kuchenteypenh for close to a year, along with about 40 north Kendall people and, for much of this time, an adventurous younger sister who had come to join me. South Kendall families and others established a small outstation across the river, at Kuli-anychen. Although an outpost of the Aurukun Mission run by Wik missionary workers had been established a few hundred metres from Kuchenteypenh in 1928 and had existed until the late 1950s, there was no infrastructure whatsoever when we arrived. Over the course of that dry season, we built basic shelters, sank a well, set up a solar-powered radio communication system with the mission authorities at Aurukun, and started clearing by hand an 800 m airstrip on a sand ridge a couple of kilometres away. It is a rich environment—just upriver from the Kendall estuary with extensive mangrove forests, pericoastal ridges with vine thickets and freshwater swamps. We lived well according to the season, variously on fish, stingray, estuarine sharks, crabs, ducks, wallaby, wild pigs and occasional stray cattle, with some bush foods such as yams. These were supplemented by stores brought down on a precarious journey around the coast on a small mission boat and eventually overland, comprising particularly of flour, sugar, tea and powdered milk, syrup and jam and, very importantly, tobacco, cigarette papers and matches, with the hunting and fishing made possible by fuel, fishing lines, hooks, sinkers and ammunition.

A number of languages were spoken at the Kuchenteypenh outstation, including what I now know to be Wik Ngathan, Kugu languages by those from south of the Kendall, and the lingua franca of Aurukun, Wik Mungkan. This multilingual situation complicated my learning Wik Mungkan, but I persevered with it, slowly gaining competence in everyday communication. Learning by experience, always to be careful to defer to older men, and in particular to the eldest of my Korkaktain brothers on whose country Kuchenteypanh lay, I nonetheless found myself drawn into mediating conflicts, and was considered responsible for organising matters that required cross-family cooperation or that serviced the outstation as a whole. These included operating the radio schedule with Aurukun, including ordering food and other items from the mission store, eventually running a small independent store at Kendall itself (as did Peter Sutton at Peret to the north), and along with my eldest brother, initiating work on conjoint activities such as clearing the airstrip and the track to it. Sutton (2009: 171–5) has written of similar experiences of his time at Peret outstation, now referred to as Wathanhiin.

To this point, basic support for the outstations then established (largely Peret, Ti-tree and, more latterly, Kendall River) was being provided by staff of the Aurukun Mission. In 1978, I moved into Aurukun itself to establish a distinct support service for outstations, as there were significant numbers out bush at Peret and Ti-tree, and there were increasing numbers of Wik people seeking support to move out bush and establish other outstations. I will discuss this stage below, but first it is necessary to briefly outline certain factors that were relatively unique in the Queensland context, and which were preconditions to the establishment of and support for outstations in the 1970s, largely in the Aboriginal lands south of Aurukun.

Preconditions for the 1970s outstation developments in Aurukun

Peter Sutton (this volume) has detailed a number of the factors that preceded the establishment in the 1970s of outstations south of Aurukun between the Archer and Kendall rivers. Here I will complement his discussion by briefly outlining a set of factors that in my view were significant in creating the preconditions for Aurukun's outstations in this period.

The first concerns an intersection between geography and the particularities of the history of the Aurukun Mission. While the township of Aurukun itself lies some 600 km north-west of Cairns and only 80 km or so south of the mining township of Weipa, its location close to the coast on western Cape York, with its monsoonal climate and large serpentine rivers winding their way down to the Gulf of Carpentaria, rendered it essentially inaccessible except by air and by boat. Only in the 1980s, with the construction of an unformed road linking Aurukun with the Peninsula Development Road running to Weipa, was Aurukun itself accessible overland—at least during the dry season. The extensive area between the Archer and Kendall rivers—part of the Aurukun Aboriginal Reserve—was even more remote and inaccessible, both from Aurukun where it necessitated an 8 km boat trip upstream to a precarious landing on the south bank of the river, and from the east where the only access until the mid-1980s was by a rough bush track following the south side of the Archer from Merepah Station west of Coen. This isolation rendered the movement of people between Aurukun and the developing outstations and the logistics of outstation support complex and resource intensive, but historically had insulated its population from many of the pressures of the colonial expansion into Cape York.

This geographical insulation was reinforced by the Reverend William MacKenzie, a Presbyterian missionary and the superintendent of the Aurukun Mission between 1923 and 1965, who strictly controlled access by outsiders. MacKenzie was tough, authoritarian and meted out harsh punishments to those who broke the rules or challenged his authority, including cruel floggings and, for some, banishment to Palm Island. Children were raised in separate boys' and girls' dormitories, from which the boys left to work on cattle stations in Cape York and beyond or in the bêche-de-mer fishery in the Torres Strait, while the girls left to do domestic work around the mission and marriage. At the same time, MacKenzie (along with his wife, Geraldine) appears to have supported the maintenance of aspects of Wik culture and practice, both philosophically and practically. He encouraged the use of language (outside of the fenced-in mission buildings) and the maintenance of male initiation, and was himself put through the first stage known as *uchanam*.

If partly for economic reasons, since the Aurukun Mission was starved of funding from the Queensland Government, MacKenzie required the families of children in the dormitories to bring in food they had hunted or gathered in the surrounding region, and until the early 1960s newly married couples were sent to live out bush for several months. Furthermore, while MacKenzie very actively sought to bring children into the dormitories in Aurukun, he did not force people to settle there. Consequently, in the mid-1970s, many of the senior generations of Wik people whose traditional lands lay south of the Archer River would have lived out bush for extended periods of their lives, and a number of their children (now young adults and middle-aged) were born out bush. Additionally, the Aurukun Mission established a cattle industry, largely south of the Archer River, which reached its peak in the 1960s, and whose workers were almost entirely Wik people. It was centred on Peret outstation, but created a number of hubs that formed the basis of subsequent outstation development—apart from Peret itself, most importantly Ti-tree, but also others such as Kenycherreng, Bamboo and Hagen's Lagoon. Peret and Ti-tree in particular had quite significant infrastructure, including airstrips, rudimentary water supplies, sheds and (in the case of Peret) what was by the mid-1970s a rather dilapidated homestead.

A consequence of these historical and geographical factors was that in the mid-1970s the traditional countries of a significant majority of Aurukun's residents had never been legally alienated since they lay within the southern portion of the Aurukun Reserve, and many of that majority had maintained connections to, and had a detailed knowledge of, the cultural geography of that area and of their own estates within it—although as I found when living there and as Sutton (this volume) shows, those connections were far from uncontested. That knowledge was subsequently documented in the comprehensive anthropological mapping of the region by Peter Sutton and to a lesser extent myself, John von Sturmer and others (Sutton et al. 1990), which formed the ethnographic basis on which the first stage of the Wik and Wik Way native title claim was determined in 2000.

Other factors were also at play. The history of Aurukun after the MacKenzies left in 1965 was one of increasingly relaxed controls by liberal mission authorities (for instance, the dormitories were closed the next year), intensifying exposure to the secular institutions and agencies of the outside world, and accelerating changes in the circumstances of Wik people's lives, much of it profoundly detrimental (Martin 1993; Sutton 2009). The generally liberal character of the mission administration post-MacKenzie had two interrelated effects of significance to this account. The first was that the political and administrative 'glue' under the authoritarian MacKenzie regime that bound the relatively culturally homogenous but deeply segmented Aurukun population quickly eroded, allowing the omnipresent but hitherto largely suppressed competition and conflict between and within various levels of Wik groupings to surface. The second was that in its final decade or so of administering Aurukun, the Presbyterian Church's Board of Ecumenical Mission and Relations (BOEMAR) placed increasing emphasis on self-management at the broader community level through the Aurukun Aboriginal Council, but *also* provided support for the expressed aspirations of groups from south of the Archer River to establish outstations on or near their traditional country. It is significant that the moves to establish Aayk and Peret, Ti-tree and the two outstations on the lower Kendall River, as well as in subsequent years Kenycherreng, Bullyard (Am – the Wik name) and Walngal (see Map 11.1), involved individuals from groups who had largely been excluded from holding power in the interface between the mission and Wik—a phenomenon reported in other regions (for example, Gerritsen 1982).

From the early 1970s, at the Federal level and influenced by H. C. Coombs, there were moves towards a policy of self-determination for Aboriginal people. For the Wik groups who initiated the move to establish outstations, however, the incentive to decentralise (as expressed to me) lay more with a desire to be self-determining vis-à-vis those other Wik they perceived as controlling Aurukun. Not unrelated to this was the wish to remove themselves from the increasing conflicts within Aurukun itself, rather than to be independent and self-determining vis-à-vis the wider Australian society. Indeed, there was a pivotal role played by a small set of non-Wik individuals, of whom I was one, in the development of the Aurukun outstations in the 1970s. These were all individuals who were strategically incorporated into Wik kin networks to serve Wik ends and access desired services and resources. They were the anthropologist John von Sturmer, in the region first in 1969, with deep links into Kugu groups from south of the Kendall River; anthropologist Peter Sutton, who undertook his doctoral field research at Peret from 1976 and played a major role in the establishment and life of that outstation in its earlier years (see Peter Sutton, this volume; and Sutton 2009); the Reverend John Adams and his wife, Jeanie, who had particularly close links with Ti-tree families and lived at the outstation there before moving in to Aurukun for wider community development work; and myself in relation to Kendall River people as outlined above, and subsequently in the development of an outstation support service as described below.

The Aurukun Outstation Support Group

The Aurukun Outstation Support Group was a non-incorporated resource centre independent of, but supported by, the BOEMAR administration, which I established when I moved in from Kuchenteypenh in 1978 and coordinated until I left in September 1983 to undertake a Masters degree in anthropology in London. Here, I will outline the methodology and philosophy of the resource centre, my own roles and my assumptions and expectations at that time, and the challenges to those assumptions and expectations posed by my everyday experience.

The support group grew quite substantially over the period to 1983, although it never had more than six or so staff. It aimed to be collaborative, but looking back, it was most definitely driven by me. I worked almost entirely in Wik Mungkan, and the only other non-Wik full-time employee was our mechanic, Bruce Hinchley, originally a prune farmer from near Young in New South Wales who could do truly extraordinary things with broken-down machinery of all types—a very necessary skill, as I shall discuss below. Wik male employees worked at tasks such as vehicle and boat drivers, logistics organisers, mechanic's assistants and bush builders. Initially, the support group transported food, fishing gear, ammunition and so forth, which outstation residents ordered over the morning radio schedules and which were filled by the Aurukun store. However, this was quite expensive and we ended up ordering in bulk directly from suppliers in Cairns, as I had done for the little store at Kuchenteypenh and Peter Sutton had done for its equivalent at Peret.

The support group was organic, evolving in its size, focus and complexity over time. In terms of contemporary practice and expectations, its governance would have been seen as highly deficient since it had no formal mechanisms for 'community' oversight of my work—for example, through an Aboriginal board. As I saw it at the time, my accountability was maintained through the everyday praxis of engagement with the Wik individuals and families, who were never loathe to let me know if they felt I was not being accountable to them, or was not being equitable in the allocation of support services.

At its peak in the 1978 and 1979 dry seasons, the support group serviced about 300 people on outstations south of the Kendall River, and a smaller but still substantial population in the wet season. Its focus was very much on providing the basic logistics and infrastructure to support individuals and family groups to move out to and stay on country for as long as they desired. Transport was central, and was highly seasonal; as observed above, this was a remote and inaccessible region, with most of the outstations on ridges in the extensive coastal floodplains that were intersected by river systems draining west to the Gulf of Carpentaria. In the dry season, four-wheel-drive vehicles and tractor-trailer units were used to transport food and necessities such as building materials and fuel, along with passengers. The support group provided subsidised transport for teachers, nurses and other service personnel to visit outstations, and for emergency evacuations by plane.

In order to get vehicles, stores and supplies across the Archer River and upstream from Aurukun, we designed and constructed a flat-bottom barge. In the wet season the only practicable access to all but the Kendall River outstations was by light aircraft, and eventually a charter company had a specialist twin-engine light aircraft permanently stationed in Aurukun for outstation support. Peret and Ti-tree already had serviceable wet season airstrips from the cattle days, but at the newer outstations of Kuchenteypenh, Kenycherreng, Bullyard and Walngal, airstrips were laboriously cleared using chainsaws, axes, picks and shovels by outstation residents, with some assistance from support group staff such as myself.

This was a very resource-intensive (human and capital) transport system, and although the support group received a Federal grant through the then Department of Aboriginal Affairs (DAA), this was not sufficient for the volume and complexity of transport requirements. To meet the demand, we therefore leveraged the DAA funding by negotiating and instituting a 'user pays' transport system, charging reasonably nominal seat prices for planes (varying between $20 and $30 per adult according to the distance from Aurukun), as well as for overland transport in the dry season, and for personal freight such as foodstuffs. More generally, a key principle in the operations of the support group from its inception was to encourage and support people's own initiative and self-reliance rather than simply providing services on demand. For example, we attempted to avoid getting caught up in the interminable politicking about country conducted within the township of Aurukun itself, including attempts to capture support group resources for symbolic rather than practical ends, manifested, for example, in demands for infrastructure to be put in place before people would move out.

An important operating principle was the requirement for people to demonstrate some commitment to spending time out bush before the support group would provide more than transportation in the way of assistance. For those moving to areas without existing infrastructure, we provided basic building materials such as corrugated iron and some basic tools, but in general where there were able-bodied men in the group they were expected to undertake the work themselves. As noted above, however, I and other support group staff assisted outstation residents in major tasks such as clearing airstrips, digging and lining wells, and on some occasions in constructing their basic huts of bush timber and corrugated iron. We also managed a radio communications system that was used to organise transport requirements from and between outstations, ordering foodstuffs and other necessities for delivery to outstations, organising technical assistance such as a mechanic to repair outstation equipment, and for contacting Aurukun in emergencies. Outside the morning schedules each weekday, the radio system also served for communications between kin living in different outstations.

With hindsight, it is clear that the issue of the social and economic sustainability of outstations was looming large almost from their inception, although I understood this only incompletely at the time. There are several factors relevant to this. First, as I was to find out, I was absolutely central to the everyday operations and the social sustainability of the Outstation Support Group. Despite subscribing to the 'working myself out of a job' mantra of community workers of the era, it became transparent over time that Wik people by and large were focused on keeping me working in my job (see also Peter Sutton, this volume). I was told quite explicitly by senior Wik outstation residents that they strongly preferred me rather than a Wik person to manage outstation support, because (as they expressed it to me) no Wik person could be 'fair' in allocating resources, time and support among the various outstations and family groups.

There was also no recognition—by myself or others who supported the Aurukun outstation movement, including its bureaucratic patrons in the DAA—of any need to develop local economies or productive livelihoods. The goal was moving 'back' to country and thereby reducing conflict and revitalising traditional ways. There was uncritical affirmation of the importance of hunting, fishing and to a much lesser extent gathering as valued and valuable activities that improved health and maintained traditional skills—although the cattle industry was revitalised for a while by the Aurukun Community Incorporated (ACI) in the mid-1980s and provided some local employment (as well as opportunities for significant rent-seeking by some individuals on whose country the ACI enterprise operated).

I earlier expressed the view that the impetus for people moving to outstations arose as much from the conflict and politicking among Wik in Aurukun as it did from a desire to exercise self-determination vis-à-vis the wider society. Its motivating force therefore was dependent on a social calculus among Wik in which the benefits, resources and opportunities associated with living on or establishing an outstation—importantly including significantly lower levels of conflict and violence—outweighed the disadvantages. It became clear that the factors underlying this calculus among the senior generations, who had co-opted Peter Sutton, John and Jeanie Adams and me into this enterprise, were not being reproduced in the succeeding generations, along with much else of Wik classical culture. As discussed later in this chapter, for younger generations of Wik there was an increasing disengagement from intimate connections to a deeply cultural landscape in parallel with a progressive engagement with a very different kind of life in the township of Aurukun itself.

Certainly, there were large numbers of people out on country in the late 1970s and early 1980s, particularly at Peret and Ti-tree—but this then exacerbated conflict at those outstations, particularly Peret. Furthermore, after the euphoria of the initial moves had faded, as I found at Kuchenteypenh, and after basic infrastructure had been established, there was not much to keep people engaged. The 'relentless boredom' of which Sutton (1978) wrote became a real factor. This was particularly an issue for younger people, who were highly mobile anyway and who drifted back into Aurukun, drawn there by its excitement and intense sociality. By the early 1980s, the demographics of most outstations as I recall it were comprised largely of older people, in some cases along with their young grandchildren.

There was another aspect of the work of the support group that reflected systemic issues with sustainability, and exercised me greatly in my role as coordinator. This concerned the way in which outstation services and equipment were used and abused: the radio communication system, vehicles, tractors, outboard motors, and so on. While not universal across all outstations, there was what I experienced as a widespread fecklessness and unwillingness among young men in particular to exercise responsibility in the use of equipment along with resources such as scarce and expensive fuel. One issue was misuse of the radios. There were numerous occasions when an emergency call to Aurukun would request a plane be sent to collect a sick person (often a child). There had been deaths on outstations, including two at Kuchenteypenh while I was living there, and there were no means at the time to get sick individuals back to Aurukun for treatment, so we were certainly very aware that serious problems could arise. If a Wik staff member took the emergency call, there was no way he could or would query the legitimacy of a demand for a plane be sent out; an assertion of illness axiomatically commanded support and sympathy, or risked blame and potentially severe sanctions should the individual concerned prove to be genuinely ill. If I took such a call, I would try to get a sense of the seriousness of the situation, but without medical training (or authority), I always erred on the side of caution. Many emergency calls, however, ended up not being emergencies at all, but appeared to me to be convenient ways for people to get back into Aurukun; not infrequently, the supposedly ill person would not even present at the Aurukun clinic.

Tractors were a particular problem. As a result of earlier DAA support for outstations, most groups had been supplied with a tractor-trailer unit, a number even before moving out bush. It was thought that these would be suitable for the very rough country (which proved to be the case) and robust enough to withstand the rigours of use for outstation transport (which proved not to be so). On multiple occasions, we were called to extricate or repair tractors that had become badly bogged or inundated on tidal flats, or which had a rear tyre irreparably staked by the timber used to try to extricate it from a bog, or which required a major engine rebuild because of failure to clean filters, or because of contaminated fuel, or which had just been abandoned because it could no longer be started.

The question of who had control of an outstation tractor was a major source of conflict in itself on some outstations, and senior Wik had little control over young men commandeering the outstation tractor for their own purposes, including on occasion to return to the landing on the Archer River from which to go back into Aurukun. Young men would break into the boxes in which the radio communications batteries—charged by solar panels—were secured, in order to use them for Toyotas or tractors whose batteries had been flattened by multiple unsuccessful attempts to start them. This would then leave the outstation without the ability to radio for assistance and without transport. The costs of repairing damaged equipment became beyond the capacity of the support group to manage, and in the case of tractors we instituted a regime where we would not repair one until there was agreement that it would subsequently only be driven by designated licensed drivers, and that the outstation would be responsible, paying for an hourly charge-out rate as measured by meters we installed on repaired tractors. This of course did not prevent misuse, but it did provide a culturally acceptable means for senior outstation people to at least attempt to dissuade young men from misusing the tractors, and at Kenycherreng (where there was a smaller and more solidary group with relatively clearly defined lines of authority around everyday affairs) it proved remarkably successful.

With the benefit of hindsight, and informed by anthropological understandings, I now see the nexus between the immediate consumption and use by Wik of (objectively) scarce resources (finances, fuel, equipment and so forth) on the one hand, and on the other the unrelenting pressure from demands on me and on other non-Wik staff, less adept as we were at evading such demands than the Wik men working for the support group. Both were ultimately unsustainable in light of available funding sources and personal capacities respectively, but both can be understood as forms of demand sharing (Peterson 1993), through which Wik opportunistically sought both tangible and intangible resources from others as aspects of what is still in many ways a 'foraging' economy (Martin 2011: 206). Of course, this was a system with me at its centre, which, in very large part, was my own creation. But I can now clearly see that this was a collaborative project to which Wik themselves actively contributed—a project of 'agency through dependency' in which Wik (as individuals, and in aggregations of various forms) sought to access both material and symbolic resources and strategically leverage relative advantage within a highly contested Wik polity through intermediaries or brokers such as myself (see also Sutton 2009).

As it came close to the time for me to leave Aurukun in September 1983 to study in London, the Uniting Church sourced a replacement coordinator. However, he had no experience in Aboriginal affairs or life in a remote community and lasted only a few days before having to be evacuated out of Aurukun. Outstation support was then taken over by ACI, which over the next few years made quite significant investments in outstation housing and other infrastructure in a number of locations. However, the capital investment by ACI in outstation infrastructure seems to have been in inverse proportion to the social investment by all but a few Wik in residing on outstations, and by the time I arrived back in 1985 to begin my doctoral field research, barely any Wik lived out bush.

Strategic engagements and disengagements

It is no coincidence that the gradual abandonment of most outstations coincided with very significant changes in Aurukun itself. The foundation for these changes was set by the 'takeover' of the Aurukun Mission administration by the Queensland Bjelke-Petersen Government in 1978, and the imposition of a form of local government under a compromise brokered by the Federal Fraser Government (Martin 1993: 3–5). Outstations in particular had aroused very strong opposition from the Bjelke-Petersen Government and from Killoran, the powerful director of the Department of Aboriginal and Islander Advancement, whose expressed policy at this stage was still one of assimilation of Aboriginal people into mainstream society. Departmental officers, the State police and informants such as barramundi fishermen conducted both covert and overt surveillance of Aurukun outstations and supportive mission staff such as John and Jeanie Adams during this period—part of general Bjelke-Petersen Government attempts to keep 'radicals' and their ideas out of Aboriginal communities.

The imposition of local government marked the beginning of profound changes in Aurukun. From a poorly funded and relatively simple organisational structure with a limited number of staff working for agencies actually present in Aurukun, and with comparatively clearly defined policies and practices, there quickly developed a complex (albeit ineffectual) administrative system, with a greatly increased number of non-Wik people living in Aurukun and working for the numerous agencies and organisations, and a massive increase in funding levels. The new breed of staff, by and large, were of a different order from those who had been there in the days of the church-run administration—totally unconcerned with how Wik people thought or with their worlds of meaning, and only with (ostensibly) delivering services. Those services, however, did not include outstations: successive council administrations made it clear that they would focus on the town of Aurukun itself and provide at best very limited assistance to outstations.

Concomitantly with this increasing administrative complexity, Aurukun people have been exposed ever more directly to the forms and institutions of the wider state: construction of an access road through to the Peninsula Development Road that was open for all but a few months of the year, the full introduction of a cash-based welfare economy, within a few years the opening of a liquor outlet in what had been up to that point a training centre, consumer goods, telephones and televisions, ever greater numbers of outsiders living there or passing through—all of which meant that while remote, Aurukun was no longer isolated. This period has been one of quite profound social, political and economic transformation in Aurukun; it has seen a progressive escalation of social problems such as very high levels of interpersonal violence, widespread alcohol and other substance abuse, increasingly troubled and often angry and alienated younger generations, and major health issues, such as high rates of diabetes and alcohol-related morbidity (Martin 1988, 1993, 2009; Sutton 2009). The increasing social dysfunction in Aurukun has in turn led to ever greater interventions by the courts and the legal system, and by other agencies and programs of the state (Martin 1993, 2009).

Aurukun people had come to national attention through the 1970s and into the 1990s through their feisty spokesmen and women, and their willingness to take collective political and legal action to defend their collective rights (for example, in opposing the 'takeover' in 1978, and in the early 1990s through the Wik native title claim). In contrast, more recently Aurukun has received unwanted (and resented) national prominence through its reputation for high levels of internal violence, alcohol abuse, destructive behaviour by young men, and other manifestations of a deep social malaise. The worsening circumstances of everyday life and its increasing atomism as social problems escalated—and as institutions of the state have established an ever greater presence in Aurukun, both required and legitimated by these very problems—have been paralleled by an increasing disengagement by many Wik from working to address the circumstances of their lives, whether at the individual, family or broader collective levels (Martin 2010).

The establishment of the Aurukun Shire Council created a new and powerful political institution, greatly expanded resources and new fields of endeavour for enterprising Wik politicians. Wik were as pragmatic as ever; despite the national campaign against the 1978 State Government takeover supported by the Uniting Church and involving many prominent senior Wik people, before long the council itself was front and centre in Wik politics and involved most of these same individuals. The dramatic transformation of life in the township of Aurukun itself, while frequently involving high levels of chaos and violence, also provided upcoming generations of Wik with a new and all-pervasive focus for life and meaningful action quite radically sundered from that which had underpinned the original rationale for outstations. During my own time in Aurukun and its outstations, I observed a radical deskilling, in terms of both the classical Wik world and the kinds of endeavours that the mission had focused on.

I also observed a quite profound involution in Wik life worlds. As I noted earlier, when I first encountered Wik in the 1970s, Wik people had a markedly ethnocentric and self-conscious view of themselves as the bearers of traditional culture in Queensland, but were also vitally interested and engaged in the wider world. Over the next decades, Wik increasingly turned inwards, with passion and energy devoted to the interminable inter-family feuds that paralysed life in Aurukun for days at a time (Martin 1993). I found among younger men and youths in particular widespread hostility both to 'classical' expressions of Wik culture and to what the wider society might offer. Many were angry, alienated and suffered major alcohol and other substance abuse issues.

Thus, there have been parallel processes of the progressive *disengagement* of Wik people (especially younger generations) from intimate connections to country on the one hand, and on the other *engagement* in the rapidly deteriorating life in the Aurukun township. Country has become more and more the focus of identity politicking within Aurukun itself for all generations, rather than of everyday lived experience, and knowledge of country has become progressively more attenuated. These factors—pervasive through many parts of remote Australia, in my experience—have profound implications for how we might envisage the project of realising certain forms of self-determination through outstations today within communities such as Aurukun.

New paradigms from the old: Productive livelihoods on country?

I (Bruce Martin) spent much of my early childhood between Aurukun and its various outstations and beyond them, as part of my father's ethnographic work with Wik families. The role he had played in outstation development, and ultimately in assisting Traditional Owners to record areas of cultural significance to them, had a profound impact on the way other Wik people viewed me. Members of the Korkaktain and other Kendall River families had always seen me as a Kendall River person, and reckoned their kin relationship to me through my father, as opposed to through my Wik mother. I was in a unique position from an early age in that I was 'within' the Wik system, both through my mother and through my white father, but was simultaneously seen as having a place 'outside' this system as well.

In 2009, I was partway through a Bachelor of Arts through the University of New South Wales, but by mid-year was fielding telephone calls from family back in Aurukun who were concerned about a recent declaration by the then Bligh State Labor Government of the entirety of the wetlands across the Archer River Basin and south to the Kirke River Basin as a High Preservation Zone under the *Wild Rivers Act (Qld) 2005*. This was essentially the area within which most of the outstations lay and within which the lands of the majority of Aurukun's Wik people were situated, and included my mother's country. My mother's family asked me to come back to Aurukun to help them make sense of it all, and to find out what impacts the declaration would potentially have on people's aspirations for their country. This included me spending three months based at my aunt's outstation on the Archer River, Stony Crossing. What I had known to be true (but had not realised its scale) was just how empty the outstations were to the south of Aurukun. As a boy, I had spent time visiting and living on various outstations and homelands, and at the peak of the community company ACI, some 350 Wik people lived on their homelands over a dry season. When I was there for three months in 2009, I was the only person out there.

The *Wild Rivers Act* issue forced Wik people from the region subject to the declaration to consider what 'country' meant to them, and what it might mean to succeeding generations, and raised questions about their ability to pursue sustainable development opportunities. The Wild Rivers legislation and declaration acted like a catalyst for Wik people to have in-depth conversations about what role they wanted to play in the continued management of both cultural and biodiversity values of their own lands. With the assistance of some external agencies, individuals and the Cape York regional organisations, we initiated a process of mapping people's own aspirations for country, family group by family group, based on their potential roles in the management of its cultural and biodiversity values, as well as economic opportunities. After more than 15 years of fighting for our native title rights through the Wik claim, the Wild Rivers declaration had shifted the focus to the right to (and need for) sustainable use and development of our lands, and therefore how to create development opportunities from our native title rights. My father used to joke with me that native title only entitled us (Wik people) to be native. This same argument around development was articulated in a very different way by the head of my own family group and ceremonial head of my broader clan group, Silas Wolmby. During our aspirational social mapping and planning processes in late 2009 and into 2010, Silas said to me:

> Our old people looked after this country, story place, sacred site, hunting and fishing ground. In return, that country looked after us and our families, gave us food and water, shelter, and looked after us spiritually. We are just trying to do that same thing today, look after that country so it looks after us.

During the initial engagement process, Wik people were asked whether they wanted a regional organisation to auspice the Federal Government funding that was initially offered. The very clear message that came back was that they would prefer to discuss and plan for a longer period to be able to develop a strategy that ultimately meant they had genuine ownership of the governance structure that was created and, ultimately, the outcomes that were achieved. What I understood from this was that—more than the outcome being achieved—what was most critical to Wik people was genuine input into the decision-making processes to achieve that same outcome.

A critical matter arising out of these detailed consultations was the need to build an appropriate governance structure around the aspirations expressed. This was ultimately articulated as establishing a framework to:

- assist Traditional Owners to get back to country
- assist Traditional Owners in the transfer of knowledge to younger generations
- maintain the cultural and environmental diversity of Wik and Kugu groups
- promote economic and training opportunities for Wik and Kugu people
- promote social programs to improve health and education outcomes for Wik and Kugu people.

These objectives are reflected in the constitution of the community-owned organisation I helped establish, Aak Puul Ngantam Limited (APN Cape York), and in the projects we have initiated. From the beginning, APN had a clearly articulated aspiration to reduce our dependence on government funding (while recognising it would remain essential to achieving the goals set for it, and that meant building enterprises). The philosophy was that it was impossible for us as Wik people to be environmentally, socially or culturally resilient without also being economically resilient—and that meant working to diversify APN's income streams to manage the risk of market changes and the inherently risky circumstances of enterprises in this region. We never underestimated the social and financial challenges in achieving this. During the Wild Rivers debate in Cape York, at a community meeting, I heard one old pastoralist say, 'It's hard to be green when you're in the red', to which I replied, 'It's even harder to be green when you're in the red and you're black'.

In the work APN and its partners did and the conversations that were facilitated, it was interesting to see the shift in language and thinking around productive livelihoods on country. There was an explanation APN developed for Wik people around the principles of market economics, in terms of putting in labour, utilising deep cultural knowledge of seasons and country, and being able to bring all of these together to provide for oneself and one's family. There was also a general understanding of this in the context of Wik art and crafts, and of course cattle-rearing. There was a service or product that Wik people had and were able to provide, and this was worth something in the outside world. The benefit of these services and products for Wik people was that it linked aspiration with opportunity and brought dollars from outside the Wik system into the community—dollars that were relatively untied to government. These sustainable livelihoods on country that people had mapped out as part of their aspirational planning and that external advice had shown to be a potentially viable enterprise also helped to establish, for some, an alternative to the 'relentless boredom' referred to earlier. The ultimate aim of APN was to have a diversification of revenue streams that would help mitigate seasonality and market volatility but which were primarily focused on outstations and would require people to be on country for periods—whether it was for a week as part of a weed-spraying program, for a couple of months for feral pig control and associated turtle nest management, or indeed for most of a dry season for families wishing to be near their kin working on country.

Thus far, APN has had some success in achieving its goal, but the difficulties of its operating environment have certainly been demonstrated. Perhaps its most notable success was in attracting a substantial six-year investment from the Biodiversity Fund established by the previous Federal Government. This is focused on such matters as feral animal and weed control and sea turtle nest monitoring and protection, and has provided important multi-year baseline funding for the Wik and Kugu Ranger Service. One component of this has involved the removal of feral cattle across the region between the Archer and Kendall rivers to reduce their impact on that region's very significant cultural and biodiversity values. This in turn has allowed APN to establish the beginnings of an appropriate-scale cattle enterprise, building up an improved quality herd over suitable areas. Funding for this has been an amalgam of cattle sales, and philanthropic investment through a combination of loans and grants, which have also allowed fences to be constructed and some basic infrastructure to be put in place. Cattle have an important role in the history of Aurukun; as noted earlier in this chapter, during the mission era, many Wik men were sent to work on cattle stations throughout Cape York and beyond, and there was a cattle industry during the mission period, re-established by ACI in the 1980s. The establishment of a cattle enterprise was one of the key themes emerging from our family consultations, but the very clear message was that it needed to be both commercially viable and culturally and environmentally sustainable. The work APN has done to date with key partners such as the Commonwealth Scientific and Industrial Research Organisation (CSIRO), Indigenous Land

Corporation, Indigenous Business Australia and the Queensland Department of Primary Industries (DPI) has allowed us collectively to better understand where this balance might sit.

Figure 11.1 Wik and Kugu Rangers burning open floodplain country near the Kirke River, south of Aurukun, as part of their fire management and carbon abatement strategy. In 2015, APN received its first carbon abatement payment, quantified through a research partnership with the CSIRO.
Photo: Rex Martin

Experience thus far has shown that as a stand-alone operation, multiple factors including the distance from markets mean that a cattle enterprise based entirely on Aurukun lands is unlikely ever to be a major source of income, but that it does have the potential for delivering local social benefits as well as important synergies with other activities on country, including increasing people's ability to access and use outstations in the absence of government funding. Another instance of where local knowledge and aspirations can be brokered around market and environmental services opportunities can be seen in the work conducted thus far by APN on a carbon-farming initiative. APN had established research collaboration with the Northern Australian Indigenous Land & Sea Management Alliance (NAILSMA) and CSIRO to inter alia measure the biodiversity outcomes and quantify carbon abatement from a managed mosaic burning regime conducted collaboratively with the APN Rangers across the sclerophyll forest sectors of Aurukun lands. As mapped by DPI, these areas do not support viable numbers of cattle, but with the work APN is doing with its partners on carbon abatement, the evidentiary basis suggests that this may be another diversified income stream.

APN has also assisted the Aurukun School with 'culture camps' out on country, and has assisted with youth programs in Aurukun. Much like my father and other outstation workers in the 1970s and 1980s, and indeed myself over the past few years, APN acts as a conduit between the aspirations and opportunities people have to access their country and the information, systems, partners and resourcing that are required to better understand and ultimately realise these aspirations. In 2013, APN assisted more than 400 Wik people to return to their traditional lands, and for many of the younger generation, to see it for the first time. For most it was for a few days; for others, for the entirety of the dry season.

Figure 11.2 David Martin in 2014 at the Kuchenteypenh Well with a group of younger Wik from Kendall River families, seeing their country for the first time.

Photo: Rex Martin

It is this role as conduit, bringing in new information and ideas, coupled with APN's ability to engage employees at various levels—full-time, part-time, casual/seasonal—to perform the work required, that has allowed APN to have some success in Aurukun. Indigenous ranger programs across the country are perfect examples of investment that creates benefit for all Australians, through managing large areas of critical biodiversity, but also linking to localised aspirations and Indigenous cultural practices. This investment is, however, heavily dependent on government funding and therefore at risk due to the political cycle. For this reason, Wik people articulated the critical need to have a diversity of enterprises that were built on market economics. We engaged our membership and described this diversification of revenue streams as being like the mosaic pattern of traditional burning. APN's long-term goal is to help establish a mosaic of livelihoods and subsequent entry points for Wik people, so that they are able to engage in relation to their own skill levels and interests, and for the period to which they are willing and able to commit.

Much like APN's need to have diversity in income and therefore mitigate risk, to be truly sustainable there needed to be a diversification of income streams at both family and outstation levels. One family member might work for the cattle operation, another for the rangers, there might be some family over a dry season that collects seeds as part of Rio Tinto Alcan Weipa's revegetation program (an Aurukun community resident working in this program made a taxable income of $45,000 in the 2013 dry season, logistically assisted by APN), the station as a whole might wish to participate in the native honey industry and there is the potential for small-scale carbon abatement credits, the potential for aquaculture and myriad other economic activities. The key message APN continues to push through the work it does in Aurukun is that, in the twenty-first century, greater economic independence is true empowerment. This means reforming Wik people's perceptions of work and welfare. Our community organisation needs to lead by example by reducing our organisational dependency on government. That is easier said than done.

The aim of APN is ultimately to create a variety of opportunities that will allow different people, with different skill sets, abilities and aspirations, to engage in meaningful, productive activities, especially those based on country. The strength of these sorts of programs, as I see it, is that they cater to people with those various levels of ability and understandings of work. Take someone who has only ever had the experience of CDEP or two days a week work-for-the-dole; it is unreasonable to expect them to manage a five-day week performing fairly rigorous work from the outset. A perfect example of this was in 2012 when we needed to do 47 km of fencing leading up to Christmas between the Kirke and Love rivers to help muster and truck out cattle. We had roughly six weeks to do this work. APN went through 46 casual workers during this six-week period; eight were offered full-time work starting the next year. Of the eight, four are still working for APN.

Earlier in this chapter, during his experiences in the 1970s and 1980s, David wrote of the ways in which Wik people realised their 'agency through dependency'. Through my own experiences, I found this to be true in the period from 2010 to 2014 in the work I did with APN. There seemed to be an incapacity and general unwillingness to take personal responsibility for even menial tasks and deliverables. Even senior rangers avoided requesting or directing others to perform work-related tasks, due to the impact this might have on inter-family relations. Much like my father in the 1970s at Kendall River and with the Outstation Support Group, I often found myself being made responsible for matters that required cross-family cooperation. Wik people who are truly within the Wik kin, cultural and political system find it highly problematic to engage across family and clan groups. This was not only an issue within the workforce, but was also particularly apparent when family put pressure on individuals to utilise company assets. The demands were often around using a ranger's time and APN vehicles to drive family out hunting or to take boats out fishing; the demands were incessant. At a critical start-up and growth phase for the organisation, these pressures could ultimately affect the companies' ability to deliver on contracts and to manage works within a budget. At the individual level, the demands on some employees during APN's fortnightly pay cycle were enough to make them quit, with one young ranger having to give up his hard-earned pay to close kin, some of whom had threatened him with violence. For him, the easier option seemed to go back into the system everyone else was in.

To me at least, it seemed that 30 years of CDEP and the new policy paradigm, Remote Jobs and Community Program (RJCP), are the destination rather than a transitionary program, and 30 years of relaxed expectations of what constituted a full day's productive work for the Aurukun Shire Council has meant that many younger generations of Wik have low expectations of themselves around work. It is this enculturation into a relaxed work ethic that has become a major barrier for many Wik people seeking more mainstream employment.

There were of course the exceptions, and in the APN experience these were a few older men who were respected for their knowledge of culture, ceremony and country. However, both of these senior men had experiences during the mission era of working outside the Aurukun community, on pastoral properties around Queensland and even in the logging industry in Papua New Guinea. Ultimately, this 'agency through dependency' has created a wicked dependency on agencies in Aurukun, both government and regional organisations. A by-product of this is that it has in turn inadvertently disempowered Wik people from being critical players in the decision-making processes within Aurukun. The other by-product is that the process has totally alienated an unskilled younger generation that has neither the deep cultural knowledge nor the ability to work between two worlds, which the Aurukun Mission previously supported.

The key strength in APN during the initial engagement, incorporation and early operations phases centred on governance. It was the approach pushed by key elders in those early days that, rather than be auspiced by an external entity to attract funding quicker and get programs happening sooner, we needed to concentrate on creating our own vehicle to achieve our own ends. The decision-making structures and accountability systems that were created were developed internally, Wik owned and led, but with external advice. Although there were mistakes and lessons along the way, it was a critical process as it created a mandate and therefore legitimacy in the decision-making.

Conclusion: What does the Wik experience say about 'self-determination'?

Here, we limit our conclusions to the Wik situation; we have not as yet given sufficient thought to whether they can be generalised beyond it. David Martin's 1970s understanding of 'self-determination' was that it entailed Wik people running their own affairs in a form of cultural and political autonomy, and that his role was to work collaboratively with them towards this end, and indeed under their ultimate direction. As he outlined it previously, his obligation was to 'work himself out of a job'. He was drawn into supporting the outstation movement in Aurukun, initially through personal connections with the Kendall River people and then more broadly, because it seemed clear to him that it was an expression of the desire of those Wik people for self-determination. The desire to be supported to move 'back to country' was strongly expressed (and to some extent, among some older Wik people, still is). We are of the view that there continue to be at least three compelling but largely pragmatic arguments— pragmatic in the sense of not having to rely on arguments for Aboriginal rights, important though these are—to support Wik people maintaining close connections to traditional lands.

The first concerns the imperative for the development of a mixed or 'hybrid' economy (Altman 2005) for Aurukun, which now has a working-age Wik population of perhaps 400 people but very low employment. In such situations, livelihoods on country of the kind being instituted across northern Australia, including in the Aurukun region through the work of APN, provide an important avenue for socially meaningful and productive employment. However, the APN experience demonstrates that only a small proportion of the working-age population—probably less than 10 per cent—can be involved in working on country, which, if sole reliance on welfare payments is to be avoided, suggests there needs also to be a substantial parallel move for many to engage with the market and state-subsidised economic sectors.

The second argument, and one linked to the above, concerns the involvement of Wik people themselves in the management and enhancement of a landscape that is of considerable national significance in terms of its biodiversity, through the provision of environmental services, carbon farming and the like. However, while the philanthropic and private sectors are investing in this arena, its sustainability is heavily dependent on government funding, and current political and economic circumstances suggest that this will be increasingly under threat.

The third argument centres on the significance of country to the transmission of central elements of distinctive Wik culture to future generations—and thereby also to the management and transmission of elements of a locally and nationally significant cultural landscape. For this culture to involve more than increasingly essentialised forms that are divorced from the realities of people's everyday experience, it is critical that there is a core of Wik people actively involved in gaining livelihoods on country, as well as those (visiting kin and so on) who orbit between Aurukun and outstations.

Each of these three elements would necessarily entail profound individual and collective transformation, and would require in particular significant changes in the dispositions and practices of Wik people—especially upcoming generations of Wik men—around the nexus between work and more generally productive activity on the one hand, and value and reward on the other. However, our own experiences in the Aurukun region spanning nearly four decades would suggest that there has been entrenched resistance to such transformations, or if not active resistance, certainly a pervasive unwillingness or an incapacity to change. Furthermore, any potential for 'working on country' and other such government programs to resource social transformation around these matters has been completely undermined by a lack of long-term commitments in funding and shifts in policy driven by ideological fads.

Finally, the twenty-first century is making new demands on the old thinking underlying outstations as manifestations of people wishing to run their own affairs in their own way. In the earlier period of David Martin's engagement with Aurukun, he gave little intellectual attention to what Wik people themselves variously saw as significant in 'their own affairs' or what they actually wished or were willing to manage themselves, or to how his own role might be understood, or more broadly to the interrelationship between 'their affairs' and matters arising from Wik people's interaction with the institutions of the wider society.

We suggest that 'self-determination', at least in the ways the term was used in the 1970s and 1980s, is best understood as shorthand for particular ideological and sometimes essentialised representations of Aboriginal agency, individually and collectively, and of the relationship between that agency and the engagement of Aboriginal people with the broader Australian society. 'Self-determination' has historically been determinedly focused on the collective Aboriginal group or community—here Wik people, for example, or the 'community' of Aurukun.

It leaves unexamined the critical role that individuals play in social change (of whatever kind), and assumes that it proceeds by some sort of consensus or collective agreement to a course of action within the group in question. However, we have come to the view that Wik agency, manifested in what we have termed 'agency through dependency', required and requires outsiders, or even better 'insider-outsiders' (such as Bruce Martin) and 'outsider-insiders' (such as Peter Sutton and David Martin), for the achievement of certain purposes, both internal (so to speak) to Wik society and relating to its engagement with the broader society. This is far from a novel argument more generally: in matters concerning Aboriginal health, it has long been proposed that doctors can be agents of social change (Cawte and Kamien 1974; Brady 2000), in part because, as Brady (2000: 8) puts it, they are an authorising 'other', a person who is outside the individual's immediate kin network and who can legitimate the transformation of particular behaviours (see Sutton 2001: 150).

And how could it be any other way? If we accept the thrust of the notion of Aboriginal life-worlds as constituting 'intercultural' social fields proffered in the Australian context by Merlan (1998) and Hinkson and Smith (2005) and others (for example, Martin 2003), it is no longer defensible to think, or act, in terms of a supposedly separate Aboriginal domain, Wik or otherwise. An inescapable consequence therefore is that social transformation requires 'brokers' or 'change agents' or 'social entrepreneurs' (to use common terminology) who are adept across the diverse repertoires to be found in these intercultural fields.

And this is never more the case than in contemporary Aurukun, where living and working on country are not in any meaningful way to be seen as revitalisation of some traditional world, but are absolutely a transformative project: multiple new skills, many drawing on modern technologies; working collaboratively with other Wik and with non-Wik and engaging in productive activities that serve common goals rather than aimless self-aggrandisement; structured time allocation; having regard to scarce resources; and more generally transformed ways of being and acting in the world that resonate with those of the classical past but are not limited to them.

References

Altman, J. C. 2005. Development options on Aboriginal land: Sustainable Indigenous hybrid economies in the twenty-first century. In L. Taylor, G. Ward, G. Henderson, R. Davis and L. Wallis (eds), *The Power of Knowledge, the Resonance of Tradition*. Canberra: Aboriginal Studies Press, pp. 34–8.

Brady, M. 2000. Introducing brief interventions for Indigenous alcohol misuse: Can doctors make a difference? Paper presented at Australian Institute of Aboriginal and Torres Strait Islander Studies Seminar, Canberra, 18 September.

Cawte, J. and Kamien, M. 1974. The doctor as a social change agent in Bourke, NSW. In B. S. Hetzel, M. Dobbin, L. Lippmann and E. Egglestone (eds), *Better Health for Aborigines (Report of a National Seminar at Monash University)*. Brisbane: University of Queensland Press, pp. 151–60.

Gerritsen, R. 1982. Outstations, differing interpretations and policy implications. In P. Loveday (ed.), *Service Delivery to Outstations*. Monograph. Darwin: North Australia Research Unit.

Hinkson, M. and Smith, B. 2005. Introduction: Conceptual moves towards an intercultural analysis. *Oceania* 75(3): 157–66.

Martin, D. F. 1988. Background paper on social and family factors for the Aurukun case. *Report to the Royal Commission into Aboriginal Deaths in Custody*, November 1988.

Martin, D. F. 1993. Autonomy and relatedness: An ethnography of Wik people of Aurukun, western Cape York Peninsula. Unpublished PhD thesis. The Australian National University, Canberra.

Martin, D. F. 2003. *Rethinking the design of Indigenous organisations: The need for strategic engagement*. CAEPR Discussion Paper No. 248. Canberra: Centre for Aboriginal Economic Policy Research.

Martin, D. F. 2009. Domesticating violence: Homicide among remote dwelling Australian Aboriginal people. In *Domestic-related homicide: Keynote papers from the 2008 international conference on homicide*. AIC Report No. 104, Research and Public Policy Series. Canberra: Australian Institute of Criminology.

Martin, D. F. 2010. The art of Wik politics and the politics of Wik art. In S. Butler (ed.), *Before Time Today, Reinventing Tradition in Aurukun Aboriginal Art*. Brisbane: University of Queensland Press, pp. 118–31.

Martin, D. F. 2011. Policy alchemy and the magical transformation of Aboriginal society. In Y. Musharbash and M. Barber (eds), *Ethnography and the Production of Anthropological Knowledge: Essays in Honour of Nicolas Peterson*. Canberra: ANU E Press, pp. 201–15.

Merlan, F. 1998. *Caging the Rainbow: Place, Politics, and Aborigines in a North Australian Town*. Honolulu: University of Hawaii Press.

Peterson, N. 1993. Demand sharing: Reciprocity and the pressure for generosity among foragers. *American Anthro* 954: 860–74.

Sutton, P. 1978. Wik: Aboriginal society, territory and language at Cape Keerweer, Cape York Peninsula Australia. Unpublished PhD thesis. University of Queensland, Brisbane.

Sutton, P. 2001. The politics of suffering: Indigenous policy in Australia since the 1970s. *Anthropological Forum* 11(2): 125–73.

Sutton, P. 2009. *The Politics of Suffering: Indigenous Australia and the End of the Liberal Consensus*. Melbourne: Melbourne University Press.

Sutton, P., Martin, D. F., von Sturmer, J., Cribb, R. and Chase, A. 1990. *AAK: Aboriginal Estates and Clans between the Embley and Edward Rivers, Cape York Peninsula*. Adelaide: South Australian Museum.

12

Peret: A Cape York Peninsula outstation, 1976–1978

Peter Sutton

Leaning on memoir, and extensive photographic and written records, this chapter presents an eyewitness account of just one of many Aboriginal outstations that broke away from population centres in remote Australia in the 1970s and later. The context is western Cape York Peninsula, Queensland. The event was the re-establishment in 1976 of Peret Outstation, named after the well Pooerreth near a cattle yard, as a homeland centre rather than the mission pastoral operation for which it had been created. It was, in part, a staged return to the countries of origin of Cape Keerweer people, who had in recent decades become settled in the Presbyterian Mission township of Aurukun to its north (Map 12.1). It was also a time of hope, adrenalin, politicking and pre-eminence, desperate shortages, bogged vehicles—Land Rovers, tractors, small planes—the luck, feasting and starving of hunting, happy children dancing by firelight, old people singing now forgotten song verses, the strains of camp life, and yet also a curiously sedate existence, as yet largely without media, alcohol, drugs or crispy fried chicken wings. Each character seemed larger than life. Perhaps they were.

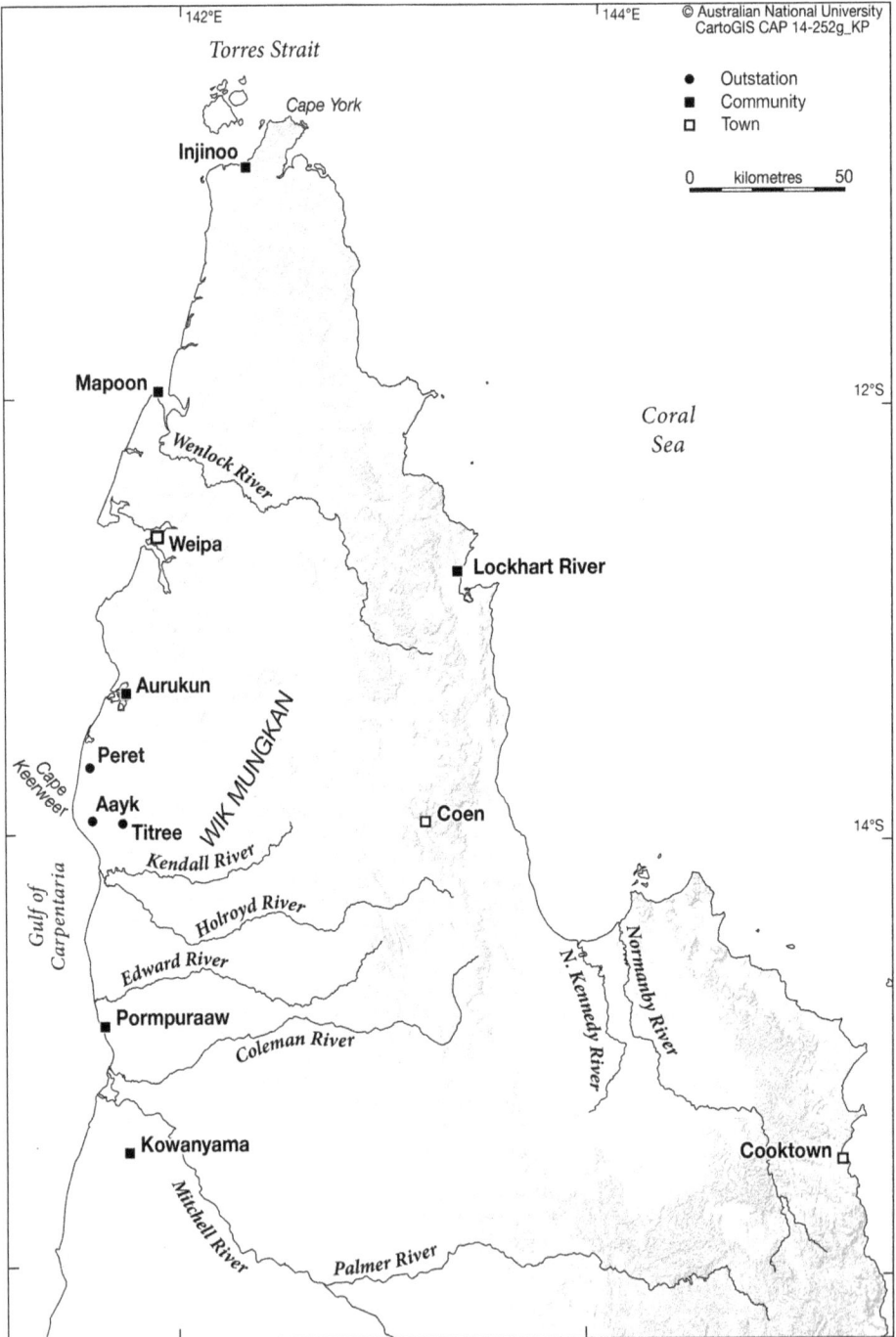

Map 12.1 Cape York Peninsula and Peret Outstation.

Source: Karina Pelling, CartoGIS, ANU College of Asia and the Pacific

Pre–land rights era outstations of Cape York Peninsula

Several mission 'outstations' (rarely 'mission extensions') had been established in western Cape York Peninsula by the 1920s. For example, the Aurukun Mission records mention an 'outstation' of Weipa Mission, which lay north of Aurukun, called Myngump.[1] This place on the Embley River is more latterly known as Moyngom (Hey Point), a key estate site for members of the Flying Fish clan of Lenford Matthew and kin.

Further north from Weipa was Mapoon Mission, which Presbyterian Mission chronicler of the interwar period George Kirke referred to as 'the station'. It had at least two 'outstations' in 1919:

> Along the Batavia River frontage is found the out-station, where the majority of the married people live. (Kirke 1919: 6)

> About 14 miles up the Batavia River is another out-station, where there are about a dozen families wrestling with the forest and bringing the land into subjection by the gardener. (p. 7)

Twelve years later, Kirke also reported the visit of Mr and Mrs Miller of Mapoon to 'the outstation on the Batavia River, where several sick people were attended to and helped' (Kirke 1931; see also Anon. 1932).

The vast Mitchell River Delta is south of Aurukun on the same Gulf of Carpentaria coast. By the time Robert Logan Jack published a map of the lower Mitchell River in his 1922 book *Northmost Australia*, the 'head station' of Trebanaman Anglican Mission had three 'outstations', Angeram, Koongalara and Daphne, and a fourth, Yeremundo, was projected (Map 12.2). The settlement was later known as Mitchell River Mission and is now a town called Kowanyama.

---

1   'Saul Mammus, Wusarangot H[usband] of Big Archiewald, from Weipa Outstation, Myngump.' Data card for Saul Mammus, c. 1896–1942, Aurukun Papers, Australian Institute of Aboriginal and Torres Strait Islander Studies (AIATSIS) Library.

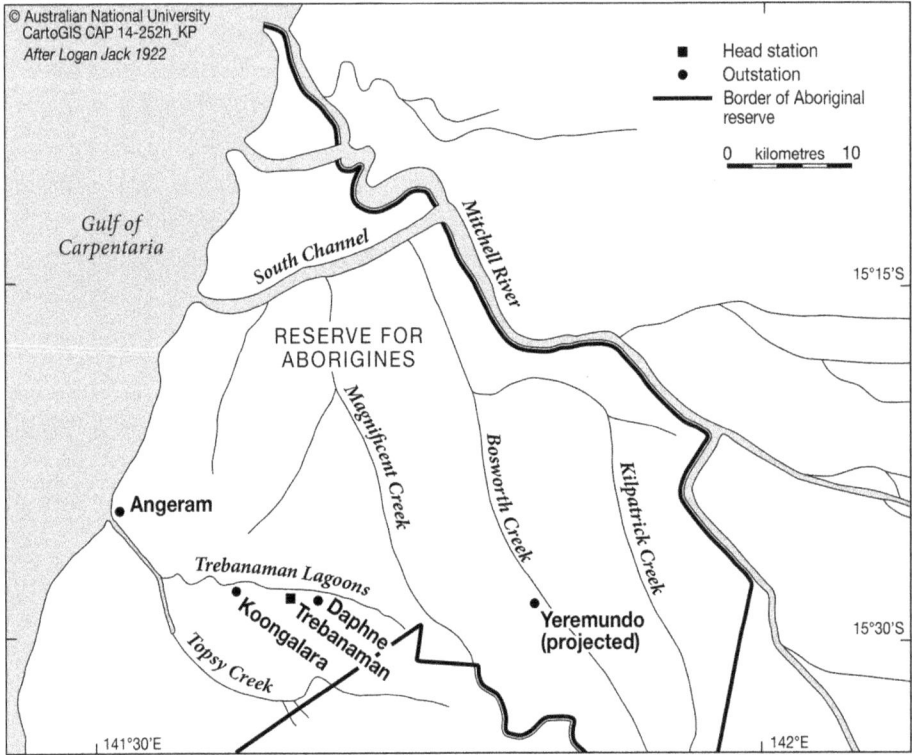

Map 12.2 Lower Mitchell River, Cape York Peninsula.
Source: Karina Pelling, CartoGIS, ANU College of Asia and the Pacific, after Jack (1922: Map F [detail])

This language of 'head station' and 'dependent outstation' was the language of pastoral properties (sheep and cattle ranches). It was a language established long before the outstation movement of the 1970s. In the Cape York Peninsula cases I have looked at, these older mission outstations were ostensibly based not on the traditional home countries of inhabitants, but on function. There was a division of labour. There were outstations for married couples, for horticultural projects, for stock operations, for isolation of the sick or for the isolation of the well from the sick. In the pastoral industry, outstations were similarly set up for particular functions—mostly mustering points with yards and pens for drafting, castrating, dipping and branding during the season. I saw and stayed at a number of these industrial outstations in the 1970s while carrying out linguistic salvage work in far north Queensland.

Before ever reaching Aurukun, I had worked recording Gugu-Badhun with Old Harry Gertz at a mustering camp on Valley of Lagoons Station on the upper Burdekin River, in the time the boss allowed him between a day in the saddle, food and hitting his swag. In 1970, I had recorded the languages of Doomadgee stockman Big Arthur on Seaward Outstation of Iffley Station, out west on the

Gulf of Carpentaria, again between mustering and dinner. It was run on the old lines. The 'ringers'[2] (stockmen) slept on the ground on canvas swags—whites and blacks apart—with their saddles as pillows, dining by the light of infernally dangerous carbide lamps, and eating beef, beef and beef, Burdekin Duck (salt beef fried in batter), damper (unleavened bread) and brownies, a traditional bush cake. The only entertainment was talk.

By 1928 the 'Kendall River Extension' of Aurukun Mission, staffed by Uki and Archiewald Otomorathin, husband and wife Christian converts from further north, was being maintained remotely from the mission's head station at Archer River. This was a difficult sailing journey through shoaly water off the Gulf of Carpentaria coast. Links were improved when the mission bought a launch for the Kendall run in 1935. Still, Uki and Archiewald had to walk back and forth at times (it is more than 100 km to Aurukun, as the crow flies, including multiple river-mouth crossings in notorious crocodile country). On one of these walks, Uki was killed by a taipan bite at Munpunng in 1948. His grave lies there today. His widow, Archie, as she was known, continued to manage the Kendall River Extension for about another decade after this, largely on her own, administratively. I knew her and worked with her in her old age. She was without doubt a strong personality and might under other circumstances have been an original Boadicea (Brown 1940). At Kendall she organised buildings, food gardens and Christian services, and gathered people for the mission visits when Superintendent Bill MacKenzie came to treat eye disease and other illnesses. All of the 'settlement' she and Uki set up disappeared after she left. When the location was reoccupied in the 1970s under the new secular dispensation, with David Martin (see this volume) as outstation adviser, nothing of Archie's work remained in a tangible sense.

Much of the way of life at Kendall in Archie's time was superficially the same in the Aurukun outstations of the 1970s. But the political economy that underlay it was now radically different. Carbohydrates were bought with small pensions from my tiny store at Peret, where I ran a line of credit with the Pacific Ocean victualling company Burns Philp. These supplies—mainly of tea, sugar, flour, powdered milk, tobacco, matches and ammunition—were shipped from Cairns via Torres Strait to Aurukun, reloaded into dinghies and hauled upriver to Bamboo Landing, then re-hauled into my Land Rover and driven south to Peret. All the protein, however, was hunted.

In the Aurukun Mission case, during the interwar period, temporary camps were set up north of Archer River and mostly within a day's walk from Aurukun for children's holidays, for isolation during times of epidemics, and for working

2   That is, 'shit-wringers', men who wrung the shit out of bulls, cows, calves, mickeys, heifers and bullocks as they pushed them to movement and production.

the mission dairy herd, coconut plantation or food gardens. Waterfall, Ikalath, Cowplace, Wutan and Possum Creek were the main ones, and all were on the northern side of the Archer River, where Aurukun lay.

A further set of mission-inspired outstations was set up for the mission cattle operations, which were in full swing by the 1960s—this time largely south of the Archer River. Access here was far more difficult as Aurukun lay north of the vast and intricate Archer system. The most substantial of these south-of-Archer establishments, at Peret, Ti-tree and Bamboo, had worksheds and stockmen's quarters, yards, bush airstrips, radio aerials, generators and concrete-lined wells with windmills to supply water. There were also a number of other, more temporary, cattle-related outstations south of the Archer, such as Hagen Lagoon, Donny Yard, Moonpoon, Kencherung, Wayang, Big Lake and Dish Yard, where cattle were yarded, drafted, castrated and branded seasonally. This work was carried out by Wik stockmen under supervision of a part-Aboriginal head stockman Jerry Hudson, or, later, other mission staff, but no outside stock workers were employed. Stock were annually turned off for market by being walked south roughly 300 km to Mungana railhead, and later, by being loaded on shallow draught boats from the coast (MacKenzie 1981: 174). In the wet season, Aurukun stockmen did maintenance jobs, and made useful things like belts from greenhide.

On first arriving at Peret Outstation in 1976, I found such a belt abandoned and hanging on a tree next to the cattle outstation manager's house. Pecked into the belt was a poignant statement of a stockman starved of company: 'ASLONE [sic] WHY WORRY ME GORDON HOLROYD.' Gordon Holroyd, a man from Pormpuraaw, was in a relationship with Jinny Gothachalkenin of Aurukun in that period.[3]

The old life and the new overlapped in the Aurukun cattle outstations in the 1960s, when two, and finally one, of the last of the mobile bands of bush Wik were recorded as visiting the cattle camps south of Aurukun asking for food. They were regarded as a bit of a nuisance by at least one staff member. In 1966 mission staffer Ken Cobden reported seeing 'two children about three years old down there [in the Peret area] amongst the nomads. We know of no such children. The youngest woman is over 55 and is almost certainly barren' (Gillanders 1966). These were the last Wik children known to have lived in a foraging band.

---

3   He was the father of Jinny's daughter Donna May Gothachalkenin, born in 1978. Jinny was killed by her later de facto Ken Wolmby in 1989. See Sutton (2009: 87–8).

Aurukun outstations in the land rights era

The first of the modern Wik outstations, in the 1970s sense, was established at Aayk on the Kirke River estuary by Victor Wolmby in 1971 (see Figure 12.1). This date is before the election of the Whitlam Government in 1972, from which the shift of policy to self-determination is often reckoned, so it is not part of the Whitlam era strictly speaking. However, 1971 is the same year as the initiation of the federal policy shift towards self-determination as expounded in Prime Minister William McMahon's Cairns address written by H. C. Coombs (Rowse 2000: 53–5). Still, that level of policy shift was not likely to have been felt on the ground at a place like Aurukun, where federal involvement was as yet minimal. More importantly, 1971 belongs to the period in which the Presbyterian Church (which became from 1977 part of the Uniting Church) was moving towards local self-administration as mission policy, and the very liberal Reverend Robert Bos was an Aurukun staffer. The influence of anthropologist John von Sturmer on the Aurukun outstation movement is undoubtedly relevant, though hard to quantify. He had worked at Aurukun beginning in 1969.

The earlier Cape York outstations lay squarely within the era when the churches and their missions, with the maritime and pastoral industries and State Governments in the background, dominated the political economies of settled Aboriginal people in Cape York Peninsula and the Australian outback generally. The missions acted as employment brokers for the labour needs of the lugger and cattle industries. Economics was soon to shift radically to unemployment, government transfer payments and the spending and gambling of unearned incomes.

In January 1976, I was visiting Aurukun with colleagues Peter Ucko, Athol Chase and John von Sturmer. During this time, von Sturmer introduced me to Victor Wolmby, also known as Victor Coconut (1905–76). The latter was no ridiculing nickname. One of his clan totemic titles as a man was Thiinethengaycheyn ('[He] Saw a Coconut'). 'Wolmby' was the mission rendering of Waalempay— that is, he was from an estate-owning group whose Shark men could be named after the parallel ripples (*waalempay*) of a shark's fin slicing the estuarine waters of the Kirke River where his country of Aayk lay. He was *Pam Aweyn* (a 'Big Man') ritually and politically. He was the top man for the Apelech regional ceremonial group and also the top man for the Cape Keerweer regional political sphere—a sector of the Aurukun population that was at that time dominant politically and demographically.

Victor's fellow patriclan members actually formed the best-organised and most coherent entity within the social field in which I found myself. This stood them in good stead for the struggle ahead. Their structural unity was mirrored in realpolitik. Not all Wik clans' members enjoyed this state. It was a target, not a commonwealth. Its varied achievement struck hard at less organised subgroups.

Victor recruited me as his son, as a fellow Wolmby clan member, and as what was known in remote Australia then as an outstation adviser. He wanted to lead his people back to the country from which they had gradually gravitated to Aurukun since about the 1920s. Peret Outstation was not his first choice—that had been Aayk, south of Peret, in his own clan estate, where he had paid young men out of his pension to cut trees for an airstrip, where he had in the early 1970s put in a wet season with his wife, Isobel, being thrown tobacco from the mission plane as it reconnoitred his lonely and perhaps stubborn isolation on occasions. But there were existing facilities at Peret: two airstrips, a house for the cattle manager, sheds, workers' accommodation, yards, a well with a windmill—all of them in poor condition or actually broken, but in theory (rarely in practice) capable of being rescued. No electric power, no running water, house wood rotting, fleas infesting the outside dwelling area, the house masterfully commandeered by cockroaches, the odd taipan in the (non-functioning) toilet waiting for a green tree frog to arrive—but a certain order of settled proxemics and understood responsibilities formed quickly among us in the first weeks. We were a manageable number so long as that number was smallish—about the same as the band level. Twenty-five to 50 was okay. Above that population sociality became exponentially more difficult and, ultimately, a nightmare at 125. Even in a post-conquest, hunter-gatherer context, demography can be destiny.

Peret was a politically workable alternative to Aayk partly because it lay in Victor's mother's clan estate, that of deceased Wikatukkin, whose estate was Small Lake, including Peret, and who was buried at Aayk. This now gave his widow, Isobel, a link to it as her mother-in-law's country. Wikatukkin was also the mother of several of Victor's siblings. Two of Victor's living siblings, sister Oothekna and brother Frank, and several of the adult children of their other siblings born from the union of Wikatukkin and Peter Pumpkin Wolmby, were in a position of successional claims on the deceased estate in which Peret lay.

On her first night back at Peret after many years, Oothekna (*Uthikeng*, 'Catfish') sang and keened for her mother and the mother's country in which she was now resident again. So although Peret was planned by Victor and later participants as a jumping-off platform for the reinvestment of the patriclan estates south of it, especially Aayk, it was also, in a clear sense, a prize of its own. In a sense, its whiteness underpinned its newness as an Aboriginal possession in the post-nomadic world of settlement. On classical lines, it also rapidly became the eye of a storm over who had rights to claim it, since its own patriclan had died out. Succession to the Uthuk Eelen (Small Lake) estate in which Peret lay was suddenly everybody's business.

I accepted both of the roles Victor had chosen for me. The Presbyterian Board of Ecumenical Mission and Relations accordingly made me a voluntary member of Aurukun Mission staff, under the title of 'Outstation Advisor, Peret' (Coombs 1976). My post-belief secular position was not, apparently, an obstacle to mission status. Actually, I didn't notice much demand for Christianity at Peret, unless the Reverend Silas Wolmby was there to act as a part-time catalyst of the MacKenzie paradigm that had also been the Uki and Archie paradigm at Kendall in the 1930s to 1950s, where Christianity, school, work and foraging blended.

Victor died in May 1976 before I could return. I got to Aurukun in time for his house-opening ceremony in July, bringing my wife, Anne, and baby son, Thomas. I intended to be based at the mission where my nuclear family would be living, and to help those moving out to the bush on a part-time basis. I had a Land Rover utility truck, a two-way radio, a .222 sporting rifle good enough for pigs and a Flying Doctor kit. I would do bush fieldwork and return to Aurukun to write up and rest up. But Victor's close kin had other ideas. I was to move out with them. Family had been augmented and redefined. And Victor's widow, Isobel, emerged from her silent mourning period as an elemental force, and as my chief mentor, in her late husband's stead.

Figure 12.1 Isobel Wolmby loading native bamboo spear shafts in her clan country south of Cape Keerweer, 1977.
Photo: Peter Sutton

Moving to Peret[4]

On 9 September 1976, we were preparing to leave en masse for Peret the next day. People were saying 'we gotta pull together'—an early indication that this was going to be an exercise in the reinvention of collective action under a new dispensation. It looked like it might be a tough call. It was.

We were nearly ready to leave the next morning when the manager (acting superintendent) of Aurukun, Syd Thomas, called me to a meeting in the main mission building. Also present were the mission liaison officer, Gordon Coutts, school principal, Alan Bailey, council chairwoman, Geraldine Kawangka, councillor Rex Walmbeng, and Bruce Yunkaporta, who was there as a parent of numerous schoolchildren. He was also my pseudo-actual brother-in-law, married to Victor's daughter Marjorie.

The problem was Alan Bailey's worry about the schoolchildren going out to Peret and failing to get an education. Argument ensued, words between Gordon and Bruce being the most heated. Then Geraldine had a 'tongue-bash' with me. Propositions flew. Bruce stressed the necessity of burning Victor's clothes and other possessions at his home country of Aayk, and of showing children the country; most had lived their lives thus far in the mission. In reply, Alan stressed the need for educated Aurukun people to take on the mining companies and other modern forces. Geraldine made some vitriolic remarks about 'these white dictators coming in and dragging people out'. David Martin and myself were the dictators. My journal comments here say:

> I stood up to her as well as I could, but must admit she knows the ropes of conflict a lot better than I do. (Sutton Field Book 22: 3)

> [I later that day] had a second confrontation with Geraldine (in public this time) with a little invective from both sides, BY [Bruce Yunkaporta] trying to soothe the flames. Afterwards, BY told me not to argue with her, and that I'd been mistaken in saying that C Keerweer [Bruce's and my group] and Tea Tree [Geraldine's husband's group] didn't get on together, the latter being a dangerous statement which could cause fights (!! Clearly proving the statement, and the extreme foolishness of anyone making it in a *public* context). i.e. the conflict 'officially' doesn't exist (unlike the Kendall–CK [Cape Keerweer] conflict which is open and results in actual fighting), though in private people say nasty things about the other group.

> AW's [Alan Wolmby's] advice was to play it very quiet & cool in my 3rd talk with GK (which she had requested 'this evening', with the concerned people present—i.e. Paul [Peemuggina], Johnny [Lak Lak], Clifford [Toikalkin],

---

4   This section is based on my field notes (Sutton Book 22: 1–29).

JA [John Adams] (*et al*?). I approached her straight away, a full 15 minutes after our [second] tongue-bash, and she was conciliatory, flattering, and shook my hand several times. BY apologised for not having introduced us before, and she & he both stressed the fact that if she'd known I was her classificatory father the argument would not have developed. There may be *something* to that. In any case I learned how rapidly changeable she can be, and how unrelated to reality are her arguments as statements of opinion. (Book 22: 3–5)

Rather pompous at the end, but I was trying hard to overcome what had been a fairly crippling shyness of youth during the 1960s in the cauldron of Aurukun in the 1970s. I could not afford to be a walkover.

I learned later how Bruce was able to act as conciliator between Geraldine and myself. They had been childhood school friends—a modern and innovative tie that bound them across something of a gulf of ancient structure: she was an inlander; he was a sand-beach man. Furthermore, her family was an established elite long at ease in the mission structure, and indeed she was named after missionary Geraldine MacKenzie and had been partly raised in the Mission House by the MacKenzies. Bruce was born in the bush among myalls, and his father, Charlie, had fought Bill MacKenzie in hand-to-hand combat over the issue of Charlie permitting his children to go to school in Aurukun.

But the mission agenda had been one of deliberate homogenisation of the children, and the children did a fair bit of homogenising themselves—rapidly adopting a single village lingua franca for regular interaction, for example, and engaging in these school friend pairings.

That night Alan Bailey got so drunk he could not get up the next morning to talk with Bruce, who went to see him. Bruce then saw Syd and Gordon, who agreed that the children could go out to Peret for two to four weeks. So on that day, 11 September 1976, we assembled at Aurukun Landing, got ourselves and swags and food into dinghies, and took them about 40 minutes upstream to Bamboo Landing. At Bamboo cattle outstation, we left Isobel, her mother, Yukwainten, and Isobel's siblings Rupert and Eembinpawn for the night, to be picked up and taken to Peret the next morning. The rest of us somehow fitted into and on to my Land Rover ute. My journal recoded that '[t]he trip to Peret was arduous and worrisome, and mostly done in pitch darkness'—because the young men were sitting on the bonnet and front mudguards as well as the caving roof. Oothekna, Victor's aged sister, 'was car-sick all the way, and vomited all over herself (and Marjorie)' (Sutton Book 22: 10). Apparently, Oothekna had never been in a motor vehicle before. By my calculations, we were 25 people on that Land Rover that night, inching along for more than 30 km in the gloom on a rough bush track. Alan took the ute back and picked up Isobel's group from

Bamboo the next morning. So ,by the afternoon of the next day, those who had arrived to inaugurate Peret Outstation in its new incarnation were as follows, numbering 28 plus myself:

Alan Wolmby and his son Rex.

Adrian Wolmby, son of Alan's brother Morrison and close classificatory brother and age-mate of Rex.

Kornomnayah, Alan and Morrison's mother. She was also a sister of Isobel Wolmby and Billy Landis.

Isobel Wolmby, widow of Victor, with her ancient mother Yukwainten (born c. 1899), her brother Rupert Gothachalkenin and sister Eembinpawn Yantumba and Eembinpawn's son Munroe.

Marjorie Yunkaporta, Isobel and Victor's only child, with her husband Bruce Yunkaporta and most of their children: Vicki, Iris, Cynthia, Perry, Ursula, Bruce Jr, and Charlie Victor. Bruce's (and thus his children's) patriclan country was Um-Thunth, widely known as 'Moving Stone', immediately south of Cape Keerweer on the coast.

Isobel and Kornomnayah's brother Billy Landis, with his Lamalama wife Lily Chookie (they met at Palm Island), and most of their children: Marjorie, Margaret, Gladys, Billy Jr and Janet.

Kornomnayah, Isobel, Billy Snr, Rupert and Eembinpawn were among the numerous offspring of Billy Wildfellow who had had eight wives. His estate, Thaangkunh-nhiin, abutted Bruce Yunkaporta's on its south.

Three apparently floating young men were also present: Roger Kalkeeyort, Roderick Coconut, and Derek Yunkaporta.

This skewing towards Isobel's clan, whose country lay south of Cape Keerweer on the same coast, was soon to be counterbalanced. Victor, Oothekna and Alan and Morrison's father, Colin, were children of Peter Pumpkin. He was the still-remembered root of the Wolmby clan with its estate, Aayk, lodged in prime country just inland of Cape Keerweer itself, on the banks of the Kirke River estuary (*Man-Yelk*, 'Neck-Road'). The estate within which Peret lay had belonged to Pumpkin's wife, Wikatukkin, and her patriclan. Pumpkin and Wikatukkin were the parents of Colin, Victor, Oothekna and their youngest son, Frank Wolmby. Frank arrived at Peret with his wife, Topsy, and two children on 25 September. Within the year, other Wolmby clan siblings of Alan and Morrison arrived, offspring also of the late Colin but by a different mother: Silas, Caleb and Ray Wolmby. Alan and Morrison thus consolidated their position at the core of the power spectrum. The Wolmby brothers were solid as a wall.

Figure 12.2 Marjorie Yunkaporta and some of her children cleaning up Peret airstrip, 1976.
Photo: Anne Sutton

Pumpkin had a brother, Bob, who had two sons, Noel and Paul Peemuggina. On 14 September and in the days just afterwards, Noel arrived at Peret with his son Peter, Peter's three children (Peemugginas, but the same clan as Wolmbys) and four of Peter's sister Chrissie's eight children (Namponans). These were all people with abutting clan estates immediately inland in the peri-coastal country of Cape Keerweer. The father's mother of the Namponan children was Yewimuk, Noel and Paul's oldest sister, another Wolmby. After Yewimuk there had been her younger sister, Mabel. Mabel's widower, Jack Spear, who was Noel and Paul's brother-in-law, also came to live at Peret that year and stayed continuously many months. He was among the most senior exponents of Apelech ceremony. He taught me many things at Peret and while mapping the sites of his own clan estate on the middle of the Kirke River system. He figured significantly in the MacDougalls' film made at Cape Keerweer, *Familiar Places* (MacDougall 1980; and see Sutton 2014).

Noel's wife, Mikompa, was a Yunkaporta from Knox River, south of Cape Keerweer, hence a 'southern Yunkaporta'. Her siblings Jack Sleep and Eeng (a sister) were to come a little later and settle at Peret as well, followed by Reg Yunkaporta of the same clan, whose sister Diane had married Paul Peemuggina. Reg raised Victor's natural son, Ron Yunkaporta, born of an affair between Victor and Reg's future wife, Moira. Ron visited Peret too about this time. The southern Yunkaportas were present but not influential in Peret's dynamics, even though they were so intertwined genealogically with the others.

Mikompa's sister Eeng and her husband, Johnny Lak Lak Ampeybegan, arrived on 25 September. Johnny rapidly took a formal frontline role as a senior man, though he, like other older men, tended to look to Alan Wolmby for ideas and positions. Alan stood behind the old men of this upper generation, but held much of the real power to determine outcomes.

Clans and landscape as political agents

The Peret estate was closely linked to Johnny's: Peret lay in the Uthuk Eelen (lit. 'Small Milky Way') estate, which drained, during the wet, through Johnny's Uthuk Aweyn ('Big Milky Way') estate on its way to the Kirke River estuary. These paired and adjacent estates were named in English Small Lake and Big Lake. The estuary to which they drained debouched into the Gulf of Carpentaria at Cape Keerweer. The Big and Small lakes people were thus geopolitically part of the Cape Keerweer group. Drainage was alliance politics. Structure here was not merely something reproduced by action, because collective action also relied heavily on structure. A 'history of consociation' by itself could not account for the formations of Peret politics.

Soon Noel's younger brother Paul and his three children had arrived at Peret, along with Isobel's sister Telpoana and Telpoana's doggedly traditional bushman husband, Paddy Yantumba. These last two persisted in the foraging life more than most, often camping together in isolation for long periods, Telpoana in fact dying at Aayk with only Paddy's company one subsequent wet season.

Thus far, two main patriclans dominated the demography of Peret: the descendants of Peter Pumpkin Wolmby and his brother Bob, and the descendants of Billy Wildfellow Gothachalkenin (such as Isobel), including people who were both (such as Marjorie and Alan, the two main contenders for boss-ship). The third part of the eventual upper mix, the northern Yunkaportas, was still building.

One northern Yunkaporta had been there at the start, on the first day. Bruce Yunkaporta was there by right as Marjorie's husband. His siblings could be there with him by right also. Soon, Bruce's full brother George Sydney Yunkaporta, and his half-siblings Clive, Francis, Mikompa and Annie and their spouses and sometimes their offspring were also living at Peret. These were all descendants of Charlie Yunkaporta. The two mothers of the senior sibling set were wives of Charlie, who were both called Arkpenya, and were Wolmby sisters. This marital alliance between Wolmbys and northern Yunkaportas had been going on for generations. The two clans were referred to by shorthand at Aurukun as 'W and Y Families'. Bruce's siblings included many of the most bush-bred and knowledgeable and articulate people of Peret. They held numbers but generally refrained from being at the heart of the regular disputations and screaming matches erupting between the Wolmby and Gothachalkenin factions.

This dominant threesome was, however, to meet its match.

The triumph of a late starter

By the end of September 1976, Marjorie and Bruce's oldest surviving son, Roy Yunkaporta, had moved to Peret with his wife, Sandra, and their new baby, Richard, and Sandra's brother, Trevor Bowenda. Little Richard was in the same camp as his father, father's mother, father's mother's mother and father's mother's mother's mother. This made my investigation of the perpetual cycling of kin terms rather easier than it might otherwise have been.

Sandra and Trevor were Bowendas, from their father, Denny Bowenda. Originating in the Nicholson River region of the Northern Territory when young, Denny was one of a tiny minority of Aurukun people recruited from outside the immediate region. His family had long been adopted into the same clan as Johnny Lak Lak's Uthuk Aweyn, so he was a Big Lake man. Denny was to come to Peret in later months, accompanying me as we mapped the Peret estate (Small Lake), and asking me for copies of the maps for his own use. 'The land *is* a map', he once told me. Indeed. And he kept his cards close to his chest.

What I did not see coming was that, to make short of a long and winding story too extensive for here, within just a few years Denny Bowenda managed to sideline both main contenders for leadership of the Peret outstation—Marjorie Yunkaporta and Alan Wolmby, both Wolmby clan members with Wik-Ngathan as their language—and wrest that leadership for himself. Succession to an abutting and linked estate of the same language as his own adoptive tongue (Wik-Ngatharr, not Wik-Ngathan), to an estate united to his own by a single drainage flow, and united by a neatly dyadic toponymy, together with Denny's adroitness, persistence, superior command of English and of the ways of Australian law and bureaucracy, all worked together to score a successful outcome for Denny.

The achievement of collective action

Before Denny's late coup, in my 1978 report to Peter Ucko, principal of the Australian Institute of Aboriginal Studies (which was then funding my work at Peret), I addressed the question of 'Organisation of authority and work within the outstation' (Sutton 1978: 2–5). I will quote that section at length, as it was written within the period and has a certain freshness as a result:

> Victor Wolmby was clearly both 'boss of Cape Keerweer' (a secular role) and 'boss of Apelech' (a ritual role). On his death, the ritual leadership passed without dispute (as known to me) to Clive Yunkaporta … Many people told me that his secular leadership passed by tradition to his [Victor's] wife, who had waived it in favour of their daughter Marjorie (married to Clive Yunkaporta's brother Bruce). Victor had no [legitimate] sons. His wife and daughter have struggled with tremendous vigour to hold onto the role of secular leadership, but it has been effectively wrested from them by Alan Wolmby, Victor's older brother's son. He is not the oldest of the Wolmby brothers (there are two older than he), but he is clearly the most politically adept and has carried through his involvement with the outstation movement from the very start with dedication and great concentration. Conflict between Alan and his brothers on the one side, and Marjorie and her mother (Isobel) on the other, continues, and has resulted in public verbal battles involving the whole Peret population from time to time.
>
> It will be seen from the data on population below [omitted here] that the Wolmbys, the northern Yunkaportas (Clive and Bruce's family) and the Gothachalkenins (Isobel's family) have between them accounted for a large proportion of the Peret community. The Wolmbys are not only numerically dominant, they are also politically unified and well-organised. The northern Yunkaportas, apart from Bruce, have not made any significant moves to assume any dominance in this community at Peret, and Bruce's moves have all been through his wife.[5] In conflicts, most of them try to cool the flames and often go away for a few days at a time afterwards. During one recent argument, Marjorie publicly renounced her status as a Wolmby, saying Aayk was 'a desert place, no water' and spoke only in her husband's language [Wik-Mungkan]. The third family, the Gothachalkenins, are completely fragmented politically, and their political thrust consists solely of the enormous and skilful efforts of Isobel.

---

5   In December 1976, Bruce Yunkaporta dictated the following handwritten statement to Syd Thomas, manager of Aurukun (spellings as in original): 'After Victor Walamby died the land at Cape Keeweer that belong to him his daughter took charge of the place (her name Marjarie Yangaporta) Allen tried to assume the Area as his & his brother Morrison did also, but Majorie is the only boss for the whole Area & no notice should be taken of Allen & Morrison. The Area in question is approximately 10 sq. miles & Majorie is the only one to allow any orders or work or changes to be carried out. Also her husband is helping her.' (MS held by Peter Sutton.)

By late 1977, it was abundantly clear that Alan Wolmby was, in most people's eyes, the 'boss' of Peret. A number of matters came up for decision while Alan was in Cairns getting a Toyota utility, and the older men decided to wait for his return before anything was done.

Figure 12.3 Alan Wolmby, 1976, with the tree he inscribed in 1971 marking the first day of his work on Victor Wolmby's outstation at Aayk with Victor.
Photo: Peter Sutton

Decisions are not made, ostensibly, in camera, but the essential power lies among the mature Wolmby brothers. Alan usually consults with his older brother Silas and younger brothers Caleb and Ray, but they all have a different mother from himself and Morrison. Alan and Morrison have the same parents, and are married to two actual sisters. They are the centre of the power spectrum. They and their wives do more of the practical jobs at Peret than any other definable group.

Major decisions are made by informal (but highly structured) public meetings. Males sit in a circle, females sit in a group a short distance away. Males are frequently grouped by clan, though only approximately. Each speaker claims to speak 'only for myself'. One speaker may put two or more opposed views on the same subject, without committing himself to any one of them, particularly in the early stages of discussion before a consensus has emerged. If the matter is important this type of meeting will occur several times over a few days before resolution is reached. Unless the meeting develops into open conflict, it is not a debate but a forum where views are simply launched into space. Younger men, frequently those with the most influence on the course of events, publicly renounce actual power and claim only to 'go by what you old fellows say'. The 'old fellows' usually make sure they know the mood of such younger men before coming out with a decision. The Wolmby brothers, for example, have made it explicit that they see themselves as 'standing behind' the older men. If government or other officials visit Peret, 'you old fellows march up to them and speak in language; then we come behind and explain it to them'. The use of older men in such cases amounts to making them figureheads and is only one of a number of instances where go-betweens, front-men and ombudsmen are used in political life in the area. The three older men who have signature rights over the Cape Keerweer bank account really wield very little primary influence in Peret affairs, and this is in accord with the norms of decision-making.

Collective work efforts, such as the clearing of airstrips by teams of up to 20 or 30 people, are generally initiated by one person (usually Alan) starting the job alone or with someone over whom their authority is not a matter of dispute (Alan takes his son Rex to help him). Others who wish to help do so. The giving of orders, or even the making of 'polite requests', is not normally how things are done among adults. Whether one is told or asked, the fact that someone else is trying to initiate one's own activity is not happily borne. Two statements most frequently heard above the din of squabbles in the camp are: 'You make yourself boss for me—you're not a boss, I'm boss for myself', and *'ngay ngay* (I am myself = I am different)'. These attitudes mean that collective work is possible, at least for short periods, but cannot be organised 'efficiently' along European lines, and does not need to be.

By general consensus, a rule emerged that no alcohol was to be brought in and drunk at Peret. This was broken in late 1976 when one person brought a number of bottles of rum from Coen. That evening a fight erupted (between Alan's brother Silas and Marjorie's son Roy) which resulted in a number of people sustaining bruises and cuts. This was the worst conflict that has occurred since the outstation began. I contacted the Royal Flying Doctor Service in Cairns for advice on the treatment of an infection [Silas's] resulting from this clash, and the radio message was overheard by DAIA [Queensland State Government Department of Aboriginal and Islander Advancement] personnel at Kowanyama, who notified Aurukun. The Aurukun manager (Syd Thomas) then arrived [at Peret] by plane with the community chairman [Geraldine Kawangka] and local policemen [that is, Aboriginal police aides; State police were not stationed at Aurukun until later], concerned to institute a structure which would maintain law and order. Virtually without consultation, he 'suggested' Peret have a community council of the Aurukun type, and also suggested who might be on such a council. The chairman was to be Francis Yunkaporta, because of his previous experience as chairman of Aurukun Council (a man who is definitely on the periphery of affairs at Peret). The other members of the Peret Council (some suggested by Thomas, some by local people) were Francis's brother Clive, Alan's brother Silas, and one of the older men … Johnny [Lak Lak] Ampeybegan.

Thomas also suggested that there should be a policeman. By local decision two older men, Jack Spear Karntin and Paddy Yantumba (the latter renowned for his spearing and fighting ability in former years) were appointed.

This structure came to nothing almost immediately, since the new 'chairman' soon chaired the biggest showdown to date between Alan and Isobel, the result of which was Alan's assumption of control in Peret. The need for an outsider had been significantly lessened, and the 'council' disappeared. One of the 'policemen' was given the job of emptying the toilet tins.

In broad outline, the politics of Peret have gone from relative unity at the beginning [1976] to greater fragmentation more recently [1978]. As population increased, the different 'mobs' emerged more clearly, and people more peripheral to the group arrived. Fission began to take place more often. This represents the re-emergence of the groupings and pressure points that may be reconstructed for the pre-mission period of fifty years ago. The politics of these groups has not essentially changed but, while the settlement life of Aurukun demanded it, they could be rendered fairly invisible to European eyes. The camping arrangements at Peret and in bush camps reflect alliances and divisions very clearly, since these are fluid residential situations. In the Aurukun town plan, it is often difficult to reserve village areas to those groups that are most close-knit. (Sutton 1978: 2–5)

The future in 1978

I closed that report with a section called 'Aspirations of Peret community'. I will reproduce that same coda here as my coda 36 years later. It is, as is inevitable, poignant. One needs to read this poignancy in light of the fact that Peret, renamed Watha-nhiin ('White-tailed Water Rat Sitting') after the humble bush well at its epicentre, never became a permanent outstation. It has been occupied, deserted, occupied and deserted again many times over the intervening years, and its purposes have altered with the times also. But that is another chapter.

Aspirations of Peret community [1978]

The establishment of Peret was aimed at the future, not a 'return to tribal ways' as has sometimes been thought. The immediate concern was to establish independence for the group, without forgoing the ability to come to grips with the European or 'outside' world. This meant that economic considerations and the need for education were paramount.

The basis of the economy of Peret and other outstation communities was, and still is, intended to be cattle. The low prices for cattle and the extent to which voluntary labour based essentially on kinship obligations can meet the demands of a beef producing operation were both against them. There was hardly any money available from the mission to pay to stockmen, and this was quickly used up. Fencing and odd jobs such as fixing windmills are done voluntarily, and several sheds have been built.

A Weipa barramundi fisherman [Neville Bagnall] has offered to continue to employ casual labour from the group, but on an increased scale, if they will make a deal over the location of a freezer within country 6 [Wolmby's Aayk estate], and if they will agree to exclude other fishermen from Kirke River. They have invited him to a point on the Kirke River to discuss the matter, but are wary. Some (notably close brothers of one of the erstwhile permanent employees [Peggy Kelinda, a Wolmby and daughter of Colin]) see a future in such work, while others see it as yet another case where they will be labouring for a European boss in their own country.

One enterprising individual [Billy Landis, sr, Isobel's brother] agreed to sell salt from the Kirke River saltpans to a cattle station on the Coen Road (Meripah Station [that is, to Bill Witherspoon]), since it is an expensive commodity on which freight is high. He collected the salt from another man's country [Johnny Lak Lak's, who later confronted Billy about stealing his salt]. On returning to camp that night, [Billy] collapsed apparently unconscious. Old ladies began to mourn. As he revived [that is, while I administered powerful Flying Doctor smelling salts that had a miraculous effect on his thespian torpor] they attempted to divine whether he had drunk from an increase centre. He suggested that the ancestors of the salt-place were getting at him. In any case, their principal living descendants tackled the salt-stealer the following day and, after a vigorous public dispute, the latter moved to Ti-Tree [another outstation]. One of the rightful claimants to the salt, however, collected more and took it up to Meripah [courtesy of my Land Rover]. This may be a minor source of income in the future.

I do not have any figures on incomes, but the principal source of money other than social services appears to be artefact making. If it were better organised, this could be more profitable, but would exclude the young since the principal makers of traditional bags, spears etc. are over 35 years old.

Gardens have been planted at Peret. Coconuts, bananas and watermelons are most commonly planted. The crops have been insignificant. By and large, the exercise is symbolic rather than pragmatic, and is aimed particularly at ensuring the maintenance of support from mission and other authorities. This is probably a legacy of earlier superintendents who stressed the importance of agriculture, and it has come to assume a kind of ritual importance. The kinds of things, which grow easily in the areas, are not considered basic food, except for the yams which were always there and which are still plentiful.

Some individuals have suggested that tourists be brought to Peret and sold artefacts, taken on a brief trip around the country, and generally told something of local culture. This would undoubtedly bring in money, but no great enthusiasm has been shown for it. People like Alan Wolmby would rather run their own enterprise. His purchase of a Toyota utility represents a move in this direction, and he will undoubtedly make money out of it by providing transport.

To a significant extent, Victor Wolmby's plans have been realised. Six or seven years ago it was determined that Alan Wolmby would be head stockman, Morrison would be the carpenter, Silas would hold the church services, and Peter would build fences. By the end of 1976, Alan had organised a joint muster of cattle with Ti Tree and sent four Peret men there to take part in it (all outsiders to the core Cape Keerweer group), had done some fencing, and took charge of killing a beast once a month to supplement hunted meat. Morrison had, with Peter, built a shed at Aayk requiring more than 50 sheets of iron for the roof alone, and had done jobs of similar nature around Peret. Silas was holding a regular church service (in the Wolmby's dialect) on the sand at Peret, whose attendance was many times that of any similar events held in the great church at Aurukun. (Sutton 1978: 10–1)

References

Anon. 1932. Aboriginal mission notes. *The Presbyterian Outlook* 14(2): 14.

Brown, D. A. 1940. Our mission stations. *The Presbyterian Outlook* 22(11): 7.

Coombs, K. V. 1976. Letter to Peter Sutton. 15 December. Sydney: Board of Ecumenical Mission and Relations.

Gillanders, J. E. 1966. Letter to Sam Edenborough (Australian Presbyterian Board of Missions), Aurukun. 10 February. MS1525/7. Canberra: Australian Institute of Aboriginal and Torres Strait Islander Studies.

Kirke, G. K. 1919. Letter to the editor. *The Presbyterian Outlook* 1(7): 6–8.

Kirke, G. K. 1931. Aboriginal mission notes. *The Presbyterian Outlook* 13(8): 5.

Logan Jack, R. 1922. *Northmost Australia: Three Centuries of Exploration, Discovery and Adventure in and around the Cape York Peninsula, Queensland.* 2 vols. Melbourne: George Robinson.

MacDougall, D. (dir.) 1980. *Familiar Places: A Film about Aboriginal Ties to Land.* Canberra: Australian Institute of Aboriginal Studies.

MacKenzie, G. 1981. *Aurukun Diary.* Melbourne: Aldersgate Press.

Rowse, T. 2000. *Obliged to be Difficult: Nugget Coombs' Legacy in Indigenous Affairs.* Cambridge: Cambridge University Press.

Sutton, P. 1978. Report on Peret Outstation, via Aurukun, Queensland. Unpublished typescript. University of Queensland, Brisbane.

Sutton, P. 2009. *The Politics of Suffering: Indigenous Australia and the End of the Liberal Consensus*. Melbourne: Melbourne University Press.

Sutton, P. 2014. Filming at Cape Keerweer, Queensland, 1977. *Journal of the Anthropological Society of South Australia* 38: 155–65.

FRUSTRATED
ASPIRATIONS

13

People and policy in the development and destruction of Yagga Yagga outstation, Western Australia

Scott Cane

I have called this contribution 'people and policy in the development and destruction of Yagga Yagga outstation' because it seems to me that the relationship between people was more significant than that between policy and people in the social experience of residents at Yagga Yagga. Yagga Yagga was an outstation of Balgo Mission in the Great Sandy Desert of Western Australia (see Map 13.1). My exposure to the story of Yagga Yagga situates the primacy of the community's experience in an amorphous middle ground, across the interstice of policy development and policy delivery that begs exemplification if the successes and failures of Yagga Yagga are to be understood and learnt from. The consideration here is less about the nature of policy and its consequences for people and more about the interdependent relationship between government policy, its agents of administration and the people who are affected by that policy and its administrators.

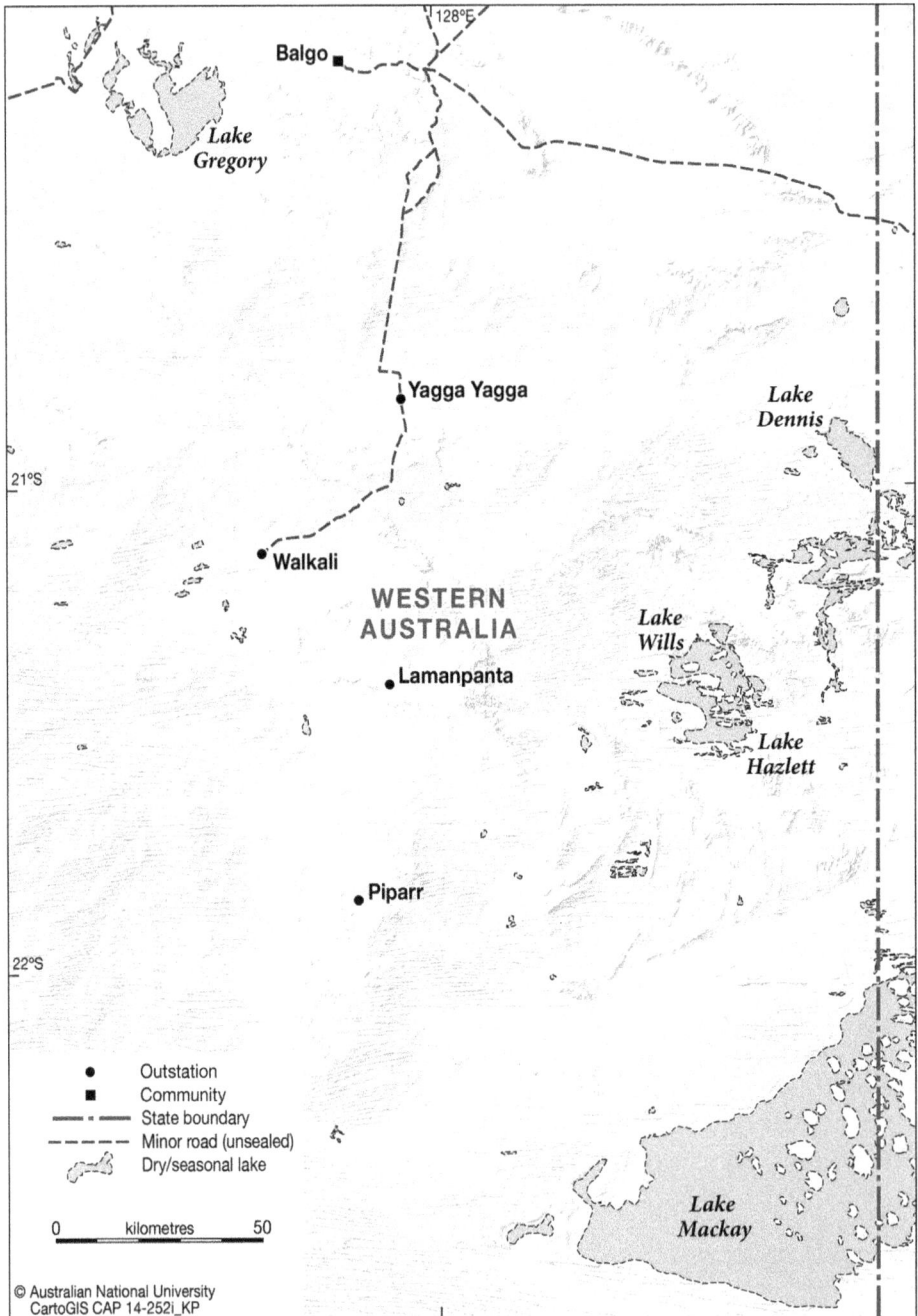

Map 13.1 Yagga Yagga outstation.
Source: Karina Pelling, CartoGIS, ANU College of Asia and the Pacific

Policy is, as a social and political goal, an expression of human experience—a formulation by one group of people in recognition and response to the needs of another. Policy is therefore necessarily subjective, formulated and implemented as an intersubjective action that necessitates, in significant part, a serial expression of interpretation and assessment: discretion hinged on proportional measures of comprehension, capacity, responsibility and accountability in a bureaucratic world of differentiated possibilities filtered through the personality, opinion, energies and commitment of the people constituting the agencies dispensing it. The administration of policy necessarily situates people, and so the discretion of those people is an important articulating force of social change.

The experience of people at Yagga Yagga raises a number of questions in this regard. What, for example, were the processes that played out in the development and delivery of policy for Yagga Yagga? What factors influenced the implementation of policy, why was the policy needed and how was the policy solution managed on its return journey from the community to the Government? How were the social needs of the people received, understood and transformed into effective policy delivery and how was that delivery transformed into social benefit concordant with the original need? How did the relationship between the needs of the people and the directives of policy translate across the amorphous area of bureaucracy positioned between them? What was the social consequence of the nature of translation?

It is my experience of Yagga Yagga that the people in the administrative process had great influence in the development and destruction of the community; and perhaps this 'agency effect' also has great consequence across Aboriginal affairs generally. People and the agencies they inhabit have, I suspect, an unrecognised (and easily overlooked) centrality in the effective and ineffective delivery of Aboriginal policy.

There is, I believe, an unaccountable space here as Aboriginal policy is essentially rights-based policy, articulated and administered broadly within the covenant of self-determination. This means that the policy configuration must be loose, in so far as 'loose' equates with and allows for the social and geographic flexibility necessary for free and unfettered political expression. Free and unfettered expression translates into variable (and at times idiosyncratic) form and directive that implicitly lack definition and contingent regulation and accountability—the allowable consequence of which is that policy delivery is articulated between the policymakers and the policy-takers in a manner that is itself self-determined. Everyone in the chain of delivery has a qualified 'voice' such that no voice resonates particularly and no voice is particularly authoritative, responsible or accountable. The intersubjectivity of the multiple voices of self-determination—between the desert and the desk—necessitates (and must result in) indeterminate consequences for the people in need of the policies developed for them. There is, in other words, a space between policy and people across which policy generally, and homelands policy particularly, succeeds or fails as a consequence of the discretionary powers conditioned by self-determination and configured by the political perceptions, sympathies, aspirations and abilities of its administrators.

Success or failure is itself a matter of perception, but the notion of unfettered discretion as a consequential hallmark of self-determination suggests that the aspirations of people and the intentions of policymakers may be lost in translation; policy intentions and people's aspirations may be subverted in favour of the intentions and aspirations of the individuals and agencies situated in relation to them. The inevitable conclusion is that 'discretion' becomes a central and significant component in the delivery of successful policy outcomes and the positive realisation of community well-being. The history of Yagga Yagga indicates that, regardless of the policy approach or the aspirations of the community, outcomes were largely determined by the middlemen and women operating in relation to them, without particular accountability to either.

The voice of self-determination

I want to start the chapter in 1979 because in that year one hears the emerging voice of self-determination from the northern margins of the Great Sandy Desert. It is heard in the original sense of the policy, as a political voice regarding 'future development' and 'control of policy and decision making' (Snowdon 1990)—not the later, conflated agenda of self-management, administration and 'responsibility', with its attendant notions of 'freedom' as eventually articulated by the Fraser Government (Fraser and Simons 2010: 390).

In 1979, the call from north-western Australia was for self-determination alone—as a political voice. This was the era of Noonkanbah (Hawke and Gallagher 1989) and saw the birth of the Kimberley Land Council (KLC). It was also the first public record of an intelligent and charismatic young Balgo spokesman, Mark Moora, on the newly formed KLC executive (KLC 1979: 2). Mark would become the voice of Yagga Yagga.

In that year, he wrote to the director of the WA Aboriginal Lands Trust, 'seeking rights to his communities traditional lands'.[1] Those lands had been mapped by Ronald Berndt in 1972 and lay south of Balgo, extending as far south as Lake Mackay, with Yagga Yagga near their northern margin.

---

1   Letter to Director of Aboriginal Lands Trust, 20 January 1979. Hevern 1979: 18.

By 1980, people were travelling widely through their homelands on the back of heritage surveys associated with oil exploration (Akerman 1980, 1981, 1982; Palmer 1980; Cane and Novak 1980, 1981), driven largely by the policy commitments of the Liberal State Government and the duty of the minister under Section 10 of the *Aboriginal Heritage Act* (*AH Act*), and the proximal vision of the Noonkanbah conflict. Regional oil exploration necessitated large-scale archaeological and anthropological surveys and saw the arrival of Kim Akerman, Kingsley Palmer, Peter Bindon and myself on the scene. The combined fieldwork capacity of these individuals, knowledge of senior men and exploration requirements placed people back in their country for the following years and led to the discovery of potable water in the sand plains on the northern margin of that exploration area. This was very close to the country of Mark's father and the birthplace of his sister, Nellie Njamme.

By 1980, the larger homeland movement across the desert had been under way for some time—and, as an articulation of self-determination, people were determining a preference to leave the violent communities established for them outside their country and return to a quiet, simple, autonomous life in small camps in country. The homeland movement here was a movement born more from the desires of people than the direction of policy, although the Federal Government had created a political platform, a place and a possibility (through its policy of self-determination, land rights legislation and grants of $10,000 from the Council for Aboriginal Affairs) (Cane 1989).

The homeland movement was, at that time, a movement ahead of Federal and State policy preparedness: Federal administration was struggling to keep up with the momentum and character of the movement that, as I recall, was seen as an event of some social, economic and political concern. It was an unmanaged movement of colossal geographic scale: there were five desert homeland settlements in 1975, 41 by 1980 and 72 by 1984. By the late 1980s, there were more than 100 outstations across the desert, accounting for more than 3,000 people. More widely in remote Australia, there were 165 homelands in 1981 and a population of 4,200 people, 400 to 600 homelands in 1986 with a population in the order of 10,000 people and growing to about 1,000 outstations housing between 13,000 and 32,000 people across Australia by the late 1990s (Myers 1976; Penny et al. 1977; Stead 1982; Nathan and Japanangka 1983; Cane and Stanley 1985: 32; Blanchard 1987; Altman et al. 1998).

Balgo Hills community

In the early 1980s, Balgo Hills Mission, a Catholic mission established in 1939, was a large and sophisticated enterprise. It was an artificial community incorporating a mission, cattle station, service station, store, service centre, fuel agency, bank, post office and air charter service, as a multi-million dollar jigsaw of religious fundamentalism, community management, government accountability, financial management, unprofitable business enterprises, community upkeep and welfare, technical maintenance and servicing, education and health in an isolated, demanding environment, occupied by about 300 naive and traditional desert nomads facing rapid social change who had been trained, in part, to fix fences, make beds and serve food in the community kitchen.[2]

At the same time, regional governmental perspectives regarding self-determination shifted into a policy of self-management and 'self-government'— and in the case of Balgo, sought the transfer of community responsibility to the local people, unmindful of their notable lack of capacity to carry it. None of the Aboriginal people I knew wanted to take over the management of Balgo, although regional bureaucrats were enthusiastic on their behalf. Desert people were not equipped to deal with the necessary management and decision-making to ensure the continued smooth operation of Balgo. Self-management was effectively thrust on them.

At the regional level the mission was being starved out of operation: in 1982, government funding allocation was reduced to $3,900 per quarter, or $37 a day.[3] Not surprisingly, social problems that did not exist began to appear: community confusion in 1982 became a community crisis in 1984 and, after the dismissal of Father Ray Hevern, Balgo became a community in chaos.[4] Balgo Hills was formally incorporated as an Aboriginal Association in 1984 and that same year saw riots, communal drunkenness, the sexual assault of a female employee, violent intimidation, vandalism and theft, assault at knife-point and break-ins: an 'almost schizophrenic change' towards anger, petulance and violence, unprecedented in the 'missionary years'.[5]

---

2   Brief to the Minister dated 19 August 1983, from B. W. Easton, Acting Director, Department of Aboriginal Affairs [hereinafter DAA], Western Australia. For ethnographic background on the Balgo community, see Poirier (2005); McCoy (2008).
3   Letter to Minister of Aboriginal Affairs from Father R. Hevern, 27 December 1982.
4   Letter from P. Sheridan, 8 November 1983, to Senior Assistant Director Community Development Branch, of Aboriginal Affairs, WA; Report on Visit to Balgo Mick Marshall 17/2/1987, File Note DAA19/1984 Department, Cane 1989.
5   Community records 1984: handwritten, S. Cane 1989.

Non-Aboriginal people began running grog into the community; there were 11 drunken assaults on white staff between 1985 and 1987, by which time the handful of missionaries had been replaced with 40–50 white staff. By 1987, conditions at Balgo were described as 'appalling', but in a speedy repositioning of history, this disaster was now seen as the community's fault by the Department of Aboriginal Affairs (DAA). The Community Council was described as 'having lost direction, credibility and the ability to manage' (as if they had once had it). The problems facing them were recognised, somewhat belatedly, as being 'beyond their control'.[6]

It is not surprising therefore that some within the community sought an alternative solution that was in their control, involving fewer people, fewer problems, and among family in home country. People began moving south to the water point established by Mobil Oil and acquired by Mark Moora in 1984.

Meanwhile, back at Balgo, office workers had fled the community, children had vandalised a charter plane, thefts continued and brawling was common (Guild 1988). There were two large riots between police and Balgo residents at Halls Creek, both of which were stopped by senior men who travelled up from Yagga Yagga for that purpose. When I was asked by the Community Council to visit Balgo in 1989 and reflect on its future, I was formally advised by the regional office of the DAA that the Government could not guarantee my safety.

Yagga Yagga

1980s: Peace and tranquillity

Yagga Yagga was established as a homeland in 1985 largely independent of government funding, with the assistance of the Institute for Appropriate Technology in Alice Springs. It was a local movement inspired by regional developments among the Pintupi to the south (see Myers 1986; and this volume) and driven by local people—in opposition to and in contrast with Federal and State Government policy initiatives at the time.[7]

---

6   Telex 30 December 1982 from DAA Perth to Balgo; File note DAA5/2/85 and 18 February 1985; Marshall 1987; Anon. 1989, Confidential report: 42-443; DAA file note 31 December 1987; Phelan To Community Health Derby, 21 October 1987; DAA confidential paper, 'Balgo—New Management Plan', 9 April 1987; also File Note 16 April 1987 from Cedric Wyatt, Telex to DAA 2 July 1984; Cane (1989).
7   Undated Council minutes and DAA file note 26/2/86, DAA file note 16/3/1987, Cane 1989.

The name Yagga Yagga is taken from the Wati Kutjarra ('Two Men') *Tjukurrpa* (Dreaming) and means 'to be quiet' (in the context of the Two Men walking quietly across the plains to avoid waking a large sleeping snake). The name was applied to the small settlement and was indicative of the circumstances that gave rise to it: a place of intended peace and tranquillity.

Yagga Yagga was not, in this sense, a product of nostalgic desire for a return to the past,[8] nor a confused attempt to mix the past with the present or amalgamate traditions with modernity. It was a local solution to the terrible social problems at Balgo Hills, created, in the final instance, by policy directives engendered and driven by the regional office of the DAA. Yagga Yagga emerged as an escape from the consequences of poor government policy configured by the intentional manipulation of the emergent policy of self-determination redressed as an opportunity for Aboriginal self-management, which was, at root, a poorly disguised excuse for removing the missionaries. Yagga Yagga was less a return to the past than a solution to the present.

In 1986, Yagga Yagga consisted of four galvanised-iron sheds with verandahs and a series of corrugated-iron shelters and was occupied by about 60 Ngarti, Kukatja, Warlpiri and Pintupi-speaking people. In the same year, Mark Moora acquired $68,000 for refrigeration units, an airstrip upgrade, a bulldozer, a second-hand four-wheel-drive and fuel. Discussions were taking place for a part-time school. There was also a chook pen and a communal tap and bath fed by a header tank filled each morning with a diesel pump.[9]

The first 'Desert Women's' project began with the involvement of Sonja Peters. Balgo painting had started; the majority of painters painted and lived at Yagga Yagga, in country. An account of their experiences was published (Tjama et al. 1997).

In the late 1980s, Yagga Yagga was officially recognised as 'a refuge for those who wanted to escape the drunkenness and unrest at Balgo' (Anon. 1989: 40). It was well-managed and strategically placed in terms of traditional country and resources. The community model was copied from Nyirrpi, with part-time schooling, fortnightly store runs and health visits from Balgo.

The new settlement and associated community aspirations required some additional infrastructure, and I drafted and costed a proposal for a four-year, $4.5 million homelands program in 1989. The program was intended to provide infrastructure (and associated opportunity) proportional to the needs and

---

8   But broadly in line with homelands motivation as summarised in Coombs et al. (1983: 220).

9   Balgo Community council allocated $68,000 for these items in 1986–87. Undated Council Minutes and DAA File Note, 26 February 1986.

capacity of its intended occupants: basic houses, airstrips, roads, solar-powered radios and refrigeration, water bores with hand pumps, tractors for local use, and unregistered vehicles for use on the lands (Cane 1989; Cane and Stanley 1990).

The Federal Government was by then supportive of the homeland movement and, after the House of Representatives, *Return to Country* report (Blanchard 1987), had allocated some $50 million in support of the larger movement. Minister Gerry Hand made a special, discretionary grant of $4.5 million for the Yagga Yagga program.[10]

In contrast, the State Labor Government had conducted its own 'Task Force Investigations' into Balgo's problems and expressed 'serious' but unspecified 'concerns' about the homelands program and proposed instead the establishment of a police station at Balgo.[11] In 1990, community violence and vandalism at Balgo almost ceased. The police station was not yet built.

The Aboriginal and Torres Strait Islander Commission (ATSIC) replaced the DAA in 1990. ATSIC was not prepared to carry on DAA's funding commitment to Yagga Yagga, and I was asked by the regional office of DAA to commit the remaining allocation—more than $3.7 million—in the remaining 17 weeks of the 1989 financial year (between April and July 1990).

The homelands program was thus established rather more quickly than planned, with Yagga Yagga completed, along with smaller outstations at Walkali, Lamanpanta and Piparr, within a radius of 80 km. The program saw an almost immediate resettlement of the area that lasted for several years—about the duration that recurrent funding was provided to maintain communication across the larger area.

As funding evaporated (and vehicles broke down), people fell back to Yagga Yagga, which then housed about 150 permanent residents.[12] Yagga Yagga was described as a magnificent success—notably, as a community relying on minimal non-Aboriginal personnel. There were just two white people (Chris Carey first, followed by Robert Taylor) employed sequentially across that period, with cyclical visits of nursing and teaching staff.

---

10   I discussed the Yagga Yagga program with the minister at Oak Valley in South Australia during negotiations for the establishment of an ATSIC regional council. The grant was made in 1989.

11   Letter to DAA from Aboriginal Areas Protection Authority (hereinafter AAPA), 19 April 1989; and see Anon. (1989), addressed in detail in Cane and Stanley (1990).

12   Current list of names and addresses at Yagga Yagga as at 30 June 1997, List of names, Kimberley Public Health Unit, 10 April 1997. The numbers swelled to about 500 people during one period of initiation ceremonies in the early 1990s.

With exceptions in each case, there was no drinking at the outstations and no vandalism. Traditional landowners asserted authority in the context of their gender, family and seniority without the assistance of white people or police. Vehicles were relatively well maintained, with people paying for the repairs from their own savings.[13] The local tractors were used as intended for local foraging and wood collection. One of those tractors was still operating as intended in 2008—18 years after delivery. People regularly travelled the 8–15 km to adjacent waterholes and sweet potato fields for recreation and food.[14]

ATSIC's initial engagement with Yagga Yagga was, however, problematic, as it stumbled with staffing and management problems in its first years. Part of the new management regime presented the desert people with a cycle of relatively inexperienced Anglo-Aboriginal middle-class administrators who had their own views of what was good and acceptable for desert people and, as Aboriginal people themselves, no longer saw the need for advice from non-Aboriginal specialists like myself.

When I went to meet new ATSIC staff in Kununurra in 1991, no one knew anything about the homeland developments at Yagga Yagga; no one had been there or read reports written relating to the movement, and there were no copies in the office. Policy programming and implementation were difficult for other reasons as well. In the early 1990s, for example, ATSIC's administrative structure was divided into three program areas, 19 subprograms with 47 components and 109 subcomponents and 115 sub-subcomponents (ATSIC 1992), and in the two areas in which I was principally involved, serviced from Kalgoorlie and Kununurra, there were eight different regional managers and 13 different project managers in the first two years.

By 1992, however, ATSIC had a National Homelands Policy and Yagga Yagga met its funding criteria: it had land tenure, occupancy, potable water and servicing (O'Donoghue 1992: 5) and began to reap material benefits. Recurrent and capital funding increased from just more than $50,000 in 1992 to more than $750,000 in 1993. Yagga Yagga was given new architecturally designed three and four-bedroom homes with flushing toilets, a huge new store, a new clinic, a new multi-roomed office, larger fuel storage, community lighting, electricity in every home and a massive generator to run them.

---

13   Notable exceptions are recorded in Cane and Stanley (1990).
14   The resources in this area are described in detail in Cane (1989).

The material growth brought bigger budgets and more complicated machines and systems that necessitated increased specialised support. Yagga Yagga crept happily beyond its own management capacity[15] and successfully grew into a small Balgo—but was a more distant community and thus more difficult to service.

Yagga Yagga thus became materially rich but logistically poor. In 1996, for example, it had a recurrent budget of more than $1.3 million but 'only had a nurse visiting the community on 6 1/2 days' over a six-month period.[16] In 1997 there was only one visit by the nurse each fortnight, the road was 'bad' and the 'telephone service' was 'intermittent'.[17] There were 126 adults receiving wages at Yagga Yagga in that year,[18] suggesting a population of more than 200 people. Decisions were still made by the Traditional Owners of the land, the community was described as 'cohesive' and enjoyed the benefit of 'good community staff'.[19] Funding peaked in 1998 at more than $2 million dollars that financial year.

This period coincided with a change in State Government from Labor (Premier Carmen Lawrence) to Liberal (Premier Richard Court), and the Ministry of Aboriginal Affairs came under the direction of five different ministers between 1990 and 1997.[20] They pursued an alternative policy of communal consolidation and control in the context of modernisation with an emphasis on law and order, with dubious success, as implied by the drunken riots by Balgo residents at Halls Creek in 1996 that saw the siege of the police station for more than five hours and led to 66 arrests.

The State's policy solution was to strengthen the police presence, add night patrols, create Aboriginal wardens, provide vocational training and employment, improve access to sport and recreation, and teach various short courses for which the State Government allocated $1.76 million that financial year; 20 students at Balgo were enrolled in short courses in literacy, numeracy, arts and crafts.[21]

At that time, Yagga Yagga was busy, fully occupied and healthy. Trees had grown and there were no litter or vandalism. Something of its vitality can be seen in a kind of Yagga Yagga scrapbook prepared by Tjama and others (1997) between 1987 and 1995. Balgo, in comparison, had just seen the fatal stabbing

---

15   Details of these budgets were recorded by myself from files held (and copied) at Yagga Yagga in 2002.
16   Letter from Community to Tommy Stevens MLC, 26 March 1997.
17   Letter from Yagga Yagga, 3 February 1997.
18   Yagga Yagga wages sheet (signed), 6 June 1997.
19   Conversation with the then regional manager for ATSIC, at Kununurra (Cane Diary 2002: 145).
20   These being: Carmen Lawrence (1990); Judith Watson (1991); Kevin Mison (1993); Kevin Prince (1994); Kim Hames (1997).
21   August 1996: Legislative Council questions on notice, 30 October 1996 and 5 November 1996; Blagg and Valuri (2003).

of a girl and the severe beating and spearing of the accused, whose fingerprints, unfortunately, were not on the knife. The police had been stationed at Balgo for two years by this time.[22]

1990s: The stress of success

The success of Yagga Yagga in its first decade of occupation attracted the interest, engagement, opinion and influence of various agencies and individuals. Intentions were generally good, but, as I recall them, the outcomes were bad, usually unintended.

The sense of purpose, for example, generated by the successful settlement at Yagga Yagga created interest in other land-related matters, and in 1993 the community was keen to have their residential status in country matched by recognition of their traditional rights and interests in their homelands. Mark Moora organised a meeting to that effect. The meeting was attended by the KLC, which, in company with their lawyer, subverted the community's aspirations and drafted a letter instructing the KLC, its lawyer and anthropologists 'to act on the community's behalf in relation to mining on the land and the defense of the Mabo title for the lands'. The community was told that 'everyone … must sign the letter before they go. The people filed up to sign and the meeting closed'.[23] Nothing happened, and despite repeated requests by the community for engagement and assistance,[24] Yagga Yagga would wait 13 hard years before its native title was recognised—then through the efforts of others.[25] By that time, Yagga Yagga had been destroyed.

The late 1980s and early 1990s were also a period of 'fertility and creativity' and 'flowering of expression' among Balgo artists, who were in fact living at Yagga Yagga (Watson 2003: also footnote 30, p. 366). This was a problem for Yagga Yagga, as the art centre, art coordinators and buying public were in Balgo. Initially, the painters travelled backwards and forwards. But people complained and asked for the industry to be based at Yagga Yagga where the painters lived and the country they painted was located.[26] The non-Aboriginal people associated with the industry, however, were not interested in living at Yagga Yagga and the new artistic direction was away from their country. The establishment of 'Warlayirti Artists'—named, revealingly, after the Kingfisher Dreaming of the Balgo area,

22 Cane Diary 13–18, 1995.
23 Confidential: Minutes from Yagga Yagga Meeting, 13–14 May 1993.
24 Letter from Mark Gregory, Kimberley Regional Land and Heritage Unit, ALRS WA, 1 March 1996, and again on 25 June 1996.
25 *Payi Payi on behalf of the Nguurrpa People v the State of Western Australia* (2007 FCA 2113 [October 2007]); Cane (2006).
26 DAA Field Notes 123/6/87, point 5, 'Painting—Old people should paint at Yagga Yagga and not return to Balgo anytime sister calls'.

and not a Dreaming from the country to which the painters belonged[27]—and the establishment of a multi-million dollar art complex at Balgo sucked people from Yagga Yagga (Cowan 1994, 1999; Watson 2003; De Ishtar 2005).

The art business also created a more immediate social problem: senior painters earned upwards of $300,000 per year, with resultant direct and indirect community disengagement, family conflict, suicide, alcoholism, substance abuse and jail terms. The eventual establishment of a Women's Law and Culture Centre, as a kind of gender-restricted outstation for ageing women near the water tank at Balgo, furthered competition for Yagga Yagga's human resources (De Ishtar 2000).

Both attractions created a demographic tension that destabilised Yagga Yagga, and ultimately the Balgo-based agencies effectively extracted the majority of grandparents then living with family at Yagga Yagga, seemingly unaware of the importance of that generation in desert society.

Another strain on Yagga Yagga's viability in the 1990s emerged from the unconsidered and unintended impacts of royalty payments from goldmining in the adjacent Northern Territory. Gold discovery and mining took place in the Granites region of the Tanami Desert between 1987 and 2000, driven largely by the significant discovery of the 3-million-ounce Callie gold deposit in 1992— one of the great modern gold discoveries, and leading to some 260 exploration licences granted and pending, and 53 agreements between the Central Land Council (CLC) and different companies across the area by 2000. Royalty payments were described as considerable in 1997 and amounting to millions of dollars to Aboriginal communities and individuals (Manning 1997, quoted in Ellias 2007; Manning 2002; also Altman and Levitus 1999; ABA 2006; Scambary 2013). No beneficiaries lived at Yagga Yagga, but all those with country on the eastern side of the homelands were related to people who were.

The consequence was that approximately one-quarter of Yagga Yagga's population regularly left the community to join cashed-up relations: the community destabilised, families fragmented and fought over access to vehicles, money and alcohol, which in turn led to inter-family feuds and fuelled community conflict and a more permanent drift away from Yagga Yagga.

As the 1990s drew to a close, these emerging problems were aggravated by the poor selection of white staff, including one who had a violent relationship with the residents, abusing them regularly and ultimately threatening them with a loaded gun. Residents left Yagga Yagga in droves at this time. The regional manager at the time told me 'we drove them away'.

---

27   And incorrectly attributed to Pai Pai Napangarti from Yagga Yagga in Nichols and Williams (2006).

During that same period, Mark Moora had sought and won election to the ATSIC Regional Council. He, like many other Western Desert men I knew in this process, was seduced by the experience and the meretricious charms of city life, money, girls and alcohol, which accompanied regular Regional Council board meetings. The absence of his consolidating influence on the residents at Yagga Yagga began to tell.

2000s: Inconspicuous compassion

When I visited Yagga Yagga in 2000, the population had declined to about 30–40 people, and included a large proportion of children.[28] The infrastructure surrounding them was so large and complicated they could not meet its technical and administrative requirements. There was also a distinct breakdown in communication and servicing from Balgo, leading to a decline in health and education, vehicle failure and shortages of food and fuel. Lack of road maintenance made access to Yagga Yagga increasingly difficult after each wet season's rains. The population (and perhaps their emotional stamina) seemed to have dropped below its critical mass: people were increasingly drawn back to Balgo, where everybody else lived.

The regional ATSIC office now took a hard line in response to the community's difficulties. As people left the community and financial requirements went unmet, ATSIC threatened to cut funding for their Community Development Employment Projects (CDEP) and administrative costs. The regional manager told me his office simply sent a fax to Yagga Yagga 'saying CDEP was no more'.[29]

In response, Mark Moora and other community members drove to Kununurra with a view to protest. They entered the ATSIC office (sober) and, after asking the staff to leave, smashed it to pieces with wooden clubs. Mark told me 'they are trying to destroy Yagga Yagga, so I do the same to them'. This was a calculated act of civil disobedience after which Mark and those involved went to the police station to be arrested. The police released them. The regional manager at the time felt Mark was 'trying to get justice. He wanted to be heard'.[30]

This period of difficulty and decline coincided with, and was probably aggravated by, a shift in national policy that sought to mainstream services, develop established communities at the expense of outstations and homelands

---

28 Cane Diary entry, November 2000.
29 Notes from discussion with regional manager at the ATSIC Office in Kununurra, 2001.
30 Cane Diary 2002: 146.

yet, somewhat inconsistently, was also intended to listen directly to the desires of 'individuals, families and communities' (Collins et al. 2003; and see Sanders 2004).[31]

But the regional arm of ATSIC (soon to be Aboriginal and Torres Strait Islander Services, ATSIS) appeared not to be listening. By 2003, Federal policy was beginning to walk hand-in-hand (Vanstone 2005b) with State policy, so was now inclined to more authoritarian solutions. The regional office ceased to be sympathetic to the ensuing social fragmentation at Yagga Yagga and began a pointed bureaucratic attack regarding compliance with 'Terms and Conditions', appropriate vehicles use, 'breaches of Grant Conditions' and the increasing likelihood of 'withholding funds' and, people felt, closing the community.[32]

The community responded that ATSIS staff visited Balgo but refused to visit Yagga Yagga to discuss the ongoing problems; phone calls were never answered or returned; vehicles were misused after attending ATSIS and Council of Australian Government (COAG) meetings in Halls Creek; computer software required to manage CDEP was inoperable due to dated software; and, in the absence of a functioning CDEP program, people were leaving to obtain money at Balgo.[33] The community subsequently approached the CDEP help desk and was advised to send their computer discs to Adelaide.[34]

The correspondence points to a degree of departmental obstinacy that is both consistent and inconsistent with incongruent Federal Government policy at the time. That policy stressed accountability, on one hand, and compassion (with implied understanding and flexibility), on the other: 'Indigenous Australians, as individuals, in their families and communities can only be said to have a real voice when governments actually listen directly to them' (Vanstone 2005b).[35]

---

31   ATSIC's fiscal powers were transferred to a new independent organisation, ATSIS, in 2003, proposed for abolishment in 2004 and abolished in 2005. Vanstone (2005a, 2005b, 2005c); Curtis et al. (2005). Peter Shergold, Department of the Prime Minister and Cabinet Management Advisory Committee, Speech to launch 'Connecting Government: Whole-of-Government Responses to Australia's Priority Challenges', Report No. 4, 20 April 2004, p. 4, quoted in McCausland 2005: 16.

32   Letter from Regional Manager, ATSIC Kununurra, to Chairperson, Yagga Yagga, Re use of CDEP, December 2003; Letter from Field Officer to Yagga Yagga Chairperson, Re 2002/2003 Audit report—initial follow up, 7 October 2003.

33   Letter to Alastair Brown, Regional Manager ATSIS, from Julian Carson, 4 December 2003; Letter from Bernard Njamme to Nita Warren, ATSIS, re CDEP schedule and Computer, 24 November 2003; Letter from Quality Assurance Officer, ATSIS, Kununurra, to The Chairperson, Yagga Yagga, 27 August 2003; Letter from Field Officer to Yagga Yagga Chairperson, Re 2002/2003 Audit report—initial follow up, 7 October 2003, compare Yagga Yagga Aboriginal Corporation Financial Statements for Year ended 30 June 2000, Barry Hansen, Chartered Accountant, Darwin.

34   Three letters faxed to ATSIS from Yagga Yagga, 24 November 2003.

35   Shergold, Speech to launch 'Connecting Government'.

In the case of Yagga Yagga, it would seem the regional office of ATSIS was not listening. It was, instead, overtly hostile to the community's requests for help. The lack of administrative assistance and the active removal of departmental support had a debilitating effect on the community's sense of purpose and state of mind. External problems were exacerbated by internal ones: almost all the old people had gone, teenagers who had grown up at Yagga Yagga and knew no other home were left without role models and saw their families, home and community dissolving.

The desert had become a lonely, pointless place and Yagga Yagga had become an environment of uncertain opportunity and certain boredom. Their world might be inferred from the neon and nightmarish visions the children painted of it on the walls of their empty four-bedroom homes. These are not the images of desert nomads sold by the Balgo Art Centre, but they are the visions of young lives coloured by the neon of TV and violent videos; they are visions of despair, boredom and frustration: clear social commentary for anyone who was willing to look.

The sense of disempowerment was compounded by insecurity, compounded by despair among occupants who, for their own part, knew their community was on the verge of closure yet lacked the skills and experience to do anything about it. The available correspondence in 2003 suggests an intentional effort to close the community by forcing people to leave and receive Centrelink payments elsewhere.[36]

Despair and disillusionment created inter-family and inter-community conflict as residents at Yagga Yagga accused those who had moved back to Balgo of failing to support Yagga Yagga. In counter-accusation, those Balgo families claimed they stopped visiting Yagga Yagga because of the proprietorial anger launched against them by those still living there. Community conflict thus replaced community consensus and this further destabilised the settlement.

Administrative issues receded into the background in the presence of more immediate and pressing social problems. Yagga Yagga residents found themselves increasingly isolated from the broader social environment of Balgo, and the compounding social disorientation led to greater personal despair and a general sense of irrelevance and futility. Bouts of drinking at Halls Creek increased exponentially. The latter consequence further aggravated the attitude of DAA officials, who felt, with some justification, that the residents at Yagga Yagga should spend more time in their homelands and less time in Halls Creek.

---

36   Letter from Bernard Njamme to Nita Warren; Letter from Quality Assurance Officer, ATSIS; Letter from Field Officer to Yagga Yagga Chairperson, Re 2002/2003 Audit report.

Matters were made worse as Mark Moora began to suffer extreme anxiety and depression: he was, quite literally, being driven mad. His mental state was aggravated by the development of cataracts and increasing blindness, by the manslaughter of his daughter-in-law, and his wife's cancer and subsequent death. Mark believed his wife had been 'sung' and he told me he had 'spirits in his head' after she died. He was so disturbed he went to the Balgo cemetery one night, where he was found by his family trying to retrieve her body and bring her back to life.

Mark continued to live at Yagga Yagga and speak at meetings, pursuing his aspirations for native title commandeered by the KLC some 13 years previously. But he was a shadow of himself, under heavy medication and otherwise catatonic—and spent most of the day sitting alone in front of the Yagga store staring into space.

Eventually just one family remained permanently at Yagga Yagga—along with five male teenage petrol-sniffers taken there under care. The sniffers were exposed to frequent drinking, homosexual behaviour and explicit heterosexual pornography. They were taken to Halls Creek by the carer one night, where, perhaps in imitation of the pornography they had been exposed to, they raped a young girl so violently that she subsequently required a colostomy bag. They were tried for the aggravated rape and sent to jail.

That same night a young man, Calwyn, left alone at Yagga Yagga with his grandmother, hanged himself from the swings in the school playground. The young man was buried with sand brought from his grandfather's country at Piparr, where he had lived as a child in the far south of the homelands. The boy's family returned to Yagga Yagga after three months in sorry business and a distressing funeral. They made another trip to the young man's country at Piparr—in the same, now decrepit, vehicle I had provided for them in 1991. They broke down 100 km south of Yagga Yagga in the heat of early summer and were saved by the boy's uncle, Peter Njamme, who walked alone to Yagga Yagga with a dog that died on the way.

That same week a journalist from the *West Australian* newspaper arrived in Yagga Yagga. Unaware of recent events, she described Yagga Yagga as a 'picture post card community' under the headline 'Community turns into ghost town' (Paganoni 2003).

In 2004, ATSIS advised Yagga Yagga that its funding would be cut if the family could not 'do the wages bill', the information for which was 'in the computer' that no one could operate. The family rang me, I rang ATSIS, but the field officer was rude, uncomprehending and completely unwilling to do anything to help.

The next year, ATSIS hired contractors to place a locked gate over the road leading to Yagga Yagga, actively blocking occupation of the settlement and its homelands. In July 2006, Yagga Yagga was advertised for sale: the 'remote community infrastructure, buildings, power plant and mobile equipment' at Yagga Yagga would be auctioned on Friday, 28 July 2006.[37] That same year, in the absence of any visitation at Piparr, and perhaps to prevent any further visitation, the last nomads living uncontacted in the far south of the homelands burnt the place to the ground.

Figure 13.1 The locked gate.
Photo: Scott Cane

And so, after many blows to the body, Yagga Yagga and its homeland movement were destroyed. The last residents were forced to live at Balgo, which continued its nightmare of death, injury, violence, drunkenness, substance abuse, delinquency, vandalism and brawling—despite an enlarged police presence and the establishment in 2005 of 'multi functioning policing facilities' that were apparently 'a holistic approach, designed to provide a total environment for safety and security' (DIA 2005: 166). By 2007, women were calling for even more policing, a greater police presence and female as well as male wardens (Kapululangu 2007). In 2008–09, the suicide rate at Balgo was 100 times higher than anywhere else in Western Australia.[38]

---

37   Evans and Clarke National Valuers and Auctioneers Australia Wide, [Advertisement], *The Advertiser*, [Adelaide], 8 July 2006.
38   Hope Coroner's report, 2011.

Hindsight as foresight

After a quarter of a century, many broken lives and some $17 million in expenditure, everyone is back at Balgo or scattered in various degraded and drunken conditions across the fringe of the Kimberley. Peter Njamme, who walked to save his family after the funeral of his nephew Calwyn, was buried in December 2013, having been found dead on the street in Broome. The grandchildren of the original residents are dead, alcoholic, unhappy, despairing or depressed. Their Facebook posts reveal troubled minds: insomnia ('staying up all night coz I can't sleep. I have sleeping problem. I need to buy sleeping pills'; 'still watching cartoon with my son. And its nearly 3:00 o'clock [am]'); substance abuse, violence and gambling ('I had a dream because people are smoking too much Gunja, fighting, too much jealousy. Gambling too much'); nightmares ('I was on top of the pit looking down as they were falling. I heard them crying out to me in language 'help, help' … I tried to reach out but their hands split away from my hands'); and salvation ('I love Jesus with all my heart, mind, soul and strength. Nothing can separate me from his love'; 'when you ignoring Jesus it's like you choosing hell. No air, no light, no love, no peace, no joy, no water, no happiness, there is no rest'). They could be describing life at Balgo.

Figure 13.2 Bundles of newly collected spear shafts.
Photo: Scott Cane

And this unhappy consequence happened despite the desire of the local people and despite the evolution of policy that was designed for better things. In the broader scheme of those things, and despite inconsistencies in Federal and State policy, the homeland movement fell at the local level, through lack of support, overcapitalisation, bad and unsympathetic management, and disparate competing and destabilising influences.

The 'politics of suffering' (see Sutton 2009) was, in this case, an 'administration of suffering' in so far as things might have been significantly better if those situated between the policies and the people had made more informed, discerning and compassionate decisions in relation to the people they were employed to assist; if policies had not simply been reduced to police, and if the aspirations and agendas of intermediaries had been conditioned by expert advise, experience, communal consensus, moderation, compassion, understanding and practicality.

In the case of Yagga Yagga, policy direction and personal aspirations did not dictate or necessitate negative outcomes; these outcomes were largely realised by agents and administrators on the ground. The choices made across Yagga Yagga's history might reasonably have been otherwise. Hindsight is a regrettable historical device, but it does not take a great deal of reflection to imagine things differently and see how life at Yagga Yagga might have been rather better— particularly as that vision was readily apparent at the time, to almost everyone who took the time to look, listen and think about the orientation of policy formulation and regional decision-making impacting the small community. The future was relatively plain to see.

Figure 13.3 Yagga Yagga in 2002.
Photo: Scott Cane

We might reflect, for example, on how things might be at Balgo had the voice of self-determination not been confused (and manipulated) for a desire for self-management in those early years of transition. And would it have been too much to expect State and Federal governments to develop complementary policy solutions to the emerging problems at Balgo in those transitional years? It is not unreasonable to imagine that everyone may have benefited if local administrators had listened more carefully to community concerns and solutions. And, as some of us recall, there was a time when local lawmen had sufficient authority to manage community conflicts. Might they not have been supported instead of sidelined by an enforced presence of foreign and transient police? And, to the extent that different policy solutions were manifested through different government agencies, might things have been different if the homeland option was allowed to run its programmed course, and not rushed by changes in departmental structure and discordant funding policy? Should I have refused to develop the program in haste and let the remaining $3.7 million return to Treasury?

One might also reflect that the communities at both Balgo and Yagga Yagga may have been more stable if royalty payments from the Tanami goldmines had been managed in accordance with conditional parameters of positive communal and personal outcome. And similarly, Yagga Yagga might not have been destabilised if its artists had been encouraged to stay in their homelands and not lured to Balgo. How might the children of Yagga Yagga have prospered if the Balgo art and women's centres were built at Yagga Yagga and had not extracted their grandmothers and grandfathers for resettlement and financial gain in Balgo?

And how much more energised and enriched might Yagga Yagga have been if the KLC had not commandeered the community's native title aspirations in 1993? And what if ATSIC's urban vision for Yagga Yagga had been qualified by the cultural context of the population it was intended for? What if ATSIC had not turned Yagga Yagga into a sophisticated community that required external administration, coordination and support? And, one might ask, if the departmental vision was to develop the outstation in such a manner, might it not have been reasonable to expect its population to be trained accordingly? And, in lieu of appropriate training, might it have seemed reasonable for the regional officers to obsess less about the community's financial and managerial obligations and accountability and more about the means and mechanism to resolve them? Might not someone have recognised that the emergent community conflict, violence and alcoholism needed attention and could be traced back to the social dislocation and distress paralleling it? Perhaps there was another solution to the community's difficulties other than cutting funds, blocking access, closing the community and selling its infrastructure.

And, in the final event, as State and Federal policy began to accord, authority was regionalised and ministerial presentations ostensibly lent an emotive eye and ear to the needs of people, might not it have been reasonable for regional officers to actually listen to and work with the people they were paid to assist? Is it unrealistic to expect government employees to be properly trained, properly informed, have analytical compassion and be skilled in management directed towards positive social outcomes in the context of the funding made available to them? Might it not be reasonable to ask that government officers and community employees in remote and regional Aboriginal Australia be trained in relevant cross-cultural disciplines? And might it not be reasonable to expect that those same employees and agents be accountable to their clients and the broader population in accordance with the success or otherwise of their activities in the context of reasonably measured and qualified policy goals and outcomes. In other words, with the benefit of hindsight, as the catalyst of foresight and the reasonable expectation of sound public servicing, it is foreseeable that had Yagga Yagga been supported moderately and sensibly, with responsible degrees of compassion, understanding, professionalism and practicality, it might still be there, the homelands might still flourish and people's lives might be healthier and happier than they are today.

References

Aboriginals Benefit Account (ABA) 2006. *Aboriginals Benefit Account Annual Report 2006–2007*. Canberra: Office of Indigenous Policy Coordination.

Akerman, K. 1980. *Survey of Sites of Ethnographic Importance in the Area of Mobil Oil Australia Ltd., 1980 Seismic Program in Ep's 219 and 134*. Broome, WA: Kimberley Land Council.

Akerman, K. 1981. *Survey of Sites of Ethnographic Importance in the Area of Mobil Oil Australia Ltd., 1980 Seismic Program in Ep's 219 and 134*. Broome, WA: Kimberley Land Council.

Akerman, K. 1982. *Survey of Sites of Ethnographic Importance in the Area of Mobil Oil Australia Ltd., 1980 Seismic Program in Ep's 219 and 134*. Broome, WA: Kimberley Land Council.

Altman, J. and Levitus, R. I. 1999. *The allocation and management of royalties under the Aboriginal Lands Rights (Northern Territory) Act: Options for reform*. CAEPR Discussion Paper 191. Canberra: Centre for Aboriginal Economic Policy Research.

Altman, J., Gillespie, D. and Palmer, K. 1998. *A national review of outstation resource agencies, 1998*. Confidential Report to ATSIC. Canberra.

Anon. 1989. *Report by the Balgo Aboriginal Task Force, October 1989*. Perth: Aboriginal Areas Protection Authority.

Aboriginal and Torres Strait Islander Commission (ATSIC) 1992. *Aboriginal and Torres Strait Islander Commission Corporate Plan: 1992–1996, Attachment C*. Canberra: Commonwealth of Australia.

Blagg, H. and Valuri, G. 2003. *An Overview of Night Patrol Services in Australia. Crime Research Centre. University of Western Australia*. Canberra: Commonwealth Attorney-General's Department.

Blanchard, C. A. 1987. *Return to Country: The Homelands Movement in Australia*. House of Representatives Standing Committee on Aboriginal Affairs. Canberra: Australian Government Publishing Services.

Cane, S. B. 1989. *Return to the desert*. Report to Department of Aboriginal Affairs and Wirimanu Aboriginal Council.

Cane, S. B. 2006. *Countrymen: An ethnography of the Ngurrurpa Native Title claim*. A Connection Report to Ngaanyatjarra Council and the Office of Native Title, Department of Premier and Cabinet. Perth: Government of Western Australia.

Cane, S. B. and Novak V. 1980. An archaeological survey of the White Hills prospect area EP134, north western Australia.

Cane, S. B. and Novak, V. 1981. *Archaeological Survey of EP 134 West of Stansmore Range*. Perth: Department of Aboriginal Sites, Western Australian Museum.

Cane, S. B. and Stanley, O. 1985. *Land Use and Resources in Desert Homelands*. Darwin: North Australia Research Unit.

Cane, S. B. and Stanley O. 1990. *Returning to the desert: Stage two*. A Report to ATSIC and Yagga Yagga Community.

Collins, B., Huggins, J. and Hannaford, J. 2003. *In the Hands of the Regions—A New ATSIC: Report of the Review of the Aboriginal and Torres Strait Islander Commission*. Canberra.

Coombs, H. C., Brandl, M. M. and Snowden, W. E. 1983. *A Certain Heritage*. CERS Monograph. Canberra: The Australian National University.

Cowan, J. 1994. *Wirrimanu: Aboriginal Art from Balgo Hills*. London: Gordon & Breach International.

Cowan, J. 1999. *Balgo, New Directions*. Sydney: Craftsman House.

Curtis, J., Hooland, I., Kelly, A., Watling, T., Rogers, B., Babyack, S. and Drinkwater, C. 2005. *After ATSIC: Life in the Mainstream*. Canberra: Select Committee on the Administration of Indigenous Affairs.

De Ishtar, Z. 2005. *Holding Yawulyu: White Culture and Black Women's Law*. Melbourne: Spinifex Press.

Department of Indigenous Affairs (DIA) 2005. *Overcoming Disadvantage in Western Australia Report. Key Indicators 2005*. Perth: Department of Indigenous Affairs.

Ellias, D. 2007. The measure of dreams. In J. Weiner and K. Glaskin (eds), *Customary Land in Tenure and Registration in Australia and Papua New Guinea: Anthropological Perspectives*. Asian Pacific Monograph 3. Canberra: The Australian National University, pp. 233–46.

Fraser, M. and Simons, M. 2010. *Malcolm Fraser: The Political Memoirs*. Melbourne: Miegunyah Press.

Guild, F. 1988. Office workers flee as violence hits mission. *West Australian*, November.

Hawke, S. and Gallagher, M. 1989. *Noonkanbah: Whose Land, Whose Law*. Fremantle, WA: Fremantle Arts Centre Press.

Hope, N. 2011. *Record of investigation into death. Suicide of five young men between 2008 and 2010*. Coroner's Court Western Australia 2011 23/11. Perth.

Kapululangu 2007. *Aboriginals Have Answers Themselves: Report of the Balgo Women's Law Camp, 24–27 August 2007*. Balgo, WA: Kapululangu Aboriginal Women's Association.

Kimberley Land Council (KLC) 1979. *Newsletter* 1(1).

McCausland, R. 2005. *The new mainstreaming of Indigenous affairs*. Briefing Paper No. 3. Sydney: Jumbunna Research Unit, University of Technology.

McCoy, B. 2008. *Holding Men: Kanyirninpa and the Health of Young Aboriginal Men*. Canberra: Aboriginal Studies Press.

Manning, I. 1997. *Native Title, Mining and Mineral Exploration: The Impact of Native Title and the Right to Negotiate on Mineral and Mineral Exploration in Australia*. Canberra: Aboriginal and Torres Strait Islander Commission.

Manning, I. 2002. The Aboriginal Benefits Account: Its management, investments, performance—A history. Paper prepared for the Northern Land Council, Darwin.

Myers, F. R. 1976. To have and to hold: A study of persistence and change in Pintupi social life. PhD thesis. Bryn Maw College, Pennsylvania.

Myers, F. R. 1986. *Pintupi Country, Pintupi Self: Sentiment, Place, and Politics among Western Desert Aborigines*. Washington, DC: Smithsonian Institution Press.

Nathan, P. and Japanangka, D. 1983. *Settle Down Country*. Melbourne: Kibble Books.

Nicholls, C. and Williams, S. 2006. *Luurnpa, the Magical Kingfisher: A Dreaming Narrative Belonging to Bai Bai Napangarti*. Adelaide: Working Title Press.

O'Donoghue, L. 1992. Message from the Chairperson: Taking control. In *ATSIC Corporate Plan 1992–1996*. Canberra: Aboriginal and Torres Strait Islander Commission.

Paganoni, L. 2003. Community turns into ghost town. *West Australian*, 1 December.

Palmer, K. 1980. *Aboriginal relations to the land west of the Stansmore Range: An anthropological study of Aboriginal land tenure and religious beliefs in an area west of the Stansmore Range in the Great Sandy Desert, Western Australia*. Report prepared for Mobil Oil.

Penny, D., Davis, K. and Hunter, J. 1977. *Papunya: History and future projects*. Report to DAA. Alice Springs, NT: Department of Aboriginal Affairs.

Poirier, S. 2005. *A World of Relationships: Itineraries, Dreams, and Events in the Australian Western Desert*. Toronto: University of Toronto Press.

Sanders, W. 2004. *ATSIC's Achievements and Strengths: Implications for Institutional Reform*. Canberra: Centre for Aboriginal Economic Policy Research.

Scambary, B. 2013. *My country, mine country: Indigenous people, mining and development contestation in remote Australia*. CAEPR Research Monograph 33. Canberra: Centre for Aboriginal Economic Policy Research.

Snowdon, W. E. 1990. *Our Future Ourselves: Aboriginal and Torres Strait Islander Community Control Management and Resources*. House of Representatives Standing Committee on Aboriginal Affairs. Canberra: Australian Government Printer.

Stead, G. 1982. Kintore review. Unpublished report. Department of Aboriginal Affairs, Alice Springs, NT.

Sutton, P. 2009. *The Politics of Suffering: Indigenous Australia and the End of the Liberal Consensus*. Melbourne: Melbourne University Press.

Tjama, F., Pay Payi, N., Martingale, M., Kuninyi, R., Nanyuma, R. and Skeen, M. 1997. *Yarrtji: Six Women's Stories from the Great Sandy Desert*. Canberra: Aboriginal Studies Press.

Vanstone, A. 2005a. Address to the National Press Club, Canberra, 23 February 2005.

Vanstone, A. 2005b. Beyond conspicuous compassion: Indigenous Australians deserve more than good intentions. Lecture, 7 December 2005.

Vanstone, A. 2005c. Indigenous communities becoming cultural museums. Transcript, *ABC Radio*, 9 December.

Watson, C. 1999. Touching the land: Towards an aesthetic of Balgo contemporary painting. In H. Morphy and M. Smith Boles (eds), *Art from the Land: Dialogues with the Kulge-Ruhe Collection of Australian Aboriginal Art*. Virginia: University of Virginia, pp. 163–218.

Watson, C. 2003. *Piercing the Ground: Balgo Women's Image Making and Relationships to Country*. Fremantle, WA: Fremantle Arts Centre Press.

14

Imagining Mumeka: Bureaucratic and Kuninjku perspectives

Jon Altman[1]

Mumeka is the name of a place; it was once the location of a seasonal camp. Since the late 1960s it has been called an outstation or homeland. The name first appears in the archive in the late 1960s, but the immediate precursor to its establishment was the blazing of a vehicular track from Oenpelli to Maningrida in the Northern Territory in 1963 that crossed the Mann River adjacent to this wet season camp (see Figure 14.1). That place was inhabited by members of a community that speak what we now refer to as the Kuninjku dialect of the pan-dialectical Bining Gunwok language (Evans 2003).

In this chapter, I want to say something about the lives of Kuninjku people over the 50 years since 1963 through the locational lens of Mumeka and their engagements with the Australian state and capitalism, including during a policy period termed self-determination. I then want to say something about current Kuninjku circumstances and the indeterminacy of their future, even as the future of Mumeka, the place, seems reasonably assured.

1   I would like to thank John Mawurndjul and the Kuninjku community for productive collaborations over many years; Melinda Hinkson, Chris Haynes and Dan Gillespie for helpful comments on an earlier draft; Ben Heaslip when at the National Archives of Australia; and anonymous referees for their constructive comments.

Map 14.1 Mumeka and outstations in the Maningrida region.

Source: Karina Pelling, CartoGIS, ANU College of Asia and the Pacific

Opening vignette

In 1979 and 1980, I lived with John Mawurndjul at Mumeka. Balang, as he is generally referred to using his subsection name, was a young aspiring artist, hunter, ceremony and family man who decided in the 1980s to focus much energy on painting. By the 1990s, he had become Australia's best-known bark painter. In 2003, he won the Clemenger Prize; in 2004, he was the lead artist at the major retrospective *Crossing Country* at the Art Gallery of New South Wales in Sydney. In 2005 and 2006, he had a major retrospective, *Rarrk John Mawurndjul*, at the Museum Tinguely, Basel, and the Sprengel Museum, Hannover; he had books published about him and his arts practice. In 2006, he was heavily involved as the only Australian artist working on site at the Musée du Quai Branly commission, and in 2009 he received the Melbourne Art Foundation Artist of the Year Award—the first Indigenous artist to do so.

Figure 14.1 An aerial view of Mumeka outstation.
Source: Google Earth

These were happy times; Balang was at his peak, living entirely and very comfortably on his arts earnings. In 2010, he was awarded a Member in the General Division of the Order of Australia '[f]or service to the preservation of Indigenous culture as the foremost exponent of the Rarrk visual art style' (Eccles 2010).[2] All this is thoroughly documented in the arts literature (see Kaufmann 2005; Volkenandt and Kaufmann 2009).

What is not yet well documented is that after 2009 his career nosedived as his relationships with a string of short-term arts advisers soured; as his arts organisation, Maningrida Arts and Culture, and its parent, Bawinanga Aboriginal Corporation, got into financial difficulties; and how with the Global Financial Crisis (GFC), the demand for Maningrida fine art declined rapidly. That rapid decline for both Balanga and Bawinanga has been exacerbated by changed policy circumstances that have seen a shift from a local form of self-determination and community control to imposed mainstreaming and normalisation and a less-effective mediated relationship between Kuninjku people and the state.

---

2   See also: www.gg.gov.au/sites/default/files/files/honours/qb/qb2010/Media%20Notes%20AM%20%28M-Z%29%20%28final%29.pdf (accessed 30 April 2014).

In 2010, I saw Balang in hospital in Darwin for the first time ever, unwell and psychologically distressed by his rapidly declining arts career. In 2011, he told me of his deep dissatisfaction with the new arts adviser, who was subsequently dismissed. By 2012, he was living in a 'side camp' in the township of Maningrida on Newstart, a social security benefit for the unemployed, dispirited. He had no vehicle to return to his outstation and art studio at Milmilngkan from where he had decentralised from Mumeka in the early 1990s; three years earlier in 2009, he had three four-wheel-drive vehicles in excellent working order: a hunting truck, a family truck and an arts truck.

In September 2013, he told me he had given up painting; there is a large stock of his art at Maningrida Arts and Culture. I watched him, aged over 60, walking to the Ye Ya workshop in the Maningrida industrial precinct looking for a 'real job' as a tyre repairer, as required by the new Remote Jobs and Community Program if one is not to be breached and left destitute with no Newstart and no cash.

I cannot pretend that our relationship is not sadly strained. Balang imagines that I have the power to assist in the repair of his career and to restore the fortunes of Maningrida Arts and Culture and Bawinanga Aboriginal Corporation, institutions that I have worked with closely over many years. I in turn feel deeply frustrated and angry at my inability to make a difference and lament my powerlessness to facilitate a more secure livelihood for his 'retirement'. There is a degree of cross-cultural tension about who is responsible for whom and for what.[3]

This vignette captures metaphorically much of what I want to cover here: the history of the repopulation of Kuninjku outstations in the south-west of the Maningrida hinterland underwritten and then sustained by state transfers and a successful engagement with the global arts market mediated by a local organisation and managed by highly qualified, well-meaning and committed non-Indigenous outsiders; the pursuit of a particular form of highly mobile lifestyle by Kuninjku loosely connected to mainstream services institutions like education and health in Maningrida; and the risks that this way of life entails. I end by pondering what avenues might exist to restore the fortunes of Balang in particular and Kuninjku people more generally if their main avenue for engagement with capitalism continues to decline.

---

3   This tension has been greatly ameliorated by our ongoing friendship and collaborations, most recently at the successful exhibition *Rarrk Masters* at Annandale Galleries in Sydney, which I opened in April 2015 with Balang in attendance. Balang received significant second payments for barks and hollow log coffins painted before he retired in 2013. He bought a second-hand four-wheel-drive vehicle with this payment and, now aged 63, is considering rejuvenating his arts practice.

The Gunwinggu problem

Archival records document what we call today Kuninjku-speaking people living in the upper Tomkinson/Mann/Liverpool rivers region in 1939, 1946, 1949, 1955 and 1963 (Altman 1987: 18–20). Maningrida was established as a government settlement in 1957 and the last of the Kuninjku were coaxed there after a bush track was blazed in 1963 that connected them to Maningrida and Oenpelli, where some had previously lived and worked for short periods. The key catalyst for in-migration was the thoughtful establishment of a leprosarium at Kurrindin near Maningrida, which meant that those afflicted by the disease did not need to be evacuated to East Arm near Darwin, where some Kuninjku had gone, but not returned. Mawurndjul was one among several Kuninjku afflicted with early stages of leprosy—in his case, evident in his hands (Kettle 1967: 206).

The Kuninjku adapted badly to settlement life and its project to sedentarise, civilise and assimilate them. There is archival documentation of what became known as 'the Gunwinggu problem'.[4] One insightful commentary is provided in a 1969 report on Maningrida by project officer E. C. (Ted) Evans in a National Archives of Australia file, 'Social and cultural change—Maningrida'.[5]

Referring specifically to the Gunwinggu, Evans (1969: 27–8) notes:

> The alleged non-school attendance of the children of the Gunwinggu tribe was one of the matters I was specifically asked to investigate at Maningrida. I am afraid that my findings are, so far, inconclusive in respect of this phenomena and that I will need to do further investigation before attempting any valid conclusions. However, some very interesting and significant situations were revealed and which justify detailing at this stage.

> The Gunwinggu at Maningrida have always given the impression that they are *in* the community not *of* it [emphasis in original]. They had their origins in the upper Liverpool River and it is important to note that they have always established their camp on the extreme limits of the Settlement on the shores of the river and in the direction of their tribal country … I have not been able to establish conclusively that this arrangement has its origins solely with the Gunwinggu or has been partly imposed on them by other groups. However, whatever the cause, this apartness plays some part in the attitude of the Gunwinggu children to schooling.

---

4   When using historical material, I replicate text and spellings of the time—in particular, the words Mumeka and Kuninjku/Kunwinjku, actually two different dialects of Bining Kunwok, are spelt in a variety of ways, as are a number of placenames.

5   NAA 1973/5087, National Archives of Australia [hereinafter NAA], Darwin. When quoting directly from archival material, I refer to the date of the document (not the date of the file) and to the folio numbers in the file.

I have deliberately used the expression 'the attitude of the Gunwinggu children' because one fact that I was able to establish quite definitely is that the degree of non-attendance at school by these children is as much, if not more, as a result of their attitude as that of their parents. The quite extraordinary lengths to which some of these children have gone to in their efforts to avoid apprehension for schooling is ample evidence of their determination in this regard.

A persistent theory found among staff members to explain this state of affairs is that children of other tribes 'rubbish' the Gunwinggu children in the school situation. There would appear to be some grounds for this view, as adult members of other tribes have been heard to refer to the Gunwinggus as 'myalls' and 'like animals because they eat bush tucker'. This strange disparagement by sophisticated and semi-sophisticated Aborigines of those who continue to exploit the economy of the traditional life is quite common.

… There is also a strong cohesiveness among this group suggesting that they derive strength and confidence only from within the tribe. I was informed by the Superintendent that on the occasions the Gunwinggu attend the picture shows they arrive in a compact body and remain together throughout the performance. On returning the dancers and their audience to their camp following the abovementioned dancing trials [for Expo '70] I noticed a loud continuous chant emanated from the back of the truck to the effect 'Gunwinggu the best'.

And later:

There is a strong move among the Gunwinggu to move back to the upper reaches of the Liverpool and settle at a place called Mormaka. To facilitate this … they have purchased and driven to Maningrida a Fordson tractor and a diesel Landrover. The status of the Gunwinggu on their acquiring these vehicles rose astronomically within the Maningrida community … their plans are by no means as well structured or crystallized as those of the Jinang, nor are they seeking any assistance from the Government … Again I would adopt the attitude of 'let them have a go' provided adequate provision can be made to meet their emergency health requirements.

Reverting to the education problem, I consider that here we have an opportunity to experiment with a compromise form of schooling. We should do nothing to impede the acquiring of traditional hunting and tracking skills by children where the desire for such skills is still manifest. But if education in these skills could be harmoniously married to more formal education, then the end result may be an even more complete being with a valuable contribution to make to both cultures. My mixing with the Gunwinggu children satisfied me that, despite their broken or lack of education, they have nevertheless acquired good competence in English and in number, which suggests that they are ready and anxious to learn, but that other as yet undefined factors inhibit their going about this in the accepted and established manner. (Evans 1969: 26–7)

Somewhat presciently and very progressively, Evans suggested that if Kuninjku moved to Mumeka, a young, motivated, male teacher could be placed with them and what we might term today a 'two-way curriculum' could be delivered.

The response from the director of Welfare Services, Harry Giese, was predictably swift and equivocal. In particular, he noted:

> Whilst the proposal to establish an outstation for Gunwinggu at the upper reaches of the Liverpool and the suggestion relating to the development of a special curriculum for the children of this group offer some provocative views, I think we need to look very carefully at this proposal if it meant that this group developed a strong feeling against Maningrida as the servicing point for the various communities which would be established in this area …
>
> I would like to visit Maningrida early in the new year to have discussions … so that we can point out some of the problems in carrying health and education services to these communities and the limitations which these areas may well place on them in the development of economic projects of various kinds. In saying this, however, I would not like it to be thought that I do not support the proposal.[6]

This exchange is noteworthy on three counts.

First, while 1969 preceded the policy era termed 'self-determination' (from 1972), one does not get the impression that the Gunwinggu were asking permission to move to Mumeka; indeed Evans makes it clear that they are not seeking assistance from government.

Second, Giese's response was interestingly uncertain, suggesting that he was unsure about how to respond to the Gunwinggu initiative. This uncertainty gave his subordinate, John Hunter, scope to act on his own judgment.

Third, there is no attempt to acknowledge that the Gunwinggu were experiencing what we might term today 'structural violence' (Farmer 2005) living in Maningrida; they lived a marginal existence on the edge of the settlement, they experienced discrimination and their physical and psychological health status, as well as access to food, was low.

---

6   Harry Giese, Correspondence in response to report of Mr Evans dated 25 November 1969, in 'Social and Cultural Change—Maningrida', NAA 1973/5087, folios 38–42, NAA, pp. 40–1.

The Kuninjku (Gunwinggu) solution

The Kuninjku did not hang about for Harry Giese's permission to go back to Mumeka; they took off in their tractor and Land Rover back along the road that had been made six years earlier 'to open up that part of the Arnhem Land Reserve adjacent to and west of the Liverpool River' in an expedition led by the very same Ted Evans, then chief welfare officer.

Back then, Evans outlined some advantages to be derived from the road link:

> The first immediate advantage from this road link will enable the Superintendent of Maningrida to have ready and easy access to those areas to the south where native peoples for varying reasons still choose to live away from settled areas …

> A second important advantage … is the opening up of good pastoral country to the west of the Liverpool River. The presence of cattle and buffaloes in excellent condition … would seem to confirm that these pastoral areas have considerable potential and should be developed. (Evans 1963: 12)

Indeed, somewhat ambitiously, Evans (1963: 12–3) notes:

> Out of this I see emerging a plan for Maningrida whereby its forestry, agricultural and small livestock projects will be developed on the eastern side of the Liverpool River and its cattle and buffalo development will be undertaken on the western side.

These earlier observations and the subsequent use of the road for reoccupation are poignant on two grounds.

First, the Kuninjku found an unexpected ally in the form of the quietly spoken but formidable superintendent John Hunter (Gillespie 1982).[7] Hunter set up a bank account for the Kuninjku and facilitated savings by them via a voluntary 'chuck in' of saved cash, mainly from art sales, which allowed them to purchase vehicles. Hunter also used the road himself (he loved driving, often at night) from the earliest days of decentralisation to maintain a communications and supply line to Mumeka (and other embryonic outstations) on a fortnightly basis. Perhaps more aware than anyone of the destructive impact of settlement life on Kuninjku—as its long-serving superintendent, he was there when they centralised in 1963—he became the champion of decentralisation.

---

7   Gillespie relates how in 1974 Hunter was moved from Maningrida when he stood down a number of white DAA staff there because he perceived that Aboriginal people were being smothered, and how subsequently members of the Maningrida Council occupied the DAA offices in Darwin and demanded his return—a demand the DAA acceded to (Gillespie 1982: 6).

Hunter meticulously kept annual Aboriginal contact tables, one of a number of governmental record-keeping tools that the state forged to ensure legibility (Scott 1998), as required by the Welfare Branch. And so he provides a record of the precise time of Mumeka's administrative birth; in 1969–70, Hunter (1970: 72) enumerated '11 people at Mormaka'.

Second, Evans' developmental optimism took a very different direction. Such optimism had begun in 1884, when explorer and surveyor David Lindsay (1884) had promising things to say about the pastoral potential of some of the savannah grasslands in the region of the Liverpool River—an assessment repeated in almost all patrol officer reports; it was hard to quell. Evans (1963: 19) even thought that the imminent exploitation of bauxite deposits on Gove Peninsula would create a future important market for locally produced beef and other foodstuffs.

The development that did occur was very different from that anticipated in 1963. Hunter's (1974) handwritten documentation provides early information on this new form of local economy: he notes that the 51 Gunwinggu at Mormega community are 'very active hunters and gatherers' and that 'they are also one of the better sources of craft work for Maningrida Arts and Crafts that fully supports their work'. He notes that they have erected traditional housing at Mormega (dry season) and Manbulugadi (wet season). Elsewhere, Hunter notes:

> This group is evidently determined to stick it out at Mormega this year. I have been visiting the place each fortnight over the dry season and I am impressed by their determination and production capacity when they decided that they need a vehicle to stay on in the wet. They cut 8 miles [13 km] of track through eucalypt forest in just over 6 days, no mean feat, in order to demonstrate that there is an alternative to moving out during the wet. The M.P.A. [Maningrida Progress Association][8] has since agreed to carry their supplies each fortnight to the landing. (Hunter 1973: 2–3)

In 1963, Evans (1963: 10) observed that '[h]istory has shown that throughout Australia road access and links with other settled areas has been a necessary prerequisite for the opening up of undeveloped areas'. Not only did the existing track between Maningrida and Mumeka open up the means to export art and craft and import Western supplies, but it also opened up new hunting grounds. Kuninjku clearly saw the value of such bush roads for external communications when they made their own to Manbulgardi.

---

8   The Maningrida Progress Association is a community-owned retail operation established in 1968 that delivered supplies via a 'tucker run' to outstations from the early 1970s until 1999, when the operation was purchased by the Bawinanga Aboriginal Corporation.

Mumeka and the new policy environment

From 1972 and the election of the Whitlam Government, three important things happened: first, the emphasis on managed assimilation and colonial domination in remote regions was relaxed and there was talk of self-determination; second, there was a commitment to land rights and so greater authority was vested with Traditional Owners; and third, the Federal Department of Aboriginal Affairs (DAA) was established. This in turn opened up possibilities for greater support for outstations, policy advocacy on their behalf and much policy angst in Canberra about the future of outstations, with reference often focused on outstations as places of residential fixity.

Hunter implemented the new policy quickly, moving to operate as an enabling community adviser. And in 1974, in that role, he assisted people at Mumeka with an application for a now formalised and properly bureaucratised establishment grant, with a ceiling of $10,000 (Hunter 1974).

The grant was quickly approved. In correspondence, it was emphasised by the department that the funds approved and assets purchased should be used only for the purposes for which they were provided; there was a requirement for quarterly financial statements, audited annual statements and auditor's reports, together with a certificate that funds had been used for the purposes stipulated. On 23 October 1974, Anchor Gulumba, leader, put his mark, 'X', to the acceptance form, acknowledging that 'I accept the funds approved in the above letter on the terms and conditions stated therein'.

This exchange is instructive on a number of counts. To get assistance—in this case, a boat and some rudimentary building material and hand tools—groups needed to show commitment. And there was a hint in Hunter's application that support would enhance engagement with commerce via a fishing venture. The application was for a group living between two places, Mormega and Manbulugadi; and while Mumeka was unincorporated, a Mormega Society Account was established to receive the cash. Bureaucratic entanglements and legal obligations for the illiterate Gulunba came with self-determination and government support.

Direct links between the Commonwealth and places like Mumeka and people like Gulunba, who did not speak English, were clearly not sustainable. Benign John Hunters would not be there forever; something had to change.

In June 1975, H. C. ('Nugget') Coombs made one of his visits to Maningrida and travelled to Mangallod outstation (near Mumeka) as a member of the Council for Aboriginal Affairs. The council had its own concerns about the survival prospects of outstations; the most basic long-term threat to their future was identified as environmental, with a concern that a combination of sedentarism, new technology and population growth would deplete resources (see below). Other important observations included a view that if decentralisation was to meet the psychological needs of participants, it needed to remain an Aboriginal initiative (Council for Aboriginal Affairs 1976).

An important paper from 1974 was 'Decentralization trends in Arnhem Land' by Bill Gray (1977). Gray was a DAA official, who coincidentally accompanied Evans in 1963 in the patrol to establish a road link between Oenpelli and Maningrida. Like others at the time, Gray noted the need at outstations for communications and services, highlighting that groups did not want resident non-Aboriginal people in their communities and so the need for flexible service delivery models (Gray 1977: 114–23).[9]

Pondering the future of decentralisation and whether it was a passing phase, Gray predicted:

> [W]hether it is or not will depend in large measure on the attitude taken by those who administer and determine government policy and its translation into action. If services and resources (financial and otherwise) are restricted to established settlements and mission stations, then no doubt decentralization will have a limited future. On the other hand, if our organization (i.e. the Department of Aboriginal Affairs) is designed to be responsive to the needs of Aborigines, as determined by them, then we will be committed to assisting these groups in their endeavours to re-establish themselves in their own traditional countries … Finally, I should underline that I believe decentralization constitutes one of the most positive steps taken by 'tribal' Aborigines to regain their independence and, most importantly, to re-establish their relationship with the land. (Gray 1977: 120)

Andy Hazel, community adviser for a short time at Maningrida in 1974, provides a somewhat different perspective. Much of his report (Hazel 1974) is focused on the continuing involvement of non-Aboriginal staff at Maningrida and the issue of dependency, but his report is also one of the few that mentions self-determination and the interdependence between Maningrida and outstations. Hazel suggests that while Aboriginal people resent the presence of too many Europeans in Maningrida, they are paradoxically highly dependent on them. He observes that people at outstations exhibit a great deal of independence and self-reliance, and notes: 'The out-stations are perhaps the most important feature of Maningrida. I personally feel that the future of Maningrida lies not in developing Maningrida proper but the outstations' (Hazel 1974: 94).

---

9   The paper was originally presented at the Australian Institute of Aboriginal Studies Symposium on Social and Cultural Change in Canberra in 1974 and was widely circulated and quite influential prior to publication.

And later: 'Self "determination" is most certainly the key note with regard to "outstations" and any interference with the exception of support sought by the people themselves must be discouraged' (Hazel 1974: 97–8).

The most significant upshot of all this policy work was recognition of an urgent need for a formal outstation resource agency based in Maningrida to service outstations.

What happened to Mumeka and the Kuninjku, 1979–2009?

I lived at Mumeka during 1979 and 1980 and have been back there on more than 50 visits since. It is not easy to summarise what has happened there and why in a short space, but I will try, using the past tense until 2009.

When I lived at Mumeka, and even now when I am there, I used it as a lens through which to look at what I refer to as the Kuninjku 'hybrid or diverse' economy (Altman 2010)—a productive economy that is deeply socially and environmentally embedded. I find it difficult conceptually to differentiate Mumeka-the-place from the people who own the place and the people who inhabit it. In many ways, Mumeka has become more of an infrastructural node and less of a real, or even imagined, community.

The fortunes of Mumeka-the-place have been intricately linked to the role played by the Bawinanga Aboriginal Corporation, incorporated in 1979. I have written about this organisation elsewhere (Altman 2008); it was constituted to assist people at outstations as a charitable resource or service organisation. It superseded the Maningrida Outstation Resource Centre, which disappeared in 1977 when Minister for Aboriginal Affairs Ian Viner illegally revoked the permits of three of its white staff, Dan Gillespie, Peter Cooke and David Bond, protégés of the Hunter approach, for being too progressive, but that is another story (see MacCallum 1978).

Over the 30 years to 2009, Bawinanga grew as an organisation to become the second-largest incorporated by the Registrar of Indigenous Corporations. Its spectacular growth began in the 1990s, when it became the largest and most financially successful Community Development Employment Projects (CDEP) organisation in remote Australia. Bawinanga was an institution born of the self-determination era that advocated for its members and delivered on multiple objectives: it was the provider of key services, mainly housing and community facilities, roads and regular supplies; it ran employment and training programs; and it successfully established a range of community and commercial enterprises over many years, the most significant of which have been Maningrida Arts and Culture and the Djelk Community Rangers. Bawinanga has always been Maningrida-based, and as it has expanded as a development agency, many of the opportunities it has provided have been in the township. And while Bawinanga has advocated vigorously for health, educational and social security services on behalf of its members, it has never been responsible for their delivery.

Bawinanga's activities have transformed Mumeka in a physical sense as a place, as evident in the aerial photograph from GoogleMaps (Figure 14.2): two three-bedroom houses, two earlier tin houses on concrete slabs, a school and preschool, a women's centre and teacher accommodation, as well as reticulated water and ablution facilities, and a fine gravel airstrip. Mumeka is a far more solid infrastructure node than it was in 1972 when people lived there in bark shelters and on sleeping platforms, or in 1979 when people lived in corrugated-iron sheds with dirt floors and nothing else.

Figure 14.2 Mumeka house and school.
Photo: Jon Altman

Figure 14.3 'Development' comes to Mumeka, July 2012.
Photo: Jon Altman

Through its responsiveness, Bawinanga has also assisted Kuninjku with the development of a number of other smaller infrastructural nodes, as the group associated with Mumeka has splintered for reasons of family politics and new outstations have been established, each connected by formed tracks. The improvement in the road between Maningrida and Mumeka has also facilitated travel, even by two-wheel-drive sedan, between the two places for longer periods in the annual seasonal cycle than in the past.

Bawinanga also assisted Kuninjku people with livelihood; it has helped people save for, purchase and maintain vehicles; it has helped people with the tricky business of getting a gun licence and firearms; and, most importantly, it has purchased, marketed and promoted Kuninjku art to such an extent that by 2008–09, I estimate that more than $1 million per annum was returned just to Kuninjku artists. And art was the only significant commodity export from this region.

Paradoxically perhaps, the enduring characteristics of Kuninjku—hunting skills and adherence to tradition including art and craft production and high ceremonial participation—that saw them marginalised in Maningrida in the 1960s now gave them very different heightened regional status as people who could control their own destiny. And so Maningrida became a more welcoming place for Kuninjku, and for more and more it became their principal, if not permanent, place of residence. Through their arts expertise, Kuninjku came to dominate some Maningrida-based institutions like the Babbarra Women's Centre, where they worked (and still do) as highly creative screen-print artists.

The improved roads, greater access to vehicles and discretionary cash from art sales made the Kuninjku more and more mobile; people increasingly drove from Mumeka to Maningrida for day shopping trips and from Maningrida to Mumeka for day or night hunting trips; some people even commuted for work. This high mobility made the delivery of services to Kuninjku either in town or in country extremely difficult, especially if provided on an orthodox basis. One consequence has been that getting medical attention to Kuninjku has been difficult, as alluded to by Evans in his 1969 report. Kuninjku are a high death-rate, high birth-rate community. Another hurdle is that getting standard Western education to Kuninjku, whether in Maningrida or at Mumeka, is extremely challenging. And, so, as in 1969, while Kuninjku school attendance is minimal and functional English literacy among Kuninjku is almost absent, the maintenance of a full array of Kuninjku clan-lects and other fine-grained linguistic expressions of identity, as described in the work of Murray Garde (2013), which is extremely rare in Australia today, continues strongly. And while a few Kuninjku do hold regular jobs, they are notorious for absenteeism, irregularity of work hours and employment mobility owing to competing priorities.

The great crash

Until 2009, one interpretation of what happened to the Kuninjku might suggest that they have engaged with capitalism and the state on their own terms with some success. Another interpretation is that the Kuninjku way of living is socially dysfunctional and an abject failure. This latter view came to dominate popular and policy discourse even as some Kuninjku like Mawurndjul were meeting Jacques Chirac in Paris in 2006 and being hailed as cultural diplomats. Bawinanga, an institution born of the self-determination era, valiantly tried to shore up the defences against the latter demeaning interpretation, but the national tide of policy history, aided and abetted by some black and white public intellectuals such as Noel Pearson (2009) and Peter Sutton (2009), seems to have won the day: there is now a dominant public perception that the government project to 'close the gap' in Indigenous disadvantage is not possible at outstations and that the maintenance of fundamentally different cultural norms by groups like the Kuninjku is primarily responsible for their slow or unsuccessful integration into the mainstream. The GFC of 2008–09 also played a part, as Kuninjku engagement with capitalism via their creation of fine art declined rapidly as market demand eroded.

In chronological order, the following events rocked the established Kuninjku and Bawinanga order: in 2004, the abolition of the Aboriginal and Torres Strait Islander Commission (ATSIC), an institution (like Bawinanga) with certain defined functions, which was blamed for all ills in Indigenous affairs; from 2005, the reform of the CDEP and the demeaning of outstations as 'cultural museums' by the then Minister for Indigenous Affairs, Amanda Vanstone; in 2007, the NT Intervention, which Bawinanga strongly opposed[10] and Kuninjku largely avoided by retreating back to outstations; in 2008–09, the GFC; and, perhaps of greatest significance, also in 2009, the departure of CEO Ian Munro, who had worked at Bawinanga for 18 years. The last marked the end of the committed manager from the self-determination days; suddenly it was the era of fly-in-fly-out (FIFO) management and a new breed with limited local experience and little business acumen.

Looking to curry favour with the new neoliberal approach in Canberra, the newly recruited management at Bawinanga promoted 'fake capitalism' (Wiegratz 2010) not seen in the region since the 1960s. And the new approach failed so spectacularly that in just two years, Bawinanga went from surplus to being insolvent with a $10 million debt. In the name of development, a moral space has emerged for vulture capitalism (Lowenstein 2013) and incompetence.

This new approach of imagined development was visible in July 2012, when on a visit to Mumeka, I saw the construction of wooden chicken coops (imported as kits from Denmark), market gardens with trickle irrigation and pizza ovens—all delivered with copious Canberra money from a program called the Community Action Plan. In October 2012, Bawinanga went into special administration, where it remains at the time of writing (May 2014):[11] the chicken coops were wrecked before they hosted a chicken, the market gardens are now in disrepair, and the pizza oven has never been used to my knowledge (it looks splendid in the middle of Mumeka, not far from a white cross, as a symbol of some as yet to be fathomed cargo).

---

10   Including underwriting the unsuccessful High Court case *Wurridjal v Commonwealth* in 2008 that challenged the constitutional validity of the compulsory acquisition of Aboriginal townships for five years under the NT Intervention.

11   Bawinanga came out of special administration on 1 July 2014, having most of its public liabilities forgiven and its private liabilities covered by a loan from the Maningrida Progress Association. As this volume goes to press, it remains on relatively shaky financial footings compared with the pre-2009 period.

The Kuninjku enigma

Not long ago, in 2006, I suggested a little prematurely that at the start of the twenty-first century through their art and by maintaining other aspects of their local economies like hunting, Kuninjku living at or associated with outstations have succeeded in realising a hybrid form of economy that is thoroughly geared to their own emergent aspirations. But I also noted that this is not enough, because while they might be doing what the state wants, they are not doing so in accord with the broader Australian imaginary of how success should be constituted. I also suggested that the strategic use of art as a source of political and economic power has allowed people associated with Mumeka to define their identity and differences, mark social and geographic boundaries, and find an economic means to live on country when they so wish (Altman 2006, 2010).

Arguably, what had been defined as 'the Gunwinggu problem' in the 1960s emerged by the early twenty-first century as 'the Kuninjku enigma'. It was precisely because Kuninjku were 'like animals eating bush tucker' and because of their 'innate pride in traditional skills', as Evans put it in 1969, that Kuninjku were able to construct a hybrid form of domestic economy that at once engaged successfully with capitalism and provided sustenance.

This way of living was risky because it became increasingly predicated on an ever-expanding arts market and mediation provided by a politically robust and commercially successful Bawinanga Aboriginal Corporation managed by skilled outsiders empathetic to Kuninjku aspirations; and it needed state support that facilitated relative autonomy and local self-determination. In a very short time, all the conditions for relative Kuninjku success evaporated and now many are more impoverished and dependent than ever. Aspects of their hunting economy have declined owing to loss of many edible species, particularly from the invasion of the cane toad, but also other feral pests like buffalo, pig and cats, and exotic weeds. The Council for Aboriginal Affairs' (1976) environmental concerns of endogenous degradation have proven unfounded, while the Australian state and its agents have never considered compensation for loss of livelihood owing to such resource depletion and declining food security. In similar vein, as the arts economy has crashed—Kuninjku in 2013 received just 15 per cent of what they received in 2008–09—there has been no thought given to restructuring bailout packages of $100 million, as occurs for already heavily subsidised Holden car workers or employees of the nearby Gove alumina refinery, which was mothballed in early 2014.

There is no doubt that until recently the livelihood that Kuninjku eked out for themselves met their aspirations; but what of the bureaucratic imagination? Back in the 1970s there was considerable angst about ensuring that outstations received adequate access to health and education services, but that angst was never converted into effective state action in terms of either the level of investment or a search for innovative delivery options. Indeed, as Kuninjku became more and more mobile, the prospects for delivering education and health services declined even before the effective, flexible models that might have been envisioned by Gray (1977) had been tested on a longer-term basis.

There were in fact a few experiments along the lines suggested by Ted Evans in 1969, but for short periods, and finding teachers with 'the motivation and physical attributes' to be both a teacher and a pupil proved difficult, although there have been some rare outstanding examples among Kuninjku, like Murray Garde. Bill Gray's (1977) concerns proved at one level unfounded: resources were largely limited to townships, yet outstations continued. But his observation that services needed to be responsive to needs as determined by the people, as the rhetoric of self-determination implied, never eventuated. And because such services were not a high priority for Kuninjku, who were happy to trade-off a less-serviced life for the sake of autonomy on country, this left a convenient space that resulted in education and health services being a conveniently low priority for all parties. As for the prediction by Andy Hazel (1974), among others, that the future of the Maningrida region lay in outstations, not the township, this does not seem to be the case at present, with the demographic pendulum swinging back heavily in favour of Maningrida, at least according to the most recent five-yearly census.

Where does all this leave Mumeka and Kuninjku? Some remain committed to the outstation and the way of life there, preferring it to the prospects of living in what is called 'new sub' or Palmerston, the new bland housing estate in Maningrida, eking out a living on welfare and much-diminished art sales and driving out at night to shoot and bone out feral buffalo or pigs to supplement meagre township diets. Others choose town living over country. What is undeniable is that after decades of engaging successfully with capitalism through their mediated arts practice of high domestic and global reputation, having fired their best entrepreneurial and individualistic shots, Kuninjku are again impoverished, as they were in the 1960s, and highly dependant on the state. Almost all lack Western education and norms—the supposed elixir for mainstream economic integration imagined by politicians, bureaucrats and others. And Kuninjku are unprepared for and uninterested in any precarious FIFO work that might be available in industries like mining or tourism on other people's country in Gove or Kakadu National Park.

One would not want to prematurely write off the enigmatic Kuninjku, exposed in 2013 as they were in 1963, or their outstations. In the 1960s, they combined hunting and artistic skills as a lifeline to reassert their identity, rights in land and relative autonomy; and for a time this strategy, promoted by many, including me, worked, at least in regional terms. What will now emerge as the imagined hope and future for the children of John Mawurndjul, many already fine artists, and his grandchildren remains unclear. It should not, I think, just be a choice between the risk of being an artist and the mundaneness of being a tyre fixer at the Ye Ya workshop. In today's precarious late-capitalist world, there have to be other less risky alternatives to living at Mumeka, or in Maningrida, or most likely living between both.

References

Altman J. C. 1987. *Hunter-Gatherers Today: An Aboriginal Economy in North Australia*. Canberra: Australian Institute of Aboriginal Studies.

Altman, J. C. 2006. The invention of Kurulk art. In J. C. Altman (ed.), *Mumeka to Milmilngkan: Innovation in Kurulk Art*. Canberra: Drill Hall Gallery, The Australian National University, pp. 17–33.

Altman, J. C. 2008. Different governance for difference: The Bawinanga Aboriginal Corporation. In J. Hunt, D. Smith, S. Garling and W. Sanders (eds), *Contested Governance: Culture, Power and Institutions in Indigenous Australia*. Canberra: ANU E Press, pp. 177–203.

Altman, J. C. 2010. What future for remote Indigenous Australia: Economic hybridity and the neoliberal turn. In J. C. Altman and M. Hinkson (eds), *Culture Crisis: Anthropology and Politics in Aboriginal Australia*. Sydney: UNSW Press, pp. 259–80.

Council for Aboriginal Affairs 1976. *Report on Arnhem Land*. Canberra: Australian Government Publishing Service.

Eccles, J. 2010. Queen honours Aboriginal artists. *News: Aboriginal Art Directory*, 18 June.

Evans, E. C. 1963. Patrol to establish road link between Oenpelli and Maningrida. In *Proposed road between Oenpelli and Maningrida*, NAA 1966/3790, folios 10–19. National Archives of Australia, Darwin.

Evans, E. C. 1969. Maningrida. In *Social and cultural change—Maningrida*, NAA 1973/5087, folios 11–35. National Archives of Australia, Darwin.

Evans, N. 2003. *Bininj Gun-wok: A Pan-Dialectical Grammar of Mayali, Kuninjku and Kune*. 2 vols. Canberra: Pacific Linguistics.

Farmer, P. 2005. *Pathologies of Power: Health, Human Rights and the New War on the Poor*. Berkeley: University of California Press.

Garde, M. 2013. *Culture, Interaction and Person Reference in an Australian Language*. Amsterdam: John Benjamin.

Gillespie, D. 1982. John Hunter and Maningrida—A chorus of alarm bells. In P. Loveday (ed.), *Service Delivery to Outstations*. Darwin: North Australia Research Unit, pp. 1–7.

Gray, W. J. 1977. Decentralization trends in Arnhem Land. In R. M. Berndt (ed.), *Aborigines and Change: Australia in the '70s*. Canberra: Australian Institute of Aboriginal Studies, pp. 114–23.

Hazel, A. 1974. Community adviser report—Maningrida, 27-5-74. In *Maningrida—Continuing involvement of non Aboriginal staff*, NAA 1974/700, folios 89–98. National Archives of Australia, Darwin.

Hunter, J. 1970. Aboriginal population contact table, Maningrida settlement, 1969/70 dated 27.8.70. In *Population movement and statistics Maningrida settlement*, NAA 1976/844, folio 72. National Archives of Australia, Darwin.

Hunter, J. 1973. Request for loan money, Mormega community. In *Movement of Gunwinggu People to Mormega*, NAA 1973/8239, folio 2–3. National Archives of Australia, Darwin.

Hunter, J. 1974. Report on application for funds detailed considerations dated 16/9/74. In *Re-location of Mormega Group—Maningrida*, NAA 1974/1466, folios 1–2 (double-sided). National Archives of Australia, Darwin.

Kaufmann, C. (ed.) 2005. <<rarrk>> *John Mawurndjul: Journey through Time in Northern Australia*. Basel: Schwabe Verlag.

Kettle, E. 1967. *Gone Bush*. Sydney: F. P. Leonard.

Lindsay, D. 1884. *Mr. D. Lindsay's explorations through Arnheim Land*. South Australian Parliamentary Paper No. 239, 1883–84. Adelaide: Government Printer.

Lowenstein, A. 2013. *Profits of Doom: How Vulture Capitalism is Swallowing the World*. Melbourne: Melbourne University Press.

MacCallum, M. 1978. Viner muscles in on Maningrida. *Nation Review*, 27 April – 3 May.

Pearson, N. 2009. *Up from the Mission: Selected Writings*. Melbourne: Black Inc.

Scott, J. C. 1998. *Seeing Like A State: How Certain Schemes to Improve the Human Condition Have Failed*. New Haven, Conn.: Yale University Press.

Sutton, P. 2009. *The Politics of Suffering: Indigenous Australia and the End of the Liberal Consensus*. Melbourne: Melbourne University Press.

Volkenandt, C. and Kaufmann, C. (eds) 2009. *Between Indigenous Australia and Europe: John Mawurndjul*. Berlin: Reimer.

Wiegratz, J. 2010. Fake capitalism? The dynamics of neoliberal moral restructuring and pseudo-development: The case of Uganda. *Review of African Political Economy* 37(124): 123–37.

15

Thwarted aspirations: The political economy of a Yolngu outstation, 1972 to the present

Frances Morphy and Howard Morphy

The outstation movement and the Aboriginal art movement have something in common: they are both often said to have originated, even to have been invented, at the beginning of the 1970s. Each is associated with myths of origin that privilege the agency of non-Indigenous actors. One is that the rise of contemporary Aboriginal art was initiated by a Papunya schoolteacher in 1971; another is that the outstations were an initiative of the Whitlam Government associated with land rights. Some have given H. C. ('Nugget') Coombs a primary role in influencing the direction of both: in the case of Papunya, the important contribution made by the Australia Council; in the case of the homelands, Coombs' romantic socialist imagination (Hughes 2007). Aesthetics and socialism come together in Helen Hughes' articulation of the primary motivations of those white intellectuals and public servants who supported the outstation movement: 'The homelands were designed to enable Aborigines and Torres Strait Islanders to enjoy their traditional lands as hunters and gatherers with culturally rich lives' (Hughes 2007: 5); and they were thought 'to have inherited communitarian social structures that were free of private property concepts' (p. 12).

Myths of origin typically designate an originating moment or event, thus creating the very phenomenon they are trying to explain. They provide a uniformitarian perspective on events that may have a family resemblance but which arise from quite different historical trajectories and situational logics. In the case of the 'homelands movement', our argument will be that when we survey homelands or outstations in the north of Blue Mud Bay, in the Northern Territory, from the perspective of the *longue durée* we can see them as the outcome of a complex historical process of transformation that was influenced by a multiplicity of factors, both local and national in origin. There were factors that were particular to the circumstances of Yolngu people and that influenced the subsequent trajectory of the Yolngu homelands; these are factors that are commonly ignored, or that are, indeed, unknown at the non-local level, yet which need to be taken into account when planning for the future.

Figure 15.1 An aerial view of Yilpara.
Photo: Frances and Howard Morphy

We do not deny that the national initiatives introduced by the Whitlam Labor Government were a factor in facilitating the outstation movement—the move of Aboriginal people in many regions away from mission stations and government settlements to establish smaller communities on country (Coombs et al. 1980). And the prospect of land rights certainly provided one stimulus. However, in eastern Arnhem Land, it is possible to see the outstation movement as an outcome, in part, of the struggle for the recognition of rights and for relative autonomy, to position the movement as part of a continuing process of adjustment by Yolngu to the process of colonial encapsulation (Morphy and Morphy 2013). But to see the government initiatives as being the primary cause of the homelands movement is to deny Aboriginal inventions of the outstation movement in all their diversity.

In this chapter, we will argue that the development of outstations in eastern Arnhem Land allowed Yolngu to re-emplace a regional system of relationships (*gurrutu*) that had been disrupted in the early decades of the twentieth century as the region came increasingly under Australian Government control. While systems of alliance have changed over time, genealogical data confirm the Yolngu perception of the existence of enduring regional systems of marriage and affinity that link sets of clans together in connubial relationships. The establishment of government settlements and mission stations in the 1920s and 1930s created an externally imposed spatial framework for the relocation of the Yolngu population that was shaped by the pragmatics of the time.

Our primary case study focuses on a south-eastern Yolngu connubium, the Djalkiripuyngu, centred on the north of Blue Mud Bay, whose members had been dispersed among a number of different communities. This dispersal, and the fact that they were not the primary landowners in any of the communities to which they had moved, created long-term problems of adjustment. Regional alliances had always been shaped by external as well as internal relationships, and the outstation movement provided a context and an opportunity for the reconstitution of local political relationships that were perceived to be in continuity with past trajectories. Peterson has characterised the outstation movement as an example of an Indigenous life project, in which Indigenous people 'seek autonomy in deciding the meaning of their life independently of projects promoted by the state and the market' (2005: 7). The Djalkiripuyngu example is a clear case in point; however, such life projects cannot be pursued except in the context of articulation with state projects for Indigenous people, and state projects may either help or hinder.[1]

---

1   As Fred Myers has pointed out to us, the Yolngu case shares elements in common with outstation dynamics elsewhere in Australia in 'which people wanted to withdraw in order to re-establish some sort of political standing that was diminished by incorporation into another space' (personal communication). Myers' research on the Pintupi outstation of Yayayi shows how the Pintupi initially attempted to integrate themselves as 'one countrymen' within the population of the government settlement of Papunya before the tensions presented by the increased scale of social life became too great (Myers 1986: 40 ff., 257). The trajectories of the outstation movements, however, have been different in part because of the differences between Yolngu and Pintupi political structures (cf. Myers 1986: 295).

Yilpara in history

The homeland settlement of Yilpara or Bäniyala has existed since 1972 as one of the initial outstations supported from Yirrkala mission. It has always had a large population. Mission records show that in 1974 there were about 70 people there, and in the 2000s there were periods when up to 170 people were regular residents.[2] Yilpara is situated on a peninsula that juts out into the north of Blue Mud Bay (see Map 15.1). The settlement site was chosen in part because of its excellent permanent freshwater resources. Yilpara had always been a major, seasonally occupied settlement site. It is associated with a Yingapungapu burial ground and a restricted *Ngärra* performance space, both of which are of regional significance. However, the overall tenor of the surrounding land is *garma*, associated with more local ancestral forces: a good and safe place to camp. Yilpara is well resourced for living off the land and sea, with offshore reefs and seagrass beds, seasonal abundance of dugong and turtle, patches of vine thicket for yams and accessible wetlands and rivers.

Yilpara was also one of the sites of long-term trade with Macassans; nearby are the remains of a Macassan trepang-processing site. Oral history recounts the exchange of names between Wirrpanda, a senior member of one of the local clans, and a Macassan captain, 'Bäpa Basu' (quite possibly Pobasso, mentioned in Matthew Flinders' 1814 account of his 1803 visit to the east Arnhem Land coast)—an exchange that must have occurred in the late eighteenth or early nineteenth century. There is much evidence to show that Yilpara was, in geographical terms, a central node of the Djalkiripyungu, the connubium of Yolngu clans of the northern Blue Mud Bay region.[3] And there is evidence that external trade relations with the Macassans resulted in Blue Mud Bay becoming a zone of connection and interaction, linking groups together around its perimeter. In particular, the southern Djalkiripuyngu clans developed very close relations, including intermarriage and trade, with the Anindilyakwa-speaking peoples of Groote and Bickerton islands. Yilpara was also a site of occasional interaction with the Europeans who serviced the Overland Telegraph and established cattle stations and mission stations in the Roper River region to the south.

---

2   These figures come from research in 2001 and 2006 on the national census in eastern Arnhem Land (F. Morphy 2002, 2007) and on subsequent as yet unpublished population research undertaken in the region in 2010 (see F. Morphy 2012).

3   This evidence was gathered by the authors in the course of the research for the Blue Mud Bay case (H. Morphy 2003), and is referenced in F. Morphy (2010).

Map 15.1 Yilpara and the Laynhapuy homelands area, north-east Arnhem Land.

Source: Karina Pelling, CartoGIS, ANU College of Asia and the Pacific

This brief regional sketch provides a background to understanding the situation that developed after European colonisation. European intrusion into eastern Arnhem Land was a slow and at first intermittent process. It began with the visit of Flinders in early 1803, when Yolngu people had congregated at major coastal sites for turtle hunting and for the anticipated arrival of the Macassans. Flinders' crew had a violent encounter with Yolngu on Morgan Island in which one and possibly two Yolngu were killed. Over the next 130 years, Yolngu continued their trading relationships with outsiders, with the Macassans until 1907 and subsequently with Japanese and European visitors. European encroachment on Yolngu country took place on the western and southern boundaries with the development of cattle stations at the turn of the nineteenth and twentieth centuries. There were documented massacres in the region of the Arafura Swamp (see Dewar 1989) and another about 1911 at Gängan, within the Djalkiripuyngu region (Berndt and Berndt 1954: 101; H. Morphy 2003: 27).

These encroachments from the outside had an impact on Yolngu society internally. Some of the massacres were facilitated by Aboriginal people who were in effect clients of the Europeans at the advance of the frontier. Internal and external pressures came to a head in the early 1930s with the Caledon Bay killings. The crew of a Japanese pearling and trepanging vessel was killed in 1932, and in 1933 Constable McColl, one of the policemen sent out to investigate the deaths, was himself speared to death on Woodah Island (Egan 1996). The time of the Caledon Bay killings proved to be a watershed in the recent history of the region, which, from the present-day Yolngu perspective, brought an end to domains of conflict; it resulted in an end of conflict with Europeans through the process of missionisation and it greatly reduced the level of internal warfare. External evidence tends to support the Yolngu view of their history (see, for example, Clarke 2010: 22 ff.).

The establishment of the mission settlement of Yirrkala in 1935 was an element in a broader regional process of missionisation. However, Yirrkala's location on the far north-eastern corner of the Yolngu region also had consequential effects on the subsequent history of the region that are essential to understanding the distribution and composition of contemporary outstations of the eastern Yolngu area. Members of the Djalkiripuyngu clans made the decision to move a considerable distance from their clan lands centred on the Blue Mud Bay and Caledon Bay region. Some moved north to Yirrkala, and this entailed establishing stronger relationships with the clans of the northern coast, which was achieved in part by broadening the connections through marriage. In part because of the recent history of warfare, a number of Djalkiripuyngu never relocated permanently to Yirrkala and chose instead to move south to Numbulwar, Ngukurr (Roper River), Wugularr (Beswick) and Groote Eylandt.

1935–1970: 'Mission time'

In the era between 1935 and 1970, Yolngu from Blue Mud Bay moved widely about the entire Yolngu region and beyond. People resident at the main settlements to the north and south maintained contact with their clan lands, going there for regular visits, trading crocodile skins with the missionaries, and travelling along the coast to meet up with relatives and participate in ceremonies (see Greenfield 1954a, 1954b). Some Yolngu remained permanently on country away from the settlements, and a number of semi-permanent settlements were developed across the Yolngu region, at Caledon Bay, Baykurrtji, Gurrumuru and Mirrngatja.[4]

Yolngu from the Djalkiripuyngu clans tried to get support from the Government and missions to establish their own settlements in the southern Yolngu area at Caledon and Blue Mud bays. In 1954 Brian Greenfield, a patrol officer for the Department of Native Affairs, noted a movement away from Yirrkala by people he refers to as the southern clans, including members of the Dhaḻwangu, Dhuḏi Djapu, Märi (Gupa) Djapu, Maḏarrpa, Munyuku, Manggalili and Marrakulu clans. Settlements had been established by Djeriny Mununggurr of the Gupa Djapu clan at Caledon Bay and by Mäw' Mununggurr at Trial Bay. Greenfield also refers to plans to establish a settlement in Manggalili clan country at Cape Shield (Djarrakpi). It is worth quoting from Greenfield's report as it provides a degree of evidence about Yolngu motivations at the time:

> This reversion to their own tribal areas is evidence of many things, but mainly emphasises the original mistake of trying to mix two historically opposed factions [the north-eastern and south-eastern connubia: Laynhapuyngu and Djalkiripuyngu]. To my knowledge this is the first occasion that natives have quite without assistance, taken such decisive steps to regain a little of their independence that they originally sacrificed for the comforts and assistance of the mission welfare facilities.
>
> They show no antagonism towards the mission itself. Their attitude to its endeavours is becoming cynical, but at the same time they are very much aware of the need of such an organisation for their ultimate development. The plans of these rebel groups is to place their children in the care of the mission to be schooled. When schooling is over, they will come back 'home' to help on the 'property', and carry on, peasant like in their fathers' footsteps. (Greenfield 1954b)

---

4   No histories of these settlements have been published. In a sense, they were continuing hunter-gatherer camps, occupied on a semi-permanent basis—sometimes unoccupied as people moved to other places and other settlements. Links with mission stations were facilitated by the building of airstrips, allowing regular visits from the missionary Harold Shepherdson, based at Elcho Island. Shepherdson was a missionary in Arnhem Land from 1927 to 1977 and began flying after he built his own plane in 1932. Ella Shepherdson's book, *Half a Century in Arnhem Land* (1981), provides an account of their lives in Arnhem Land. She writes that 'Baykurrtji a place on the Koolatong River was commenced in 1959. This was the ideal place for a garden because it had good soil and plenty of water. Our Fijian agriculturist, Penuia Sari, went down there and stayed for a fortnight to fence a garden and help the people plant sweet potato runners. They reaped the first crop but did not continue to plant, evidently preferring their own way of hunting in the bush. On one occasion at Baykurrtji, two women went washing clothes by the river when a crocodile caught one of them. She was never seen again. This upset the people of course, and they immediately moved camp to another place called Gängan. This place is still open and is contacted by the Yirrkala people' (Shepherdson 1981: 37). No date is given for the departure from Baykurrtji but when Nicolas Peterson visited the settlement in 1965, it had been reoccupied. Bandipandi Wunungmurra (personal communication, 2000) recalls the event.

Envisaging futures

A number of themes recur in Yolngu visions of a future mode of existence adapted to the circumstances of colonisation. Some of these are reflected in Greenfield's report. The vision of a relatively autonomous existence for the homelands is clearly linked to the enterprises introduced by the missionaries and others who in their own interests had to create a local economy. The Methodist (later Uniting) Church had a strong ideology of making people work in return for rations. At Yirrkala the main economic activities involved the development of gardens to help make the community self-sufficient in food and the marketing of art and craft as a source of income. Most other enterprises, such as sawmilling and attempts to establish a fishing industry, were based primarily on a subsistence model. The people from Blue Mud Bay had a second source of inspiration when they worked for Fred Grey to establish the settlement of Umbakumba on Groote Eylandt. Grey's belief was that, free from the control of the missionaries, Yolngu would be able to establish small communities that were largely self-sufficient and develop a life independent of missionary or government. But his model for the economy was very similar to the mission's. And under the governance of the missionaries and Fred Grey, the major settlements of the region were moderately successful.

Yolngu also understood that another component was vital to sustain the kind of communities they envisaged: transport. The Djalkiripuyngu were in many respects people of the sea. Not only were they coastal hunters and gatherers, but also boats (principally dugout canoes) had provided a major mode of transport and opportunities for employment when working with the Macassans. The missionaries and Fred Grey, equally, built on this tradition; Yolngu worked on the mission lugger, which provided an essential mode of communication between settlements. Recurrent themes, in both Yolngu and missionary thinking, concerning what a settlement should comprise included: self-sufficiency in food and housing, schooling for the children and a ready means of transport. These are all themes that resonate still today in discussions of regional development. Matters of scale, which are still a factor today (as we shall see later), were sometimes invoked to characterise these aspirations as unrealistic. In response to Narritjin's requests for a barge to help found and supply a settlement at Djarrakpi, Greenfield was dismissive: 'Narritjin and another of his big ideas' (1954a).

Seizing opportunities

The history of eastern Yolngu interaction with outsiders has been a combination of resistance to the impositions of the colonising society and the seizing of opportunities it provided. The early 1970s gave opportunities for both. Yolngu had been engaged over the previous decade in a struggle for land rights as a result of the granting of leases for bauxite mining on the Gove Peninsula near Yirrkala (see Williams 1986). The ultimate outcome of that struggle was not yet evident, for although they had lost the Gove land rights case, the incoming government had commissioned Justice Woodward to report on ways in which Aboriginal people in the Northern Territory could gain recognition of their title to land.

As we have seen, Yolngu people had, with some support from the mission, already begun attempts to move back on to country. Concern with what might happen to their land if they did not occupy it more permanently had now increased as a result of the Gove case. Conditions at Yirrkala mission were becoming more difficult with the development of the nearby mining town of Nhulunbuy and the opening of the Walkabout Hotel.

The advent of the Whitlam Government, with its support for the idea of self-determination for Aboriginal people, provided the opportunity to act decisively on the desire to move back to country; it did not create that desire. The new policy environment facilitated the establishment of small, dispersed communities while increasing support from the Uniting Church, which had been actively supportive of the Yolngu in the Gove case, allowed the maintenance of links with and support from the settlement at Yirrkala.

A number of other factors must also be taken into account. The development of the mining town of Nhulunbuy had marginally improved regional transport infrastructure, and the Methodist Aviation Fellowship began to provide efficient and relatively low-cost air transport. Toyota four-wheel-drive vehicles provided the land equivalent of the dugout canoe for travelling between settlements, and indeed in the Yolngu case Toyotas received names previously reserved for canoes. The mission provided each outstation with minimal resources in the form of sheet iron for housing, water pumps and access to equipment such as graders. Some government subventions began to flow, but on the whole the outstations were built with minimal resources. The airstrips were laboriously cleared by hand and houses built by members of the community trained in basic construction methods by the missionaries and using local timber. The initial economy was based on hunting and gathering of food and art and craft production, supplemented by welfare payments that had recently begun to be a significant input into the region. Quite early on education followed the establishment of the outstations and Yolngu teachers' and teaching assistants' salaries began to make an additional contribution.

The establishment of the outstations did not simply involve a movement of people away from Yirrkala. Members of Djalkiripuyngu clans, such as the Maḏarrpa, Dhuḏi Djapu, Munyuku and Dhäpuyngu, who had for various reasons not wanted to move to Yirrkala mission, took the opportunity to join those moving from Yirrkala back to their country. To a considerable extent, this enabled the regrouping of the Djalkiripuyngu connubium, whose interactions had been disrupted by people's dispersal to settlements in distant places.

Yilpara is established

Yilpara was among the first of the Yolngu outstations to be established, on Maḏarrpa country. The initial population was built on a set of core individuals of the Maḏarrpa, Munyuku, Dhäpuyngu and Dhuḏi Djapu clans—all clans of the northern Blue Mud Bay Djalkiripuyngu connubium. Not all intended to remain there permanently but rather to use Yilpara as the springboard for establishing their own homelands in neighbouring places. In subsequent years, further outstations were built nearby, at Rurrangala on Munyuku country and at Dhuruputjpi on Dhuḏi Djapu country. Together with Gängan, Djarrakpi and Waṉḏawuy, which were established at the same time as Yilpara, these form an interconnected set of settlements with shared histories that long predate the homelands movement itself—a region within a region. Over time at Yilpara, the Maḏarrpa were joined by some members of other clans from the connubium, particularly Gupa Djapu and Marrakulu—clans of the opposite moiety. Many Maḏarrpa have Marrakulu mothers, and many Djapu have Maḏarrpa mothers.

Ian Dunlop's film *We are the Landowner* (filmed in 1982; released in 1985) provides an excellent record of aspects of life in Yilpara during its formative period and illustrates the aspirations of some of its leaders. Djambawa Marawili and Gumbaniya Marawili emphasised their long-term connection to the country. They took Ian to the area of jungle behind the settlement:

> We can see this tree, *wangupini*, our grandfather planted it—a tree he brought from Barratjala—and it reminds us of his presence in this country. This is the old people's land and this is why we have come here to live ... I am here in my own land and I am moving around in my own area—I know how ... and where to walk—we have got everything here, no reason to go back to Yirrkala. (Dunlop 1985)

And virtually everything at that time had been built by the people who lived there. At the heart of the outstation was the school, housed in a tin shed, which began with more than 30 students, from infant to post-primary, divided into three classes. The school was established initially as an outpost of the Yirrkala School, with additional support provided by the Isolated Students Allowance (ISA). The senior teacher was Galuma Maymuru (Djambawa's mother-in-law to be), who had previously been a teaching assistant at Yirrkala. The available educational funding covered the costs of two teachers, with a third paid out of the ISA monies. This was Galuma's idea, and she also started a canteen to provide children's lunches, funded by the parents. Her ambition was to make a profit to plough back into the school budget to acquire a school vehicle. The school was an English-language school since it was felt that the children gained sufficient education in their own language and culture outside school hours. This has continued to be the policy applied to homeland schools since that time. The main non-benefit income apart from the teachers' salaries was derived from art and craft production. In the years immediately after the establishment of the homelands, the income from the sale of craft through Yirrkala increased tenfold, with most of the production coming from the outstations.

In the years since its establishment in 1972, Yilpara has maintained a sizeable population of more than 100 individuals, with considerably more present at ceremonial times. Over time the infrastructure of the community has developed slowly. Bore water is sourced via a solar and wind generator pump and, since 2006, electricity has been generated by a substantial diesel-powered generator that is able to supply the entire community. But it is costly to run. Housing improved greatly in the 1990s, with more substantial houses being built under the auspices of the Laynhapuy Homelands Association, the local outstation resource centre, on the footprints of the original outstation buildings. Schooling came under the management of the Yirrkala-based homelands school, and a new school was built. The teaching system used a combination of locally resident teaching assistants and visiting (mostly non-Yolngu) teachers from the Yirrkala base, who stayed in the community for three days a week. The community also gained a small building to house the office and the clinic. Yilpara has a small store, the fortunes of which have waxed and waned; it is now operated as an IGA.[5] The economy was built around welfare payments, salaries of teaching assistants and health workers and subsidised employment facilitated by community development schemes of which the most important was Community Development Employment Projects (CDEP). The last enabled the provision of local services such as refuse collection and community grounds maintenance. Hunting and gathering and art production continued to be important non-subsidised sources of income and subsistence. Yirrkala outstations continued to

---

5   An independent chain of supermarket stores.

be the main source of production for what became Buku Larrnggay Mulka art centre. The art centre developed in the decades after the 1970s into a considerable business in which the return from art alone brought in an annual income of more than $2 million, most of which was generated by the southern homelands. The art centre also became one of the main conduits for communication and interaction with the wider Australian community and resulted in some Yilpara community members having regional and national roles.

Linkage within the broader economic framework was also facilitated by the development of a regional ranger program covering the Laynhapuy homelands. The Yirralka ranger program was instituted in 2003 and the later declaration of the Laynhapuy Indigenous Protected Area (IPA) created further opportunities for employment for both men and women. People from Yilpara had been leading players in the establishment of the ranger group and the IPA, which came in part out of the work they undertook for the Blue Mud Bay native title claim. The Yolngu view the establishment of the IPA as being in continuity with the struggle for land and sea rights and the homelands movement, reflecting the need to occupy and protect country. As Waka Mununggurr put it:

> I am the child of this country, its manager and caretaker. I care for the land and the laws of this Madarrpa clan, for their sea and their land. Yes, it was for this that we established the Rangers. We wanted to have them care for the country, the sea and the inland together. Yes, this was needed because we have seen some bad things happen here before. [Professional] fishermen despoiled this country, they came in ignorantly … Then we provided evidence [to the Blue Mud Bay court hearing]. Because of this, we then wanted a Ranger program. The Rangers will patrol and monitor the boundaries in the sea and care for the land. This is the reason why we undertook that sea rights claim. (Translation from the original in Yolngu matha, cited in LHAI 2006: 6, 9)

The past decade has also seen the slow emergence of cultural tourism as a possible industry, with a number of initiatives now in place.

Thwarted aspirations: Recurring themes

Measured in terms of the stability of their population, the Yirrkala homelands, including Yilpara, have been successful communities. Today they comprise about 50 per cent of the regional population, and there is no evidence of population decline.[6] However, there has been a long history of dissatisfaction with the way the homelands have been treated and the people of Yilpara have led much of the critique. The main criticisms have centred on housing, schooling and employment opportunities.

We returned to work at Yilpara in 1997, using it as our base for research for the Blue Mud Bay case. The concerns displayed then by the community have remained essentially unchanged and until recently have been largely unaddressed. In the case of housing, the resources available from government for homelands became scarcer and the cost of housing increased exponentially. Government funding for new homelands community housing ceased altogether in 2008. Over the years, the Government's model of housing delivery had resulted in building regulations and tendering processes that had the effect of taking construction out of the hands of Yolngu. In the period from 1997 to 2007, not a single house was built to address the significant overcrowding in the community. Moreover, limited resources were available for other community facilities, including spaces for art production, visitor accommodation and tourism development. The Laynhapuy Homelands Association (LHA), established in 1985 to service the homelands, had limited resources to satisfy the demand, and regulatory structures meant it was difficult for them to provide cheaper solutions using government funding.

With schooling, the desire for full-time residential teachers in an enlarged school premises to match the increasing school-age population was also slow to be satisfied. It required changes in the policy of the homeland school; creating different models for different outstations was both ideologically and logistically difficult.

The economic development of outstations had never been a government priority, and again limited resources were available. LHA's main function was as a resource centre supporting the infrastructure needs of the homelands; economic development was a secondary concern, inadequately resourced and funded. The main resource that was available for LHA to manage in this area was the CDEP program. CDEP was designed to help support and generate employment in remote areas but, beginning in the time of the Howard Coalition

---

6   This figure is derived from as yet unpublished research by Frances Morphy, who conducted a regional population survey in 2010. The survey covered Yirrkala and Gapuwiyak, and all the homelands serviced from those major communities. The figure of 50 per cent relates to the community of Yirrkala and the set of homelands originally serviced from Yirrkala by the Laynhapuy Homelands Association (LHA) (now Laynhapuy Homelands Aboriginal Corporation). In the late 2000s, LHA assumed responsibility for servicing a group of homelands that had previously been serviced from Gapuwiyak. For this larger region as a whole, the homelands population comprises one-third of the population.

Government, it was increasingly subject to ideologically motivated criticism.[7] Organisations like LHA, which managed CDEP programs, increasingly spent much of their time defending an uncertain resource, rather than deploying the energy necessary to make it work more effectively in achieving the objectives for which it was set up.[8]

The rhetoric from government that emphasised the creation of 'real' jobs had considerable purchase within the Yilpara community, yet there was little understanding (in the community or indeed in governments and the local bureaucracy) of where those jobs would come from. Indeed, in many respects, government policy (of all complexions) in the spheres of both employment and housing was increasingly directed towards moving people away from the homelands to the hub settlements, rather than providing solutions where people lived.

At Yilpara, it was a case of 'shoot the messenger'. The community leaders became increasingly disillusioned with and even hostile to the LHA. For its part, LHA, in attempting to fulfil a development role, overextended itself financially. It has only just recently emerged from a period of special administration under the new title of the Laynhapuy Homelands Aboriginal Corporation (LHAC).

Pragmatic Yilpara: Seizing opportunities again

Recent developments at Yilpara have involved a complex relationship between community demands and the response of a number of competing non-Indigenous organisations and interests operating in the public and private or voluntary sectors. Developments in the areas of infrastructure, education and housing can be only briefly summarised here.

The involvement of the Centre for Independent Studies (CIS) and Sydney Cove Rotary Club began in early 2000. The Rotary Club responded to requests from the community to build facilities, successfully bidding for contracts to undertake work and providing skilled volunteer labour. They worked with local Yolngu labour, also voluntary, to build an artists' studio and a women's cultural centre, and subsequently built a visiting officers' quarters (VOQ), comprising a kitchen, two bedrooms for visitors and a lecture theatre/dining room. The Rotary volunteers also worked with Yolngu to construct a permanent campsite for guests

---

7   The saga of the demise of CDEP is a topic in itself. For the beginning of the end, see Peter Shergold's (2001) contribution to a volume dedicated to an evaluation of CDEP (Morphy and Sanders 2001). At the time, Shergold was the secretary of the Commonwealth Department of Employment, Workplace Relations and Small Business.

8   For an analysis of the governance of LHA in the mid 2000s, and the tensions generated by serving two masters—the Yolngu residents of the homelands and government paymasters—see F. Morphy (2008).

taking part in a planned future program of cultural and environmental tourism. The concept for the latter had been developed by Stepwise, a consultancy organisation with loose connections to The Australian National University. The VOQ has served a number of different purposes, providing accommodation for visiting researchers, leaders of tour groups and volunteers. Latterly, it served as accommodation for the manager of the Yilpara store after it had been taken over by the Nhulunbuy IGA. It is also used as a training centre, for Laynhapuy-wide training courses as well as purely local training.

Members of the Yilpara community had long been demanding that the NT Education Department provide a school staffed by full-time teachers resident in the settlement. They also wanted the school buildings to be upgraded to provide more classrooms and better facilities. Yolngu faced two main problems in pursuing these demands. They required the school to be set up on a different basis from other homeland schools and they required that a larger budget be allocated to cover the costs of resident teachers. Their case had a strong national political dimension to it since it was strongly supported by researchers associated with the CIS, whose discourse involved a critique of bilingual education (despite the fact that Yilpara school was not a bilingual school), of government schools and of the ideological basis of public education. The Education Department, after many years of discussion and lobbying, agreed to fund a school for Yilpara that fitted in with Yolngu wishes. The building of a new school was funded by the department, as was the construction of two houses for the resident teachers. Although Yolngu and others often refer to the new school as 'independent', it is run by the NT Department of Education. Its curriculum is similar to those of other government schools and, as is the case with other homeland schools, it is not bilingual. Its difference from other Yolngu outstation schools is that it has been set up as an autonomous local 'small school' and does not come under the umbrella of the Yirrkala Homeland School.

The houses for the teachers were the first to be built at Yilpara in more than a decade and highlighted the community's overall housing problem. Indeed, changes in government policy in recent years have made it impossible for local organisations such as LHA (now LHAC) to be able to build new houses in homelands. This has opened up the opportunity for the rhetoric of private home-ownership as a solution to Indigenous housing problems to gain some purchase. Yilpara (aided by CIS) petitioned the Federal Government and the Northern Land Council (NLC) for the granting of 99-year leases to individuals in order that they can become owners of (or, rather, take out mortgages for) private dwellings. The NLC did not respond positively. Yilpara (via their CIS/Rotary advisers) enlisted the aid of the Australian Indigenous Chamber of Commerce (AICC), whose executive chairman is Warren Mundine. The following appears on the AICC website:

> In 2012 the ICBF [Indigenous Community Benevolent Fund] arranged for two transportable and fully furnished and equipped homes to be transported and installed at Yilpara. These homes cost $150,000 each, ready to move in (as compared to Government-built houses on remote communities which cost about $450,000 or more). The homes are being leased back to two Yilpara families and are intended to be sold to them if and when 99-year leases are implemented.
>
> The Chamber saw first hand these two homes in Yilpara. Nearly a year old they now have pretty gardens out the front and are obviously well cared for.[9]

The issue of continuing repairs and long-term infrastructure support for the houses has yet to be finally negotiated with LHAC, which continues to have the main responsibility for homeland support. We do not have space here to fully describe the complex networks of influence that led to this interim solution to the Yilpara housing problem.

It is deeply ironic that the ideological critique of the outstation movement associated with neoliberal organisations, in particular the CIS, had one of its bases in the community of Yilpara itself. The irony is that the CIS, while critiquing homelands as a form of apartheid (Hughes 2007), simultaneously provided the opportunities for Yilpara to increase its resources locally and remain relatively autonomous of the hub communities. The support of the CIS and the Sydney Cove Rotary Club also enabled the community to remain on a trajectory that utilised the value of its cultural production, to continue to exploit what Helen Hughes referred to as their 'culturally rich lives'.

Conclusion

Yolngu desires for facilities and services at Yilpara have been consistent since the outstation was set up. Over time, they have wanted to see a continual, incremental improvement of the facilities available to them and increasing employment opportunities. Over time, supporting government-funded institutions have been more or less able to meet their aspirations depending on government policy, available expertise and resource availability. The CIS and Rotary essentially stepped in when LHA as an organisation became chronically unable to satisfy community aspirations. Yolngu strongly supported CIS-sponsored efforts on their behalf, because they provided an opportunity to improve their housing situation and also to create a school that was more directly under their local control. There is some evidence that the rhetorical stance of the CIS/Rotary alliance was synergistic with community feelings of dissatisfaction with service provision. There was a strong belief that too many

---

9   See: www.indigenouschamber.org.au/.

decisions were taken at a distance from the community and that the ways in which LHA resources were distributed did not take sufficient account of the needs of large communities. And from the beginning the homeland movement in eastern Arnhem Land emphasised local autonomy.

While the LHA inevitably had to take account of its regional responsibilities and hence could not appear to unduly favour one outstation over another, the outcomes achieved at Yilpara by the collaboration with CIS/Rotary were largely ones that the organisation supported, sometimes reluctantly, and which it facilitated, where it was able to do so. Many of the ventures were in effect collaborative, with LHA managing the budgets and providing infrastructural support—for example, in plumbing, waste disposal and electricity supply. However, LHA was becoming increasingly handicapped by government policy settings that favoured the hub communities, which in effect put the outstation movement into reverse. These policy settings had been heavily influenced by the very position that the CIS and other neoliberal theorists had long advocated, including their critique of the homelands as a factor contributing to Aboriginal disadvantage. The policies of government, which were designed to advantage the townships and take advantage of imagined mainstream job opportunities and economics of scale, did not differentiate between outstations. Detailed evaluation of the potential of different communities was not relevant to the policy agenda. So how was it that CIS/Rotary provided such strong support for Yilpara? What was it that government policy had overlooked, in this particular case, that made Yilpara an exception to the viability rules?

The answer must lie in the space between rhetoric and reality. Yilpara is among the most distant of Yirrkala outstations and has all the locational and logistical 'disadvantages' that make outstations an expensive proposition. At the same time, however, it is a community that has long shown itself to be determined to continue existing. It is a strong community that has achieved a high profile through its outstanding artists, through the 'Saltwater' collection of paintings and by successfully taking on the NT and Federal governments in the Blue Mud Bay native title claim. Yilpara has a number of leaders who have taken on national roles. Djambawa Marawili, in addition to having an international reputation as an artist, has been the long-term chairman of the Association of Northern, Kimberley and Arnhem Aboriginal Artists (ANKAAA). He is now a member of the Prime Minister's Indigenous Advisory Council. Yilpara was also instrumental in the establishment of the Yirrkala rangers. In short, Yilpara has cachet and cultural capital! It is precisely because of its high profile and the determination of its residents that Yilpara provides a suitable case for treatment and exposure. But we would argue that the factors that made it seem to be an unviable proposition are what need to be taken into account if communities like it are going to be part of the solution to Indigenous disadvantage in the future.

Our own position is that neither governments nor CIS/Rotary have built into their analysis or vision the necessity to build a viable regional economy. Indeed, as far as recent government policy is concerned, the development of regional economies in remote Australia almost seems to have been ruled out as too difficult. The economic solution is mainstreaming and enabling Indigenous Australians to work in the resource-extraction sector. One of the many problems with that model, in eastern Arnhem Land, is that it depends on major transformations of the aspirations, motivations, mobility patterns and educational status of the Yolngu population—a social engineering project for which there is little supporting evidence for likely success (see Morphy and Morphy 2013). The CIS/ Rotary intervention at Yilpara has arguably been equally unrealistic because it has taken no account of the factors required to maintain the trajectory of the community, to enable the incremental improvements to their living standards that people desire, in the absence of regional economic development. The CIS initiatives have been based, in effect, on a massive subsidy, both financial and in terms of activating networks to which Yilpara would otherwise have had no access, unaided. Rotary has provided a resident builder/engineer at no cost, and has engineered a version of private ownership that is at least two degrees removed from the 'real' market. The developments have also been helped by the LHA, which has borne a number of hidden costs. Using community members as a volunteer labour force (subsidised by CDEP) has also facilitated the affordability of the housing.

The next stage in maintaining the trajectory of Yilpara requires addressing the matter of the regional economy, and addressing that requires a much broader focus than Yilpara itself. While mining is likely to be a long-term contributor to the NT economy, it is not likely to provide direct employment for most of the residents of the Laynhapuy homelands. It does seem that those cultural assets that have undoubtedly been one of the factors that attracted CIS/Rotary to Yilpara will continue to play an important role—for example, in the form of the craft industry, land and sea management and cultural and environmental tourism. Moreover, Indigenous knowledge and capacities are likely to provide the basis for development of new businesses—fishing being a recurrent imaginary. And nearly all of those enterprises need to be developed as part of a regional system, which requires cooperation and the sharing of resources between the various outstations and associated hub communities. It is no coincidence that Buku Larrnggay Mulka art centre has operated on the basis of a distributed production model across the homelands, nor that the recently established Lirrwi model for Indigenous tourism has developed on a hub and spokes model. Similar considerations apply in the area of infrastructure, where regional transport and services can only be supplied using a regional model of collaboration. The model of individual achievement and enterprise advocated by the CIS can only be supported if there is an element of communitarianism in the system. The logic of the situation also requires government to take a more active role in the development of regional economies rather than using the absence of a regional economy as a constraint on developing futures.

While Yilpara residents unquestionably desire resources that enable them to have better housing for their families and greater economic opportunities, they also wish to sustain their community as one that is integrated within a regional system. Yilpara does not see itself as a community in isolation, but as one of a set of 'suburbs', as Djambawa once put it to us, that form a distributed Djalkiripuyngu 'town'. These are the communities from which come Yilpara's wives and mothers, husbands and mothers-in-law; these are the people who come to support them in ceremony and whom they in turn support. The regional population continues to be structured by a complex web of kinship with its attendant obligations and responsibilities (F. Morphy 2010). This is something that an individualistically focused model takes no account of, and to which it attaches no significance. In short, taking a regional view of development is synergistic with Yolngu aspirations to maintain the locally grounded and interconnected, kin-based nature of their society.

References

Berndt, R. and Berndt, C. 1954. *Arnhem Land, Its History and Its People.* Melbourne: Cheshire.

Clarke, B. 2010. *Larrpan ga Buḏuyurr: The Spear and the Cloud.* Adelaide: Bernard Clarke Publisher.

Coombs, H. C., Dexter, B. G. and Hiatt, L. R. 1980. The outstation movement in Aboriginal Australia. *AIATSIS Newsletter* [NS]14: 1–8.

Dewar, M. 1989. Strange bedfellows: Europeans and Aborigines in Arnhem Land before World War II. MA thesis. University of New England, Armidale, NSW.

Dunlop, I. (dir.) 1985. *We are the Landowner … That's Why We're Here.* [Film]. Sydney: Film Australia.

Egan, T. 1996. *Justice All Their Own: The Caledon Bay and Woodah Island killings, 1932–1933.* Melbourne: Melbourne University Press.

Flinders, M. 1814. *Voyage to Terra Australis, Volume 2.* London: G. & W. Nicol.

Greenfield, B. 1954a. Killing of Aborigine Urubulu, Caledon Bay area. Unpublished report, 5 February. Northern Territory Archives, Darwin.

Greenfield, B. 1954b. Caledon Bay natives: Further report on happenings in the Trial Bay area. Unpublished report. Northern Territory Archives, Darwin.

Hughes, H. 2007. *Lands of Shame: Aboriginal and Torres Strait Islander 'Homelands' in Transition*. Sydney: Centre for Independent Studies.

Laynhapuy Homelands Association Incorporated (LHAI) 2006. Laynhapuy Indigenous Protected Area: Management plan, April 2006. Unpublished draft, version 11/04/06. Yirrkala, NT: LHAI.

Morphy, F. 2002. When systems collide: The 2001 census at a Northern Territory outstation. In D. F. Martin, F. Morphy, W. G. Sanders and J. Taylor, *Making Sense of the Census: Observations of the 2001 Enumeration in Remote Aboriginal Australia*. CAEPR Research Monograph No. 22. Canberra: ANU E Press.

Morphy, F. (ed.) 2007. *Agency, Contingency and Census Process: Observations of the 2006 Indigenous Enumeration Strategy in Remote Aboriginal Australia*. CAEPR Research Monograph No. 28. Canberra: ANU E Press.

Morphy, F. 2008. Whose governance, for whose good? The Laynhapuy Homelands Association and the neo-assimilationist turn in Indigenous policy. In J. Hunt, D. Smith, S. Garling and W. Sanders (eds), *Contested Governance: Culture, Power and Institutions in Indigenous Australia*. CAEPR Research Monograph No. 29. Canberra: ANU E Press.

Morphy, F. 2010. (Im)mobility: Regional population structures in Aboriginal Australia. *Australian Journal of Social Issues* 45(3): 363–82.

Morphy, F. 2012. *The Yolngu in place: Designing a population survey for northeast Arnhem Land*. Agreements, Treaties and Negotiated Settlements Project Working Paper Series. Melbourne: University of Melbourne.

Morphy, F. and Morphy, H. 2013. Anthropological theory and government policy in Australia's Northern Territory: The hegemony of the 'mainstream'. *American Anthropologist* 115(2): 174–87.

Morphy, F. and Sanders, W. (eds) 2001. *The Indigenous Welfare Economy and the CDEP Scheme*. CAEPR Research Monograph No. 20. Canberra: Centre for Aboriginal Economic Policy Research.

Morphy, H. 2003. An anthropological report in relation to their claim to recognition of native title in the land and sea by the Yolngu people of Blue Mud Bay. Unpublished report prepared on behalf of the claimants at the instruction of the Northern Land Council, Darwin.

Myers, F. R. 1986. *Pintupi Country, Pintupi Self: Sentiment, Place, and Politics among Western Desert Aborigines*. Washington, DC: Smithsonian Institution Press.

Peterson, N. 2005. What can pre-colonial and frontier economies tell us about engagement with the real economy? Indigenous life projects and the conditions for development. In D. Austin-Broos and G. MacDonald (eds), *Culture, Economy and Governance in Aboriginal Australia*. Sydney: Sydney University Press, pp. 7–18.

Shepherdson, E. 1981. *Half a Century in Arnhem Land*. Adelaide: H. & E. Shepherdson.

Shergold, P. 2001. The Indigenous employment policy: A preliminary evaluation. In F. Morphy and W. Sanders (eds), *The Indigenous Welfare Economy and the CDEP Scheme*. CAEPR Research Monograph No. 20. Canberra: Centre for Aboriginal Economic Policy Research.

Williams, N. 1986. *The Yolngu and Their Land: A System of Land Tenure and the Fight for its Recognition*. Canberra: Australian Institute of Aboriginal Studies.

16

A history of Donydji outstation, north-east Arnhem Land

Neville White

The first official exploration of Yolngu country was by David Lindsay, who, in 1883, travelled the western edge of Wagilak land, following the Goyder River into the Arafura Swamp, where he first encountered Yolngu people and in large numbers. Soon after, in 1885, the Florida cattle station was established when a herd of cattle driven from Queensland arrived (Berndt and Berndt 1954). This was a short-lived but violent frontier, with memories of conflict and atrocities persisting today. Soon after the closure of Florida, a Methodist Overseas Mission was founded, in 1923, on Milingimbi Island, off the north-western coast of north-east Arnhem Land (Berndt and Berndt 1954). This mission settlement attracted Yolngu people from a wide area, many of whom settled on the mission. Others, like the families who set up the Donydji outstation, visited periodically for supplies such as tobacco and sugar—commodities that were also occasionally obtained from the Mainoru cattle station and Roper River Mission Station to the south. These journeys often took many months.

During World War II, Milingimbi came under air attack by the Japanese, and the Reverend Harold Shepherdson moved to a new Methodist mission site on Elcho Island, a little to the east. Shepherdson later transported, in his own single-engine plane, some food supplies and clothes to the newly created Mirrngadja outstation, using an airstrip he had helped construct in 1959 (Shepherdson 1981). In 1969, the Reverend started Lake Evella (now known as Gapuwiyak) as an outpost of the Elcho Island Mission, so as to engage with

Yolngu people further inland and to mill native cypress pine growing in the vicinity (Shepherdson 1981). Shortly before Lake Evella was set up, a mining survey party constructed a rough road connecting Katherine, south-west of Arnhem Land, to the Gove Peninsula, in the north-east. This track has become the Central Arnhem Highway, which is about 5 km further north than the original road that ran through Donydji. The construction of the bauxite mining town of Nhulunbuy began in the late 1960s, followed soon after by an alumina refinery. This has become the main service centre for all of north-east Arnhem Land and further afield, attracting Yolngu people from the entire region, who come for health and other services, such as banking, the purchase of food and other provisions, as well as motor vehicles and spare parts.

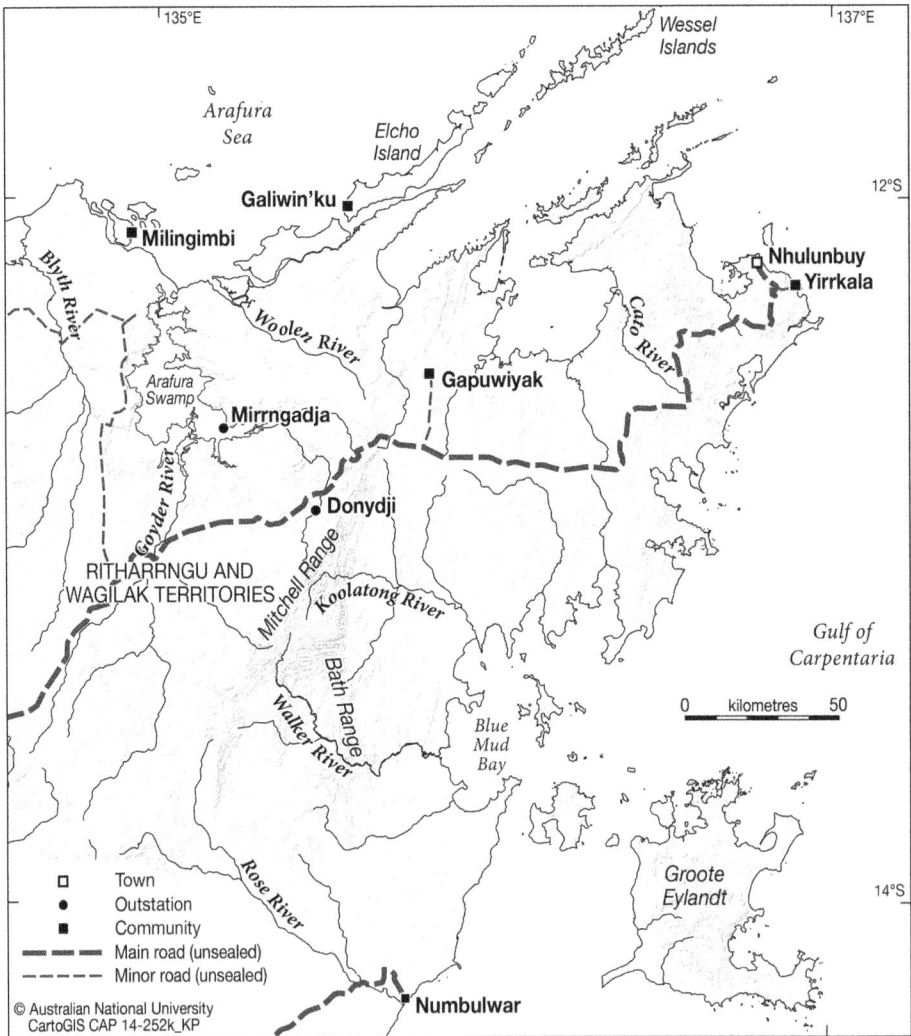

Map 16.1 Doyndji outstation in north-east Arnhem Land.

Source: Karina Pelling, CartoGIS, ANU College of Asia and the Pacific

In outlining here the origin and history of Donydji (now Gurrumala) outstation, I suggest that it was not established as a move away from the larger centres in rejection of the settlement lifestyle, although I think it has become such. Rather, the aim was to protect the area from outside interference by mining companies as well as the utilitarian desire to stay near the airstrip (constructed by a mining survey team) so as to obtain food, materials and, it was hoped, health services. Strong emotional attachment to this place was just as important: the two senior Ritharrngu brothers who chose to establish the permanent camp at Donydji had never left their land. Three years ago, I recall two elderly Djarrwak women living at Balma, to the east, telling me that these old men never left their country during the Yolngu 'wartime': 'They were strong and stayed. That's what we think about them.'[1]

Figure 16.1 View of the Donydji (Gurrumala) Homeland community, taken in 2012. Most of the buildings were constructed by Vietnam veteran volunteers, working with community members using charitable funds provided through the Rotary Club of Melbourne.

Photo: Neville White

---

1   This is probably a reference to the conflict taking place in north-east Arnhem Land during the 1930s, both with outsiders and internally (see Berndt and Berndt 1954).

The young generation, however, sees living in the homelands as an assertion of self-determination—a need to show the outside world that they care for their country and choose to live on it. In fact, some young people—men and women— see it as an act of defiance in the face of increasing pressure from governments, miners, tourism interests and others to have them give up their homeland and move into the government-defined 'hub centres' with the promise of better servicing and social control through police surveillance.

Since 1974, I have spent about two months every year living in Donydji, conducting research and working with the residents as an advocate and in community development. Starting in 2003, this has been as project leader of the Mittjiwu Djaaka (Caring for Our Community) Project funded by philanthropy with support from volunteers, especially Vietnam veterans with whom I served as an infantry conscript. The story I tell here, then, is based on a long-standing relationship with the Yolngu in and around Donydji.

Donydji outstation takes its name from a very important Ritharrngu sacred site nearby. The wider area, called Gurrumala, was (and is) seen to be a 'company' area under the custodial jurisdiction of three Ritharrngu clans with ceremonial connections to different species of paperbark trees growing along the river close to where the outstation is located. Before 1968, the Ritharrngu and Wagilak families now resident at Donydji were, to a considerable degree, nomadic, largely dependent on traditional wild food resources. Much of their time was spent exploiting the area between Donydji and Mirrngadja to the north, although their economic range also covered the country of Ritharrngu and Wagilak clans with whom they had strong marriage relationships, and extended over about 4,000 sq km. These people were among the few remaining Aborigines living in, and off, the bush, although they had substantial contact with mission stations in the region.

In 1967, several of the people who later took up residence in Donydji were engaged occasionally in walking from the long-standing Mirrngadja outstation to a mining camp that had been set up on the Donydji River at Gadadhirri, a little downstream from where the outstation is now. In return for their efforts, they received sugar and tobacco, according to some of those who were involved.[2]

In 1968, a bush airstrip was constructed near its present location by the mining survey team with the assistance of some of the Yolngu. About this time, geologists damaged a sacred site by removing a core from one of the granite boulders that form the Djawk constellation, which both represents and embodies the Ritharrngu clans. These events prompted the establishment of a permanent camp at Donydji: the airstrip added to the resource base by providing access to tools,

---

2   Nicolas Peterson, while carrying out fieldwork at Mirrngatja, confirmed these reports.

food and occasionally medical care, while the damaged sacred site emphasised to the Aborigines the need to guard their land. Since then, the outstation has functioned as a permanent base camp, with households moving in and out in response to the availability of resources, and to social tension. In recounting to me the history of the outstation, Yolngu placed far greater emphasis on site protection than on the acquisition of Western goods that Nic Peterson, working at Mirrngatja, saw as the imperative.

During 1975, the community was swelled by a number of families and single men from the Malabarritjarray (also known as Madarrpa) Ritharrngu clan, who travelled up from Roper River. These people came to try to resolve the responsibility and subsequent compensation for the damage to the Djawk. Not then having a working knowledge of Wagilak, I had to rely on my friend Yilarama to explain some elements of the meetings and ceremonies. His English was not good at that time and my Wagilak was much worse. It seems that the Birdingal and Gulungurr clansmen were held responsible for allowing the mining company to drill into the stone. I still do not know what, if any, material compensation was paid to the Madarrpa Ritharrngu and other custodial clans. I did record, however, that the same groups came together soon after for a *Marradjiri* ceremony, which was taken west into Rembarrnga stone country.[3] It was only in recent years that these stone country and eastern Ritharrngu clan members returned to Donydji to reside for short periods, to participate in ceremonies or join in negotiations over mining exploration (all rejected), roadworks and other development proposals. In late 2013, representatives of these groups and other custodians gathered in Donydji to consider the gas pipeline proposed by Rio Tinto for its alumina plant in Nhulunbuy.

During the 2013 pipeline negotiations, there was strong disagreement between men from the southern clans—who anticipated a financial windfall but who, it was made clear, had never been carers for the country in dispute—and those opposed to economic development of this kind. After sometimes heated and dramatic discussions over two days, and unlike the earlier applications, approval was finally given for a pipeline to be constructed across Ritharrngu and Wagilak estates in the vicinity of the outstation. However, not long after this meeting, the plans were shelved by Rio Tinto.

---

3   Six months after this ceremony, an elderly Wambukungu Rembarrnga widow came to Donydji as the first wife of one of the Birdingal Ritharrngu.

Missionaries and evangelism

An important influence in Donydji's history has been the presence of Methodist missionaries. In particular, the Reverend Harold Shepherdson from the Elcho Island Mission was instrumental in supporting a number of homelands in their early years, among the earliest being Mirrngadja from which Donydji was a spinoff, by flying in some basic food staples, and of course, Bible study materials (even though no one at Donydji could read English and few could speak it).[4] 'Bapa Sheppy' had a good relationship with these homeland residents and was understated in his proselytising. He believed that people should be helped to stay on their country if that was what they desired. Taking the 'good works' of the mission to the Yolngu living on their traditional lands rather than drawing them into the mission would, he claimed, reduce conflict in the large centres. Cole (1980: 89) visited the area as a missionary in 1979, and wrote that 'only Dhonydja [sic] continues during the wet season', and the people were 'a happy integrated group, hunting and living largely off the bush'. His observations were made before the wider decentralisation movement in eastern Arnhem Land, and demonstrated the commitment that those Yolngu people made to stay on their traditional land.

Cole (1980: 89) 'reported the 'local aboriginal church worker' spoke of the [Donydji people] as 'good and faithful people, part of God's family and sharing the gospel with each other'. During the 1980s, a form of Pentecostalism, which I believe was associated with a Billy Graham-inspired crusade, spread through Yolngu country, including Donydji (see Bos 1988). Among its manifestations was a type of cargo-cult mentality by which men would gather in a crowded bark hut calling out through prayer for food and asking God to send some buffalo bullets. There was also a very strong fellowship movement in which young men and women danced around a large crucifix and practised faith healing. People travelled widely to fellowship gatherings, thereby substantially expanding their social connections, including marriages, beyond Yolngu country.[5] Before these evening fellowships, the single men would spend a great deal of time viewing themselves in fragments of mirrors, brushing their hair, rubbing oil over their skin and generally preening themselves; so, too, did the women. These were times when Jesus gave permission for single men and women to hold hands and praise the Lord. They would then pile on to a dilapidated tractor-trailer with no springs and be towed 27 km or more to another crucifix arena in the then deserted outstation of Dhunganda.

---

4   See also Morphy and Morphy, this volume.
5   My notebooks during that time are replete with expletives, bemoaning the hallelujah-ing of the late-night fellowships that deprived me of sleep.

The current, self-proclaimed leader of Donydji is a 58-year-old Birdingal Ritharrngu man I shall call Henry. In 1986, at the very start of the Christian fellowship in the homeland, Henry appointed himself a lay minister and led the night-time fellowship gatherings, providing sermons and hymns very often in a largely unintelligible form of English. The only obvious English words that I understood were 'Praise the Lord', 'God Jesus' and 'Hallelujah'. On the occasional Sunday morning, Henry conducted something that resembled a Catholic Mass in which he used red cordial in a cut-down plastic bottle and pieces of damper as the sacrament. In these gatherings, males and females were kept apart. The first kit-house sent to Donydji was destroyed when the aluminium frames were cut up to manufacture crucifixes. Through his Christian leadership, Henry gained considerable secular authority among missionaries and homeland support agencies that no doubt contributed to his current leadership role in Donydji.

This Christian activity peaked from late 1988 to 1992. Faith-healing sessions became important. I believe this resulted from the death, in 1987, of Henry's older brother and favourite son of the two senior Ritharrngu clansmen. As is the case with most unexpected deaths, it was attributed to sorcery or a '*Galka*'.[6] As far as I am aware, the 'murder' was blamed on a failure to pay properly for participation in a *Nara* ceremony (see Warner 1958) that was held near the Arafura Swamp.

A consequence of this religious movement in Donydji was the return to the community of a number of women, young and old, many with their children. Christian leaders such as Henry had stressed in their sermons the importance of following Jesus as a way to bring people together and stop the fighting and harm that Yolngu were causing each other. The fellowship emphasised the role of the homeland in proving a more secure and safer environment, especially for women and children, away from the larger centres such as Gapuwiyak, the hub settlement about 130 km to the north-east by road, where there was growing social dysfunction, substance abuse and anxiety from threats of sorcery and *Galka*. Some of the women were torn between their desire for life in Donydji and what they saw as the need for at least some Western education through the school at Gapuwiyak. At that time, and indeed until very recently, the Gapuwiyak School authority did not support schooling in the homelands; if carers wanted a Western education for the children, they were expected to move to the nearest 'hub' school.

---

6   Said by some Yolngu to be a murdering manifestation or operative of a malevolent spirit that can take many forms.

The school

Residents were vocal in their desire to have a school at Donydji, recognising that unless their young people learned to read and write English and had numeracy skills, both they and the community would continue to struggle in negotiating for community infrastructure and their aspirations for the future. They were adamant that Western schooling should occur on their own land in the safety of their homeland community, where children and young people could also learn about their own language and culture. As one man said, 'the place needed to know their smell'. It was at the end of 2001, about 26 years after their own brief experiment with running a school was ended, and after continual lobbying, that Shepherdson College in Galiwinku on Elcho Island sent a teacher to Donydji, where she spent three days a week teaching under a bark and plastic shelter that had no protection from the hot gusting winds of the late dry season or from wet season rain. The education authorities were approached for a classroom, but the response was that the children needed to demonstrate their commitment to learning for a further 12 to 18 months before funding would be considered. Working with one of my postgraduate students, I decided to seek funding for a schoolhouse from charitable organisations in Melbourne through the Rotary Clubs of East Keilor and, later, Melbourne—a highly successful relationship that continues to this day. This, then, was the start of what has been the most significant development in at least the recent history of Donydji: the Mittjiwu Djaaka 'Caring for Our Community' Project, which has brought together philanthropy, volunteerism and, at times limited, government-funded organisations that should be providing infrastructure and services to homelands.

The first building completed was the schoolhouse in 2003, which soon had 35 students. A new government-funded school and teachers' residence were constructed once the original school was shown to be a success, with the children and their carers committed to a community-based Western education that incorporated local cultural studies. A number of families subsequently returned to Donydji to take advantage of the school. As a consequence, additional housing was needed. Since that time, charitable organisations operating through the Rotary Club of Melbourne (RCM) have provided close to $1.7 million for the construction of a trade training workshop, four small houses and a three-room single men's quarters built to a design developed by the local people, all of which have solar power, three ablution blocks with laundries and solar hot-water, and three outdoor hearth-kitchens, also designed by the residents. The RCM not only raises funds for the purchase of equipment and materials for the Mittjiwu Djaaka Project, it also provides travel and support for a group of mainly Vietnam veteran volunteers. These and some other volunteers have worked with the youth and young men (mainly) for one to two months each year since 2004, imparting practical skills in constructing the buildings and providing basic literacy and numeracy in the workplace.

In 2013, for the first time, there was a five-day school week. This was the initiative of the Mittjiwu Djaaka Project after the principal of Shepherdson College informed the community in November 2012 that government funding would only permit effectively two days of teaching each week. Before this, there was rarely a week when the school ran for more than three days; often children gathered at the school waiting for the teacher to come. The week-long teaching program, available to other children throughout Australia, was made possible by a young volunteer from La Trobe University. He agreed to live and teach in the school for the first semester of 2013. This proved to be very successful and he returned in the second semester on a salary, 40 per cent of which was provided through the RCM. The daily attendance was between 18 and 25 children. This was about 85–90 per cent of the school-age residents, compared with the 30 per cent or so regularly attending school in the hub communities.

In semester one 2014, teaching days were once again irregular and some children reluctantly moved temporarily to Gapuwiyak. Some community members complained that they were being neglected by Shepherdson College, supporting their view that 'the Government' wanted to force them from their homeland. As a consequence of what they saw as inadequate teaching, residents held a meeting in Donydji in May with the principal of Shepherdson College. They expressed their view that the operation of the Donydji School should be transferred from Shepherdson College to the Gapuwiyak School. Teachers would then drive to and from Donydji rather than use costly and irregular charter flights from Elcho Island. They argued that this arrangement would ensure at least four teaching days per week for the Donydji pupils. Following a letter to the regional director of education with their request, the transfer occurred in time for the second semester. The NT Education Department almost certainly made the decision on financial grounds rather than education outcomes.

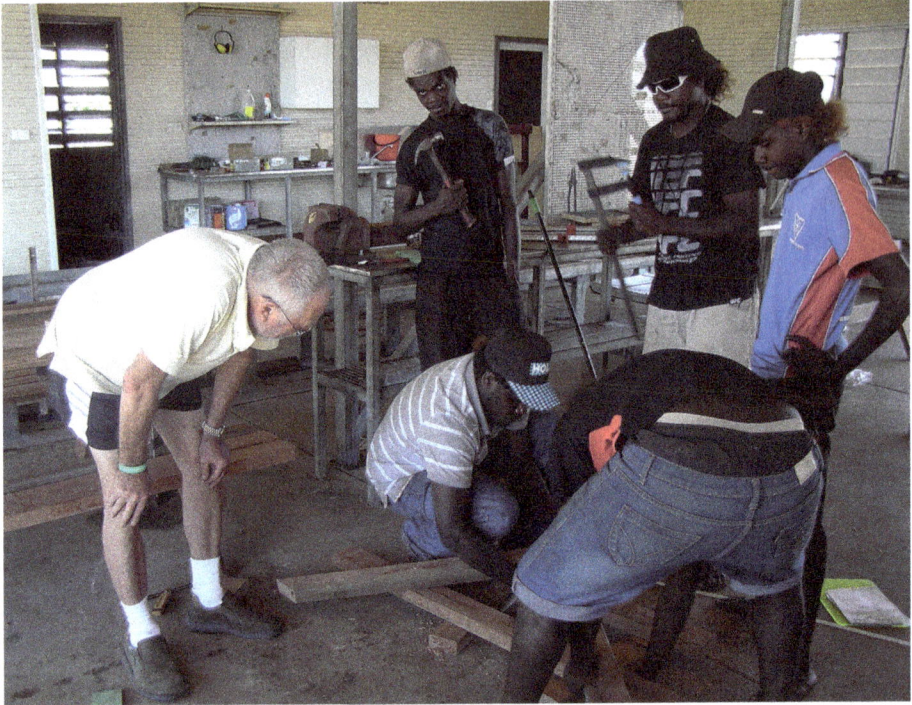

Figure 16.2 Workshop activities: Vietnam veteran volunteer, Graham Singleton, in 2013, mentoring single men in the construction of furniture for community use and sale to other homelands and organisations in the region. The workshop was constructed in 2005, by volunteers and local men using charitable funds.

Photo: Neville White

The Donydji experience has shown that homeland education would benefit from being community-based and individually targeted rather than following the national curriculum and its inappropriate benchmarks. Most of the young people in Donydji over the age of about 14 have not acquired basic primary-level literacy and numeracy skills, and are thus not academically equipped to enrol in the middle and senior school classes corresponding to their age groups. Therefore, workplace-based literacy and numeracy and vocational education could replace the formal structure of a primary through secondary curriculum. A community-based approach would also recognise the important role that elders have in passing on cultural heritage, including local languages and an understanding of traditional values.

The recently deceased community leader of Donydji said to me shortly before he died that 'my language [is] Ritharrngu: this place [is] Ritharrngu, why they come and teach our children in a different [Yolngu] language? Young people are forgetting their fathers' tongue.' Shortly after this conversation, I raised his concern with the assistant teacher, a young literate Djambarrpungu woman who was the only person in Donydji, indeed in the wider Yolngu community, who could write in her own as well as her mother's Ritharrngu dialect. It was decided that she would teach the older students Djambarrpuyngu, which was commonly spoken in Donydji, and Ritharrngu. Not a single student of any age could write or read his/her own dialect. Classes were given on Fridays, one of the days when there was no visiting teacher. English translations were also given. Back in Melbourne, I received a rare phone call from a 16-year-old young man, who thanked me for helping set up the Yolngu literacy class, saying that it made him feel proud and want to learn more at school.

Apart from the mentoring provided by the volunteers, there is still no formal vocational education and training course provided to the young men in Donydji—that is, those aged between about 14 and their late 20s—despite the construction of a fully equipped community training workshop. The NT education authorities no longer include vocational and adult education in school programs and hence funds are not available to run teaching programs. The Mittjiwu Djaaka Project has, however, demonstrated that vocational education and training is popular and can be successfully implemented.

For the first year after the workshop was built in 2005, there were 12 trainees who wanted to continue the training program established by the volunteers. Not long after the latter departed, a visiting teacher wrote saying the young men had approached him 'in high spirits and full of enthusiasm', anxious for more training and work experience. There were other young men from surrounding homelands and, indeed, the hub communities who wished to participate, but there was insufficient accommodation and food in Donydji to support them. The then principal of Shepherdson College recognised the value of the youth training initiative and provided a trade-qualified teacher to develop a workshop program for the next 12 months. The technical teacher later wrote to me saying that the students had displayed a 'real enthusiasm and motivation in working towards improving their own situation', and it was 'this willingness to work and learn that was his initial motivation to go and teach them'.

The young men acquired sufficient trade skills and team spirit to undertake building maintenance work under the supervision of the Vietnam veterans, who tendered for the job on their behalf. This work was satisfactorily completed for less than half the amount demanded by outside contractors. It was the first paid work any of them had ever done. Individual and collective self-esteem blossomed, and participants were keen to continue training and work. Sadly, the college's new principal decided not to continue this arrangement, saying it was not for him to provide technical training since Donydji's 'was not a real school'; it was a 'homeland learning centre'. The supportive and technically qualified teacher was moved to another school to teach the primary school curriculum where his vocational training skills were not utilised. As an alternative, the principal instructed the primary schoolteacher to provide cooking lessons for the young men. Most of these youths wanted to learn the skills of a motor mechanic or builder, for example, and found it difficult to fit into the mixed-age primary to early secondary classroom with boys and girls, their kin, who ranged between five and 15 years of age. As a consequence, Donydji school enrolments fell by 50 per cent, with most of the youths and young men moving away from the community due to boredom.

Figure 16.3 The three rooms in the single-man's quarters, constructed by volunteers and community members in 2008. Philanthropic funds donated through the Rotary Club of Melbourne financed the project.
Photo: Neville White

The NT Education Department's withdrawal from vocational education and the low level of literacy and numeracy of Donydji people have meant that they would not be offered apprenticeships anyway. However, a recent Federal Government initiative does revive the possibility of vocational training and local employment prospects for the majority of young adults in Donydji who desire it. 'I want to live here in Gurrumala; there is too much humbug in Gapuwiyak', one teenager said to me recently. 'We can go hunting here but sometimes we get bored like it is there, and I don't want to sit around or just cut grass and clean up rubbish.'

In August 2014 the Vietnam veteran volunteers and I established a fruitful working relationship with field staff of the recently established Miwatj Employment and Participation Limited (MEP) group in Yirrkala. This is the local contractor for the Commonwealth Government's new Remote Jobs and Community Program (RJCP), set up to supervise work-for-the-dole and be a replacement for Community Development Employment Projects (CDEP).

> It is designed to increase the level of participation in the mainstream economy by encouraging and fostering new employment and training opportunities. It is also intended to foster self-sufficiency, resourcefulness and community participation where jobs are scarce—such as in the homelands.[7]

Figure 16.4 Inside the single-men's quarters: the TV was used to view Australian Football League videos, which remain popular. Electricity is from solar energy.
Photo: Neville White

MEP has agreed to continue the Donydji Workshop program. Materials were supplied by MEP to enable the volunteer mentors to train 11 young men to manufacture furniture and food boxes requested by Yolngu in Donydji and other centres. Many of the products will be sold, with the money to be returned to the workshop to pay top-up wages and buy the required tools and materials. As with many initiatives in Aboriginal Australia, apparently straightforward solutions to problems in community development become entangled in bureaucratic

---

7   Email, 11 July 2014, from the acting CEO, Laynhapuy Homelands Aboriginal Corporation.

incompetence or oversight. In this case, while RJCP policy is focused on training and employment, it appears to have made no provision for paying participants or setting up businesses in the homelands. A solution needs to be found.

Responses to mining and other development interests

As indicated above, people living in Donydji have traditional custodial rights over a substantial area of inland Yolngu country. For this reason, members of the outstation community are continually being called on to attend meetings on mining exploration proposals. The custodians' frustration about these meetings and their determination to resist these pressures are evident in a speech by my late companion Roger Y. Birdingal, which I recorded. It was made to a public meeting at Gapuwiyak on 11 January 1983, held to respond to applications for mining exploration and a gas pipeline corridor:

> We are not going to change our law the way you white people keep changing yours. Every year you question us about our land. We will not give it to you. You argue strongly for mining, but you will not destroy us … There are plenty of minerals for you in your own country. You have no permission from us. We are the landowners here. The trees are ours. The water, the rocks, the turtles and all the animals in the bush—all are ours. (McKenzie et al. 1984)

The next year, Roger again expressed his frustration and anger over the constant pressure on him and his family from mining companies through the Northern Land Council.

It was evident that a different strategy was needed if the cultural and biodiversity values of the region were to be both respected and protected. To this end, I travelled with Roger to Canberra in the early 1990s to meet with senior staff in the Australian Heritage Commission. They encouraged us to nominate this unique cultural and natural landscape for inclusion on the Register of the National Estates. This would provide national and global recognition for the Yolngu custodians and their lands as well as legislative protection from environmental damage.

Roger and his kin decided to proceed with a nomination. For the next three years, consultations and additional scientific and anthropological research were conducted at Donydji and other homelands and settlements. The nomination was based on the area being recognised as a cultural landscape, arguing that there were both high cultural and natural values that were intimately connected with and dependent on the ongoing Aboriginal occupation of the region, especially by homeland residents. The Arafura Wetlands and Surrounds was finally interim-listed—a decision celebrated at a ceremony in Yirrkala in June 1993.

In 2001, the Arafura Wetlands and Surrounds was placed on the Full Register of the National Estate. This followed further field research with the communities involved and having to deal with strong opposition from a number of organisations, including mining companies, the NT Chamber of Mines and the Northern Land Council. The listed area of 600,000 ha became the largest Aboriginal cultural landscape on the list. However, despite the ceremony and promises, the Yolngu custodians were badly misled: there was no apparent benefit to them in the face of growing development pressures from mining companies for major roadworks, the construction of a fibre-optic cable through Donydji and proposals such as a gas pipeline to Gove.

Apart from the failure to conduct the appropriate social and environmental impact studies supposedly required by the heritage legislation, the promised economic, social and environmental benefits have not eventuated. Certainly, the Yolngu have no greater control over, or protection of, their cultural landscape than before the listing. Furthermore, it was recently discovered that the 'Arafura and Surrounds' has been transferred to the Non-Statutory Archive of the Register of the National Estate, rather than being added to the new National Heritage List. This 'provides recognition but not protection', according to an officer of Australian Heritage in a recent telephone conversation. The change in status was done without any consultation, explanation or even notice of the decision to those involved in the nomination.

Nevertheless, one positive development resulted from the nomination exercise: the formation of the Arafura Catchment Ranger Program, which brought together five homelands in the southern wetlands and the southern catchment. The communities worked together on occasions, particularly on biological surveys and in land management workshops. They each had their own rangers wearing their own carefully designed logos, who worked in the vicinity of their homelands addressing local natural and cultural resource issues. The ranger network was formed in 1996 and ran until 2002, funded by small grants obtained though the National Heritage Trust. During this time a number of intensive biological surveys were conducted in partnership between rangers from each of the five communities and scientists from the NT Parks and Wildlife Service and La Trobe University. One such survey centred on the top of the Koolatong River in the Mitchell Ranges. It was here I discovered how rapidly detailed knowledge of the cultural landscape is being lost. The last Traditional Owner raised in this rugged country, a Madarrpa Ritharrngu man, had died six months before the expedition. The other senior men in the ranger group who travelled through the country in their youth could not recall, if they ever knew, details of placenames and sites of cultural significance. All were pleased to have returned and strongly expressed their emotional attachment to the place, promising the country that they would return and better care for it in the future. There are few remaining Yolngu who have detailed knowledge of the cultural landscape on which they were raised and with each death the world loses forever an irreplaceable fragment of a deep intellectual tradition and understanding of our world.

In 2011, the Gurruwiling Ranger group based in Ramingining employed the Donydji leader as one of its rangers to allow them to extend their carbon credit fire management program through Ritharrngu and Wagilak country. To date, there has been no attempt to train and employ other people from the community.

Service delivery

One of the major problems and ongoing frustrations for Donydji has been the poor provision of infrastructure maintenance and community services. Service delivery is far from rational; services and resources do not come from a single hub. For example, again the teacher travels by charter flight to and from Elcho Island (until this semester there were sometimes four flights per week); food and irregular health visits come from Gapuwiyak, about 90 minutes away by road; while maintenance and municipal services are supposed to be provided by the Laynhapuy Homelands Aboriginal Corporation at Yirrkala, some 300 km to the north-east, along the main road that runs past Gapuwiyak. Logic would suggest that Gapuwiyak would be the hub for all these services that have been so poorly organised and coordinated. In the words of the historian and writer Don Watson, who has visited Donydji on six occasions in recent years, 'the daily life of the people is conducted in the shadow of this incompetence, waste and neglect. The stories are funny, in the manner of Russian satire, but the reality, like the Russian one, is corrosive and dispiriting' (2007).

Donydji homeland today

On my first visit to Donydji almost 40 years ago, there were 58 people in 12 households; 11 of these were headed by Ritharrngu or Wagilak, with only one of them Djambarrpuyngu (at that time identifying as the Liyadhalingmirri, but now calling themselves Guyula). On my most recent visit, one month ago (May 2015), there were 56 residents, 22 of whom are under the age of 17. Now, however, of the nine households, only two are Ritharrngu, none is Wagilak and the rest are Guyula. Most of the Ritharrngu are widows (sisters) of the Djambarrpuyngu men (mainly brothers). Of the bachelor Ritharrngu men who were there in 1974, and who stayed until their deaths, only three established married households at Gurrumala. There is now a much larger social range with greater marriage distances than was the case in earlier years. As a result, there has been a breakdown in customary marriage relationships. A source of recent conflict has been a number of irregular 'marriages' that would once have resulted in serious injury or death to one or both of the couple involved.

In the early years of the outstation, there were nearly always families in residence, although numbers fluctuated as family groups resumed a nomadic lifestyle or moved away due to tensions and conflict. This stemmed from pre-outstation life where band size varied through fission and fusion in response to economic, social and religious imperatives. People are now more reluctant to leave their houses and personal possessions, because others, especially visitors, might take or damage them. This is the reason for the continual demand for locks on doors, boxes and bags! As a consequence, tension and conflict rise within the community. For this reason, among others, there is a strong need these days for community-focused leadership rather than authority imposed within and among close families.

In the early days of the outstation, the elderly Ritharrngu brothers who were largely responsible for its establishment were respected and feared in equal measure. Their reputation as ceremonial leaders and fighters was far reaching, and they had sons and sons-in-law who could defend their interests. Their authority generally went unchallenged in the community. After they died, one of their sons, TGB, took on the mantle of leadership. TGB was also widely respected, and in contrast with some of the other male members of the homeland, he considered the interests of the wider outstation community. After TGB's death, his younger brother has become leader—the 'number-one landowner'. He is yet to command the same respect and authority as his 'fathers' or older brother and is finding it difficult to adopt a community perspective in his decision-making.

Tradition-orientated social groups in Aboriginal Australia did, and still do in many cases, function through nepotism and self-interest. Despite the widely held view of a caring and sharing society as well as the anthropological literature on ideal customary sharing and generosity, there is very often reluctant reciprocity.[8] It is not uncommon for much desired items such as honey or tobacco to be hidden or remain undeclared when requests are made to share, or they are consumed out of sight of others. As in all societies, there were, and still are, greedy people who will bend the customary rules to satisfy their own interests. The same applies to the other base emotions, jealousy and envy.

---

8   Peterson (1993) uses the term 'demand sharing', while B. Schebeck, footnoted in Peterson's article, calls it 'mutual taking'.

Many Yolngu, particularly men, are secretive about their bank and credit union accounts, and carefully guard access to them, unlike most women, who commonly hand over their debit cards and bank details to their kin. Often this is on demand. The great imperative of men is to acquire a motor vehicle, the most prized being four-wheel-drive Toyotas. Invariably, they seek money from their sisters, mothers and grandmothers and thereby have a substantial negative impact on food supplies and other necessities.

Money, mainly from social welfare (only two people, both working in the school, now earn wages), is being spent not only on the purchase of cheap four-wheel-drives, but also on their repairs and fuel. On my visit to Donydji in November 2013, there were 13 'dead'—that is, unserviceable—motor vehicles in the outstation, not including a similar number in the community rubbish dump. While there is a good deal of 'bush mechanic' work done on the homeland through the workshop, the only qualified mechanic and spare parts outlet is in Nhulunbuy. In desperation, men from Donydji try to drive their mechanically unsound vehicles to Nhulunbuy, almost a day's travel to the north-east, where not only is servicing very expensive but also police sometimes confiscate the un-roadworthy vehicles. Frequently, vehicles do not complete the journey and are left by the roadside, where they are very often stripped. In addition, there have been many occasions when people have taken a four-wheel-drive bush taxi to Nhulunbuy to purchase parts and food and sometimes sell their craft work— at a cost of $950 for the return trip (this is cheaper than a charter flight). On one occasion known to me a family spent $950 to sell $1,200 worth of craft that was to have been used to purchase clothes and food for the community.

In addition to wanting to buy food and goods not available in Gapuwiyak, a number of the residents have established bank accounts in Nhulunbuy because they do not trust the Yolngu in Gapuwiyak. This means even more frequent trips to the town in their own dilapidated vehicles, or by bush taxi or air charter, and less money for food and essential supplies. The Yolngu in Donydji, especially children, often complain that they are hungry, and despite the introduction of school breakfast there is a need for improved strategies to ensure food security, particularly for the schoolchildren and older women.

These demands on the cash economy of the outstation create the major source of tension among the residents. It has led to public accusations of greed and placed particular strain on the few wage-earners, who have suffered from the envy and jealousy of others, to the point where one young woman rejected an offer of paid employment. More frequent and extravagant funerals have contributed substantially to the financial and resource burden on the community in recent years. Associated pressures on resources have also been responsible for members of the Ritharrngu landowning group challenging people from other clans over their right to take up residence in Donydji.

Apart from changes in leadership, social composition and the economy, there has been a substantial change in the diet and foraging and hunting range of the Yolngu. In the early 1970s, families still traversed an economic range of 3,000–4,000 sq km. At that time, the bulk of the diet was vegetable, foraged by the women, while the men went out less often and over longer distances to procure fish and small game with the occasional kangaroo or wallaby, emu and, very infrequently, the big game of buffalo and wild cattle (White 1985). About 80 per cent of the annual food intake was wild food. Today, most of the fishing and hunting expeditions are undertaken in four-wheel-drive vehicles using shotguns and rifles. Fewer locations are visited, but the hunters and fishers can travel further and bring more meat back to camp than was possible previously. Now that people travel less on foot, at least over wide areas, patterns of burning and fire management of biodiversity and bush foods have changed in ways detrimental to the landscape. As noted above, knowledge of the country and its resources among the younger Yolngu is also being lost—or was never learnt. A more subtle consequence of this is a poorer understanding of songs and myths that often require a detailed knowledge of particular places through time.

The focus on hunting big game has meant an increase in wild meat and fat in the diet. Women, especially the young ones, are reluctant to forage, particularly in the thickets and swamp land, because of their fear of buffalo and pigs, the numbers of which have increased dramatically over recent years. Furthermore, with many people living in the homelands throughout the year, local vegetable foods and fruit have been hard pushed. Indeed, even in earlier times the economic range around Donydji over the seasonal cycle would have struggled to support the number of people now living in the homeland. Women now spend more time purchasing store foods from Gapuwiyak, where they use their Government Basics card.

With less foraging over a reduced range and changing food preferences, there has been a noticeable decline in ecological knowledge among the younger Donydji residents. Between 1972 and 1985 at Yirrkala, I found there to be an approximately 30 per cent loss of knowledge of plant names among men and women under early middle age. This figure is probably greater today in Donydji in the mid-teens to mid-20s age group. Of 106 species of roots, fruits and seeds in the diet in the early years of Donydji, only about 18 to 20 are now being commonly eaten (White 2001). Foods such as cycad seeds that were once carbohydrate staples for much of the year are now, like many other wild plant foods, used only as emergency foods. Today, while wild foods remain important to the community, with almost all meat being hunted and all fish caught, only about 20 per cent of the fruit and vegetables consumed during the year are from the bush. Exceptions are fruits during the wet season and early dry, and wild honey during the dry season. There is evidence that these dietary changes, particularly the greater dependence on the Arnhem Land Progress Association store in Gapuwiyak, are leading to a decline in nutritional health when compared with the indicators of nutritional status that were recorded nearly 30 years ago (O'Dea et al. 1988). Body mass index (BMI) and abdominal fat—both indicators of the risk of cardiovascular disease and type 2 diabetes—remain lower in the long-term Donydji residents than for those living in the settlements and towns of the region (Jones and White 1994), but their increasing reliance on store food could undo this.

With the improvements in infrastructure and amenity in Donydji, largely through the Mittjiwu Djaaka project, there has been an increasing number of Yolngu visitors and short-term residents who have links to the homeland through either country or close family association. Families and young men often arrive on weekends to go hunting. Against the wishes of the community, some young men sometimes bring *ganydja* (marijuana), although most people reject it and the police at Gapuwiyak have been asked by residents to intervene. The visitors are coming mainly from Gapuwiyak but there are others from large centres such as Roper River, Numbulwar and Beswick, where there is considerable social dysfunction and where many of the children display antisocial behaviours.

Concluding remarks

There are a number of external and internal forces that threaten the ongoing development and future viability of Donydji outstation. For the community to develop in line with the aspirations of most of its residents, solutions must be found to the following urgent issues:

- the failure of government-funded Homeland Resource Centres to effectively service homelands, and the general lack of coordination between government and local agencies
- the lack of educational and training opportunities for youth and young adults who are not equipped for formal secondary education
- the lack of local employment opportunities despite the willingness of residents to participate
- the need for the newly initiated RJCP services to be given the necessary personnel and resources to achieve their aim of fostering 'self-sufficiency, resourcefulness and community participation where jobs are scarce'
- the lack of *community*-focused leadership and financial skills
- major health concerns among homelands residents; among the most urgent are dental disease, parasite infections and the availability of fresh food, especially during times when bush foods are scarce.

Donydji residents have expressed a strong desire for employment programs such as those trialled with the volunteers. With outside supervision in the early phases, there are opportunities for commercial craftwork by men and women, and possibly, ecotourism and/or study tourism involving small special interest groups. These might include university students from relevant disciplines, bird watchers and botanists. Local ranger-supervised hunting has been suggested, but this needs careful consideration for a range of environmental and social reasons. A successful educational exchange program involving Eltham High School (EHS) in Melbourne has been in place since 2010. Students from EHS spend approximately two weeks with their peers at the Donydji School learning about local Yolngu culture and languages. The high school makes a financial contribution to the Donydji community as well as building mentoring partnerships among the students. These will include visits to EHS by some of the older Donydji students, where they will undertake short vocational education and training courses.

Apart from the social justice and moral arguments that justify support for homelands, the land management practices of these communities are crucial for the maintenance of biodiversity; funds would be well spent in this area since it not only provides particularly satisfying work for many young Aboriginal people, but also allows Australia and Australians to preserve the natural and cultural values of these places for the benefit of future generations—black and white.

I strongly believe that, for this part of Aboriginal Australia at least, homelands provide the best opportunity for the Indigenous people to acquire the skills and education necessary to engage with wider Australia in the longer term, while living as they wish on their traditional lands away from many of the serious problems confronting the larger communities and towns. They also function as rest-and-recreation or respite centres for Yolngu who live in those larger centres. This benefits their mental and physical health and allows social bonds to be reinforced.

There is an additional and compelling reason to invest in outstations, one that should be attractive to economic rationalists. Evidence is mounting from medical doctors and health economists (Rowley et al. 2008; Campbell et al. 2011) that it is cheaper for governments, and taxpayers, to help people stay in their outstations than to have them migrate to the larger settlements, towns and fringes of cities such as Darwin and Alice Springs. In these centres, they do not have the social, emotional and physical support as in the homelands and are more likely to participate in substance abuse, self-harm and social disorder as 'long-grass people'.

I conclude with two quotes: the first, by Watson (2007), expresses the pessimism of many in the wider Australian community, and I sense, of the NT and Federal governments, towards the future of homelands:

No white community would stand for [the ineptitude of the bureaucracy] but then, in general, white communities are not so heavily dependent on the Government. Some are, of course; and some, like the Aborigines of the outstations, chose to live in remote and unproductive places. But the white people who do this are commonly esteemed as authentic, if not 'iconic' Australians, and the passing of their way of life is reckoned a national tragedy. There was a time when it seemed possible the country would think this way about the Aborigines living on their homelands, but it now seems certain that this time has passed.

The second quote is from a letter written in 2012 by Joanne Yindiri Guyula and her sister Sonia Gurrpulan. The former was then the assistant teacher at Donydji School but is now completing a tertiary teaching degree in Darwin. The young women asked me to deliver their letter to the Rotary Club of Melbourne. It conveys their desire to remain in their homeland, while recognising the need for ongoing outside support to secure its, and their own, future well-being:

> *Napuya yakuy djaal'thirr ... Bilinu nhumaya latjuwatju dhuya gunggayunanu napuunha.*

> We would like you to be friends of our Donydji community and help us to build a happy future for our young people. At Donydji we don't have grog or drugs and we look after our kids and the old people. Before we only had bark huts and no school. Already you good people have helped us.

The RCM responded by establishing the 'Friends of Donydji' to raise funds for education and training in the homeland and provide support for volunteers to work with the residents.

Unlike Don Watson, I believe that with a more sympathetic, considerate and competent approach to homelands by the Federal and NT governments and their agencies, their value will be recognised by a majority of Australians.

In its *Outstations policy* Discussion Paper of July 2008, the NT Government (2008) claims that it 'values the contribution of outstations to the economic, social, and cultural life of the Territory, and the important role they play for Indigenous Territorians who have chosen to live on their traditional lands'. If this is the case, the NT and Australian governments should put their words into action and show a stronger commitment to ensuring their survival.

References

Berndt, R. M. and Berndt, C. H. 1954. *Arnhem Land: Its History and Its People*. Melbourne: F. W. Cheshire.

Bos, R. 1988. Jesus and the Dreaming: Religion and social change in Arnhem Land. Unpublished PhD thesis. University of Queensland, Brisbane.

Campbell, D., Burgess, C., Garnett, S. and Wakerman, J. 2011. Potential primary health care savings for chronic disease care associated with Australian Aboriginal involvement in land-management. *Health Policy* 99: 83–89.

Cole, K. 1980. *Arnhem Land: Places and People.* Adelaide: Rigby.

Jones, C. O. H. and White, N. G. 1994. Adiposity in Aboriginal people from Arnhem Land, Australia: Variation in degree and distribution associated with age, sex and lifestyle. *Annals of Human Biology* 21: 207–27.

Jones, R. and White, N. G. 1988. Point blank: Stone tool manufacture at the Ngilipitji quarry, Arnhem Land. In B. Meehan and R. Jones (eds), *Archaeology and Ethnography: An Australian Perspective.* Canberra: Department of Prehistory, Research School of Pacific Studies, The Australian National University, pp. 51–87.

McKenzie, K., White, N., Jones, R., Winingbir, R. A., Shebeck, B., Sekars, M. and Yilarama, R. 1984. *The Spear in the Stone: A Study Guide.* Canberra: Australian Institute of Aboriginal Studies.

Northern Territory Government 2008. *Outstations policy.* Discussion Paper. Darwin: Northern Territory Government.

O'Dea, K., White, N. G. and Sinclair, A. J. 1988. An investigation of nutrition-related risk factors in an isolated Aboriginal community in northern Australia. *Medical Journal of Australia* 149: 177–80.

Peterson, N. 1973. Camp site location among Australian hunter-gatherers: Archaeological and ethnographic evidence for a key determinant. *Archaeology and Physical Anthropology in Oceania* 8: 173–93.

Peterson, N. 1993. Demand sharing: Reciprocity and the pressure for generosity among foragers. *American Anthropologist* 95(4): 860–74.

Rowley, K., O'Dea, K., Anderson, I., McDermott, R., Saraswati, K., Tilmouth, R., Roberts, I., Fitz, J., Wang, Z., Jenkins, A., Best, J. D., Wang, Z. and Brown, A. 2008. Lower than expected morbidity and mortality for an Australian Aboriginal population: 10-year follow-up in a decentralised community. *Medical Journal of Australia* 188: 283–87.

Shepherdson, E. 1981. *Half a Century in Arnhem Land.* Adelaide: E. & H. Shepherdson.

Warner, L. 1958. *A Black Civilization: A Social Study of an Australian Tribe*. New York: Harper Bros.

Watson, D. 2007. Drugs banned, kids healthy, but community feels the heat. *The Age*, 20 October: 9.

White, N. G. 1985. Sex differences in Australian Aboriginal subsistence: Possible implications for the biology of hunter-gathers. In J. Ghesquiere, R. Martin and F. Newcombe (eds), *Human Sexual Dimorphism*. London: Taylor & Francis, pp. 323–61.

White, N. G. 1995. Inside the Gurrnganngara: Social processes and demographic genetics in northeast Arnhem Land, Australia. In A. J. Boyce and V. Reynolds (eds), *Human Populations: Diversity and Adaptation*. Oxford: Oxford University Press, pp. 252–79.

White, N. G. 1997. Genes, languages and landscapes in Australia. In P. McConvell and N. Evans (eds), *Archaeology and Linguistics: Aboriginal Australia in Global Perspective*. Melbourne: Oxford University Press, pp. 45–81.

White, N. G. 2001. In search of the traditional Australian Aboriginal diet: Then and now. In A. Anderson, I. Lilley and S. O'Connor (eds), *Histories of Old Ages: Essays in Honour of Rhys Jones*. Canberra: Pandanus Books, pp. 343–59.

Contributors

Jon Altman

Jon Altman is an Emeritus Professor of The Australian National University currently with the Regulatory Institutions Network in the College of Asia and the Pacific. Trained in economics and anthropology, he was from 1990–2010 the foundation director of the Centre for Aboriginal Economic Policy Research (CAEPR) at The Australian National University. In 1979 and 1980, he lived with Kuninjku-speaking people at Mumeka outstation in western Arnhem Land while undertaking doctoral research; he continues his friendships and collaborations with this group, whom he has since revisited on more than 50 occasions. Altman's political advocacy highlights the rights of Indigenous peoples to live on their lands.

Diane Austin-Broos

Diane Austin-Broos is Professor Emerita of Anthropology at the University of Sydney, a Fellow of the Academy of Social Sciences in Australia and a doctoral graduate from the University of Chicago. Her two main research areas have been in the Caribbean, with a focus on Jamaica, and in Central Australia among Western Arrernte people at Ntaria/Hermannsburg. Her principal research themes have been social and economic marginalisation and cultural change. She has published eight books, including *Jamaica Genesis*, *Creating Culture*, *Arrernte Present, Arrernte Past* and *A Different Inequality*. Her current research concerns the politics of moral order in market societies.

David Brooks

David Brooks has been working as an anthropologist in the Ngaanyatjarra Lands for more than 25 years. He has researched and written on a wide range of matters there, including relationship to country, youth affairs and art. His PhD thesis was entitled 'Dreamings and connections to country among the Ngaanyatjarra and Pintupi of the Australian Western Desert'. For nearly 10 years, David worked on the various native title claims in the area, in the course of which he gathered ethnographic material on recent Ngaanyatjarra history, including the period of the outstation movement.

Scott Cane

Scott Cane has worked throughout Australia, with a particular focus on Australian desert environments. He has a PhD from The Australian National University, has co-authored a monograph on Aboriginal land use and homelands in Central Australia (1986) and has written two books: *Pila Nguru* (2002) about the Spinifex People from the Great Victoria Desert, and *First Footprints* (2013), based on the award-winning TV series of the same name. He has published some 30 papers and 140 reports, including 37 expert opinions regarding native title, resulting in the determination of rights and interests to more than 400,000 sq km of land.

Bill Edwards

Reverend Doctor W. H. (Bill) Edwards was ordained as a Minister of the Presbyterian Church in 1958, and was superintendent of Ernabella Mission (1958–72), superintendent of Mowajnum Mission (1972–73), and minister of the Pitjantjatjara Parish based at Fregon (1973) and at Amata (1976–80). He lectured in Aboriginal studies at Torrens College of Advanced Education (1975) and at the South Australian College of Advanced Education, and from 1991, the University of South Australia (1981–96). He has interpreted in Pitjantjatjara in courts and hospitals. In 2008, he was awarded a PhD in History at Flinders University for his thesis, 'Moravian Aboriginal missions in Australia'. He is the author *An Introduction to Aboriginal Societies*. He was awarded membership of the Order of Australia in 2009.

Sarah Holcombe

Sarah Holcombe is an Australian Research Council (ARC) Future Fellow in the School of Archaeology and Anthropology at The Australian National University, undertaking an ethnographic project exploring the local effects of human rights discourse in Aboriginal Central Australia. She has a diverse research background in remote Aboriginal Australia, which includes applied anthropology with NT land councils and research management as the social science coordinator for the Desert Knowledge Cooperative Research Centre (CRC). She has undertaken research on the social sustainability of mining in Indigenous communities; alternative economies; Indigenous community governance; and integrity systems in research with Indigenous peoples. Her research is increasingly focusing on legal and political anthropology.

Jeremy Long

Jeremy Long, a graduate of the University of Sydney, joined the Department of Territories as a clerk in the Welfare Branch of the Northern Territory in Darwin and worked as a patrol officer and settlement superintendent in the Alice Springs area (1955–59). Returning later as a research officer, he travelled widely among Aboriginal communities in the Territory (1960–68). In 1965, he spent a year as research fellow with Charles Rowley in the Social Science Research Council's research project 'Aborigines in Australian Society' and wrote a book, *Aboriginal Settlements, A Survey of Institutional Communities in Eastern Australia* (ANU Press, 1970). He transferred to Canberra and served in the Office, and later Department, of Aboriginal Affairs (1968–82). After serving as commissioner for community relations with the Human Rights Commission (1982–86), he left the Commonwealth Public Service to work as a consultant, and wrote a book, *The Go-Betweens, Patrol Officers in Aboriginal Affairs in the Northern Territory 1936–1974* (North Australia Research Unit, 1992).

Bruce Martin

Bruce Martin's traditional Wik country lies within the Aboriginal lands south of Aurukun. He was instrumental in establishing Aak Puul Ngantam (APN Cape York), a community-based organisation focused on developing productive livelihoods on and off Wik lands. Bruce is still on the board of APN, but is now also engaged in establishing an institutional architecture for leveraging government, private and non-governmental organisation investment in Wik country and beyond it.

David Martin

David Martin is an anthropologist who worked as a half-time research fellow at the Centre for Aboriginal Economic Policy Research (CAEPR) for a decade until 2006, when he returned to full-time consulting. He lived in Aurukun and worked there as outstation coordinator for eight years from 1976, before undertaking a Masters in Anthropology at the London School of Economics. He returned to Aurukun for his doctoral research in 1985 and 1986, and visits and works there on a regular basis. His research and applied work in Aboriginal Australia has focused on such areas as policy, development, governance and social continuities and transformations.

Frances Morphy

Frances Morphy is a Visiting Fellow at the Centre for Aboriginal Economic Policy Research (CAEPR) at The Australian National University, where she was formerly a research fellow, and is a research affiliate of the Center for Advanced

Study in the Behavioral Sciences at Stanford University. An anthropologist and linguist, her major field site for the past 40 years has been in north-east Arnhem Land, in the Northern Territory. She has also worked recently in the Fitzroy Valley in Western Australia. Her current research concerns the anthropological demography of these two regions, and the (mis)representation of Indigenous ways of being in demographic datasets.

Howard Morphy

Howard Morphy is Distinguished Professor of Anthropology in the School of Archaeology at The Australian National University. He is an anthropologist of art and visual anthropology with a major theoretical focus on the nature of cross-cultural categories. His most recent book is *Becoming Art: Exploring Cross-Cultural Categories* (Berg, 2007). His involvement in e-research and in the development of museum exhibitions reflects his determination to make humanities research as accessible as possible to a wider public and to close the distance between the research process and research outcomes. His current research working with colleagues at the British Museum and the National Museum of Australia centres on the concept of the relational museum linking distributed collections to source communities.

Fred Myers

Fred Myers is the Silver Professor of Anthropology at New York University. Myers has written frequently on questions of place and personhood, on Western Desert painting, and more generally on culture, objects and identity as they are understood within Indigenous communities and circulated through different regimes of value. His books include *Pintupi Country, Pintupi Self: Sentiment, Place and Politics among Western Desert Aborigines* (1986), *Painting Culture: The Making of an Aboriginal High Art* (2002) and edited volumes *The Traffic in Culture: Refiguring Anthropology and Art* (co-edited with George Marcus, 1995) and *The Empire of Things* (2001). His current project involves the repatriation and 're-documentation' of film footage from 1974 with the two current Pintupi communities.

Kingsley Palmer

Kingsley Palmer has worked in many areas of Aboriginal Australia. Formerly senior anthropologist with the Northern Land Council, he was appointed director of research and later deputy principal at the Australian Institute of Aboriginal and Torres Strait Islander Studies in Canberra. In 2001, he became a private consultant, working extensively in native title anthropology as well as on cases brought in relation to the *Aboriginal Land Rights Act* (NT), criminal trials and research on social impacts, community planning and management.

This included reviews and planning for agencies servicing outstations, and he was joint author of the report on a national review of resource agencies, published in 1998.

Nicolas Peterson

Nicolas Peterson is Professor of Anthropology in the School of Archaeology and Anthropology at The Australian National University. His main areas of fieldwork have been in north-east Arnhem Land and the Tanami Desert. His research interests include economic anthropology, land and marine tenure, Fourth-World people and the state, and the anthropology of photography. Since working for the Royal Commission into Aboriginal Land Rights as its research officer, he has been involved in the preparation of 12 land and native title claims.

Vikki Plant

Vikki Plant, a historian, has been associated with the Ngaanyatjarra Lands for more than 20 years. She researched the documentary history of the region for the native title claims and, like David Brooks, has also long worked on a personal basis with Ngaanyatjarra people. In 2002, Vikki co-curated *Mission Time in Warburton*, an exhibition exploring aspects of the Warburton Mission history at Tjulyuru Regional Art Gallery.

Peter Sutton

Peter Sutton is an Affiliate Professor with the South Australian Museum and University of Adelaide. He is an anthropologist and linguist who has lived and worked with Aboriginal people since 1969, and is a specialist on the Cape York Peninsula region. His publications are mainly in the fields of Aboriginal languages, visual arts, land tenure, history and policy. These include *Dreamings: The Art of Aboriginal Australia* (1988), *Country: Aboriginal Boundaries and Land Ownership in Australia* (1995), *Wik-Ngathan Dictionary* (1995), *Native Title in Australia: An Ethnographic Perspective* (2003) and *The Politics of Suffering: Indigenous Australia and the End of the Liberal Consensus* (2009).

Peter Thorley

Peter Thorley is Head of the Aboriginal and Torres Strait Islander Program, National Museum of Australia. He was a resident of Warlungurru (Kintore) for four years in the mid-1980s, where he worked as a teacher and teacher-linguist. He subsequently studied archaeology and was employed by the Ngaanyatjarra Council Native Title Unit. Since joining the National Museum in 2006, he has worked on a range of exhibition, collection and research projects featuring Western Desert artists, including the *Pintupi Dialogues* ARC Linkage project as a partner investigator.

Neville White

Neville White, a biological anthropologist, is an Emeritus Scholar at La Trobe University. His early research investigated social, cultural and environmental influences on population genetic diversity in Aboriginal Australia. Situated since 1971 in north-east Arnhem Land, his research has widened to include medical anthropology, nutritional health, ethnobiology and the Yolngu management of their natural and cultural landscapes. Over the past decade, his work has focused on community development in the Donydji homeland, with the help of volunteers and philanthropic funding.

Index

www.ingramcontent.com/pod-product-compliance
Lightning Source LLC
Chambersburg PA
CBHW061217270326
41926CB00028B/4666